Humana Festival 2010
The Complete Plays

Humana Inc., headquartered in Louisville, Kentucky, is one of the nation's largest publicly traded health and supplemental benefits companies, with approximately 10.4 million medical members and approximately 7.2 million specialty-benefit members. Humana is a full-service benefits solutions company, offering a wide array of health and supplemental benefit plans for employer groups, government programs and individuals.

The Humana Foundation was established in 1981 as the philanthropic arm of Humana Inc. The Foundation's mission is to support charitable activities that promote healthy lives and healthy communities.

For more information, visit www.humanafoundation.org.

Humana Festival 2010
The Complete Plays

Edited by
Adrien-Alice Hansel and Amy Wegener

Playscripts, Inc.

New York, NY

Published by Playscripts, Inc.
450 Seventh Avenue, Suite 809
New York, New York, 10123
www.playscripts.com

Cover Design by Matt Dobson
Cover Image by Richard Wilkinson
Text Design and Layout by Jason Pizzarello

First Edition: April 2011
10 9 8 7 6 5 4 3 2 1

LCCN: 95650734
ISSN: 1935-4452

ISBN-13: 978-0-9819099-6-7

Contents

Acknowledgments

The editors wish to thank the following persons for their invaluable assistance in compiling this volume:

Jennifer Bielstein
Zach Chotzen-Freund
Cathy Colliver
Sean Daniels
Matt Dobson
Julie Felise Dubiner
Emily Feldman
Kirsty Gaukel
Kory Kelly
Sarah Lunnie
Marc Masterson
Whitney Miller-Brengle
Mik Mroczynski
Jessica Reese
Jeff Rodgers
Sarah Rowan
Emily Ruddock
Zan Sawyer-Dailey
Wanda Snyder
Stephanie Spalding

Beth Blickers
Polly Carl
William Craver
Seth Glewen
Ronald Gwiazda
Craig Harris
Jonathan Lomma
Selma Luttinger
Kate Navin
Mark Orsini
Bruce Ostler
Thomas Pearson
Rude Mechs
Derek Zasky

Actors Theatre of Louisville Staff
Humana Festival 2010

Artistic Director . . . . Marc Masterson
Managing Director . . . . .Jennifer Bielstein

ADMINISTRATION

General Manager. . . . . .Jeffrey S. Rodgers
Human Resources Coordinator . . . . .Cora Brown
Systems Manager. . . . . .Dottie Krebs
Executive Secretary. . . . . Wanda Snyder
Administrative Services Coordinator . . . . Alan Meyer

Marketing

Director . . . . .Kory P. Kelly
Public Relations Manager. . . . . Matt Porter
Marketing Manager. . . . . Cathy Colliver
Marketing Associate . . . . Sarah Rowan
Graphic Designer . . . . .Matt Dobson
Festival/Events Manager . . . . Stephanie Spalding
Group Sales Manager . . . . .Sarah Peters
Group Sales Assistant Manager . . . . J. Stephen Smith

Development

Director . . . . Schuyler Heuser
Manager of Patron Relations . . . . .Trish Pugh Jones
Manager of Foundation and Government Relations . . . . Emily Ruddock
Manager of the Annual Fund. . . . . Gretchen Abrahamsen
Manager of Corporate Relations . . . . Danielle Manley
Development Coordinator . . . . .Andy Nusz

Finance

Director . . . . .Peggy Shake
Accounting Coordinator. . . . . Erin Bukowski
Accounting Assistants. . . . . Rebecca Price, Brunhilda Williams-Curington

Operations

Director . . . . Mike Schüssler-Williams
Operations Manager . . . . Barry Witt
Maintenance. . . . . Alan Reed
Receptionist/Administrative Assistant . . . . Griffin Falvey
Housekeeping. . . . . Patricia Duncan, Liosha Finn, Hank Hunter, Eliott Lasten,
Dion Lovett, Lavettis Morris, Charlene Patterson,
Michael Seargent, Sharon Sloan, Michelle Willis

AUDIENCE SERVICES

Ticket Sales

Director . . . . Kim McKercher
Senior Box Office Manager . . . . Saundra Blakeney

Training Manager . . . . .Steve Clark
Subscriptions Manager . . . . Julie Gallegos
Senior Customer Service Representative . . . . Kristy Kannapell
Customer Service Representatives . . . . Cheryl Anderson, Christie Baugher,
Amanda Blair, Alicia Dossett,
Carol Niehaus, Kelli Thompson

Volunteer and Audience Relations
Director . . . . .Allison Hammons
House Managers . . . . .Navid Afshar, Dana Cooley, Elizabeth Cooley,
Kyle Sawyer-Dailey Ethridge, Stephanie Lawson
Coat Check Supervisor . . . . .Cory Vaughn
Coat Check Attendants . . . . Cyndil Davis, Tanisha Johnson

ARTISTIC

Associate Artistic Director . . . . Sean Daniels
Associate Director . . . . Zan Sawyer-Dailey
Company Manager . . . . .Dot King

Literary
Director of New Play Development . . . . .Adrien-Alice Hansel
Literary Manager . . . . Amy Wegener
Resident Dramaturg . . . . Julie Felise Dubiner
Literary/Education Associate . . . . .Sarah Lunnie

Resident Designers
Costume Designer . . . . Lorraine Venberg
Lighting Designer . . . . Brian J. Lilienthal
Sound Designer . . . . Matt Callahan

Education
Director . . . . .Steven Rahe
Coordinator . . . . .Jacob Stoebel
Education Fellow . . . . .Jeffrey Mosser
Teaching Artists . . . . Liz Fentress, Jessica Leader

PRODUCTION

Production Manager . . . . .Kathleen Kronauer
Assistant Production Manager . . . . .Paul Werner
Production Stage Manager . . . . .Paul Mills Holmes
Resident Stage Managers . . . . .Kathy Preher, Kimberly J. First

Scenic
Technical Director . . . . .Jason Grant
Assistant Technical Directors . . . . .Alexis Tucker, Justin Hagovsky
Shop Foreman . . . . Javan Roy-Bachman
Carpenters . . . . Charles Ames, Braden Blauser,
Noah Johnson, Ben Passafiume, Pierre Vendette

Technical Production Assistant . . . . Rebecca Price
Pamela Brown Deck Carpenter . . . . Seth Holder
Bingham Theatre Deck Carpenter. . . . . Ryan Harvey
Scenic Charge. . . . . Kieran Wathen
Painters. . . . . Sabra Crockett, Ron Temple

Costume
Shop Manager . . . . Margret Fenske
Assistant to Shop Manager/Wardrobe Manager. . . . . .Cristy Smith
Assistant to Designer . . . . Lindsay Chamberlin
Craft Master. . . . . Shari Cochran
Head Draper . . . . Shana Lincoln
Technician . . . . Mary Lee Younger
First Hands. . . . . Christi Johnson, Karen Merrill
Stitchers . . . . Elizabeth Hahn,
Bonnie Jonus, Amanda Sox
Wig Master/Designer . . . . .Heather Fleming
Wardrobe Technicians. . . . . Jade Biviano, Asia Bloemmer,
Stephanie Adams, Regina Harris
Journeyman . . . . Jordan Bivens

Lighting
Supervisor . . . . Nick Dent
Assistant Supervisor . . . . .Lauren Scattolini
First Electrician. . . . . Rob Brodersen
Technicians . . . . .Katy Atwell, JohnBen Lacy,
Rosie Cruz, Derek Miller

Sound
Associate Designer . . . . Benjamin Marcum
Engineer. . . . . .Paul Doyle
Technicians . . . . .Stowe Nelson, Jacob Rosene

Properties
Properties Director . . . . Mark Walston
Props Master. . . . . Doc Manning
Carpenter . . . . .Joe Cunningham
General Artisan. . . . . William Griffith
Soft Goods Artisan. . . . . Heather Jakubisin
Journeyman . . . . .Jessie Combest*
Artisans . . . . Karl Anderson, Doug Aycock, Scott Rygalski

Video
Media Technologist. . . . . .Philip Allgeier

APPRENTICE/INTERN COMPANY

Director . . . . .Michael Legg
Associate Director. . . . . .Amy Attaway

Apprentices

Erin Adams, Natalie Allen, Dan Applegate, Alexis Bronkovic, Patricia Cancio, Brandon T. Chinn, Daniel Conway, Michael Cox, David Darrow, Kara Davidson, Gwen Ellis, Erin Fried, Zane Johnston, Courtney Moors, Brittany Parker, Jessica Rice, Brett Ashley Robinson, Tyler Jacob Rollinson, Shayan Jazy Shojaee, Robbie Tann, York Walker, Matt Whitfield

Members of the Apprentice Company receive additional training at the Louisville Ballet.

Interns

A/I Company..Navid Afshar
Arts Administration .... Cyndil Davis
Costume Crafts ....Lisa Weber
Development ....Cary Thale
Directing ....Jay Briggs, Gretchen Taylor Wright
Education........................... Rebecca Lynn Davis, Caitlin Puckett
Festival ....Christie Pettitt-Schieber
Graphics.. Jen L'amour Dorman
Lighting .... Dominique Luster,
                          Sarah Resnick, Rachel Fae Szymanski
Literary...Zach Chotzen-Freund,
                                        Emily Kate Feldman
Marketing... Angel L. Chichester
Public Relations.................................. Whitney Miller-Brengle
Scenic .... Matthew Krell*, Merced Rodriguez
Sound .... Marisa J. Barnes
Stage Management............................. Nicholas Bussett, Lizzy Lee,
                                        Jessica Potter, Katie Shade

KENNEDY CENTER/
WILLIAM R. KENAN FUND FOR THE ARTS FELLOWS

Lighting .... Andrew Cissna, John Burkland,
                          Brahim Pettis, Paola Rodriguez
Scenic ....Ryan Wineinger

Usher Captains

Dolly Adams, Marie Allen, Libba & Chuck Bonifer, Tanya Briley, Pernell & Maria Brown, Maleva Chamberlain, Donna Conlon, Terry Conway, Doris Elder, Reese Fisher, Joyce French, Tom Gerstle, Marilyn Huffman, Sandy Kissling, Barbara Nichols, Teresa Nusz, Judy Pearson, Nancy Rankin, Nathan Rome, Bob Rosedale, Amanda Simmons, Miranda Stone, Christopher Thompson, Tim Unruh, David Wallace, Bette Wood

Actors Theatre's company doctors:

Dr. Andrew Mickler, F.A.C.S.
Dr. Edwin Hopson, DC, CSCS
Dr. April Hopson, DC
Dr. Bill Breuer, MCH, DC, FAPHP

Foreword

Like most aspects of the arts in America, the ecosystem for new American plays has evolved over time from a monolithic idea of what constitutes a "well-made play" to a multifaceted arena where different voices have a chance to find their place. The effect of this shift on the Humana Festival of New American Plays has been positive and profound: of the many kinds of work we produce each year, 86% of the plays premiered in the Humana Festival's last decade have found subsequent productions in theatres large and small across the globe. Roughly half have opened in New York, and most of the rest have enjoyed multiple productions in theatres around the country. In spite of concerns about the state of new play production today, the success of this endeavor at the Humana Festival and beyond is strong evidence that theatres are producing lots of new work, and offering opportunities for its continued life—and that audiences are game to go on the ride.

One of the most notable developments in the contemporary theatre is the emergence and proliferation of ensemble-developed work—sometimes in partnership with playwrights and sometimes devised by the actors (or both). Most of these plays are only performed by the companies who develop them, and the ensembles' work is disseminated via touring, which has been rare in the American theatre until recently. Actors Theatre of Louisville has taken a lead in developing and showcasing this work over many years, with productions by SITI Company, UNIVERSES, New Paradise Laboratories, The Civilians, Marc Bamuthi Joseph, and others. In this volume you will find three such works: one by Rude Mechs in partnership with company member/playwright Kirk Lynn, another by four playwrights from Minneapolis' Workhaus Collective, collaborating with author/director/performers Dominique Serrand and Steve Epp, and an ensemble of actors. The third ensemble was formed to concoct a site-specific performance starring the 22 members of Actors Theatre's Apprentice Company, created by playwright Deborah Stein and director Sean Daniels, who built the event in collaboration with the actors and a team of animators.

As the style and substance of new plays have diversified, so has our methodology for development. The longstanding philosophy of the Humana Festival is to develop plays by producing them. We've recently committed resources to expand the amount of time that we devote to workshops and readings of work selected for the Festival. Every project has its own needs—and we believe strongly in letting the artists set the agenda for how much time they want to spend in development prior to rehearsals. Each of the plays in this volume has taken a different path to the Festival.

The economy has been rough over the past several years, causing all sorts of stress for businesses and individuals. Artists have been hit particularly hard. And yet there is cause for hope. The 34th Humana Festival enjoyed record attendance, and interest in these new plays is already strong. As this latest crop of new work moves out into the world, we reaffirm the power of theatre to speak to us in ways that matter. We value the different approaches to making plays and the wide range of people and organizations who will bring them new life—both in the imaginations of readers, and in theatres and conversations around the country.

—Marc Masterson
Artistic Director
Actors Theatre of Louisville

Editors' Note

Just remember, any moment, any moment
I could run through and eat the person you are most bored with
or the person you are most interested in
or the person you are sitting next to. Be careful.

This warning, delivered by an amiable Tiger, isn't just for the audience watching Rude Mechs' *The Method Gun*, but hits on the danger and risk that run through all the plays of the 2010 Humana Festival. The risks are different—bombing on Broadway, losing the ever-retreating memories that tell us who we are, chasing that fleeting sense of perfect love that's packaged in an effervescent pop song— but each of these plays considers a delicate balance of venture and danger, on and offstage.

The Austin-based company Rude Mechs created *The Method Gun* to explore what actors will do in pursuit of a truthful moment on stage, and the toll that pursuit takes on their lives and relationships. The play follows a company that has been abandoned by its guru, Stella Burden, but continues rehearsing her last project—*A Streetcar Named Desire* without any of the major characters— for nine years. The contentious and intermittently rewarding rehearsal process becomes an interrogation of the nature of failure and success itself, as the sum of all the love and the little disasters along the way.

Fissures (lost and found), another play created by a company of writer/director/ actors, examines discovery and loss more internally, by staging the experience of memory. The authors' interest isn't just in what happens when we forget, but the imaginative act of remembering: how much do we reinvent? How do we make sense of what's missing? As the actors lose and find the past again, the stage itself holds the memories that accumulate during the performance. Nothing less than our selfhood is at stake in this highly physical, funny, and moving look at the ephemerality of human memory.

The danger is less metaphoric and far more tangible in Lisa Dillman's *Ground*, a rich drama about a New Mexico border community whose lives are forever altered when a prodigal daughter returns to her father's pecan farm, unaware of all that's changed on the borderlands between families and neighbors. As the characters navigate a town now divided by the United States' immigration debate, the consequences of their actions radiate through the community.

The Festival's playwrights also addressed the live wire of risk that runs through romance, whether new or old. The characters in Scott Organ's winsome but unsentimental comedy *Phoenix* are so aware of the risks in every encounter that they nearly don't meet again at all. They badger, cajole, and accidentally talk themselves into what might be the risk of their lifetimes: a second date. But a lived-in relationship has its share of fear and uncertainty as well, as seen in Deborah Zoe Laufer's *Sirens*, a lighthearted investigation of couplehood at its quarter-century mark. Sam loves Rose—he really does—but in this classic comedy of remarriage, the siren's song of the life he could be living nearly overpowers his ability to see the life he has in front of him.

While some plays deliver peril in their plots, Dan O'Brien's large-hearted *The Cherry Sisters Revisited* puts failure center stage. Based on a real-life Vaudeville act, the Cherry Sisters quickly ascended from an Iowa barn to Broadway infamy when Oscar Hammerstein figured that he'd already put the best acts of the era on stage, and was ready to display the worst. With period music by Michael Friedman, the play imagines the journey of these historical figures, asking whether it's possible that an audience's mockery and disdain could still feel like love.

Also playing with the dynamic between actor and audience, danger and delight is Deborah Stein's *HEIST!*, created in collaboration with director Sean Daniels and the 2009-2010 Acting Apprentice Company. From the moment the audience arrived at 21c Museum Hotel, the art gallery for which this piece was devised, they were enveloped by the party and performance happening all around them. Soon a painting was stolen and numerous nefarious plans were unleashed— but just as adventuresome as the twisting plot was the way that the audience discovered characters and story during this madcap event.

All four of this year's ten-minute plays embraced the highest of stakes in compact form. From Gamal Abdel Chasten's song-laced portrait of the danger that the engines of technology pose to a way of life, to Dan Dietz's haunting reminiscence of a man who tried to scare his younger brother into feeling pain, to Diana Grisanti's girl-powered intervention to save a heart from an irresistible jerk, the plays' brevity made their risks all the more potent. In a metatheatrically dangerous feat, Greg Kotis even found himself trapped inside his own play, under interrogation by a couple of demanding, gun-wielding characters.

In the end, of course, all theatre is a risky undertaking—from the playwright throwing his or her imagination onto the page, to the wizardry that all the collaborators and theatre staff contribute to realize the play on the stage, to the leap of faith that the audience takes in witnessing these plays' first productions. There may be only one tiger running loose in this book, but the spirit of chance and possibility that makes the Humana Festival such an exciting undertaking still stalks every page. Be careful…

—*Adrien-Alice Hansel and Amy Wegener*

LET BYGONES BE
by Gamal Abdel Chasten

BIOGRAPHY

Let Bygones Be represents Gamal Abdel Chasten's fourth collaboration with Actors Theatre. Mr. Chasten first came to Actors Theatre as a member of *Rhythmicity*, then as a cast member of UNIVERSES' *Slanguage*, and in 2009 as a playwright and performer of UNIVERSES' *Ameriville*. Mr. Chasten's writing credits include *The Last Word* at PS 122 and *God Took Away His Poem* at the Abrons Arts Center. Mr. Chasten has been commissioned along with UNIVERSES for Oregon Shakespeare Festival's American Revolutions: the United States History Cycle. He has also written two screenplays, *Red Moon* and *Joe Bloe*, which he is currently shopping.

ACKNOWLEDGMENTS

Let Bygones Be premiered at the Humana Festival of New American Plays in March 2010. It was directed by KJ Sanchez with the following cast (in alphabetical order):

TRAVELING SALESMAN	Dan Applegate
BLACK AUTO WORKER	Gamal Abdel Chasten
WESTERN COWBOY	David Darrow
FEMALE CUSTOMER	Jennifer Engstrom
CAR SALESMAN	Dale Rivera
LAID-OFF AUTO WORKER	Tyler Jacob Rollinson
PULLMAN PORTER	York Walker
CASHIER	Natalie Allen

and the following production staff:

Scenic Designer	Brenda Ellis
Costume Designer	Lindsay Chamberlin
Lighting Designer	Nick Dent
Sound Designer	Benjamin Marcum
Properties Designer	Doc Manning
Fight Director	Drew Fracher
Video Designer	Philip Allgeier
Stage Manager	Paul Mills Holmes
Dramaturg	Sarah Lunnie
Stage Management Intern	Nick Bussett

CHARACTERS

WESTERN COWBOY/ MR. WATERS

TRAVELING SALESMAN

PULLMAN PORTER

LAID-OFF AUTO WORKER

BLACK AUTO WORKER

FEMALE CUSTOMER

CAR SALESMAN

CASHIER

David Darrow and Dan Applegate
in *Let Bygones Be*

34th Annual Humana Festival of New American Plays
Actors Theatre of Louisville, 2010
Photo by Harlan Taylor

LET BYGONES BE

Scene One

The show begins with video projections of newspaper clippings and images representing technological advancements and the auto industry.

The narrator, a WESTERN COWBOY *from the turn of the twentith century, enters strumming his guitar.*

WESTERN COWBOY. I believe it's all connected, the wanting to go
And wanting to let people know.
Whether it's a telegraph or teleport.
A chu chu train or just a train of thought.
Today's texting, or the bygone days of Edison's Multiplexing, Telegraphs
transmitting eight different messages, four in each direction.
But then the telegraph, got replaced by the telephone
the law of un-natural selection.
I remember a time when a phone call was a special event,
an after-dinner treat.
And if you called me and I wasn't home, then we didn't speak.
I remember horses. We had horses running up and down the dang streets, and
there was horse shit everywhere.
That was a hell of a time.
A time when I had to get on a horse and ride for hours…just to come see you.
I really must have wanted to see you.
Nothing like today.
Do you have Skype? Did you read my tweet? Shoot me an email.
Where I come from if I shoot you anything it's going to be a bullet.
Where I come from, traveling took a whole lot of time, energy and effort.
And if you were lucky enough to make it from point A, to point B,
The payoff was a bath, and a shot of whisky.
But along came time for change.
Exchanging the telegraphs for the telephones and horses for trains.
Trains…transporting goods and services from coast to coast.

(COWBOY THEME SONG)

I ride the rails all day
In hopes to find a better way
Sometimes I loss faith
When I see change, on the way

Ooh hu, hu hu ooh,
Ooh hu, hu hu ooh
Ooh hu, hu hu ooh,
Ooh hu, hu hu ooh

(Guitar keeps strumming.

TRAVELING SALESMAN *enters singing a song reminiscent of a Broadway musical. He exists in present day. With the help of visual aids he narrates his life as a traveling salesman, which takes us from 1950s to present day.)*

TRAVELING SALESMAN. *(Singing.)* I'm a T-R-A-V-E-L-ING Salesman
  I gotta trunk
  I got a trunk
  It's full of junk
  It's full of junk
  I gotta ride the rails and make a sale today
  Plan my course
  Plan my course
  I'm my own boss
  My own boss
  And door to door is how I spend my day
  A face to face
  A face to face
  A firm handshake
  A firm handshake
  A how do you do?
  Would you like two?
  One green, One grey
  But my luck is down
  From town to town
  Cause now a days
  Everything's a click away
  T-R-A-V-E-L-ING Salesman!
        (Guitar strum now mimics a train.)

SALESMAN/PORTER. I used to make a living doing this. Before Ozzie met Harriet. Before birth control pills and burning bras, back when we had stay-at-home moms.

PULLMAN PORTER. When Louis fought Schmeling.

TRAVELING SALESMAN. When our country grew more than just corn.

SALESMAN/PORTER. My gift of gab was my greatest gift.

PULLMAN PORTER. Next stop Bloomfield!

SALESMAN/PORTER. But not anymore. Now The Past is hung to dry on clothing lines.

TRAVELING SALESMAN. Housewives don't answer the door for Willy Loman anymore.

PULLMAN PORTER. This used to be one of the best jobs a black man could find.

TRAVELING SALESMAN. And my life has become a bad knock-knock joke.

SALESMAN/PORTER. It's hard to make a living like this anymore.

PULLMAN PORTER. Now they got recorded announcements.

(*He mimics an electronic announcement.*)

Next stop Bloomfield.

TRAVELING SALESMAN. eBay, Amazon and Overstock.com

SALESMAN/PORTER. And look at all that damn corn. It makes every town look like the last. I remember when we used to sing about our purple mountains majesty.

TRAVELING SALESMAN. When we grew tobacco.

PULLMAN PORTER. Wheat.

TRAVELING SALESMAN. And cotton.

SALESMAN/PORTER. But now I can only hum a song about corn. Don't get me wrong I love corn.

TRAVELING SALESMAN. Corn chips.

PULLMAN PORTER. Corn fritters.

SALESMAN/PORTER. And Corn Dogs.

TRAVELING SALESMAN. But working stiffs are being replaced by genetically modified cornstalks. And no one is buying innovation door-to-door. Trust me, I'm trying hard to sell it.

SALESMAN/PORTER. Yep, the car has killed the train.

TRAVELING SALESMAN. And this land is not my land anymore.

PULLMAN PORTER. Bloomfield!

(*Lights up on* COWBOY.)

Scene Two

WESTERN COWBOY. The more things change
The more things change!
I'm not saying change is bad.
I kinda like shopping more than I do hunting.
Drive down to the supermarket, food already frozen,
Meat already sliced, and canned peaches in syrup.
I like canned peaches in syrup.
I heard a guy from Kentucky is selling fried chicken in a bucket…roadside.
And it's all because of the car.
Mass-produced for our boys coming back from war.
There is opportunity in war.
Steel mills need milling.
Stockyards need stocking.

New roads need new cars.

And thanks to the interstate, now you can drive across the country and see nothing. The car is now king.

> (COWBOY *begins singing a Zydeco song accompanied by a harmonica player as images of car plants and auto workers fill the screen.*)

WESTERN COWBOY. Gotta build that car, gotta drive that car

Gotta start that car, gotta take it far

Gotta get some gas, gotta go real fast

Gotta make it last, the time has come, and

The Model T was the model car

For the average Joe that was on the go

The big three grew 'cause they had a war

To make tanks and bombs for America

I know where my God is

Pride has gone today, but

We sure need it back, in the worst way.

LAID-OFF AUTO WORKER. The car helped break my virginity, sex in the back seat

BLACK AUTO WORKER. The car helped me escape Jim Crow, let me drive in the front seat. Gave me control over my life.

LAID-OFF AUTO WORKER. That's right! Helped you navigate.

BLACK AUTO WORKER. Found my way to the middle class.

LAID-OFF AUTO WORKER. Union wages.

BLACK AUTO WORKER. And self-pride!

LAID-OFF AUTO WORKER. The road represented freedom.

BLACK AUTO WORKER. Sometimes. I had responsibility. Drove all the way from Arkansas with my two sisters, about 1950.

LAID-OFF AUTO WORKER. Tough times.

BLACK AUTO WORKER. Held tight to our tongues in every town, every time we were stopped by the cops.

LAID-OFF AUTO WORKER. Tough times.

BLACK AUTO WORKER. But we made it.

LAID-OFF AUTO WORKER. From somethin to nothin.

BLACK AUTO WORKER. And that was before Dashikis and Afros and all that Black Pride.

LAID-OFF AUTO WORKER. Got a good job.

BLACK AUTO WORKER. Bought my first house. We had everything. One house…

LAID-OFF AUTO WORKER. Two cars…

BLACK AUTO WORKER. The American Dream.

LAID-OFF AUTO WORKER. Not so much anymore. You know, I've always supported my family. It don't feel good having a daughter who just turned twenty-one supporting me. I blame them damn SUV's.

BLACK AUTO WORKER. Hell if it was. It was automation, machines replacing man. And the interstate. Remember Black Bottom?

LAID-OFF AUTO WORKER. Black folks replaced by highway and concrete.

BLACK AUTO WORKER. Roads got to go somewhere.

LAID-OFF AUTO WORKER. Usually the poor part of town.

BLACK AUTO WORKER. Driving over, to avoid a drive-by. The highway controls commerce.

LAID-OFF AUTO WORKER. And the bank controls my mortgage. Which is why I got to get out. I'm telling you SUV's

BLACK AUTO WORKER. Well, we did get the bailout.

LAID-OFF AUTO WORKER. They did. Not you or me.

BLACK AUTO WORKER. I'd like to thank the car for suburban gridlock.

LAID-OFF AUTO WORKER. Global warming.

BLACK AUTO WORKER. And lost dreams.

LAID-OFF AUTO WORKER. I'd like to thank technology for my rise and my fall.

BLACK AUTO WORKER. Cheers.

Scene Three

Two stereotypical characters from New Jersey, one is a CAR SALESMAN, *the other is a* YOUNG LADY *shopping for a car.*

FEMALE CUSTOMER. I was actually hoping for a hybrid, you know, going green and all…

CAR SALESMAN. But this is a classic. Bucket seats, dual exhaust and four on the floor.

FEMALE CUSTOMER. What about GPS? Does it have GPS?

CAR SALESMAN. GPS makes you lazy. What ever happened to our frontiersman spirit? Christopher Columbus never had no GPS.

FEMALE CUSTOMER. You sound like my ex-husband.

CAR SALESMAN. Smart man!

FEMALE CUSTOMER. He's my ex-husband! Look, I don't know, it's a beautiful car, but it looks more like a museum exhibit rather than something I'd want to drive. And I'm really trying to be more aware. Protect the environment.

CAR SALESMAN. Not to worry, cars don't cause global warming.

FEMALE CUSTOMER. (*Skeptical.*) They don't?

CAR SALESMAN. Of course not. It's caused by cow poop.

FEMALE CUSTOMER. What?

CAR SALESMAN. I read somewhere that global warming is caused by cow poop.

FEMALE CUSTOMER. Really?

CAR SALESMAN. You've never seen Al Gore ride a cow, but he does drive a car. And do you think if cars caused global warming the man who almost was president would be caught dead in one?

FEMALE CUSTOMER. I never thought of it that way before. It does bring back a lot of memories, my older brother Bobby had one like it growing up in Jersey.

CAR SALESMAN. Yeah, these cars used to be real popular with young men, but now they're real popular with the ladies. It's like having a bodyguard. No one messes with a girl driving a muscle car.

FEMALE CUSTOMER. How many miles to the gallon?

CAR SALESMAN. Ehhhhh…you'll get about 15 miles to the gallon in the city.

FEMALE CUSTOMER. That's not a whole lot.

CAR SALESMAN. But you're buying this car for more than just mileage.

FEMALE CUSTOMER. But it's got no GPS, and I'm horrible with maps. If I followed a map I'd end up in the Atlantic. My girlfriend just bought a new car, and hers has a thermal imaging camera. I drive a lot at night, and I can use a thermal imaging camera.

CAR SALESMAN. I'm not sure I know what that is.

FEMALE CUSTOMER. It can spot people and animals in the dark, up to 2,000 feet away.

CAR SALESMAN. Really?

FEMALE CUSTOMER. I swear it's like *Knight Rider*. You remember Kitt from *Knight Rider*?

CAR SALESMAN. Yeah.

FEMALE CUSTOMER. Well it's like that. My girlfriend can even voice activate her iPod. And if she gets in an accident and the airbags become employed, the car calls 911.

CAR SALESMAN. You're making this up.

FEMALE CUSTOMER. I'm not making this up. All the new technology really helps you keep your hands on the wheel and your mind on the road. I'm telling you flying cars are not far behind.

CAR SALESMAN. Personally I think it's all a bit much, all the doo-dads, and doo-hickeys. Me, I want to use my brain when I drive. I want to hit the open road, and I want to know that I am the master of my own fate. And this car right here, gives YOU the control!

FEMALE CUSTOMER. But what if you get stranded on a dark road, in a ditch or something?

CAR SALESMAN. I do believe in cell phones.

FEMALE CUSTOMER. No service. What if there's no service? You could use a few doo-hickeys then.

CAR SALESMAN. That's where you're wrong. 'Cause I never travel alone. I thrive off of human companionship.

FEMALE CUSTOMER. But then you'll both be stranded.

CAR SALESMAN. But at least I'll have company.

Scene Four

WESTERN COWBOY *plays the chords for the Cowboy Theme song.*

WESTERN COWBOY. You can surf the web, or surf a wave. You can communicate, or commute to see your date. You can ride the information super highway, or get stuck in traffic on an actual highway. Virtual reality is kinda like the real thing. But not. You can't virtually loose your job. Innovation often means OUTTA HERE! While forging forward we often leave good folks behind.

Scene Five

CASHIER. Sorry, this aisle's closed.

MR. WATERS. Hey Peg.

CASHIER. I can tell you one thing Mr. Waters, I'm not going to miss people like that.

MR. WATERS. I don't understand; did you get a new job?

CASHIER. Sort of…my new job is looking for a job.

MR. WATERS. I'm real sorry to hear that.

CASHIER. Maybe it's for the best, when one door closes, another one opens. The only problem is the other door is stuck.

MR. WATERS. At least you can collect unemployment; they keep extending the benefits right?

CASHIER. I don't qualify for unemployment. I'm a part-timer.

MR. WATERS. You're a great worker, why are they letting you go?

CASHIER. It's not just me. A bunch of us are being let go. Being replaced by automated check-out machines.

MR. WATERS. I still can't use those things. And every time someone's behind me I always feel rushed, and then I screw it up and then an employee's got to come over and help me out anyway.

CASHIER. I guess that's progress.

MR. WATERS. Yeah, progress. You know what I do for a living Peg? I trim trees. As long as we have trees, I'll have a job.

CASHIER. Maybe I should look into trees.

MR. WATERS. Yeah, how about that.

CASHIER. Cash or credit Mr. Waters?

MR. WATERS. Cash.

CASHIER. That'll be $36.29

MR. WATERS. I wouldn't worry, Peg. You're a hard worker. Anybody would be lucky to have you.

CASHIER. Thanks Mr. Waters. Have a great day!

MR. WATERS. I wish you the best Peg. I wish you the best.

> (PEG *checks out. She whistles the Cowboy Theme as she walks to her car that has all her belongings inside.* PEG *is still whistling the tune as she falls asleep in her car.*)

Epilogue

WESTERN COWBOY. It has been my understanding that the train, the car and the airplane were supposed to make life easier, bring us closer together. Allow us to go where we want, when we want in the least amount of time. Hell, for 100 million dollars you can go on a lunar mission to the moon. That's where all this is headed. Out into the great beyond. Where we'll contract space viruses. And then we'll have to protect ourselves from each other, and General Motors will build these little bubble cars, and we'll be floating out in space. Trapped in these individualized bubbles or pods. I-pods. And in these Ipods we'll have everything at our disposal, within arm's reach. We'll be able to communicate with each other by thought. Our chins will recede from all the processed foods we eat.

Spoiled by gadgets, we'll loose all our social skills, and next human interaction will become obsolete. And then we'll start to resemble domesticated animals. Scared, short legged, creatures with quick thumbs. But here is a silver lining. No more horse shit!

> (*Chorus*)
> Ooh hu, hu hu ooh, (*G chords.*)
> Ooh hu, hu hu ooh (*C/G chords.*)
> Ooh hu, hu hu ooh, (*D/C chords.*)
> Ooh hu, hu hu ooh (*G chords.*)
> (WESTERN COWBOY *exits.*)

End of Play

LOBSTER BOY
by Dan Dietz

BIOGRAPHY

Dan Dietz's plays include *tempOdyssey*, *Americamisfit*, *The Sandreckoner*, and *Clementine in the Lower Nine*, and have been seen in New York, Los Angeles, and points in between. *tempOdyssey* received a rolling world premiere from the National New Play Network, premiering at Curious Theatre (Denver, CO), The Studio Theatre (Washington, DC), Phoenix Theatre (Indianapolis, IN) and New Jersey Repertory (Long Branch, NJ). The play was also named a finalist for the 2007 PEN USA Literary Award in Drama. Dietz has been honored with an NEA/TCG Theatre Residency, a James A. Michener Fellowship, a Josephine Bay Paul Fellowship, and the Austin Critics Table Award for Best New Play. He received the Heideman Award from Actors Theatre of Louisville in 2003 for his play *Trash Anthem*, and again in 2010 for his play *Lobster Boy*. Dietz's work has been developed and presented at the Kennedy Center, the Public Theater, the Guthrie Theater, Actors Theatre of Louisville, Rattlestick Playwrights Theater, CenterStage, and the Summer Play Festival, among others. He is a two-time finalist for the Princess Grace Award, a two-time nominee for the Weissberger Award, a nominee for the ATCF/Steinberg Award, a nominee for the Oppenheimer/Newsday Award, and a four-time finalist for the Humana Festival of New American Plays. His work has been published by Dramatists Play Service, Heinemann, Playscripts, Samuel French, Smith & Kraus, and Stage & Screen. He is currently a Jerome Fellow at The Playwrights' Center in Minneapolis.

ACKNOWLEDGEMENTS

Lobster Boy was performed at the Humana Festival of New American Plays in March 2010. It was directed by KJ Sanchez with the following cast:

MAN ....Trey Lyford

and the following production staff:

Scenic Designer .... Brenda Ellis
Costume Designer.. Lindsay Chamberlin
Lighting Designer... Nick Dent
Sound Designer ....Benjamin Marcum
Properties Designer... Doc Manning
Video Designer ....Philip Allgeier
Stage Manager..Paul Mills Holmes
Dramaturg ....Sarah Lunnie

Stage Management Intern .... Nick Bussett

Lobster Boy was originally created as part of *The Scariest*, an evening of short plays produced by The Exchange in 2008 in New York City.

CHARACTERS

A Man in his 30s, calm, thoughtful, intellectual, reserved.

SETTING

Anyplace suitable for a lecture with slides.

NOTE

It is crucial that—with the exception of the Mozart aria—no attempt be made to use actual pictures or sounds in the realization of the slides. The slides are meant to be text, letters and symbols, nothing more.

Trey Lyford
in *Lobster Boy*

34th Annual Humana Festival of New American Plays
Actors Theatre of Louisville, 2010
Photo by Harlan Taylor

LOBSTER BOY

A MAN, 30s, stands, perhaps at a podium, a glass of water within his reach. Behind him a slide is projected that reads: LOBSTER BOY.

MAN. There once was a boy. He had a little brother. They were born two years apart.

Slide: PICTURES IN YOUR HEAD:
> A BOY (AGE 14)
> HIS BROTHER (AGE 12)
> A LOBSTER (AGE INDETERMINATE)

They lived in a house. In a working-class neighborhood. In that kind of dead zone between the city and the suburbs.

Slide: PICTURES IN YOUR HEAD:
> A HOUSE (SMALL)
> A NEIGHBORHOOD (ALSO SMALL)
> A LOBSTER (MEAL-SIZED)

Their father was a boxer. Their father was unsuccessful. He left to remedy this.

Slide: PICTURES IN YOUR HEAD:
> A MAN (TOUGH)
> A PAIR OF BOXING GLOVES (TOUGHER)
> A LOBSTER (CHITINOUS)

He never came back.

> *(Slide out.)*

Which meant that their mother had to work day and night shifts to support them. Which meant that "the job" fell to the older brother. The job was time consuming, intimate, and went like this: the younger brother stood in his underwear, and the older brother looked at his younger brother's body, from a distance of one to three inches. Here is a brief list of what the older brother was looking for:

Slide: CUTS
> BURNS
> PUNCTURES
> PERHAPS A MISSING TOE
> &c.

The reason for this was thus: the younger brother had been born beautiful, healthy, and entirely without the ability to feel pain. Thus what to us would be this:

Slide: SOUNDS IN YOUR HEAD:
> A KNIFE SLICING SOMETHING
> A PERSON SAYING OW!
> A BAND-AID BEING APPLIED

To him would be this:

> *Slide*: A KNIFE SLICING SOMETHING
> …
> …

Every night of every day of the older brother's life was devoted to scanning over his younger brother's body, like the way you might look up a difficult word in the dictionary.

> *Slide:* **nociceptor** (no•si•sep•tər) *n.* a sensory receptor for pain stimuli, usually found in great bundles in the body's most sensitive parts

Something was wrong with the younger boy's nociceptors. Also his brain, but the older boy never really understood that part. What he understood was that his brother's condition, combined with his father's absence and his mother's brutal work schedule, meant that any and every responsibility that placed one within any distance of a heated stove, a bladed knife, a lawnmower, etc. was up to him. So while the younger brother came home from school and did this:

> *Slide*: WATCH TV
> RIDE BIKE
> PLAY VIDEO GAMES

The older brother came home from school and did this:

> *Slide*: FIX SINK
> MOW LAWN
> COOK DINNER

And more importantly, this:

> *Slide*: HAVE NO FRIENDS

So while everyone else looked at his younger brother and saw this:

> *Slide*: BEAUTIFUL BLOND HAIR
> GOOFY BIG EARS
> AN EVER-PRESENT GRIN

More and more, he looked at his younger brother and saw this:

> *Slide*: THAT WHICH MAKES ME WORK
> THAT WHICH MAKES ME TIRED
> THAT WHICH MAKES ME ALONE

Which brings us to lobsters.

> *Slide*: PICTURE IN YOUR HEAD:
> A POT (FILLED WITH WATER (BOILING))
> A HAND (FILLED WITH A LOBSTER)
> A LOBSTER (FILLED WITH ?)

There is a bit of a debate raging over whether lobsters, upon being tossed into a pot of boiling water, feel what we as human beings with a spinal column, limbic system and frontal cortex would recognize and categorize as "pain."

Slide: SOUNDS IN YOUR HEAD:
    A KNIFE SLICING SOMETHING
    A PERSON SAYING DAMMIT!
    A SECOND BAND-AID BEING APPLIED

It's not a new debate, and the jury seems permanently out on this one, but there is some disagreement over the gray areas. However, gray areas do not fit neatly into a ninth grade biology class, nor into a fourteen-year-old boy's mind.

Slide: PICTURES IN YOUR HEAD:
    A GRAY AREA
    A FOURTEEN-YEAR-OLD BOY'S MIND
    AN AWKWARD MOMENT

Particularly a fourteen-year-old boy who has grown extremely tired of knowing about the subtle changes in his brother's body before said brother does.

Slide: CONVERSATION IN YOUR HEAD:
    A: "Dude, you've hit puberty."
    B: "Really?"
    A: "Yep: look."
    B: "Oh yeah, thanks."

So imagine this boy's ears perking up when he hears his science teacher proclaim, without a hint of doubt, that lobsters, having evolved with only a chitinous outer shell and a few ham-fisted nerve bundles, simply do not have the physical capability to feel pain during those pre-bisque preparations.

Slide: PICTURES IN YOUR HEAD:
    A POT FILLED WITH WATER (BOILING)
    A SCIENCE TEACHER (LECTURING)
    A FOURTEEN-YEAR-OLD BOY (LISTENING)

Now imagine the same ears on the same boy perking up past what seems humanly possible upon hearing this next factoid: that lobsters, lacking an apparatus capable of sensing and processing pain, almost certainly also lack the ability to feel…fear.

Slide: PICTURE IN YOUR HEAD:
    A PLAN (UNFOLDING) WITHIN A BRAIN (BOILING) BEHIND THE EYES (DISTANT, INTENSE) OF A FOURTEEN-YEAR-OLD-BOY

It was a simple plan that unfolded itself inside the boy's mind at that moment. One based more on a childhood sense of the tautological than on any depth of consideration. If animals that do not feel pain consequently do not feel fear, then the best and perhaps only way to give a good jolt of shock therapy to his twelve-year-old brother's nervous system and grow those prematurely burnt-out nociceptors into ones capable of experiencing the prick of a needle, the crack of a baseball in the face, the sizzling rush of okay-that-bathwateris-gonna-give-me-second-degree-burns-now, was to scare the complete and thorough Jesus out of him.

    Slide: A BRAIN (BOILING) BEHIND THE EYES (DISTANT, INTENSE)
    Slide: THE EYES (DISTANT, INTENSE)
    Slide: THE EYES

       (*Slide out.*)

    Slide: A PAUSE

       (*A pause. A sip of water. Slide out.*)

The thing about drowning is, it's not about the pain.

    Slide: DROWNING = PAIN?

It hurts, by all accounts, but that's really secondary to the experience. No, the thing about drowning is, it's all about the horror.

    Slide: DROWNING = FEAR

It generates in one a fear that comes from a place deeper than logic, deeper even than the brain. It comes from the body itself. It's as though every organ, every cell within you recognizes that something is going horribly wrong, and if that something is not fixed, and soon…. In short, it brings about absolute physical panic.

At least, this was the thought inside the fourteen-year-old boy's mind…

    Slide: THOUGHT = (DROWNING = FEAR)

…as he rushed back from his school to his neighborhood…

    Slide: (NEIGHBORHOOD (HOUSE (POOL)))

…within which sat his house…within which (or just outside of which) sat its swimming pool…over which rested a simple yet crucial feature: a heavy, black, tightly-fitting tarp which snapped into place via a series of hard metal studs circling the pool.

    Slide: (NEIGHBORHOOD (HOUSE (POOL (TARP))))
                        WATER

The tarp had a history of being employed in a manner not intended by its creators. For it could not help but be noticed by the two boys that their father had left behind a number of pairs of used, torn, pungent-smelling gloves.

    Slide: PICTURE IN YOUR HEAD:
          BOXING GLOVES

And it also could not help but be noticed that the tarp, once in place, etched out a space roughly analogous to that of a boxing ring.

    Slide: (TARP) = BOXING RING
          WATER

It supported the boys surprisingly well at six and eight, began to sag beneath their weight at nine and eleven, and now…well, they liked to think of it as adding an advanced level of difficulty to an otherwise rote form of entertainment. Besides, it was black, which concealed bloodstains from their mother. The snaps took a surprising amount of effort to pry loose, and in the end the boy could only uncover about a quarter of the pool before his fingers were rubbed raw and the pain forced him to stop, as it would anyone with a normal body. But a quarter, positioned directly over the deepest end of the pool, was enough. He peered for a moment at the shimmering, stale-looking water quivering just beneath the tarp's surface. Then he gently laid the corner back down onto the concrete edge of the pool, and waited for night to fall.

Slide: PICTURE IN YOUR HEAD:
    NIGHT (FALLING)

It is astonishing to me what people assume about children. About what children are capable of.

Slide: PICTURE IN YOUR HEAD:
    STARS (TWINKLING)

Mozart composed the melody to "Twinkle, Twinkle Little Star" when he was just a boy. By fourteen he'd written his first opera.

    (*Suddenly*, *"Nel sen mi palpita dolente il core" from Mozart's* Mitridate, Re di Ponte *bursts into our ears—perhaps starting at the intense, terror-filled final 30 seconds.*)

Slide: PICTURE IN YOUR HEAD:
    A FOURTEEN-YEAR-OLD BOY WITH AN OPERA IN HIS
    EYES

An opera. At fourteen. It ends with a suicide.

    (*A moment, as the* MAN *stares beyond us, through us, into something unseen. Then the music ceases, and the* MAN'*s eyes refocus.*)

Slide: PICTURE IN YOUR HEAD:
    NIGHT (FALLEN)

When it was dark out, and the tarp's surface nothing more than a black blob in the backyard, the older brother entered the younger brother's room and tossed a pair of boxing gloves onto his bed. It was a gesture in need of no words. The routine was understood. The younger boy donned his gloves and the older boy helped him lace up. Tightly. Then the two boys raced down the stairs together, rushed through the living room and out the back door. With a howl of joy…

Slide: SOUND IN YOUR HEAD:
    JOY

…the younger boy leapt onto the surface of the tarp, while the older boy, for the first time ever in the history of their game, stopped short. The second the younger boy's feet hit the tarp, the undone corner sank beneath his weight and the water sucked him right under.

Slide: SOUND IN YOUR HEAD:
    A SPLASH

The older boy's goal had always only been to instigate fear within the younger boy. He saw it (and he knows now, believe me he knows this must seem at best bizarre and at worst rather sick) but he saw it as a sort of gift.

Slide: PICTURES IN YOUR HEAD:
    A CORNER OF A TARP (SINKING)
    A BODY UNDER THE TARP (FLAILING)
    A PAIR OF LUNGS (CONSTRICTING)

A gift given, as many gifts are, that it might benefit not only the receiver, but the giver as well.

Slide: PICTURES IN YOUR HEAD:
    A YOUNGER BOY (PANICKING)
    AN OLDER BOY (WATCHING)
    STARS (TWINKLING)

For if the younger brother were to be scared deeply enough, he might regain his ability to feel pain.

Slide: SOUNDS IN YOUR HEAD:
    CRYING
    GURGLING
    SMACKING (GLOVED FISTS AGAINST UNDERSIDE OF
        TARP?)

And if he regained his ability to feel pain, he could be as afraid of it as the rest of us.

Slide: PICTURES IN YOUR HEAD:
    AN OLDER BOY (BY THE POOL)
    BOXING GLOVES (REMOVED)
    BARE HANDS (REVEALED)

And if he was as afraid of pain as the rest of us, he would seek to avoid injury.

Slide: PICTURES IN YOUR HEAD:
    AN OLDER BOY (KNEELING)
    BARE HANDS (SWEATING)
    BLACK TARP (WAITING)

And if he sought to avoid injury, it would no longer be necessary for the older brother to carry the entire load of the house upon his back, take care of everything, all without a mother or father around to guide, to assist, to encourage, to offer more than a symbolic presence in his already ancient-feeling life.

Slide: SOUNDS IN YOUR HEAD:
    CRYING
    GURGLING
    MUFFLED SCREAM (A BOY'S NAME?)

And then, as if adding one last insult to the labor of his days, to check for injuries every night upon a body that ought to know its own damn surfaces by now.

Slide: PICTURE IN YOUR HEAD:
    STARS (TWINKLING)

A gift. To them all.

But the factor the older brother had failed to account for was the sheer disorientation that occurs when one is submerged underwater with no air and no light. Meaning that, once he slipped under the tarp, the younger boy had no way to judge which direction to swim in toward safety.

Slide: PICTURES IN YOUR HEAD:
    HANDS (SUBMERGING)
    FINGERS (GRASPING)
    TARP (RISING)

So when it came time to lift the corner and pull it back, to expose the younger brother to the darkness and stars and above all air, when he finally pulled it back…his brother wasn't there.

Slide: SOUNDS IN YOUR HEAD:
    AS BEFORE, BUT SUBSIDING

He reached into the black water then, frantically searching for something, a blond head of hair, a goofy ear, a gloved fist.

Slide: SOUNDS IN YOUR HEAD:
    SUBSIDING

He strained until it hurt, until every fiber of his arm, from the shoulder blade to the fingertips was alight with what all but perhaps the lobster would recognize and categorize as pain. Nothing.

Slide: SOUNDS IN YOUR HEAD:
    …

There was nothing he could reach.

    (*Slide out.*)

Slide: A PAUSE

    (*A pause. No water this time. Slide out.*)

In studies of the subject, the distinction is often made between two different components of pain: the physical and the emotional. The physical component is where the sensation comes from, but it is the emotional component that makes the sensation a bad one. A lobster in a pot may struggle and slam itself repeatedly against the sides, the lid…but we do not know whether the slamming and struggling comes from the experience of a bad sensation, or simply from the automatic response of its muscle fiber to a substance that is rapidly enveloping and destroying it. You will notice that nowhere in there does anyone so much as mention the third possibility: that the lobster might actually be afraid.

Slide: PICTURES IN YOUR HEAD:
    POOL
    POLICE
    POLICE LIGHTS

This is what the older boy reminded himself as the police hauled back the black tarp and shone their lights down on the body of his little brother, floating face down, gloved hands red and weirdly reminiscent of those of a smaller, more chitinous animal with whom he seemed to share a few things in common.

Slide: PICTURE IN YOUR HEAD:
    BOXING GLOVES

The older brother reminded himself that he had almost certainly failed. That his kid brother, who had always been so brave, so reckless, moving through the world with the eager abandon of a child giant…that his brother probably didn't feel a thing. And was, up to and including the final moment of his life, almost certainly not scared.

    (*Slide out.*)

Remarkably (or perhaps not so) the word "deliberate" was never used.

    Slide: **accident** (ak•si•dent) *n.* an unfortunate incident that happens unexpectedly and unintentionally, usually resulting in damage or injury.

The older brother was assumed not to have committed the crime on purpose, in much the same way that he was assumed not to have written an opera. And the events of that autumn fell away, brushed slowly aside to rest beneath the category of "neighborhood tragedy."

Which all had a strange effect on the older brother.

Slide: PICTURE IN YOUR HEAD:
    A LOBSTER

He found himself unable to feel anything about the situation. One way or the other. He recognized the absence of his brother. He recognized that at one time he had both adored and despised the little boy in an ever shifting, ever churning mixture. But now, he could feel nothing. No guilt. No sadness. And, though it probably goes without saying, certainly no pain.

(*Slide out.*)

The older brother grew up to be a teacher, and now, in a choice bit of irony, works in the very same high school he attended back in those days. He stands in a classroom all day, five days a week, and lectures on mathematics to a group of bored and vaguely angry-looking kids. Sometimes for complicated equations, he uses slides or an overhead.

But lately.

Lately, he's started doing something new. Something probably not quite legal, though it would be difficult to define the crime in it exactly. Lately, he sneaks in at night.

> *Slide*: PICTURE IN YOUR HEAD:
>   STARS (TWINKLING)

When all but the janitors are gone. Sneaks into the classroom he'd sat in long ago when that magical plan had unfolded itself inside his mind. He sets up his slides, fills a glass of water…and he lectures. The lecture he gives at night is to nobody at all, and concerns nothing anyone would understand. Pots and lobsters and a pair of young boys. If pressed, he could not adequately explain why he does it. If pressed, he would simply stare at you, silently, with a pair of eyes not quite his own.

> *Slide*: A FOURTEEN-YEAR-OLD BOY WITH AN OPERA IN HIS
>   EYES
> *Slide*: AN OPERA IN HIS EYES
> *Slide*: HIS EYES

(*Slide out.*)

If you ask me though…. If you want to know what I think…I'd say he is actively attempting, on a nightly basis, to scare the complete and thorough Jesus out of himself.

> (*The final few moments of Mozart's "Nel sen mi palpita dolente il core" rush in to fill our ears. The* MAN *simply stares at us, expressionless.*)

> *Slide*: BLACKOUT

> (*Everything, including the slide, cuts out.*)

End of Play

GROUND
by Lisa Dillman

ABOUT *GROUND*

This article first ran in the January/February 2010 issue of Inside Actors, *and is based on conversations with the playwright before rehearsals for the Humana Festival production began.*

Zelda, 35, unemployed and recently orphaned, inherits her father's pecan grove on the southern border of New Mexico. She hasn't lived in Fronteras for twenty years, since she left town with her mother at sixteen. The landscape is just as breathtaking and the work of farming pecans just as hard, but everything else has shifted profoundly. Population is way down. Most of the town's businesses—the hospital, the supermarket—have closed. Her Mexican-American ex-boyfriend patrols the border, and has married a woman whose aunt was deported. More strikingly, the place *feels* different: everyone's angry or scared. The border, which seemed immaterial to Zelda, now starkly divides opinions, sometimes within the same family. Home used to be simple; now Zelda not only has to learn how to live without either of her parents, but must also decide whether to stay in a place that looks familiar but feels as hostile as the New Mexican desert.

The impetus for *Ground* came when playwright Lisa Dillman noticed changes in and around her parents' southern New Mexico community following September 11, 2001. "Homeland Security and the Border Patrol really started to crack down," she says. "Security got super tight, and it split the community. Suddenly there was a distance between people that I'd never seen before. Undocumented workers used to cross the border all the time. They'd get deported and just come right back. But that changed. Crossing the border got tougher and more dangerous. That led to a shortage of immigrant labor for border businesses, but more striking to me was this shortage of human feeling. It was palpable." And she started hearing stories: People who had been in the country twenty years, who had put down roots and held longtime jobs were suddenly deported. Children were being raised by distant relatives to keep them on the U.S. side of the border.

Dillman didn't know she was working on a play, though, until she stumbled on several more elements, and kept thinking about their surprising connections. A visit to a pecan farm during irrigation season gave her an austere and gorgeous setting. A story in her parents' paper about a farmer in Arizona whose eight-foot steel fence on the border was financed by private donations, many from citizen-run border surveillance groups, led to Dillman's fascination with the Minutemen and similar organizations. As she researched these volunteers who patrol the border on their own time and money, she was surprised by the complexity of the anti-immigration perspective.

"The more I poked around and listened, the more fascinated I got with these questions of immigration and security and home." Dillman says. "There aren't a lot of heroes or villains. There are just people—on both sides—struggling against forces beyond their control." From these intricacies, Dillman weaves a story of interdependence and compromise between families and neighbors. Zelda is looking for home on her childhood farm. Ines, pregnant and unwell, yearns for her deported aunt, a midwife who's never lost a baby. Ines's sister Angie holds herself and her family together by almost sheer will, cleaning, cutting hair, selling food to Minutemen and immigrants alike. Angie's determined to help her sister, whatever the damage. Angie's husband Carl is Zelda's ex-boyfriend. He wants to take care of Ines—and keep his job with Border Patrol, which means he can't sneak a deported woman to Fronteras. Rendered with warmth and complexity, these characters disagree with each other with as much intensity as they depend on one another.

Zelda's pecan farm provides not only the play's setting, but a metaphor that promises a way forward for the divided community and families. As Zelda contemplates keeping the pecan farm, she sees Chuy, an immigrant who's worked the land since her father started the farm, bandaging a tree. When she asks him what he's doing, he reluctantly explains: "I'm grafting a piece of one cultivar onto a seedling of another. I bind them tight like this so they'll go ahead and grow together. Then down the road, when this graft bears, you got nuts with a nice traditional Choctaw shape and the better taste of the Burkett." Beyond his agricultural insight, Chuy articulates one of Dillman's core beliefs: that we live in a multifaceted, hybrid world, and that the best way to survive is to lean on one person's strength, another's flexibility. "I always write about community," Dillman explains. "How little stories connect to something else, and something else, until it encompasses a whole. And theatre has always been a haven of voluntary intimacy for me—a place where we venture beyond the edge of the living-room carpet, both literally and figuratively."

—Adrien-Alice Hansel

BIOGRAPHY

Lisa Dillman's plays include *Detail of a Larger Work, The Walls, Flung, Half of Plenty, Rock Shore, Six Postcards, No Such Thing, Shady Meadows,* and *Ground.* Her work has been produced at Steppenwolf Theatre Company, Actors Theatre of Louisville, American Theatre Company, Rogue Machine Theatre, Summer Play Festival, Hypothetical Theatre Company, and Rivendell Theatre Ensemble. Her plays have been developed by the Goodman Theatre, Victory Gardens, the O'Neill Playwrights Conference, Huntington Theatre Company, Ensemble Studio Theatre, Northlight Theatre, The Women's Project, Philadelphia Theatre Company, Next Theatre Company, and the National New

Play Network. Her short works have been seen at New York's Estrogenius Festival, Australia's Short & Sweet Festival, New Jersey Repertory, City Theatre (DE), Actors Theatre of Louisville, Theatre Lumina, Collaboraction *Sketchbook*, and others. She has received new play commissions from the Goodman Theatre, where she was a member of the inaugural Playwrights Unit; Steppenwolf Theatre; Northlight Theatre; Rivendell Theatre Ensemble; the Chicago Humanities Festival; and Imagination Theatre Company. She has received two playwriting fellowships from the Illinois Arts Council, as well as a Sprenger-Lang New History Play Prize (*Rock Shore*), the Sarett National Playwright Award (*Separate Rooms*), and a Julie Harris–Beverly Hills Theatre Guild Award (*Terre Haute*). Her work has twice been nominated for Chicago's Joseph Jefferson Award for Best New Play. She has been a writer in residence at Blue Mountain Center, Ragdale, Western Michigan University, Prague Summer at Charles University, the William Inge Center for the Arts, and the Millay Colony. Her work is published by Samuel French and Dramatic Publishing, as well as anthologized in collections from Heinemann, Playscripts, Inc., Smith & Kraus, and New Issues Press.

ACKNOWLEDGMENTS

Ground premiered at the Humana Festival of New American Plays in March 2010. It was directed by Marc Masterson with the following cast (in alphabetical order):

ANGIE (OCHOA) ZELAYA	Sandra Delgado
ZELDA PRESTON	Jennifer Engstrom
INES (OCHOA) SANDOVAL	Liza Fernandez
CHUY GALLEGOS	Ricardo Gutierrez
COOPER DANIELS	Rob Riley
CARL ZELAYA	Dale Rivera

and the following production staff:

Scenic Designer	Scott Bradley
Costume Designer	Lorraine Venberg
Lighting Designer	Brian J. Lilienthal
Sound Designer	Matt Callahan
Properties Designer	Doc Manning
Wig/Makeup Designer	Heather Fleming
Stage Manager	Kathy Preher
Production Assistant	Megan Marie Thompson
Dialect Coach	Rocco Dal Vera
Fight Director	Drew Fracher
Dramaturg	Adrien-Alice Hansel
Casting	Lynn Baber

Directing Assistant .... Mollye Maxner
Scenic Design Assistant .... Ryan Wineinger
Lighting Design Assistants .... Andrew Cissna, Brahim Pettis
Stage Management Intern .... Nick Bussett
Assistant Dramaturg .... Emily Feldman

Originally commissioned by Northlight Theatre, Skokie, Illinois (BJ Jones, Artistic Director; Timothy J. Evans, Executive Director)

CHARACTERS

CARL ZELAYA, 35, Mexican-American. Lifelong resident of Fronteras. A border patrolman for the past year.

ZELDA PRESTON, 35, Anglo-American. Originally from Fronteras, she left her father's farm when she was sixteen, returning only for sporadic visits in the intervening years. At the beginning of the play, it has been about 20 years since the farm was her home. She is of Fronteras, but also a stranger there.

ANGIE (OCHOA) ZELAYA, 34, Mexican-American. A lifelong Fronteras resident, she is married to Carl. She works the underground economy, cutting hair, cleaning houses, and selling homemade foods.

COOPER ("COOP") DANIELS, early 60s, Anglo-American. Lifelong Fronteras resident. A commercial pecan grower and the local spokesperson for the civilian border defense organization Citizens Alliance.

CHUY GALLEGOS, early to mid-50s. Born in Mexico, he came to the U.S. as a very young man. An expert on pecan farming, he was the right-hand man of Zelda's father, the late August "Press" Preston.

INES (OCHOA) SANDOVAL, 21, Mexican-American. Lifelong Fronteras resident; Angie's younger sister. Six months pregnant, she lives alone in a trailer on the outskirts of Fronteras. Her husband of two years, Georgie, is stationed in Iraq.

TIME AND PLACE

The present. On and around the U.S.-Mexico border in southern New Mexico.

Ricardo Gutierrez and Sandra Delgado
in *Ground*

34th Annual Humana Festival of New American Plays
Actors Theatre of Louisville, 2010
Photo by Harlan Taylor

GROUND

ACT ONE

In the darkness, the sound of soft guitar music layered with whispering in Spanish. No individual words are discernible. The music fades and the whispering continues for a few moments before it too begins to fade. Finally there is a soft, sustained "Shhh," and then silence as a light rises on Border Patrolman CARL ZELAYA, *alone in moonlight, listening.*

CARL. Most of the time, especially on night patrol, I come up behind them. Real quiet. Not that it matters cuz if they been out there for a few days on foot, they're pretty much cooked through. Blisters all over their feet, their lips. Sometimes their eyes are swollen shut. They don't know or care where they're at anymore, and I walk right up to them. Most times they're out of water, they got no food. Half the time they just sitting out in the open. They got on the wrong shoes—specially the older ladies in their plastic slip-ons or their church shoes, they break your heart, *ése.* They don't hardly blink when I tell them not to move. First thing I do, always, I give them water. And they take it like from a friend.

(He straps on Night Vision goggles and scans the horizon as the light on him fades and soft guitar begins to play again in the darkness. Slowly the New Mexico night comes alive with stars. The soft tinkling of wind chimes and the steady chirp of crickets. Dimly visible are the skeletal shapes of pecan trees on the horizon. Lights find ZELL PRESTON *standing next to a suitcase, gazing up at the sky. She inhales deeply, enjoying the quiet. A moment later, a rooster crows raucously from the darkness nearby.* ZELL *jerks around trying to locate the source of the noise. She pulls a cell phone from her purse, squints at it, and dials. A phone rings as another light rises on* ANGIE ZELAYA *checking her caller I.D. She turns the phone on but says nothing. Beat.)*

ZELL. …Hello? …*Hello!?*…

ANGIE. Yeah. Hello.

ZELL. Oh. I'm sorry. …Who is this?

ANGIE. Who's this?

ZELL. It's Zell Preston. I'm calling for Carlos Zelaya?

ANGIE. I thought that was you. This is Angie.

ZELL. Angie. …Angie Ochoa?

ANGIE. Angie *Zelaya.*

ZELL. Oh, jeez, that's right, I'm sorry. Listen, are you at Carlos's—I mean, you're *home*, right?

ANGIE. Yeah. You called here, remember?

ZELL. Right. Well. I'm out here at my dad's. And Chuy was supposed to be here.

33

ANGIE. He'll be by.

ZELL. Uh-huh. Is Carlos home by any chance?

ANGIE. No.

ZELL. Because apparently they changed the locks at some point? So I'm kind of stuck. You know? …Angie? …Hello-o-o.

ANGIE. I'm still here.

ZELL. Carlos used to have keys to the house out here. Does he by any chance have the new keys?

ANGIE. Nope. …I do though.

ZELL. You do? You have keys? Why?

ANGIE. You really wanna know? I clean over there sometimes.

ZELL. Oh. Well. That's great! So can you—? Um. …Is it OK if I come over and *get* the keys?

ANGIE. Why don't I just come over there.

ZELL. That would be *fantastic.*

ANGIE. OK. I'll be there in about an hour.

ZELL. Ohhhh…can you possibly make it sooner? I wouldn't put you out but I've been driving for fourteen hours, and I slept so badly last night at this awful *Marriott* in deepest Oklahoma so I'm a little frazzled and I—

ANGIE. I can be there in an hour, OK?

ZELL. Ohhh-kay. I guess I can just…I'll wait for you here.

ANGIE. *Bueno. Entonces nos vemos.*

> (ANGIE *hangs up.* ZELL *closes her phone and chuckles, deeply irritated. Then she takes a deep cleansing breath and looks up at the stars again. The rooster crows as the light on* ZELL *fades and gets brighter on* ANGIE. CARL *enters wearing his uniform.*)

CARL. Hey.

> (*He kisses her.*)

ANGIE. Whoo. You need a shower.

CARL. We got any beer?

ANGIE. How many you had so far?

CARL. Just one. With the guys.

ANGIE. You stink like the *pinche* Bucket.

CARL. You got a nose like a narc dog.

> (*He sniffs her closely. She laughs, slaps at him, and they kiss again.*)

ANGIE. Hey, before I forget. Your girlfriend's here.

CARL. Over to the farm?

ANGIE. *Sí, hombre.* Hasn't changed a bit either.

CARL. She's over there right now?

ANGIE. Yeah. That's what I'm telling you, Carl. One beer my ass. She can't get in the house cuz Chuy's not there and she don't got the new keys.

CARL. So what'd you tell her?

ANGIE. Said I'd get 'em to her a little bit later on.

CARL. Why'n'cha go now? You're not doing nothing. Take you ten minutes. ...Forget it. I'll go.

ANGIE. Chuy don't want you over there.

CARL. Good thing I don't take orders from Chuy.

ANGIE. Look at you, wagging your little tail.

CARL. You come along too, I don't mind. *Pues*, why you gotta make her wait?

ANGIE. Shoulda heard her goin' on about her rough night at the Marriott! Ay, poor thing. Was the sauna broke? Or didn't room service put enough *dulcecitos* on her pillow?

CARL. Just gimme the keys.

(She holds the keys away. He grabs her and kisses her. Laughing, she pushes him away playfully, puts the keys behind her back.)

ANGIE. Why you wanna go over there? Tell her you still dream about eating her out?

CARL. *Grosera,* you better not kiss my mother with that dirty mouth.

(He snatches the keys from her and dodges away, laughing.)

ANGIE. *Ay, cabrón!*

(CARL exits as lights cross to COOP DANIELS *standing in the glow of a circle of flashlights.)*

COOP. *"E Pluribus Unum.* Out of Many, One." These words are part of the pledge of our great nation, a nation of immigrants. But the federal government is failing here, folks. Failing to end the flood of illegal trafficking across this border. You all know that; it's why you're out here tonight. But remember this: Citizens Alliance is not about playing cowboy. We're here to assist the Border Patrol so they can maybe start getting the job done *right*. Stay calm, stay quiet, and stay with your group. Keep your eyes and ears open, and get on those cell phones as soon as you spot anything at all. Questions? ...All right, good deal. Thanks, folks. Let's get to work.

(He turns off his flashlight. The lights cross to ZELL, *sitting on her suitcase. A rooster crows again, loudly. We again begin to hear whispering in the darkness. ZELL rises and looks around. She digs in her purse for her phone. The whispering begins to fade. CARL appears. Still disoriented and staring intently out at the trees, ZELL doesn't notice him until he is quite close to her.)*

CARL. Hola, *guerita.*

(ZELL shrieks, wheels around.)

ZELL. *Váyate, pendejo! Tengo pistola!*

CARL. Whoa, whoa, whoa! Zell! It's me, it's Carl!

ZELL. Carl…?!

CARL. I brought you the keys! Damn, girl, don't shoot!

ZELL. Oh…Carlos? Oh Jesus Christ, I'm sorry! My God. It is *crazy* out here. Coyotes and barnyard noises and God knows what all—!

CARL. Hey, hey, it's OK now, you're all right, you're OK.

>   (*They take each other in for a moment and then hug a bit awkwardly.*)

You almost made me crap my pants just now. You really got a gun?

ZELL. 'Course not.

>   (*He picks up her suitcase and they enter a cramped kitchen. She gazes around the room. Then, very softly….*)

My God. I'm here. I'm really *here.*

CARL. I know, time warp, right?

ZELL. Except for us. Jeez, dude, you got old.

CARL. Not you though. You look great.

ZELL. Do I, ya big liar?

CARL. Yeah. 'Course you do.

ZELL. Just for that I'm gonna have to see if there's a *cervezita* in here for you. You still drink, right?

CARL. *Pues, ¿cómo no?*

>   (*CARL sits and ZELL opens the fridge and comes back with two beers. She hands one to CARL, who pulls a dollar from his pocket and puts it on the table.*)

ZELL. What's that?

CARL. For the beer.

ZELL. Jesus. Don't worry about it.

CARL. It's Chuy's beer.

ZELL. I'll take care of this round.

>   (*She gazes at him for a moment, taking in the full effect of his uniform. He looks right back at her.*)

Border Patrol, Carlos.

CARL. Nobody calls me Carlos anymore.

ZELL. *"La migra."*

CARL. *Sí, Zeldita.* Be a year next month.

ZELL. Good lord. …How do you like it?

CARL. It's all right. Too many of them and not enough of us, that's all.

ZELL. And when you say "them" you're referring to…?

CARL. Hours are long, but I don't mind. Even if I did, it's my job.

ZELL. You got a pair of those mirror sunglasses?

CARL. Actually I prefer to work at night. It's beautiful out there in the desert, you know. Quiet. The land. The sky. Clear nights, moon turns everything magic. …You don't need to be looking at me like that.

ZELL. Like what? I'm not your judge.

CARL. That's right, you're not.

ZELL. I understand: You're making the world safe for democracy.

CARL. Look, I'm not the bad guy, OK? I'm trying to make things *better*.

ZELL. Whoa.

CARL. One time when I was still in training in Arizona we found four of them, OK? Three ladies, one man, but he was really just a kid, you know, couldn't've been more sixteen years old. They were out there in the desert all laying together in a row. Like they were sleeping, camping out. Kid had a note pinned to his shirt. Wrote it with a purple pencil. Told who they were—their names, where they came from. And also the name of the *coyote* who took their money and left them out there to die, OK? Juan Pedro Escoveda from Jalisco told them a truck would come for them.

ZELL. I was *teasing* you.

CARL. I think about that kid out there, getting broiled alive. And then I think of Juan Pedro from Jalisco. Still in business. Still eating, drinking. Kissing his mother. Going to mass on Sundays—

ZELL. All right. I got it.

CARL. You got no idea. Six weeks back, on a highway stakeout we go to pull over this truck heading north up I-25? Driver slams on his brakes in the middle of the road, jumps out and runs. Five illegals jump out the back…right into oncoming traffic. Three of them dead at the scene. And just recently there was this older lady—

ZELL. Could you…*not* tell another really depressing story right now?

CARL. Oh. …Right. Zell, I am so damn sorry about your dad.

ZELL. Well, and since we're on the subject, my mom died too. Last fall.

CARL. I heard that. Damn, girl. That's gotta be a real lonely feeling.

(ZELL *nods. Beat.*)

ZELL. So. People around here treat you different now?

CARL. You find out who your friends are.

ZELL. Yeah? Who are they?

(*They both chuckle.*)

Where's your gun?

CARL. Back at the house.

ZELL. Ever shot an illegal?

CARL. Nope. I never shot nobody.

ZELL. But you would if you had to.

CARL. If I had to? Yeah.

(*A silence; finally with studied nonchalance….*)

ZELL. How was the funeral?

CARL. Aw, you know, it was really something. People came from all over. More than four hundred all together. Saw people I ain't seen since you and me were kids. Line out Avenida Central all the way down to the plaza.

(ZELL *nods and turns away from him, breaking down a bit.*)

Aww, hey. Hey… We *tried* to reach you.

(*He pats her arm softly. She takes his hand and holds onto it.*)

ZELL. I know. I know you did.

CARL. (*Gently extricating himself.*) Chuy told Angie you went on some kind of a…?

ZELL. Silent retreat.

CARL. Right. Right. A "silent retreat." What does that even mean?

ZELL. It means I went out in the woods to meditate and literally didn't speak a word for twenty days and twenty-one nights.

CARL. What for?

ZELL. To clear my head.

CARL. (*Chuckling.*) Did it work?

ZELL. Yes. Is that funny? (*Beat.*) OK fine, I could only stand it for seventeen days before I ran out of there screaming. (CARL *shakes his head, chuckles again.*) *Anyway.* When I got back to my voice mail I found out that on day five of my retreat, my dad had died. And on day seventeen, the good people of Fronteras buried him—

CARL. We couldn't *locate* you—

ZELL. So now I think maybe I need another retreat.

CARL. Or maybe you just need to talk about it. …Anyways, it was an awesome funeral and I'm sorry you missed it.

ZELL. My God. He's really gone. Isn't he?

CARL. Yeah. He is. Just fell over one morning out there in the grove.

ZELL. He always said that's how he wanted to go. …How's Chuy taking it?

CARL. Me and Chuy don't really talk that much these days.

ZELL. How come?

(CARL *gestures to his uniform.*)

Ahh.

CARL. What you gonna do about the farm?

ZELL. Trying to get rid of me already?

CARL. Coop Daniels still got a jones for it, ya know.

ZELL. I'm sure he does. Nothing he likes more than sucking up the smaller farms in this valley.

CARL. Last time I checked, you got one to sell.

ZELL. Maybe. I don't know yet.

(CARL *laughs.*)

CARL. Oh, what? You gonna be a *farmer* now?

ZELL. I'm kind of in a transition at the moment.

CARL. Silent retreats. Transitions. Man, you like some kinda guru or something.

ZELL. That's me. Oh, and I got fired too. Well. "Asked to resign."

CARL. No way. What happened?

ZELL. I'm not really sure. It was last fall, actually, just about a month after my mom passed. ...I was getting ready for work one morning and I just...I'd been feeling so...*disconnected*, I guess...it's hard to describe...like I'd forgotten something...or no...more like I'd *lost* something really important but for so long that I'd probably never be able to get it back...do you know what I...? ...Anyway, that morning, I don't know, this feeling of being *adrift*...it was so present...I started shaking...and I just couldn't seem to stop.

CARL. They fired you for that?

ZELL. No, no. I...well. It's actually pretty funny.

CARL. Doesn't sound too funny so far, Zeldita.

ZELL. See, I was part of this team for a new pharmaceutical product, and we had a presentation scheduled that morning. The client was coming in, it was this huge deal, and I was a mess, but I knew I had to be there. So I drag myself in...and the presentation starts...and it's all fine at first but pretty soon there starts to be this *gap* where *I'm* supposed to be because that's how it works—everybody's got a very specific *thing they do*—so my team is looking at me, *waiting* for me, and the clients are starting to shift around in their chairs and check their watches, and it's all getting pretty *dire* and...oh. Did I mention the *product*? It was this cream especially formulated to shrink and tighten the tissues of the *vagina*—

CARL. I don't needa hear that.

ZELL. So there I am, everything is spinning wildly out of control—and yet it's *also* starting to seem a little bit, um, hilarious?—but I mean, we're about to lose this account and it's gonna be *totally* my fault—so what do I do? Well. Right there on the spot, I give 'em a limerick.

CARL. ...Like...those dirty poems from when we were kids?

ZELL. It popped into my head all of sudden—everything was *so tense*, ya know?—I just went on instinct: "There once was a gal from Salinas / Whose twat was too loose for a penis…" …Oh, *shit*. I had the whole thing, and now I can't do it.

CARL. And *then* they fired you.

ZELL. They asked me to resign.

CARL. *Así es la vida triste.*

ZELL. You have not changed.

CARL. Oh, I have, though. I've changed.

ZELL. Nope. Whenever you get uncomfortable you still haul out the Spanish. Come on. That was a funny story.

CARL. *Si tú dices.* To me it's pretty sad.

ZELL. (*Getting two more beers.*) Whoo. Tough crowd. …Well. You're probably right.

(CARL *slaps another dollar on the table.* CHUY GALLEGOS *enters.*)

Chuy. …*Hey.*

CHUY. *Hola,* Zeldita.

ZELL. Oh my God, I am so glad to see you.

CARL. Hey, Chuy.

CHUY. *Officer* Zelaya.

CARL. (*To* ZELL.) I should get going.

ZELL. OK. But we'll talk, right? I'll call you?

CARL. Yeah, do that.

(ZELL *kisses* CARL *briefly on the mouth, which discomfits him a bit.*)

Oh. OK. Yeah. G'night now. …Later days, Chu'.

CHUY. You not gonna check the grove before you go?

CARL. Why? Something out there I should know about?

(CHUY *mutters something inaudible.*)

I'm off duty anyways.

CHUY. So you wear that get-up just for fun these days.

CARL. *Pues, sí.* I sleep in it. Shower in it. Can't get enough.

(CHUY *mutters again as* CARL *exits.* ZELL *hands the beer to* CHUY.)

ZELL. How you holding up?

CHUY. *Así nada mas,* Zelda. Been kind of a shitty month, you know.

ZELL. Yeah. For me too.…

(CHUY *looks at the beer bottles, pockets the bills on the table. Outside, the rooster crows suddenly, elaborately.*)

OK, what is the deal with that rooster?

CHUY. El Rey? Aww, he lives down by the Garzas farm but he struts around here like he owns the damn place. Great old fighter, that one, real champ once he gets his spurs on. Twenty-three fights and counting—and he don't just survive, *ése*—he triumphs.

ZELL. I can't believe the state hasn't banned that.

CHUY. They did. But it didn't take.

ZELL. It's barbaric.

> (CHUY *mutters something.*)

Háblame, Chuy *hombre.*

CHUY. I said. Tradition matters down here.

ZELL. Throw two birds in a ring with razors on their feet and let them tear each other to pieces. There's a tradition worth hanging on to.

> (CHUY *gives her a look.*)

Are you mad at me?

CHUY. Mad. No. I'm not mad.

ZELL. But you've got *feelings.*

CHUY. Not gonna deny a few feelings, *jefa.*

ZELL. Don't be an idiot. I'm not your *jefa.*

CHUY. Oh, you're not? I mean *sí, claro,* I worked this place thirty-two years. But fair's fair when there's a legal paper to prove it. And here you are.

ZELL. Well. I'm glad you're not mad.

CHUY. So now you're here, what you planning to do?

ZELL. I'm not sure yet. …Are you expecting an answer right this second?

CHUY. Just wondering how long I got before you unload this piece of ground.

ZELL. "Unload it." That's a little harsh, isn't it? I love this place too, you know.

CHUY. Couldn't prove that by the time you spent here these last years.

ZELL. I know it's been a while—

CHUY. A long while.

ZELL. Well, I'm here now.

> (*Beat.*)

Chuy. I don't blame you for feeling invaded. But you and I have always been friends, and I don't want that to stop. …I really need to just *be* here right now. I need the quiet.

> (*Beat.* CHUY *finally nods. The rooster crows raucously very near the door and they both jump.* ZELL *laughs and even* CHUY *smiles a little. Then from under the table, he picks up a large box packed with papers and sets it in front of* ZELL.)

CHUY. These are your bills.

ZELL. Oh, whoa. …Tomorrow for all that, I think…. Ya know, I heard a lot of action out there in the grove tonight. You got people staying out back?

CHUY. Nah. We don't do that here no more.

ZELL. You're kidding me. Wow. End of an era.

CHUY. Things are a lot tougher now.

ZELL. They used to come right up and tap on the windows during dinner. And they never went away empty-handed. Camped out all over this place. I used to love that. The music at night, the laughing, singing…

CHUY. It's not like that no more. Last year Carl and his *pinche migra* friends came by here thirty-three times to check the outbuildings, the far grove, even the back bedroom one time. Your dad, well, he finally just got tired. After a while, *migra* didn't have to bother stop by here no more. They knew they broke him.

ZELL. What about you? They break you too?

(CHUY *mutters something.*)

So Dad wasn't hiring *any* labor from the other side?

(CHUY *shakes his head.*)

You're telling me he was running this place all by himself.

CHUY. No, Zelda. We ran it together.

(*Gestures to the box on the table.*)

I'd look at them bills sooner than later if I was you. I'm gonna turn in.

(CHUY *moves to exit.*)

ZELL. You're staying in the big bedroom?

CHUY. We can switch if you want.

ZELL. That's all right. I just…remember when you used to stay out in the guesthouse.

CHUY. You mean the *shed*. Been a lot of years since then.

(*He exits.* ZELL *looks down at the box of bills, pushes it away. The sound of a Spanish language radio station as the lights cross to* CARL *and* INES SANDOVAL, *21 and six months pregnant, sitting on the steps of* INES's *mobile home eating candy bars later the same night.* INES *is really savoring the hell out of her candy bar.*)

INES. Mmm. Mmm, *mmmmm*! So what's she like now? Still pretty?

CARL. *Sí, claro.*

INES. Pretty like a movie star?

CARL. I don't know about that. She's messed up like one though.

(CARL *yawns.*)

INES. You still all tired, huh?

CARL. I tell ya. Doesn't do me no good to lay down, though. Soon as I do, I'm wide awake.

INES. When's the last time you had a good sleep?

CARL. I don't even remember.

INES. *Tía Rosita* used to make this herb tea worked really good for that. Less the person got a guilty conscience. Then nothing works. ...Mmmmm. I could eat twenty of these. More. I could eat a hundred.

CARL. Every once in a while's OK.

INES. Make me fat!

CARL. Well, you gotta eat the good stuff too. Meat and vegetables, protein. I know how you are. You sit around this trailer, get all pitiful, you don't eat. It's not right, Nezzie.

INES. I eat.

CARL. Not enough, *flacita.*

INES. (*Rising and sticking her belly out at him.*) *Flacita*, huh?

(CARL *rests his hand on her belly for a moment. She laughs suddenly, self-consciously, pulls away from him, looking across the way at another trailer.*)

La vieja Truchas. Always at her window. Ay, she's so ignorant. Makes the sign of the cross when she sees me on the street. I keep reminding her I'm *married* but she's old as the dirt, she don't know nothing anymore. She just trailer trash anyways. ...Ha. Look who's talking, huh?

CARL. Living in a trailer don't make you trash.

(INES *is suddenly wobbly and she sits down abruptly.*)

INES. Whoo. Got them bright spots in front of my eyes again.

CARL. You tell the doctor about that?

INES. *Pues*, I got my appointment tomorrow.

CARL. You got a problem, you call them up.

INES. Every time I call over there the nurse act like she can't understand me. She's all snotty and everything. Anyways I see them tomorrow.

CARL. Good. ...Now what you hear from our boy in Iraq?

INES. Oh, Georgie say they just got him digging buncha holes and laying down pipes and stuff. So that's good. And only ten more weeks till he's back with me forever, forever. Whoo, I'll be so big by then! Oh yeah, and he said to tell you you're a *pendejo.* I said I would. *Pendejo.*

CARL. Tell him for me he's a *pinche maricón.* ...But I mean it, Nez: You gotta eat. Else I'm gonna write and tell him.

INES. *Ay, mentiroso*, you would not.

CARL. If you're having a bad day, don't sit around feeling sorry for yourself. Call somebody up.

INES. Like who? You?

CARL. Yeah. Call me if you need me.

INES. And what? You'll be all like "Oh, hey, um, listen, I got a bunch of Mexicans laying here with their face in the dirt. Can I call you back?"

> (*Beat.*)

Sorry.

CARL. Bring you special treats and look how you do me.

INES. I know. You hate me now?

CARL. *Pues*, I can't stand you. Hey, you want the rest of this one?

INES. You can't finish it? OK then, but I don't wanna get fat, *ése*.

CARL. You're supposed to get fat.

INES. No, just a big belly. I don't wanna get fat for reals. You know how some pregnant ladies get that real wide butt? With those floppy things on the sides? I get like that Georgie won't want me no more.

CARL. Don't talk stupid.

INES. I'm not. *Mira*, he went out with Maricela Ortiz all freshman year and then over the summer she worked at the Dairy Queen and she gained like fifteen pounds. By start of sophomore year, he was all done with her.

CARL. That was high school. Georgie's gonna love you no matter what. You're his wife. You're having his kid.

INES. Yeah, but still…it's a really good thing Maricela got that job at the DQ.

> (*They laugh. Beat. Then, very quietly.*)

He's gonna come back, right?

CARL. Sure he is. Damn.

INES. You promise?

CARL. Yes. I promise.

INES. And he'll still be him, right?

CARL. How you mean?

INES. I see all the time on TV how when they come back here, they got all kind a shit wrong with them—health problems, you know, and mental problems too. They come back and they're like mad all the time, they're drinking, doing drugs, or they just lay around in bed all day and look at the wall—

CARL. OK now, Nezzie, just stop.

INES. Tía Rosita gotta come be here with me when I have this baby, that's *it*…

CARL. Not gonna talk about that with you, Nezzie.

INES. It wasn't right what they did to her. She lived here twenty-five years! She paid her taxes and everything!

CARL. She wasn't legal.

INES. She had a card! But somebody broke in her place and stole the Bible where she kept it.

CARL. Come on, you know that's not true. Every time somebody wanna prove a point around here they bring up the *pinche* Bible. She never had a card.

INES. She didn't do nothing. They had no reason.

CARL. They had a reason. She had no card.

INES. Used to be family was more than just some guy and his wife and kids. It was like all these people…you could go in anybody's house and they be happy to see you, they talk to you, listen and joke around with you, give you food, sodas—

CARL. You still got people, Nez.

INES. Family used to be so big…I want that for my baby—I do!—I want him to have more than just me! And now everybody's always all the time leaving this place, *always*! …You promise, swear to God, Georgie's coming back?

CARL. Yeah. And you know what else? He's going to be the same old *cabrón* he's always been. Now, if that's what makes you happy, well OK, it's too bad for you but whatever.

INES. (*Smiling a little finally and taking his hand.*) You got such giant hands. Look at that crazy thing. It's like a oven mitt.

CARL. I gotta go. Here.

> (*He pulls out a couple of bills.*)

Little something for groceries.

INES. I don't want your stupid money.

CARL. Quit being so sassy all the time.

INES. You always giving your money away. Like you so rich.

> (*But she takes the bills and sticks them in her bra, winking and giggling, then kisses his hand.*)

CARL. Señora Truchas is looking.

> (*CARL tries to pull his hand away; she holds on and continues noisily kissing it. Sound of the rooster crowing in the distance as lights crossfade to the grove. It is early the next morning. Sound of mourning doves and other birds. CHUY enters with a wheelbarrow containing a very young pecan tree with a root ball. A coyote yips from a short distance off. CHUY pulls a rifle from the wheelbarrow and moves toward the sound, scanning the trees. Seeing nothing, he sets the rifle down and returns to the wheelbarrow. He takes a branch or stub from the wheelbarrow and fits it onto the seedling, then winds the two pieces together with tape to create a single branch. After a moment, ZELL enters.*)

ZELL. Hey. I couldn't find the coffee.

(CHUY *mutters something.*)

What was that?

CHUY. I don't keep it around. Bothers my gut.

ZELL. Your "gut." …Well. Guess I'll pick some up in town.

CHUY. You'll have to go into Lluvias or up Greeley.

ZELL. Why? Yummy doesn't stock coffee anymore?

CHUY. Yummy been gone couple years now.

ZELL. No way! …Well *shit*.

(*She turns to leave, spots the rifle.*)

I don't believe it! Is that…?

CHUY. *La Matilda. Sí, cómo no.*

(ZELL *picks up the gun and points it at the horizon.*)

ZELL. Jesus. Dad always loved this rusty old thing.

CHUY. She's not rusty. She can still do her job, don't worry.

ZELL. Since when do you take Matilda out in the grove with you?

CHUY. Family of coyotes up there on the ridge been coming down here for the garbage. And chickens too if they can get them. …Hey. It's not a toy.

(ZELL *sets the rifle down.*)

Something else you need?

ZELL. Nah. Just having a look at the trees. …What's wrong with that one?

CHUY. Nothing.

ZELL. Then why are you bandaging it?

CHUY. I'm grafting.

ZELL. What for?

CHUY. Keeps the grove diverse.

ZELL. How does the bandage do that?

(CHUY *mutters something.*)

I hate to pull rank but that *is* my property.

(*She has overstepped and she knows it even before* CHUY *turns and fixes her with a steady gaze.*)

Jeez. I'm *kidding*.

CHUY. I'm grafting a piece of one cultivar onto a seedling of another. This smaller piece is a Choctaw. This seedling here's a Burkett, and you know Burketts got the best root system of any pecan. I bind them tight like this so they'll go ahead and grow together. Gotta do it in the spring so it has the summer to catch. Then down the road, when this graft bears, you got nuts with the nice traditional Choctaw shape and the better taste of the Burkett. Softer shells too. …*Entiendes*?

ZELL. *Sí, claro.* ...I don't remember my dad ever doing that.

CHUY. Didn't use to. But grafting brings a better crop over time. I taught him that.

ZELL. Want some help?

(CHUY *shakes his head.* ZELL *gazes around the grove a moment.*)

My dad sort of gave up on me, didn't he?

CHUY. I don't know about that. You were always his baby girl. Maybe he didn't understand why *you* gave up on *him.*

ZELL. I didn't give up on him!

CHUY. Then you should've stayed.

ZELL. I was *sixteen.* What was I supposed to—?

CHUY. Leaving in the middle of the night—

ZELL. That's a myth and you know it! It was broad daylight! He just didn't get up to say goodbye. *You* did. You got up.

(*Beat.*)

My mom *needed* me more. He was so...you know how he was.

CHUY. *Sí tú dices.*

ZELL. When we left, he just...built a *different* kind of family. Ya know, I think of all those people who *stayed*...made lives, *families,* right here in Fronteras... He *did* that. He made it all happen. Gave 'em work, got 'em papers, loans. He'd do just about anything for *them.*

(CHUY *mutters under his breath.*)

Hey. We used to be buddies. I could always talk to you. Even when I couldn't get through to him. So what the hell happened? Talk to me, Chu'.

(CHUY *shakes his head, doesn't answer.*)

Do I owe you money?

CHUY. *¿Cómo?*

ZELL. I say: Are you owed wages? A salary?

CHUY. End of the week.

ZELL. I have to figure out stuff with the bank, but you'll get your check.

CHUY. Your dad always paid me cash.

ZELL. Fine. And, Chuy, I hope it goes without saying you'll always have a job here.

CHUY. Till you sell, you mean.

(*Sound of car horn. They both squint toward it.*)

A la chingada...

ZELL. Who is it? ...Is that Coop? Jesus Christ, what does he want at this hour?

CHUY. What do you think?

COOP. (*Off.*) Hello there!

> (CHUY *grabs the rifle, puts it in the wheelbarrow, and takes off in the opposite direction. In a moment* COOP *strides on. He is clearly a morning person.*)

Zelda Preston! Mornin', lady! Gosh, it's good to see you. How the heck are ya?

ZELL. I'm all right, Coop. It's been a long time.

COOP. It has, it has. You look great. Did I see Chuy Gallegos skedaddle out of here just now? That guy, I swear, he's like the wind. …Zelda. My God. I can't tell you how busted up this valley's been over your dad's passing.

ZELL. Thank you.

COOP. It was quite a funeral.

ZELL. That's what I hear.

COOP. How you doing? Seriously.

ZELL. Well. I'll tell you. If I don't get a decent cup of coffee sometime this morning I'm going to shoot myself in the face.

COOP. Huh. You like French Roast?

> (COOP *reaches into a deep pocket of his jacket and pulls out a thermos. As he pours coffee, the sound of a helicopter in the distance. It slowly draws closer as the scene goes on.*)

ZELL. Oh my God, you're a lifesaver.

COOP. I do what I can.

> (ZELL *sips coffee as* COOP *gazes around the grove. Beat.*)

ZELL. I'm not ready to talk about this farm yet.

COOP. Ha. You get right to the point, don't ya? Just like your dad.

ZELL. I thought I'd save you some time.

COOP. Well, I am interested in this property, that's no secret. But it's not why I'm here. What you up to this morning?

ZELL. Oh…I thought I'd head over to the cemetery.

COOP. I was just there myself.

ZELL. Were you?

COOP. Mmm. I go just about every mornin'…Catherine died, you know. Two years ago now. Cancer. It was…real fast. Relentless, actually.

ZELL. Oh, Coop. I didn't know, I'm so sorry.

COOP. Well. We had thirty-one great years together. But I miss her every day. I do.

> (ZELL *nods, touches his arm. After a moment, he takes a deep breath.*)

I should let ya get on with your morning. But, say, you got any plans later this afternoon, Zelda? Wonder if you'd have time to meet me out by the Wagner place around three o'clock. Got something I'd like to show you.

(*They continue to talk but their conversation is drowned out by the sound of the helicopter going by. The lights cross to* CARL *getting dressed for work. He wears only his uniform pants and shoes.* ANGIE *enters in a robe. She watches in silence as* CARL *puts on his shirt and begins to button it.*)

CARL. Hey, you.

ANGIE. You still live here or what?

CARL. Couldn't live no place else but witchoo, *amorcita*.

ANGIE. Could've fooled me. I go to bed, you're not home yet. I wake up, you already on your way.

CARL. Nothing been going on in that bed anyhow, so what you care?

ANGIE. That's how it is?

CARL. Lately? That's exactly how it is.

(ANGIE *moves and stands very close to him. After a moment, he pulls her to him, kisses her, then nuzzles her neck.*)

ANGIE. Hey now, don't start something you can't finish.

(*He laughs and they kiss again.*)

You thought any more about what I asked you?

CARL. Hmm?

ANGIE. *Mira*, I talked to Tía Rosita on the phone. She says every night she has terrible dreams about Nezzie. You know *mi tía* believes in her dreams but only because most of them come true.

CARL. She can't come back here. You know that.

ANGIE. She's all worried and now she got me worried.

CARL. Once she got deported, that was it. Now I can't do nothing about that, so you gotta stop working me over. Don't put me in a position.

ANGIE. If you coulda heard her. She was really crying.

CARL. She cried all the time when she lived here too.

ANGIE. Her heart is breaking.

CARL. I'm sorry to hear it.

ANGIE. No you're not.

CARL. I love my Rosita. You know that. But she was always crying about something. "The bougainvillea is soooo beautiful"… (*Sniffles.*) "The Christmas turkey smells so good." (*Sniffles and whimpers.*) "My friend's sister's boyfriend's uncle got the cancer"… (*Sniffles and whimpers copiously.*)

ANGIE. That's real nice, Carl.

CARL. "The *mole*, it doesn't taste right"…. You know it's true. It's not fair you get her hopes up about this.

ANGIE. ¡No me digas esto! ¡Ella vivió aquí más de veinte años!

CARL. Yeah. And then she got swept back down south. Just like a million other people. And that's how it is. That's the world now, OK? You wanna blame me for it, that's your business.

ANGIE. *¡Ay cabrón, tú sabes que la pinche migra no tenía ninguna razón!*

CARL. *¿Yo? ¡Yo no sé nada!*

ANGIE. (*Pushing past him.*) Excuse me.

CARL. Come on, don't be like that.

ANGIE. This is my family I'm talking about.

CARL. I'm your family too.

ANGIE. Then act like it!

CARL. It's my *job*, God damn it. I notice you like the money it brings in. I'm not gonna have you put me in a position, now that is it.

ANGIE. You and your "position." Wasn't for you, Rosita'd be back over here no problem.

CARL. She gets picked up you really think they gonna believe I don't know nothing about it? In my town? Where I know everybody?

ANGIE. Probably turned her in yourself.

CARL. Hey. You know better than that. If it was up to me, she could come live right here with us. But it's not up to me. …Why we gotta fight? I'm so tired, baby. I got a whole big long day looking at me. Can't you just like me once in a while?

(*A beat, then* CARL *moves to put his arms around her again. She pulls away.*)

ANGIE. You overdid the aftershave, *migra.*

(ANGIE *turns to leave.* CARL *grabs her and kisses her hard on the mouth. Then he lets her go and they stand there glaring at one another.*)

CARL. Can't keep doing me like this, Angela. I don't wanna fight you all the time.

ANGIE. Then do the right thing, *mi amor.*

CARL. One day you gonna wake up and it's too late. This right here's the family you should be worrying about.

ANGIE. Why don't you go arrest some Mexicans?

(*She exits.* CARL *stares after her then slowly tucks in his shirt and straightens his uniform. The lights cross to* INES *kneeling by a grave. She is whispering comfortingly, although there is no one else around. The headstone is small but the area is swamped with flowers, candles, and other tokens. A jointed wooden skeleton is stuck into the ground next to the grave. The sound of a car pulling up and then a door slamming.* INES *takes a candy bar out of her pocket, unwraps it, and breaks it in two. She sets one half on top of the headstone and begins to eat the other. After a moment,* ZELL *enters, looking around for her father's grave.*)

INES. *Hola*, Zelda. You remember me?

ZELL. …Oh my God. …Is that little Ines Ochoa? Of course I do! But look at you! You're all grown up. …My God…I remember when you were just a little itty-bitty thing, out there in our orchard picking up windfalls.

INES. Your dad used to give me a penny each one. You come to see him? He's over here by me.

> (ZELL *approaches, looking down at the decorated grave.*)

ZELL. My God, Dad. They forgot the *piñata*…

INES. How you mean?

ZELL. I just meant there's so much…never mind. It doesn't matter. It's lovely.

INES. I know, right? You want me to leave you two alone?

ZELL. No, no, it's all right. Stay. ….How are your folks, Ines?

INES. Um. That's them right over there.

ZELL. Oh *no*.

INES. Yeah. Car crash. Long time ago now. I don't think about it that much anymore. Ha. Only every day.

ZELL. I know what you mean. …I lost my mom a while back too.

INES. Aww. I don't remember her, but I always heard she was a real nice lady.

> (ZELL *nods, looks away.*)

Getting pretty crowded in here, huh? …Those over there are illegals nobody knew. No IDs, nothing. The church paid to bury them. Pretty soon there's not gonna be no space left for nobody else, you know?

ZELL. Seems like everybody's leaving anyway. Downtown's all boarded up.

INES. Right? Almost nothing left but the diner, the dollar store, and the *pinche* Bucket.

> (INES *rises and brushes dirt from her knees.*)

ZELL. Oh, wow. I didn't even. …Congratulations.

INES. I know, I'm really big, right? You wanna feel?

ZELL. Sure, all right.

> (*She does.*)

Wow. Yes, you are. Well, that's really…um…

INES. I'm married.

ZELL. Oh, *good*!

INES. Yeah, to Georgie Sandoval. But he's over in Iraq right now.

ZELL. Ahh jeez.

INES. No, no, he's coming home real soon! Then we have our baby and after that we gonna buy a house maybe up around Cruces and Georgie's gonna go to school and work for his uncle up there doing construction.

ZELL. It's wonderful to have plans, isn't it?

INES. Yeah. …You got plans, too?

ZELL. Me? Yes. Yes, I do.

INES. What plans you got?

ZELL. I'm…Well, I mean, who knows? I'm maybe going to…grow pecans…

INES. Yeah? You staying on at your dad's place?

ZELL. Well, he did leave it to me.

INES. You married?

(ZELL *shakes her head.*)

¿Por qué no?

ZELL. I don't really know how to answer that.

INES. *Pues,* won't you be lonely out there?

ZELL. No. I've been on my own a long time, Ines, and I do just fine.

INES. I didn't mean to make you mad.

ZELL. You didn't make me mad.

INES. I'm just sorry for you, that's all.

ZELL. Why?

(INES *shrugs.*)

I'm fine. I'm so much better now that I'm back here. You have no idea.

INES. Maybe some night you can come eat with me. I got Lean Cuisines or I can fix us a pizza.

ZELL. Honestly, you don't need to do that.

INES. It's no problem. I get lonely too.

(*Beat.* ZELL *finally nods, smiles.*)

ZELL. All right. That sounds nice.

INES. Your dad and Chuy used to come over and eat once in a while. Or sometimes they'd take me out for chicken night at the diner.

ZELL. The diner still does that?

INES. *Sí, claro,* and it's really good too. They give you a *lot*!

ZELL. Mmm, I used to love chicken night.

INES. It's the best thing *ever.* …Hey, you got a car that runs good?

ZELL. Pretty good.

INES. I wonder can I borrow it for a little while.

ZELL. Um. …No. Actually, I'm using it.

INES. Oh. OK. That's OK. Maybe some other time.

(ZELL *reaches down and picks up the little jointed skeleton.*)

People come every day to bring him things.

ZELL. Just like *Día de los Muertos.*

INES. One day like last week the Correos—you know the ones got the restaurant over by Las Lluvias?—they brought a whole enchilada plate! Beans, rice, salad. Everything! Set it right there on top. I knew it was them because of their red chile. You could smell it all the way from the gate.

ZELL. You come here a lot, huh?

INES. Lotta people to visit.

> (*Silence. They stand looking down at the grave for a moment.*)

Everybody here loved him, you know. They never, ever stopped.

> (INES *touches* ZELL's *arm briefly, then exits.* ZELL *stares after her. She looks down at the grave, notices she is still holding the wooden skeleton. Suddenly overcome, she places it very gently against the gravestone.*)

ZELL. Aw, Dad. Jeez…jeez.

> (*But instead of allowing herself to cry, she takes a deep cleansing breath. Then she picks up the candy. After a moment's indecision, she pops it in her mouth. The lights cross to* ANGIE *and* CHUY. *He is sitting on a wooden chair and wearing a plastic cape. She wears a pocketed beautician's smock from which she pulls a battery-operated hair clipper.*)

ANGIE. It's a damn shame, you know? The old man didn't even like her.

CHUY. *Ay, cabróna,* he loved her, she was his family. Now listen: I *said* a *trim.*

ANGIE. You should lemme do you a favor here, Sasquatch.

CHUY. At least leave me a little on top.

ANGIE. Such a baby.

CHUY. Hey? Last time my sideburns weren't even. One was way up here like this.

> (*She points at the chair and he finally sits. She studies him for a moment and then begins to buzz very carefully at the back of his head. She stops periodically to assess her progress throughout the following.*)

ANGIE. She gonna sell out, you watch. Coop Daniels and her? Made for each other.

CHUY. You still can't get over the fact she used to go out with Carl.

ANGIE. Listen to the wise old *pendejo.*

CHUY. And she found her way outa Fronteras but you still stuck here.

ANGIE. She back now though, isn't she? …'Sides, I could get out if I wanted.

CHUY. Not you. This border's got you by the throat.

ANGIE. Nah. I just know one shithole's the same as the next. I don't see you packing it up.

CHUY. That's because I love this shithole.

ANGIE. Said one turd to the other.

CHUY. I look out the back door, I see my whole life. Right there.

ANGIE. Yeah, sure you do. Only problem is the door don't belong to you. And neither does any of the rest of it.

CHUY. I see the trees I raised. Ground that feeds 'em. And I see all the people who made it happen over the years. Not just me and Press, but your dad and mom too. Tía Rosita. The Zelayas. C'de Bacas. Correos. Most the families in this valley one time or another.

ANGIE. Half them people are dead or deported.

CHUY. Yep. That's what I see. All you see is dollars floating on the ground. Never enough of 'em and blowing all over when you bend down to get them.

ANGIE. (*Poking him with the clippers.*) Hey. Respect me.

CHUY. I do. But I worry about you too.

ANGIE. Save that for when you get a life.

CHUY. All that bile's gonna choke you one of these days.

ANGIE. You the one with the ulcer, not me. Way I see it, everybody got a choice: You can be a victim or else you can get on with your life.

CHUY. That what you doing, Ange? Getting on with your life?

ANGIE. That's right.

CHUY. You always after the money but you never gonna have enough. Know why? Because anymore you can't even remember why you want it.

ANGIE. ¿Ah, sí? Carl and me got a house. Two cars. What you got?

CHUY. And it's a waste, too, cuz you're a really smart lady.

ANGIE. (*Pulling out a pair of small trimming scissors and beginning to snip.*) Smart enough to know I don't like being poor. See, you and me, we can spend our whole life scratching in the dirt. You lived with the old man all these years, took care of his farm for him, what you got to show for that? Now here comes Zeldita, she's lookin' out at them same acres, deciding what she's gonna do with 'em. And you can't say a word about it. But you know what? When you get your orders to get off her property, you'll be all nice and trimmed up, ready to go.

> (*Though she is still snipping,* CHUY *yanks away and rises suddenly, whips off the cape, and turns to face her. They look levelly at one another for a moment.*)

You see how that is?

> (ANGIE *snaps her fingers at him and he hands over his wallet. She plucks out a bill and then hands the wallet back to him.*)

CHUY. So much for scratching in the dirt.

ANGIE. *Sí claro, hombre.* Mama gots to get paid.

> (*He jams his hat on his head and exits, as the lights cross to* ZELL *and* COOP *at the fence. The sound of drilling, pounding, and workers' voices.*)

COOP. Personally? I hate the idea of a border fence, I really do. My family did business with the Mexicans for decades, just like yours did. But get caught hiring them these days you're in a whole world of hurt. So, lookit: we can't *work* them, but they're still coming. Now, a federally funded wall from Texas to the Pacific, that would be great, and it might even happen one day, but until it does, Citizens Alliance is gonna have to go one volunteer project at a time. You look confused.

ZELL. You're building a fence for this rancher, right? But it only blocks off *his* property. So, correct me if I'm wrong, but all an undocumented immigrant's gotta do is head a little east or west to where the fence gives out. So what's the point?

COOP. Well. Last fall this particular rancher was robbed at gunpoint by illegals right here on his own land. Broad daylight. Happily for him, they didn't blow his head off. Next time he might not be so lucky. My opinion, a man shouldn't need that much "luck" on his own ground.

ZELL. Does that happen a lot?

COOP. More often than you think. Matter of fact, this movement is funded by donations from thousands of concerned citizens across this region.

ZELL. So what's in it for you?

COOP. I live here.

ZELL. And you've always done pretty well for yourself, haven't you?

COOP. I do all right. But I can't just sit by while illegals gobble up my community's social services and pave the way for the economic free-fall of the industries along this border. Now, I know your dad had his own particular philosophy about things, but this border's changed, Zelda, and ya can't just shut your eyes to that.

ZELL. I'm not.

COOP. Ya see the gal driving the Bobcat? She's an out-of-work nurse from Lluvias. Lost her job because her hospital got so overrun with illegals it had to shut down. Third one in the state. These days the nearest hospital is three hours from Fronteras, did you know that? Nearest clinic's sixty-three miles. That gal look like a vigilante to you?

ZELL. No.

COOP. Would you feel the same if she wasn't Latina? You don't have to answer that. But it might surprise you to find out that nearly a quarter of our membership is Latino. See, race doesn't matter to Citizens Alliance—*that* gal, like all of us out here, is simply an American protecting her home against further invasion. Lookit, we're not anti-*immigrant*. We're just a hundred percent anti-*illegal*.

ZELL. No offense, Coop, but I'm just really not much of a joiner, so—

COOP. Did I ask you to join anything? …Here's the deal. Your farm is a conduit and it's been hemorrhaging illegals into this valley for decades. Your dad, God rest his soul, not only let that happen, he encouraged it. Which is why your property's ended up on the Citizens Alliance hot list. …And we'd like to fence it for you.

ZELL. I've already got a fence along the back of my far grove.

COOP. That flimsy thing wouldn't keep back a blind two-year-old. I'm talking about twelve feet of high-grade stainless steel along your southern perimeter. For which you won't have to shell out one penny. Now, I know you're not quite ready to talk about the sale of your farm yet, and I understand that, but I'm tellin' you, Zelda, a fence gives that property value-added, no matter what you decide to do with it

(ANGIE *enters with a large box. She whistles sharply to* COOP.)

There she is! How many you bring us today, hon'?

ANGIE. Fifty, *jefe*. Just like you ordered.

COOP. So that's fifty at a buck apiece—

ANGIE. Buck-twenty-five, *jefe*. Inflation. Handmade by little old ladies with arthritis in their fingers.

COOP. One thing about you, lady. You don't dicker. Might dick folks around a little bit. But you do not dicker. So fifty times a buck twenty-five…

ANGIE. Sixty-two-fifty.

ZELL. Angie?

ANGIE. (*Without turning to look at her.*) I was wondering when I'd run into you, *guera*. I see it didn't take you long to hook up with this bunch.

ZELL. Me? No, no, no, I'm not "hooking up" with anybody—

ANGIE. It's OK, don't apologize, you got an investment to protect now, *¿qué no?*

ZELL. It's so not like that.

ANGIE. (*To* COOP.) You gonna pay me or what.

COOP. Take a check? Oh, relax, I'm kidding. Don't suppose you could wait a few minutes while I rustle up some cash from my crew, could you?

ANGIE. You should buy them lunch. They're building your wall for you.

COOP. Wall's not for me, Angie. It's for all of us. You included.

ANGIE. Leave me out of it, man.

(COOP *chuckles, pulls out his wallet, and counts the money into her hand. She nods and turns to leave.*)

COOP. Thanks, lady. Oh, and when you're over on Wednesday, make sure you do the smaller bathroom, OK? I think you skipped it last time.

(ANGIE *is gone.*)

Gotta love that gal. Real entrepreneur. She's on the go every blessed day mining this border for all it's worth. Bounces around like a pinball, cuttin' hair, cleanin' houses, hawkin' tamales. Bet she doesn't pay a red cent in taxes. You should try one of these things though—they're awful damn good. ...So. What do you say to my proposition?

ZELL. I'll give it some thought.

COOP. Be a win-win for you. You been back there along the far end of your property line? It's full of garbage. Dirty diapers, spoiled food, God knows what all. It's a hazard. And without a barrier? If you go out there, be real careful, Zelda. I don't want to have to worry about you.

ZELL. I really will think about it. In the meantime, I don't wanna be a jerk, Coop, but I'd really prefer you to stay out of my far grove unless you're invited, okay?

(COOP *smiles and shrugs. He hands her a business card.*)

COOP. Well now, maybe you don't know this, but I have a financial investment back there.

ZELL. And what might that be?

COOP. I own your well.

(*Beat. Then* COOP *turns and calls off to the unseen workers.*)

Who wants one of Mama Zelaya's red hot tamales? Buck-fifty apiece, no waiting.

(*He exits. Open-mouthed,* ZELL *watches him go, starts to follow him, then thinks better of it and strides purposefully off in the opposite direction as lights cross to* INES *on her steps.* ANGIE *enters with a small bag of tamales. She hands it to* INES *and sits next to her.*)

ANGIE. Tamales. Eat.

INES. My pressure's up again.

ANGIE. You're kidding me. Why?

INES. Stupid car keeps stalling out. I'm all scared I'll be late for my appointment and I'm all worried and I can feel it starting to go up and then when they put that thing on my arm, it's like my eyes are gonna squirt out my face!

ANGIE. I don't get it. You're skinny.

INES. They said I might have "the clamps" or something.

ANGIE. The clamps? What the hell is that?

INES. It's not good, that's all I know. I don't remember exactly what they said.

ANGIE. What do you remember?

INES. I'm not spoze be on my feet or get excited or drink sodas—*mira*, not even diet! And no salt and—

ANGIE. Did they give you some stuff to read about it?

INES. I forgot it there. They said if things get worse then I might gotta stay in bed till the baby comes.

ANGIE. Because your blood pressure?

INES. I *guess.*

ANGIE. Didn't you ask them anything? Do I have to go with you every single time? You got a question, why don't you ask them?

INES. They talk so fast and they don't listen to me—

ANGIE. That's their job to listen to you!

INES. Plus there's about fifty thousand million people in the waiting room—

ANGIE. You got no idea how to handle *estos putos*. How you gonna take care of a baby, huh? You can't even stick up for yourself. I swear, sometimes I think you're retarded—

INES. I am not!

ANGIE. Wake up! You don't get what you want in this world by crying about it.

INES. You don't get it by screaming all the time either!

ANGIE. Doctors treat you like that because you let them! You don't say a word!

INES. Not everybody's like you, Angie! I need somebody I can talk to! You don't even listen ever!

(INES *sits down heavily. She is breathing hard, almost gasping.*)

ANGIE. (*Kneeling next to her.*) OK, OK, take it easy, Nez. You're right. I'm sorry.

INES. No you're not! Why'n'choo just get out of here and leave me alone!

ANGIE. Come on. Don't say that. I'm glad you're not like me. I'm *glad*. Really. I am.

INES. You can't talk to me like that anymore!

ANGIE. I know. You're right. …You wanna hit me? *Ándale.* Hit me.

(INES *punches* ANGIE *on the arm.*)

Harder, man. You know you want to.

(INES *punches her again. Hard.* ANGIE *rubs her arm. Beat.*)

INES. If I tell you something, you promise you won't get mad at me? …I keep on having this dream about Georgie getting blown up. There's pieces of him on the ground and all over the side of his truck and everything.

ANGIE. Everybody needs to stop dreaming so damn much.

INES. And then later, I got the Army letter in my hands, you know—they say if you can see your hands in a dream then it's gonna come true—

ANGIE. Who says that?

INES. —and I could see my hands as plain as day! And then the baby was rotting inside me and falling out one little piece at a time. I found tiny little fingers sticking up out of the carpet all over the trailer and I woke up and my heart was going so fast—

ANGIE. OK, OK, *cálmate, hermanita, cálmate.*

(*She strokes* INES's *hair gently. Beat.*)

I'm gonna get Tía Rosita back here and she'll take real good care of you, OK? I just gotta figure out how, that's all, but I'm gonna make it happen, I promise. For reals, OK, Nezzie? Come on, don't worry.

(*She gives* INES *a squeeze as the lights cross to late afternoon.* CARL *on patrol looking through binoculars. After a moment, he takes out his cell phone, dials.*)

CARL. What you got, Joey? ...Yeah, me either. Nothing moving out there. ... What you think? They getting smarter or we getting dumber? (*Laughs.*) Little of both. You got that right. Man, it was hot as hell today, right? You wanna go over Correos for a cold one? ...OK then. I'll meet you on the ridge in fifteen.

(*He hangs up. As he turns to leave, a sound captures his attention, and he freezes. We again hear whispered Spanish, although the individual words aren't discernible. The whispering gets louder but not clearer. In fact, there is a distinctly unreal quality to it that thoroughly spooks* CARL. *Suddenly there is a sustained "Shhhhh," and* CARL *whirls around, looking this way and that. Silence. He quickly takes out his cell phone again and dials.*)

Mira, you hear that just now? ...I thought I...no, it was like talking. Whispering. I don't know. ...You didn't hear nothing? All right, yeah. I'm just checking. Probably the wires or something...Sunstroke, my ass. ...Nah, I'm OK. Probably nothing. I'm on my way, bro'.

(*He hangs up and turns, scanning the horizon. Still disturbed, he does not holster his gun. The lights cross to the grove. It is near sundown.* CHUY *is alone looking out at the trees.* ZELL *enters.*)

ZELL. Talk to me about the well.

CHUY. What you wanna know?

ZELL. Why Coop Daniels says he owns it.

CHUY. If you look at them papers like I told you—

ZELL. I'm asking you.

CHUY. *Pues*...farm needed a well. Too much drought past couple years. We couldn't count on the ditch running. But your dad didn't have no cash cuz been so long since we had an on-year crop. So he financed it.

ZELL. Through Coop Daniels? I don't believe it.

CHUY. Gotta have water if you gonna grow pecans, baby girl. Daniels gave him a better deal than the bank. *Pinche* vulture. He just hovers and waits.

ZELL. How much do I owe him?

CHUY. Fourteen grand still to go. But you pretty far behind your payments. *Más o menos* seven grand past due right now.

ZELL. That's not that much.

CHUY. It is if you don't got it. And you don't got it 'less you brought it with you.

ZELL. So what can we do about it?

CHUY. You're the boss. You tell me.

ZELL. I know you think I'm completely worthless.

CHUY. I never said that.

ZELL. And you're only staying on here because you love this land and you're loyal as hell and God, Chuy, I can't even tell you how much that means to me. But…I finally feel like I'm *home*. And I just can't see letting anyone take that away from me. I *can't*. I remember who I used to be here. And I *liked* that girl.

CHUY. *Pues sí.* She was a real good kid. But this place ain't like what you remember.

ZELL. Yes it is. It's exactly what I remember. The sky. The air. The quiet. Exactly.

CHUY. You spent too much time in the city. Anything'll look good after that.

ZELL. Just answer me this. If you and I can work the groves just like you and my dad did…can we make it?

(CHUY *looks out at the trees for a long moment.*)

CHUY. Last couple years, me and Press got real quiet, you know? We could go a week without more than a couple words at a time between us. But toward the end of every day, we'd both end up right out here. All day opposite groves, but come dusk, here we'd be. In the far grove. Just a few feet between us and night coming on. Side by side. Like a couple of rock formations.

ZELL. What's it gonna take to keep it going, Chuy *hombre*? Tell me what you need.

CHUY. Press always used to say if you scoop up a handful of the soil from this back grove, you holding a little piece my heart in your hand. It's true too. This ground and me, we belong together. Your dad knew that.

ZELL. You used to eat a mouthful of dirt out here every morning. Like vitamins.

CHUY. I still do. …You asked me what I want. That's it. I want this grove.

ZELL. Wait. Say that again?

CHUY. And I'm not talking about buying it, Zelda.

ZELL. You want me to just give you the back grove. …That's almost half this farm.

CHUY. It's what your dad owed me.

ZELL. Owed you? What do you mean?

CHUY. He knew damn well he couldn't keep this place going without me. When I came here, he didn't know nothing about this land except he bought it cheap from some *pinche cabrón* who already beat the hell out of it.

ZELL. You worked here, Chuy. You got paid.

CHUY. I did. I worked hard. For thirty-two years. He said he'd provide for me. Case he died, said he wanted to make sure I got what's coming to me. Meant a lot to me at the time, you know.

ZELL. Well, I don't know what he meant by that. He never changed his will.

(CHUY *nods stonily; beat.*)

So if I agree? What then? What's in it for me?

CHUY. I teach you how to farm this place. I help you hang onto it.

ZELL. My half.

(*Silence. Finally....*)

How would we do it? What about the well?

CHUY. We make a contract and share the water rights.

ZELL. I meant...Coop wants his money.

CHUY. He'll get it.

ZELL. I've got nothing left of my severance, Chuy.

CHUY. We just need to pay up what's past due and then we'll have a little slack. Once we're caught up we split the well payment every month.

ZELL. Yeah, but how do we get caught up?

(*Beat. Finally....*)

COOP. Leave it to me.

ZELL. You're sure?

CHUY. Just take me a little time to get things in place. If Daniels don't push us too hard too fast, we be okay.

ZELL. You got a little nest egg put away or something?

CHUY. I said I can do it. That's what you need to know.

ZELL. Right, but I mean what about—?

CHUY. You're not listening.

ZELL. I'm just trying to be sure about how things—

CHUY. Zeldita. You gonna have to trust me. So. What you say?

(*Beat.* CHUY *solemnly puts out his hand.* ZELL *steps forward, shakes his hand, and then kisses him on the cheek. He is abashed but not entirely displeased. They stand there grinning at each other. The rooster crows mightily as the lights fade. End of Act I.*)

ACT TWO

About a month later. In the darkness, sustained and ghostly, the indecipherable chorus of whispering in Spanish. Gradually this sound is replaced by music playing very softly. CARL *appears alone in light. He gazes out into the darkness for a few moments.*

CARL. I know they're out here. Sometimes I can feel them all around me in the dark. All these eyes looking back at me. So I listen. Wait for a twig to snap. Scuff of a boot on rock. A voice. Sometimes it's so quiet all I hear is my own heart beating in my ears. But I can wait. I got patience. And all the time in the world.

(*The lights rise on the desert. It is night. The sound of crickets. There are stars and moonlight.* ZELL *is sitting on a blanket drinking a beer. There is a partially emptied six-pack next to her. The music is coming from a small old-model boom box.*)

ZELL. Jeez, it's like you're at work. Come and sit.

(CARL *moves to her, sits on the blanket, pops a beer.*)

CARL. So how's it feel being back out here?

ZELL. …Strange.

CARL. Yeah? You don't like the desert no more?

ZELL. I like it.

CARL. But?

ZELL. I just…I mean…

(*She reaches over and shuts off the boom box.*)

Carlos. What are we doing?

CARL. Just hanging out. Old times, *guera*.

ZELL. Yeah? You tell Angie?

CARL. Tell her what? (*She gives him a look.*) We're just hanging out.

ZELL. Yeah. *Here*, though. We only ever came here to drink and fuck.

CARL. Don't say that.

ZELL. What? Fuck?

CARL. I don't like that word.

ZELL. Awww. How many Hail Marys and Our Fathers is it?

CARL. (*Chuckling.*) Oh, so now you gonna make fun of my faith. You come back to town, you don't hardly call me a month, and now you gonna sit up in here and make fun of me.

ZELL. You could call *me*, ya know.

(*Beat.*)

If you want the truth, I'm dead tired by the end of most days.

CARL. I know what *that's* like.

ZELL. I'm passed out by ten just about every night.

CARL. Aww. Just you and Chuy sitting home in front of the fire.

ZELL. Right. I do embroidery while he reads me poetry.

(*They laugh.*)

CARL. How is ol' Chuy these days?

ZELL. Cranky as ever. But you know what, Carlos? I'm learning so much from him. The work is *endless*. I mean, I *knew*, but I didn't really *know*. You know? Dad never had me do any of the heavy stuff. My *bones* are sore. But I'm getting *muscles*. Feel this. And Chuy's a good teacher. Man, he is so patient.

CARL. So you really gonna do it, huh? You and Chuy gonna split up that farm.

ZELL. All we need is the survey. It's gonna be a couple more weeks before they can get somebody out there. But once that's done it should go pretty quick. And then all we gotta do is pay off the well and we'll be all set, ready for harvest.

(*Beat.*)

CARL. Chuy pretty much staying home nights?

ZELL. When he's not out getting hammered at the Bucket.

CARL. I woulda seen him over there.

ZELL. (*Chuckling.*) Same ol' Carlos.

CARL. You'd tell me if there was something going on, wouldn't you?

ZELL. How do you mean?

CARL. Just asking.

ZELL. What are you asking?

CARL. Chuy keeping his nose clean?

ZELL. Well, okay, off the record? I think he's been going to the fights a lot the past few weeks. The guy always did love a good cockfight, and I know damn well he's betting. It's funny, though: he's got a real soft spot for that monster that hangs around our yard. He brings it little treats, chats away to it when he thinks I can't hear him. It's kind of adorable.

CARL. They crack down hard these days, you know. If there's something going on, you should tell me.

ZELL. Cockfighting's under *migra* jurisdiction now too?

CARL. I'm not talking about that. You just tell Chuy to keep his nose clean.

(*She gives him a mock serious nod. Silence for a few beats.*)

I miss talking to you.

ZELL. Same here.

CARL. Yeah. ...Back then...you were like my sister, you know.

ZELL. You fucked your sister?

CARL. There's that word again.

ZELL. Oh, that's right. You don't have a sister.

CARL. I just meant…it was comfortable, you know?

ZELL. I knew what you meant.

CARL. I could always tell you things. And you used to tell me things too.

ZELL. Yeah. Like I told ya you should get the hell outa here and go to college. Damn, Carlos. You wanted to be a vet.

CARL. Can't always have what you want, Zell, or ain't you heard?

ZELL. But you would have been so *great* at it! God, when the Ochoas' dog got run over, you stayed with that poor thing for days. Dribbling water into her mouth with an eyedropper. …You were so good with her, so *gentle*. You saved her life.

CARL. Yep. And then some rancher poisoned her like three months later.

ZELL. Carlos, take it from me, there's no point spending your life doing work you hate.

CARL. Easy for you to say. If you get sick of *your* job you just set fire to it and watch it burn. I told you: I don't hate my job. Besides, what else you want me to do? Military? I'd rather keep out an invasion than be part of one, thanks anyways.

ZELL. Come on. Those are not your only options.

CARL. Right, I left out Walmart. …*Mira*, your family had money and a good piece of ground, mine didn't. I'm not gonna cry about it, but it's the truth. You took off a long time ago, and you drop by every once in a while just to tell us how we supposed to be living. Me, I stayed right here. I seen my home getting choked, turning into a sewer, and that made me mad.

ZELL. Yeah, you seem mad.

CARL. I'm not mad now. I'm doing something about it. You act like I'm "betraying my people" or something. I'm not betraying nobody. I leave that to the *coyotes*. Me, I just go to work, do my job, and then go on home. It's not perfect but least I can pay on my house and look my face in the mirror mornings.

ZELL. Does your C.O. know you used to run illegals up north for my dad?

CARL. No, *pues*, I left that off my application.

ZELL. Don't ask, don't tell.

CARL. OK, that's it, let's go.

ZELL. What? What's wrong?

CARL. I wanna talk to my old friend. But all night you just trying to make me small.

ZELL. No I'm not—

CARL. Your dad used to do me like that. Talk like I was too stupid to know he was putting me down—

ZELL. Yeah, well, join the club.

CARL. Always judging me—

ZELL. I'm not judging you!

CARL. The hell you're not.

ZELL. OK, Carl. I'm sorry. I really didn't mean to make you—

CARL. This is where I *live*. You're just down here on vacation from your life. Let's go.

> (ZELL *sits down on the blanket.*)

Get up.

ZELL. No.

CARL. You gonna make me leave you out here? Cuz I will.

ZELL. Go ahead.

> (*Beat.*)

CARL. I should do it.

> (*But he sits down on the blanket. He gets himself another beer and they sit without looking at each other for a while. Eerie hooting as the coyotes start up in the distance. ZELL shivers.*)

Sounds like they got something.

> (ZELL *reaches over and switches on the boom box.*)

You have any idea how much shit I gotta eat from people around here? People I grew up with, partied with, they see the uniform and all's I am is *migra*. But you know what, I can't help that. Time for everybody to wake up and live in the real world.

ZELL. Whatever *that* is. ...I really didn't mean to upset you.

CARL. Got a message for everybody. The good ol' days are gone. And no matter how much you miss 'em, they're not coming back.

ZELL. I know that. I'm sorry.

CARL. All right.

ZELL. I don't know when I'm going over the line with you anymore.

CARL. You never did, *guera, pero no importa.*

ZELL. It *does* matter. Cuz you're my friend and I care about you.

CARL. I know you do. You're just...

ZELL. What?

CARL. "In a transition."

ZELL. No. And I'm not on *vacation* either, Carlos. I live here too.

(*Beat. She nudges him. He nudges her back.*)

We still friends?

(*He finally nods, smiles. They clink bottles and drain their beers. The music on the radio changes to a song they both recognize instantly—it's clearly straight out of their shared past. ZELL laughs and slaps CARL's arm playfully. She rises and begins to dance. She's pretty good too. CARL watches, smiling, and soon he gets up and joins her. They follow each other, each playfully challenging each other to bust a few moves.*)

You remember this.

CARL. Course I do.

ZELL. Look at you.

CARL. Look at you.

ZELL. You got fat but you still dance pretty good, *moreno*.

CARL. You got kinda stringy but you do OK too, *guera*.

(*She laughs, slaps at him again. They continue to dance. After a while, they move closer to each other. They kiss. Suddenly they are surrounded by the beams of a circle of flashlights. CARL yanks away from ZELL instantly, shielding his eyes and brandishing his empty beer bottle.*)

¿Quién es? ¡Háblame pues!

(COOP, *dressed in dark clothes, appears with a heavy-duty flashlight.*)

COOP. Carl? Carl Zelaya, is that you?

CARL. Coop? What the hell you doing?

COOP. You might wanna keep your voice down just a little.

(*Calling off in a sharp whisper.*)

It's OK, guys. Move out. I'll catch up.

(*The flashlight beams recede. COOP turns to ZELL and CARL again and just takes them in for a beat or two.*)

COOP. Sorry to disturb. We heard voices and…well. You know. I was just about to call it in.

CARL. Spoze to notify Border Patrol before you approach a suspect. You know that.

COOP. Probably just as well I didn't in this case, though, huh?

(*An uncomfortable beat. ZELL begins to fold up the blanket and COOP turns his flashlight on her.*)

Hey, Zelda.

ZELL. Hey.

CARL. Any of your guys out there armed?

COOP. Just pepper spray.

CARL. Mind if I check that out?

COOP. I do mind actually. Since I'm assuming you're not on duty.

ZELL. Come on, Carl. Let's just get out of here.

COOP. Where's your vehicle?

CARL. Up by the road.

COOP. Got a torch?

(CARL *flips his flashlight on and off.*)

OK then. Have a good night.

(CARL *and* ZELL *exit.* COOP *watches them go, shaking his head. The lights slowly cross to the grove, early the next morning.* CHUY *enters with the wheelbarrow and a seedling with a root ball—it is a bit more filled out than the one in Act I. He takes out a knife and begins to cut into the burlap around the root ball. The rooster crows raucously from nearby.* CHUY *smiles and mutters something under his breath in response.* ANGIE *enters.*)

ANGIE. Hey.

CHUY. *Buenos.* What brings you out here so early?

ANGIE. You alone?

CHUY. Far as I know.

ANGIE. *¿Dónde está la dueña?*

CHUY. Still sleeping.

ANGIE. You working twenty-four-seven while she's every night out on the town.

CHUY. What town?

(*They laugh.*)

ANGIE. How you two getting along?

CHUY. You know me. I get along with everybody.

ANGIE. Yeah *right.* Getting late for planting, *¿qué no?*

CHUY. This is the last one right here.

ANGIE. Grove's looking good.

CHUY. I've had help.

ANGIE. Yeah? So she listen to you? She don't give you a lotta shit, try to tell you she know better and all that?

CHUY. Nah. She pays attention. She's catchin' on. And she does real good on the tractor.

ANGIE. Oh, I can see it now.

(*Does an unflattering impression.* CHUY *grins, shrugs. Beat.*)

CHUY. Zeldita's all right.

ANGIE. So you trust her. Well, that's good then.

(*Beat.*)

CHUY. So what you need, Angie?

ANGIE. You know Nezzie been sick, right?

CHUY. *Pues sí,* I stopped by to see her yesterday. She says the doctor told her she gotta stay in bed till the baby comes. *Pobrecita,* she's just a kid herself.

ANGIE. Right. Plus her car's broke so I gotta drive her three, four times a week over there to the clinic just to get checked out. She's all nerved up, you know how she gets. Plus it's expensive!

CHUY. She's covered through Georgie, *¿qué no?* That's government insurance.

ANGIE. *Sí claro, pero* there's all these "extras" they don't cover. Little shit that adds up real quick. Anyways, Nezzie's a complete wreck. I got some pills could calm her down, but she can't take nothing. And now they talking about putting her in the hospital up in Cruces, which she does *not* wanna do—and I don't blame her cuz you wanna die quick just go stay in a hospital. So now I'm getting really *scared*, you know. Nobody ever lost a baby when Rosita was here.

CHUY. She had a gift, no denying.

ANGIE. She brought Nezzie into this world.

CHUY. I remember.

ANGIE. What you keep in that shed these days?

CHUY. *Nada más* tools.

ANGIE. What if I come fix it up? Give it a coat of paint, put some furniture in there. I could make it real cozy and nice. Only take me a couple days.

CHUY. What for?

ANGIE. Maybe you wanna help me bring over some nice older lady from Mexico to stay in there for cheap.

CHUY. *Estas loca.*

ANGIE. *Migra* don't bother about this place no more.

CHUY. That's cuz I don't give them no *reason.*

ANGIE. It's just till Nezzie has her baby. …People come across this border every God damn day.

CHUY. They don't stay in my shed.

ANGIE. "My" shed. Listen to you. You so cute. …That guesthouse got a long history.

CHUY. You crazy or something? You married to *migra.*

ANGIE. Don't worry about Carl. I can handle him. You gotta do this for me.

CHUY. I don't gotta do a thing.

ANGIE. After the kid is born, Rosita goes right back over. Everybody's happy.

CHUY. *Pues,* I'd like to help you but I can't. Now, you want me to drive Nezzie up Greeley for you sometimes, that I can do, but—

ANGIE. You don't care about Nezzie at all, do you? That poor kid would do anything for you but you just gonna sit by while she—

CHUY. Hey! Don't say nothing you can't take back. Nezzie's my girl and you know that. But I can't risk everything I got. Not now.

ANGIE. What you think you got? Lemme tell you something. You not gonna be laying on your deathbed one day saying "*¡Ay lástima!* I didn't work hard enough on Zelda's farm." Hell, no—you know what you gonna be saying? "*¡Idiota, yo!* I didn't take care of my *gente*, and I hated myself the next twenty years."

CHUY. You give me twenty more years of this, huh? Might interest you to know. That back grove belongs to me now.

(*Beat.*)

ANGIE. Might interest you to know I seen you at the Coronado Motel last night.

CHUY. What you talkin' about?

ANGIE. I was taking Nez home from the clinic but just as we're driving outa Greeley she remember she left her purse so we gotta go back. And when I turn my car around, there you are driving along in front of me. Going exactly the speed limit. And I think to myself, "*Pues*, what's that *pinche* Chuy up to in Greeley tonight?" And two minutes later, you turn in at the Coronado, drive all the way around the back, and I'm like "Ding! Now I see how it is."

(*Beat.*)

You gotta go at least eight miles over the speed limit, don't you know that? Otherwise *migra* come pull you over for sure.

CHUY. There's construction over there.

ANGIE. Don't matter. Speed limit equals *migra*. I used to drive for Preston back in the day, ya know. Only thing: Press didn't take no money from them people. Once they worked enough time here, he just take 'em up north or wherever so they could get on with their life. He was like a good samaritan, *verdad?* You, you're more like…I don't know. What are you like?

(CHUY *mutters under his breath.*)

Hey, I'm not your judge. Times change, huh? I understand you *completamente*. Fact I can help you. But you gotta help me too.

CHUY. *Háblame pues.*

ANGIE. You do all the driving, they gonna get you. Sooner or later, it's gonna happen. Like I said: I used to do transport for Preston too.

CHUY. I can't have her staying here. Anybody wanders over the border onto our ground, I got nothing to do with it. They on their own.

ANGIE. So? Where you pick 'em up at then?

CHUY. Down there by Los Ruidos. I don't bring 'em noplace near here.

ANGIE. *Bueno. Entonces…*you hook me up with your people. I do some driving for you, we mix it up a little bit. Then one of these days, I go over and pick up Rosita at Ruidos with the rest of 'em. Right? We just gotta find someplace safe where she can stay at.

CHUY. Gonna be tough here in Fronteras. You know how things get around. …*Mira,* how about I put you in touch with some people I know up Greeley can find a place for her.

ANGIE. Greeley. …Yeah. *Yeah,* that's *perfect.* Nezzie can stay up there with Rosita till she's ready to have that baby. Then she got the clinic *and tía.* I like it! So how soon you can get Rosita over here this side? She's ready to come any day.

ZELL. (*Calling from off.*) Chuy?

ANGIE. She don't know nothing about it?

CHUY. I got no idea what she knows. This got nothin' to do with her.

> (ZELL *calls* CHUY's *name again and* ANGIE *and* CHUY *exit together in the opposite direction, as the lights change to later that morning. The sound of a helicopter is heard.* INES *sits on her steps staring at the label on a bottle of vitamins. Nearly a month has passed since we last saw her, and she is enormous.* COOP *enters and* INES *struggles to her feet.*)

COOP. No, no, dang, girl, don't get up.

> (*He helps her sit back down.*)

What ya got there?

INES. Pregnant lady vitamins.

COOP. You're getting pretty close now, aren't you? What you got—another month?

INES. Two.

COOP. How you feeling?

INES. …I'm late with your check I know—

COOP. I heard you've been having some cash-flow problems.

INES. *Pues,* I had to quit the diner last month and so now I gotta wait for Georgie's check—but I'm gonna have it should be end of this week—

COOP. How long have we known each other, Ines?

INES. *Pues, no sé…*

COOP. *Pero muchos años, ¿verdad?*

INES. I guess.

COOP. So you gotta know better than to think I'd ever come over here to shake you down for the rent. …These trailers are a write-off for me, honey. You know what that means? It means I take a loss on them every single month. I rent them out for not much money to people like you and Georgie. Elena Truchas. The Cabreras. Know why I do that? Because I like to be good to good people. So listen. As of right now, I'm dropping your rent down to one dollar. Now I'm gonna need that dollar every single month. I don't care how you get it to me, but get it to me. All right? …You got a dollar? …Well, hand it over, girl.

(INES *pulls out a dollar from her bra and hands it to him.*)

Gracias, eh?

INES. Is this for reals?

COOP. You think I'm playing with you?

INES. How come?

COOP. I told you.

INES. Georgie wouldn't like it. He's proud you know.

COOP. Well, when Georgie's back here where he belongs, we can go back to the old rent and he never needs to know a thing about this. Hell, I'll raise it if that'll make him happy. That work for ya?

(INES *nods emphatically.*)

Oh, and I'd appreciate it if you don't mention this to anybody else. I don't want your neighbors feeling like they're getting a raw deal, know what I mean?

INES. *Ah sí, claro!* Thank you, Mr. Daniels, really, OK?

COOP. You ever gonna call me Coop? That's my name. …Well. I gotta be gettin' on back to work. You take those vitamins now, ya hear?

(ANGIE *enters.*)

Hey, how you doing, lady?

ANGIE. Is there a problem here?

COOP. Not at all. Just visiting with your *hermana*.

INES. He put my rent down to a dollar!

COOP. Now Nezzie, I thought we made a deal.

INES. Oh, shit! I'm sorry!

ANGIE. What's this?

COOP. Nothing. I heard Nezzie had some backed up bills, that's all.

ANGIE. You dropped her rent?

COOP. Is that all right?

ANGIE. It's nice of you.

COOP. I do what I can. We all gotta live here together, ya know. How you doing, Angie?

ANGIE. Well, I wouldn't mind a raise if you're still looking to help people out. Hah.

COOP. (*Studying her for a moment.*) Everything OK at home?

ANGIE. *¿Mande?*

COOP. You and Carl doing OK?

ANGIE. Why?

COOP. I just…well. With Zelda Preston back in town…I just…I hope that hasn't caused any friction, that's all.

ANGIE. Friction?

COOP. Tension.

ANGIE. I know what the word means. I just don't know why you wanna get in my business.

COOP. I'm sorry. I…I shouldn't have said anything.

ANGIE. You heard something or what?

COOP. I…no, no. Forget it. I…I spoke out of turn. I'll see you ladies around, all right?

(*He exits. Beat.*)

ANGIE. What he mean by that? You think Carl got something going on with Zelda?

INES. Carl? Nahhhh. You think?

ANGIE. I wouldn't put it past him. Old times, old *putas*.

(*She suddenly looks closely at* INES.)

What you sweating like that for? …Damn, Nezzie, you look like shit.

INES. I'm not doing so good today. My heart's thumping real hard.

ANGIE. I'm taking you to the clinic. Right now. Get your stuff.

INES. I don't got an appointment.

ANGIE. I don't care, I'm taking you. But hey. Here's something'll make you really happy, OK? I got it all set up. Rosita. She's coming!

INES. …For reals?

ANGIE. Next week or the week after. Just one thing you gotta do for me, OK? You gotta get Carl to quit coming by here all the time. I don't want you two having them big old long talks anymore. You runnin' your mouth gonna be too dangerous for Rosita, you understand me?

INES. I won't run my mouth, I promise.

ANGIE. No, you can't help how you are. So you gotta do this, Nezzie. It's all I'm asking.

INES. What I'm spoze to do when he comes over?

ANGIE. Remember when Jimmy C'de Baca used to come sniffing around after you all the time? How'd you get rid of him?

INES. Georgie kicked his ass back in junior year.

ANGIE. OK, but *before* that you told Jimmy about your boundaries, right? "You can't call me. You can't come by my house. You a nice guy, Jimmy, but you don't need to be coming by." Like that.

INES. Yeah, but Carl's not like Jimmy, though.

ANGIE. I know that. I know. But right now you gotta think of what he does all day and what that means for Rosita, you know what I'm saying? Gonna be hard, but you gotta do this. You promise? …OK then. Get your stuff, we're going to the clinic.

(*Music. The lights cross. It is about ten days later. We hear the sound of a crowd roaring, cheering, and two roosters fighting to the death. ZELDA appears suddenly. She is shaking and breathing hard. She hugs herself tightly. The sound of the cockfight crescendos and there is an offstage cheer. CHUY enters. There is a spatter of blood on his face. He holds out a pint of tequila to ZELL. She takes it and gulps.*)

CHUY. You wanted to come.

ZELL. I know.

CHUY. Gonna be all right?

ZELL. Uckk, there's *blood* on you…

(*He wipes it away.*)

Jesus, that was, I mean *Jesus!*

CHUY. You shouldn'ta come.

ZELL. Can we please just go back to the farm now?

CHUY. Not me. I got money on the next fight. El Rey's about to kick some ass in there, you just wait and see.

ZELL. So is *this* how you plan to get the money to pay off the well? By *gambling*?

CHUY. Don't you worry about that. I'm taking care of it.

(*He turns to go.*)

You coming?

ZELL. I can't go back in there.

CHUY. Nobody forced you to come. Nobody even invited you.

ZELL. I know. I know. I don't know why I came…I guess I was trying to. … Did I at least *win*?

CHUY. No.

ZELL. So my guy…?

(CHUY *nods.*)

Jesus. Poor thing.

CHUY. You're not used to it, that's all. Those birds. It's what they live for.

ZELL. Yeah? Well, *my* bird's dead. This wasn't my first, you know. My dad took me once when I was a kid. In Palomas. The real deal. Everybody kept talking about "*los gallos valientes*"—like they were heroes or something—these proud fighting birds. And then, just like tonight, the thing starts and I can see they're just panicked, they're scared to death, doing whatever it takes to stay alive another couple seconds. All that jumping and flapping, slicing at each other, people screaming, the smoke. God. I threw up. Right there by the pit. …Dad was so disappointed in me. *Again.*

(CHUY *nods silently, pats her shoulder, then hands her the keys.*)

CHUY. Go on home. Take the truck. I'll get a ride.

ZELL. No, no, I. …You sure?

(CHUY *nods.*)

You think I'm a big baby, don't you?

CHUY. No.

ZELL. Well, I am. Sometimes I can't imagine what the fuck I'm doing back here.

(CHUY *mumbles something inaudible. She sighs.*)

Yeah. OK. Whatever.

CHUY. I said. You're right where you belong.

ZELL. You mean that?

CHUY. Yeah, Zeldita, I mean it. Now go on. I'll see you at home.

(*A moment between them. Then a very loud horn sounds signaling the start of the next fight. From off, stomping and clapping.* CHUY *turns and exits.* ZELL *stands still a moment, then exits in the other direction as the lights cross to morning at the trailer.* INES *stands on her steps. She is dressed in a robe.* CARL *enters.*)

CARL. Don't you answer your phone anymore?

INES. I'm not really up yet, Carl.

CARL. That's OK. …Damn, girl, look at you! You all huge and everything!

INES. I mean I'm not ready for company.

CARL. You mad at me or something?

INES. No.

CARL. You sure?

INES. Yeah I'm sure.

CARL. Then how come you acting like that? And how come you don't call me back when I holler at you?

INES. I got stuff to do sometimes, you know. Things on my mind.

CARL. Can we sit down a second so I can talk to you?

INES. *Pues*, I'm not even dressed.

CARL. That's all right.

(*He sits. She remains standing and avoids his eyes.*)

Damn, you look even more tired than me. You're all pale and everything. How you doin', Nez?

INES. I wish everybody quit asking me that.

CARL. Seems like you're mad, but I don't know what I did.

INES. Why you wanna come over here all the time anyway?

CARL. What you mean?

INES. You over here all the time.

CARL. I haven't seen you in a week!

INES. Aren't you spoze be at work right now?

CARL. I'm on my way there.

INES. You got so much extra time, maybe you should spend it with your wife.

CARL. Whoa. I just thought I'd stop and see how you doing.

INES. So now you see me. OK?

CARL. Damn, Nezzie, what is up with you?

INES. You come by here like you my boyfriend or something.

CARL. No, like I'm family who cares about you. I really gotta explain this?

INES. (*Relenting a bit.*) No, but…

CARL. Good. Cuz it would break my heart if you and me stop being family.

INES. If you're cheating on Angie then you're no family of mine, you know that, right?

CARL. *¿Qué dices tú?*

INES. You heard me.

CARL. She tell you that? …She knows damn well I'd never cheat on her. She's trying to turn you against me just like the rest of this *pinche* town.

INES. Whatever, Carl. Anyways, you gotta call first.

CARL. I did but you don't pick up the phone.

INES. Well, maybe that should tell you something.

CARL. What's it spoze to tell me? Eh? …*Háblame, hermanita.*

INES. I don't know!

CARL. Angie been talking trash about me. That's not right, Nezzie. You and me always been tight.

INES. You don't need to be coming by here early mornings, late at night, and like that. …People talk, you know. People talk around this place!

CARL. This town's always talking. It's a hobby for them. Who cares?

INES. I gotta go back in get my feet up.

CARL. Well, you got a cup of coffee for me in there?

INES. You don't even listen, do you? Leave me alone, Carl! Damn! You always at me.

CARL. *Pues*, if that's really what you want, I can stop coming by.

INES. Just wait to be invited, that's all.

CARL. This is about la Rosita. …You and Angie just gonna gang up on me until you get your way, is that it?

INES. Don't blame *mi tía* for this too.

CARL. You sound just like Angie. *Bueno, Ines. Ya me voy.* Oh. I almost forgot. Here.

> (*He pulls a small Beanie Baby-style animal out of his pocket and tosses it at her. It falls at her feet.*)

For the baby.

> (*CARL exits. INES sits down heavily on the step, picks up the toy and puts her face in her hands, as the lights cross to the grove. CHUY enters with a wheelbarrow full of dirt and a shovel. He peers through binoculars out above the tree line. ZELL enters.*)

ZELL. I gotta talk to you.

CHUY. That damn coyote's on the ridge again. Just sitting up there with her tongue out. Been watching something down here for the last hour.

ZELL. Hey. I got pulled over by *migra* on my way home from the fight last night.

CHUY. Oh yeah? What they want?

ZELL. To check the truck. They made me get out, show my ID. And then they took everything out of it.

CHUY. It happens.

ZELL. They tailed me all the way from Tortuga Road before they pulled me over. Something's up. And have you noticed that van out there?

CHUY. Across the road?

ZELL. Two days in a row.

CHUY. Citizens Alliance.

ZELL. Why are they watching the farm? Why now?

CHUY. *Pues,* who knows? Old habits.

ZELL. That's it? You sure about that, Chuy?

> (CHUY *continues working.*)

They can't just *spy* on us. That's harassment.

CHUY. They're not on the property. They just watching to see who comes in and out. They see illegals, they call *migra.* Got nothing to do with us either way. Don't pay them no attention.

ZELL. Or. Maybe we should think about letting them fence the back grove like they want to.

CHUY. You kidding, right?

ZELL. I'm not. If they're all so worried about what's going on here, let's just show them we got nothing to hide.

CHUY. Your old man would have a fit. We fought that fence ever since they first started talking about it—

ZELL. It's not like we'd be fencing the *border.* Just the back end of *this property.*

CHUY. I said no fence.

ZELL. This is a discussion, Chuy. You don't get to just say no.

CHUY. The far grove is gonna be mine, *¿qué no?*

ZELL. You know it is.

CHUY. Then the fence'd be on my property. And I say no. You forget where I'm from, baby girl. I come a long way since Zacatecas. And I'm not gonna stop anybody doing what I did to get here. Citizens Alliance can spy on this farm as long as they want. Ain't nothing happening on this ground. You got my word on it.

ZELL. …Okay…But is there anything else you oughta tell me?

(*A sharp horn sounds. They both squint off.*)

CHUY. *A la chingada. ¡Este cabrón nunca duerme!*

ZELL. What does he want now?

(COOP *enters.*)

COOP. *Buenos días,* Zelda. And my God. Is this—? It can't be! Chuy Gallegos. How are you, sir?

(CHUY *mutters.*)

ZELL. You ever spend any time at your own farm, Coop? Seems like I see you everywhere else but.

COOP. Well, that's the good news about a big operation. I got people.

CHUY. *Ah sí. Mucha gente. Claro, señor.*

COOP. Whoo, hot today, huh?

ZELL. I'd offer you a soda but we're kinda in the middle of our workday. Was there something you needed?

COOP. Yeah. Yeah, there was. Won't take long, but…it's kind of a private matter.

ZELL. Chuy's my partner. He knows everything that's going on.

COOP. …All right. I need to talk to you about the well. See, you're coming into this proposition quite a few payments in arrears, Zelda, and I know that's not your fault. Out of respect for your dad, I did allow him to get behind on his payments without taking any legal action. And, boy, I do not want to take any action now either. But…time's marchin' on, you know?

ZELL. It's going to just take us a little while longer to get things back on track here, Coop. I'm doing the best I can.

COOP. I understand. And I think you have to admit I've been pretty patient.

ZELL. Yes you have, Coop, and I so thank you for that.

COOP. But I'm gonna need you to pick up the pace for me a little bit.

ZELL. We're really working on it.

COOP. Good deal. So. How long you figure till you can get current? Just ballpark it for me.

CHUY. *Un mes, nada más.*

ZELL. Oh. Well, I don't know about *that*—

COOP. I can live with a month.

ZELL. I'm not sure we can promise that. But we are expecting a good harvest—

COOP. Oh, I know you are. God willin' and the creek don't rise. Tell you what though. At the moment, my office needs twenty-five hundred dollars of the past-due amount from you as a show of good faith. So I was thinking. If it would help you out to sell your shaker, I'd give you a real decent price for it.

CHUY. Ain't for sale.

ZELL. How much?

COOP. Give ya twenty-eight hundred.

CHUY. It's worth nine thousand.

COOP. (*Speaking only to Zell.*) Naw. That shaker's more than ten years old. Thirty-five hundred. Apply that to the well and it puts you just about back on track.

CHUY. I said it ain't for sale.

COOP. Zelda?

ZELL. Thanks for the offer, Coop. How about we think it over and let you know?

COOP. Up to you. Just want to give you another option. I try to play fair with my fellow growers.

(CHUY *mutters.* COOP *looks at him expressionlessly.*)

ZELL. *Chuy.* …We appreciate it, Coop. Really we do. I'll let you know.

COOP. Good deal. And how about this coming Monday for that good-faith payment?

(ZELL *looks at* CHUY, *who nods.*)

I'll see you then. Meantime, you behave yourselves now, hear?

(COOP *smiles genially and exits.* CHUY *and* ZELL *stand there, staring stonily at one another, until they hear* COOP's *car start up.*)

CHUY. No way we gonna sell him that shaker.

ZELL. I bet we could get him up to four or five thousand. That gets us a lot closer. Gives us some room to breathe.

CHUY. And what we do about our trees come harvest?

ZELL. We rent a shaker!

CHUY. And you know who you gonna rent from? Besides us, he's the only farm in this valley got a shaker. Now you wanna give him ours too? You thinking like a sharecropper.

ZELL. Don't let your pride lose us this farm, Chuy.

CHUY. It ain't pride. Come harvest, that shaker brings us *income* from the little farms. We make *money* off it. …Would your dad have sold his shaker?

ZELL. Who can say?

CHUY. He wouldn't have and you know it. He would have made Daniels come get it. And he'd have been standing by it with Matilda loaded and cocked if he tried it. You gonna fence this ground, you gonna sell Daniels the shaker. Why don't you just hand him over the whole damn thing right now?

ZELL. You told me to leave it all up to you. "Just *trust me*," isn't that what you said? Well, I trusted you. But we don't have the money we owe. So you need to either come up with that money by Monday or I'm selling the shaker for whatever we can get.

(*She exits.* CHUY *stares after her as we hear police radio static and chatter as the lights cross to early evening of the same day.* CARL *is sitting alone in the semi-darkness in an easy chair. He is in uniform but his shirt is unbuttoned and he is drinking a beer. He wears his night-vision goggles.* ANGIE *enters.*)

ANGIE. Halloween come early this year?

(CARL *doesn't answer.*)

OK, so who you spoze to be? …Ahh. The silent treatment. *Bueno* bye.

CARL. What did you say to Nezzie?

ANGIE. Take them damn things off, I didn't say nothing.

CARL. I went over there this morning, she wouldn't even talk to me.

ANGIE. And you found a way to blame this on me. Maybe you should try calling first.

CARL. That's you, always in Nezzie's head, chaca-chaca-chaca-chaca.

ANGIE. I can't help it you go over there, act all weird with her.

CARL. She said you told her I cheated on you.

ANGIE. I never said that.

CARL. I see you, Angie. …Even in the dark I see you.

ANGIE. Ohhhhh. Now I get it. That's a good one.

CARL. When you turn family against family, it don't get much wronger than that.

ANGIE. I told you: I didn't say nothing. Anyways, she's not your family, Carl. She's mine.

CARL. Why'd you do it? Just cuz you could? If you hate me that much, why don't you just walk out on me?

ANGIE. You're a stupid, stupid man, you know that? I loved you since I was thirteen years old! But you're changing, Carl, and it scares me.

CARL. I don't know what you're talking about.

ANGIE. Maybe turns out you're not the person Nezzie thought you were. Maybe she's afraid she'll "put you in a position."

CARL. That's you, not Nezzie.

ANGIE. Maybe she don't trust you since you got rid of our *tía*.

CARL. For the last time: I had nothing to do with that.

ANGIE. No? What if it had been my mother? Would you let them take her?

CARL. Your mother's dead.

ANGIE. Would you?

CARL. And she was born on this side.

ANGIE. Would you?

CARL. I'm not playing what-if with you.

ANGIE. What about your mom then?

CARL. Born here.

ANGIE. Would you let them take her?

CARL. This is stupid.

ANGIE. Then it should be easy, *¿qué no?* Would you let them send her back, *sí o no?*

CARL. *Bueno*, if she wasn't born here? *Pues*, what could I do?

> (*Beat; they are both a bit stunned.*)

ANGIE. Family my ass. You don't even know who you are.

CARL. I know exactly who *I* am. I'm just not sure who *we* are anymore. How we get like this, baby? Please tell me cuz I don't know.

ANGIE. Oh what, you gonna start crying now?

> (*ANGIE's cell phone rings. She answers it instantly, keeping her eyes on CARL the entire time.*)

Yeah. …Yep. I was just leaving. *Claro, hombre, no te preocupes.* I'm on it. …*Sí, cómo no.* Mm-hm. I got it. …*Bueno* bye.

> (*She hangs up.*)

I'm going out.

CARL. Is there somebody else, Angela?

ANGIE. Would that make things easier for you?

CARL. Least I'd know what to do.

ANGIE. Would you, *mi amor?* Without a direct order?

> (*ANGIE exits. The sound of a helicopter as the lights change to later that evening. CHUY enters the grove with his rifle and a small lantern, and stands scanning the grove, listening intently. The sound of the helicopter increases until its spotlight suddenly catches CHUY, holds on him briefly as he squints up into the glare. Then it moves off once again. CHUY again scans the grove. Suddenly we*

hear offstage yipping, growling, and the sound of an outraged rooster escalating into a screaming, yowling scuffle. CHUY *exits quickly as the offstage battle continues. In a moment, the sound of a rifle blast followed by* CHUY *cursing in Spanish.* ZELL *enters the grove on the run.*)

ZELL. Chuy? …Chuy, where are you?!…

(CHUY *enters carrying a mess of gore and black feathers that was only moments before a large rooster.*)

What are you doing?! What the hell'd you shoot it for?

CHUY. I didn't shoot him. I shot that *pinche* coyote. I grazed her, but she got away.

(CHUY *sets the rooster down and kneels next to it, running his fingers gently over its ruined feathers.*)

Ay, El Rey, pobrecito, que hermoso estuvo…

(*A brief silence.*)

ZELL. He belonged to Garzas up the road, right?

CHUY. Aww, yeah, but all this land was his. He was a warrior, *ese gallo.* Lot of heart, you know? Lot of *raza.*

ZELL. I'm really sorry…

CHUY. Twenty-five fights he won. Never a scratch on him. Then along come this coyote decides today's the day. And that's all it takes. *Así es la vida,* don't matter what he do.

ZELL. Jeez, I'm so sorry, Chu'. …Do you want me to…?

(*She motions vaguely at the rooster's corpse.*)

CHUY. I don't know what you gonna do. I'm gonna go and bury El Rey.

ZELL. Don't you think you better leave that to Garzas?

CHUY. Garzas throws his dead birds in the dump. This one's gonna have some honor.

(*He gently picks up the rooster again, cradling it in his arms, looks down at it for several moments. Finally, to* ZELL.)

I ask you something? …Why you think your dad didn't leave me that far grove in his will?

ZELL. I really don't know how to answer that, Chuy.

CHUY. He told me he'd provide for me. Told me I'd *earned* it. …So I wonder about it, you know? After thirty-two years. …You said he made a different kind of family once you and your ma left here. But maybe there's really only one kind of family when it comes down to it. Or maybe I was always just one more ignorant *pendejo* from below the *frontera.*

ZELL. Aww come on, Chuy. You know it wasn't like that.

CHUY. Do I?

ZELL. Besides, I'm going to make things right with you just like we said. The back grove is already yours—the survey's just a formality. You gotta believe me.

CHUY. I do. I believed him too.

ZELL. Chuy…

CHUY. (*The rooster.*) I gotta go do this.

(*There is a sudden sweep of headlights across the grove and the sound of a car pulling in close.* CHUY *immediately reaches down and picks up the rifle.*)

COOP. (*Off.*) Zelda Preston, you out there?

ZELL. (*To* CHUY.) What are you *doing*!?

(*Calling off.*)

Be right there! …(*Whispering harshly.*) Put that thing down—are you crazy?—we don't need any more trouble with him.

CHUY. Just get rid of him. *Ándale*, Zelda. I mean it.

(CHUY *backs away into the shadows. In a moment,* COOP *enters in the glare of the headlights. He has a flashlight and a cell phone. In the distance we begin to hear the faint whine of a siren.*)

COOP. Evening, Zelda.

ZELL. What are you doing here, Coop?

COOP. Been some trouble out on the highway I just picked it up on the scanner a few minutes ago. Border Patrol pulled over a truck full of illegals. They got three of them but everybody else took off on foot, including the driver.

ZELL. And so?

COOP. There's reason to believe Chuy Gallegos is involved.

ZELL. Oh yeah? Why's that?

COOP. Border Patrol ID'ed his truck.

ZELL. Chuy's been here with me all night.

COOP. You're gonna want to be real careful what you say now, Zelda.

ZELL. (*Calling into the grove.*) Chuy. Come out here a sec', will you?

COOP. He's here?

(CHUY *edges back into the light.*)

You happen to know the whereabouts of your truck this evening, Chuy?

CHUY. Get off my land.

COOP. 'Fraid you're stuck with me till Border Patrol can get here.

CHUY. I said get off my land. I got work to do.

(*He turns in the direction of the far grove.*)

COOP. I'm gonna have to insist you sit tight.

CHUY. Yeah? How you gonna do that?

(COOP *pulls a small handgun from his pocket. He holds it loosely, not quite pointing it.* CHUY *shakes his head, laughs scornfully.*)

COOP. I got my people posted along the perimeter and at the top of the road. So I wouldn't try anything if I were you.

ZELL. Chuy? Everything's *okay*, right?

CHUY. Got nothing to do with you.

(*The siren is very close now. It winds down as headlights sweep the grove again.* COOP *turns and flashes his light on and off several times.*)

CARL. (*From off.*) Chuy Gallegos!

COOP. It's all right, Carl! I got him back here!

(CARLOS *enters preceded by the sound of his police radio, which continues to crackle and chatter under the scene.*)

CHUY. *Ay, migra.* I knew it'd be you.

CARL. Yeah, you know something? I knew it'd be you too. Sooner or later. I knew it. ...Coop, what the hell you doing? Put that damn thing away before you hurt yourself. ...Hey. You hear me? Don't make me haul you in. You know I'll do it.

COOP. (*Pocketing the gun.*) You guys just cannot accept a helping hand, can ya?

ZELL. Will somebody please tell me what's going on?

CARL. I don't know how deep you're in this, Zelda, but I got a bad feeling. So if you're in it, then please, less you say right now, the better.

CHUY. She's not in it.

CARL. Just you, huh?

CHUY. Just me.

CARL. I don't understand you, man.

CHUY. *Claro, hombre.* You never did.

CARL. All those years I looked up to you.

CHUY. You never knew where to look. You're lost right now and you don't even know it.

CARL. Chuy Gallegos, you're under arrest in connection with the illegal trafficking of undocumented immigrants across an international border. You have the right to remain silent and refuse to answer questions. Do you understand? Anything you do say may be used against you in a court of law. Do you understand? ...*Do you understand?*

ZELL. Come on, Carlos, *please*. You've got this all wrong.

(CHUY *crosses into the shadows and picks up the rooster.*)

COOP. Watch him now!

CARL. (*Putting a hand on his gun.*) What you got there, man? ...OK, I want you to put it down in front of you...real slow.

(CHUY *sets the bird down and* CARL *and* COOP *both shine lights on it.*)
A la chingada, Chuy! What the hell'd you do?

ZELL. It's just a dead rooster! Chuy's been here with *me* the whole night, I swear to God.

CARL. Just stay quiet, OK? *Please.*

    (*To* CHUY.)

You have the right to consult an attorney before speaking to the authorities and to have an attorney present during questioning now or in the future.

ZELL. It's a *mistake*! Can't we all just go up to the house and—?

CARL. *I said shut up now!* They got video surveillance from the Coronado in Greeley. Are you aware of that?

ZELL. The Coronado? The motel?

CARL. Know what they got on video? Chuy driving in. Illegals getting out. Chuy driving away. They busted the owner this afternoon. You're caught, Chuy. And don't worry. They gonna get your little friend too. He's on foot and he's not gonna get far.

    (CARL'*s radio has been crackling and there has been static and chatter. In which we suddenly hear* ANGIE'*s name.* CARL *grabs the radio.*)

One six eight, can you repeat last communication? Over.

VOICEOVER. Three nine seven, Positive ID on driver of 1987 Chevy Blazer, NM license plate F-R-W dash five oh three. Suspect is Angela Zelaya, 34, of Fronteras. Second suspect apprehended, undocumented Mexican female, fifty to sixty-five, unofficially ID'ed as Rosa Alegría Ochoa. Copy?

    (*Beat; static crackles.*)

Three nine seven. You copy?

CARL. I copy.

    (CARL *shuts off the radio and the static cuts out.*)

ZELL. Carlos…?

CARL. (*Advancing on* CHUY.) Why would you do that? Why would you get my Angie mixed up in this?

COOP. Carl, take it easy. Let's all just grab a deep breath here, OK?

CARL. You gonna answer me?! It's one thing for you, man. You're all alone, you got nothing to lose. But that's my wife! You understand me, *pendejo*? My wife!

CHUY. She didn't do nothing wrong. All she wanted was her *tía* come back here.

CARL. Yeah well, looks like she got her way about that.

    (*Sound of a far-off helicopter approaching. All look up.* CHUY *calmly reaches down again and picks up the rooster.*)

What you think you're doing?

CHUY. I'm taking an old friend back to my ground. And I'm gonna bury him.

CARL. You're not going anywhere. Put that fucking thing down.

(CARL *unholsters his gun.* CHUY *cradles the bird against his chest.*)

CHUY. What, you gonna shoot me now?

ZELL. Oh my God, Carl…it's just *us! Please* put that away!

(*As she speaks,* ZELL *takes a step or two toward* CARL, *and for a brief moment, as he turns toward her, he is pointing the gun at her. This seems to surprise them both. She stops and backs up.*)

CARL. (*Turning again to* CHUY.) Drop that bird and get your hands where I can see them.

CHUY. You got any idea how stupid you sound, *migra?*

(CHUY *turns away.*)

CARL. Coop. Take that thing away from him.

(COOP *moves toward* CHUY, *who takes a step into the shadows, puts down the rooster, and picks up the rifle. He points it at* COOP, *who stops where he is.*)

Come on, man. You do not want to do that. Put it down. I'm not gonna tell you again. Put it down. Chuy, I'm warning you. Put. It. Down!

COOP. Give me the gun, Chuy. Come on now.

CHUY. *Lo siento, señor, pero esto no puedo hacer.*

ZELL. Chuy for God's sake! Give it to him!

(CHUY *turns briefly to* ZELL *and as he does so,* COOP *takes another quick step toward* CHUY *and gets a hand on the rifle.* CHUY *struggles to regain control of it.*)

CARL. God damn you, stop where you are! *Stop! STOP!*

(ZELDA *rushes to* CARL *and puts a hand on his arm in a final attempt to defuse the situation.* CHUY *lurches and stumbles a bit, and the gun swings wildly.* CARL, *distracted by Zelda and seeing* CHUY*'s weapon in motion, panics and fires. The shot hits* CHUY *in the chest.* CHUY *lets go of the gun and staggers, staring wildly around the grove.*)

CHUY. *Oh…OK. …Déjame pues. Está bien, está bien, está bien. OK…*

(CHUY *sits down suddenly, heavily, spreads his hands over his chest and then holds them out staring at the blood with a kind of fascination. The helicopter moves in suddenly; the sound is deafening and the light blinding.* COOP *signals up at it wildly as* ZELL *runs to* CHUY *and crouches next to him. Then, stricken, she turns to* CARL *who appears dazed and stares fixedly up into the light. Then the helicopter light begins to dim as it moves off the scene and slowly trolls back and forth across the stage and out over the audience. The sound of the helicopter slows down and gradually fades to a reverberated thump that is as rhythmic and distorted as the beating of a heart. Finally the beating stops, the searchlight dissipates, and lights rise on the grove.*)

It is a bright, clear morning two months later, late summer. For a moment the only sounds are wind chimes and bird calls. CARL enters dressed in jeans and a T-shirt. He gazes around the grove, eventually making his way to the spot where CHUY died. When he's sure he is alone, he kneels and solemnly places a hand on the earth. Then he takes a small brightly painted wooden cross from his pocket and places it on the ground. Then he begins to pray quietly. ZELL enters with the wheelbarrow full of fertilizer. She stops when she sees CARL. After a moment, she sets down the wheelbarrow and crosses to him, puts a hand gently on his shoulder. He lets out a sharp cry of surprise, rising instantly and moving away from her.)

CARL. *Buenas tardes,* Zelda.

ZELL. I've been worried about you. I called you a hundred times. Well. You know that. …I'm glad you're here.

CARL. I had to see this place one last time.

> (*Beat.*)

ZELL. You going somewhere?

> (CARL *looks away and says nothing. ZELL waits a moment, then turns and crosses to the wheelbarrow and, using a coffee can, begins to scoop the fertilizer out and sprinkle it around the base of one of the trees.*)

The day after the funeral, Jimmy C'de Baca showed up here. He brought *mole* enchiladas his mother had made for me. He broke down crying when he saw Chuy's hat still lying there on the kitchen table. And he's been back every day since then to help me with the irrigation. …He and his dad worked here every single harvest. Big Jimmy and Little Jimmy, remember? Chuy used to call them "Los dos Jimmies."

CARL. …I remember.

ZELL. I sold Jimmy the far grove three weeks ago. I let him have it for the price of the well. I wanted that land to go to someone who'd worked it. Someone who knows it's special—

CARL. Zelda. You forgive me, don't you? Please. Please, tell me you do.

ZELL. Oh sweetie…

CARL. I can't stop seeing Chuy laying on the ground there. …I knew him my whole life. I took this whole place and smashed it. And that one second cost me everything I ever loved in this world. Chuy. Angie. Nezzie. …It was an *accident…*

ZELL. I *know* that, Carlos, *I* know. I was *part* of it. I live with that too. I'm up all night sometimes, trying to make sense of it.

CARL. I go up Greeley to see Angie every day but it's so hard to talk in that place. She's so tiny in there. The look on her face breaks my heart. I drive on home and I talk to her all night long in my head. I got no idea what's gonna happen to her. She don't even got a trial date yet.

ZELL. All you can do is keep going up there.

CARL. I can't. I can't do her no good, and it's killing me. …I'm leaving Fronteras, Zeldita. I won't be coming back.

(*Beat.*)

ZELL. Ya know, just about every day someone stops by here and leaves a little token. I come back from the grove, and I'll find a piece of cake on the porch. Or a bunch of onions, a little carved animal, a note with a blessing. People come and check on me at odd times of the day. Bug me to go to church. I can't quit this place. I'm a part of something here. Even after everything that's happened. And you are too.

CARL. No. Not me. There's nothing left for me here.

ZELL. You're wrong. You've still got people who *need* you. And I don't mean just Angie. Why haven't you gone to see Nezzie?

(CARL *doesn't answer.*)

You gotta to go see her.

CARL. She don't wanna see me. I'm poison, and she knows that.

ZELL. Nezzie needs her family now more than ever. She *loves* you. Go see her.

CARL. If I could change it I would. But there's *nothing* I can do.

ZELL. It's not like you to give up without even trying. Please, Carlos. I'll go with you, if you need me to.

CARL. I *can't.*

(*Silence.*)

ZELL. There was this chaplain up at the hospital in Cruces where Nezzie delivered. I guess he's kind of an amateur photographer. …And if a baby is… when a baby doesn't make it, he'll offer to take some photos of the mother and child together before…you know. …So Nezzie will always have a way to remember her little boy. …He was beautiful, Carlos, he truly was. So little. But perfect, you know. …That chaplain, that *stranger*, did a small, good thing that meant the whole world to her. You'll want to see those pictures.

(CARL *covers his face with his hands.*)

I know you think everything's been taken away from you, but, Carlos, if we don't all take care of each other, we won't have any chance at all.

(CARL *finally turns to her. For several moments the only sounds are bird calls. Then, slowly, we once again become aware of ghostly whispered Spanish rising from all sides. No individual words are discernible. It begins quietly enough but it continues to rise until it gradually takes over the space.* CARL *and* ZELDA *listen. The lights slowly fade.*)

End of Play

POST WAVE SPECTACULAR
by Diana Grisanti

BIOGRAPHY

Diana Grisanti is a Louisville native currently pursuing her M.F.A. in playwriting and fiction at the University of Texas at Austin's Michener Center for Writers. Her play *Semantics* was a finalist for the Lark Playwrights' Week and the New Harmony Project, as well as a semi-finalist for the Bay Area Playwrights Festival. Diana's adaptations of *1,001 Nights* and *Alice's Adventures in Wonderland* were commissioned and produced by Walden Theatre, a conservatory for young actors. She is a 2010 nominee for the Wasserstein Prize and received her B.A. from the University of Iowa. Before relocating to Austin, Diana lived in Cuernavaca, Mexico, where she worked as a teacher and translator.

ACKNOWLEDGMENTS

Post Wave Spectacular premiered at the Humana Festival of New American Plays in March 2010. It was directed by Amy Attaway with the following cast:

JORDAN ....Brett Ashley Robinson
ALLIE.. Alexis Bronkovic
VIVIAN...Suli Holum
JESSICA ....Liza Fernandez

and the following production staff:

Scenic Designer .... Brenda Ellis
Costume Designer....................................... Lindsay Chamberlin
Lighting Designer.. Nick Dent
Sound Designer .... Benjamin Marcum
Properties Designer... Doc Manning
Production Stage Manager ....Paul Mills Holmes
Dramaturg ....Adrien-Alice Hansel

Stage Management Intern .... Nick Bussett

CHARACTERS

ALLIE, 25, they were together briefly
JORDAN, 22, had a couple months of bliss
VIVIAN, 30, still can't get over him
JESSICA, 28, the outsider, currently wrapped around his little finger

SETTING

A tea parlor that's not exactly a tea parlor. Cave-like. Spooky.

NOTE

A slash "/" indicates where dialogue should overlap.

For Sherry K. For the confabs.

Suli Holum, Alexis Bronkovic,
Liza Fernandez and Brett Ashley Robinson
in *Post Wave Spectacular*

34th Annual Humana Festival of New American Plays
Actors Theatre of Louisville, 2010
Photo by Harlan Taylor

POST WAVE SPECTACULAR

JORDAN, ALLIE, *and* VIVIAN, *three spectacular women with fabulous accessories, drink tea. They're a little larger than life.*

JORDAN. In this post-post-post era of post-post-post feminism,
my girls and I call a meeting of the minds.
A chat. An afternoon tea.
A little confab about this thing we've been thinking about.
About this *guy* who's been weighing us down.

ALLIE. And like, we're cool. We get it.
We know we're not supposed to stereotypify all the men on the planet.
Because where does polarization get us?

JORDAN. Somewhere polar.

ALLIE. Sub-zero. Glacial. Cold.

JORDAN. Totally.

ALLIE. And we don't want that.

JORDAN. So we won't polarize. We won't typify.

ALLIE. We'll be very, very specific.

JORDAN. Cause this boy?

ALLIE. This one particular Y chromosome?

VIVIAN. Is totally under our skin.

ALLIE. And he thinks he can get away with it because he's all charming and unassuming and he has a really sweet grin and this mysterious limp—no really, nobody knows why he limps, it's a total mystery—but we're wise to his shit.
Cuz we've been there.
We've been witness.

VIVIAN. Many times.

JORDAN. A few dozen for me.

ALLIE. And eight and a half times for me.

JORDAN. And a half?

ALLIE. Blowjob. Without reciprocity.

VIVIAN. If I had a nickellll...

JORDAN. Viv was with him for a year.

VIVIAN. A long year.

ALLIE. And like, duh, we know we're tiptoeing on thin ice here.
We're bordering on some neo-essentialist self-victimization toxic trash but like—

JORDAN. Whatever.

VIVIAN. Dude's a dick.

ALLIE. You see? See how he drives us to betray our undergraduate foremothers? Gendering our words, codifying our vocabulary, dragging us down the slippery slope of linguistic stratification?
But like we said.

JORDAN. He's a douchebag.

> (*A knock.*)

ALLIE. She's here!

JORDAN. I'll get it!

VIVIAN. Is everything ready?

ALLIE. Yes.
Oh Wait.
Eyelash.

VIVIAN. Thanks.

ALLIE. Make a wish.

VIVIAN. (*Blows.*)

ALLIE. Wish for something good?

VIVIAN. Mmhmm.

JORDAN. Okay. Ready?

VIVIAN and ALLIE. Ready.

> (*In walks* JESSICA. *The door slams, startling her.*)

JESSICA. Ah!

VIVIAN. Sorry about that. It's an old house. Heavy doors. Hard to open, but very weather resistant.

JORDAN. Jessica! Come in! Come in! You look fabulous!

ALLIE. You did your eyebrows. Plucking? Waxing?

JESSICA. Threading.

JORDAN. Amazing.

ALLIE. They complement the hell out of your cheekbones.

JORDAN. Totally.

JESSICA. Thank you.

ALLIE. Did you have trouble finding us?

JESSICA. No, not at all.

ALLIE. So the directions were helpful?

JESSICA. They were great.

ALLIE. Excellent.

JORDAN. And thank you for RSVPing. You know, replying really has become a lost art.

ALLIE. So true.

JORDAN. Would you like some tea? We have loose leaf, fair trade, decaf, caf, green, black, brown, red, full-bodied, slender, docile, affable, churlish, and mint.

JESSICA. I'll have the mint, I guess.

JORDAN. That's my favorite too.

JESSICA. I'm sorry but. Do I know you?

JORDAN. I am so sorry. I'm a social disaster sometimes.

I'm Jordan. You were my TA for Postmodern Feminisms in Contemporary Architecture. I wrote the paper about Pansexual Desire in Midwestern Outlet Malls?

JESSICA. Oh, right. You're Jordan. That was a great paper.

JORDAN. Thank you.

ALLIE. And I'm Allie. We volunteer at the clinic together. Opposite shifts though. You never see me.

JESSICA. Allie? The Allie who introduced the flavored dental dams?

ALLIE. Guilty.

JESSICA. You're a legend. And the pineapple is to die for.

ALLIE. I know, right?

VIVIAN. And we've never met. I'm / Viv

JESSICA. Vivian.

VIVIAN. Viv.

JESSICA. Viv.

Hi. I just, I know you 'cause—

VIVIAN. I used to date—.

JESSICA. You used to date—.

VIVIAN. Right.

JESSICA. He talks about you is all.

VIVIAN. Don't tell me that.

JESSICA. I mean, he doesn't say anything bad, / it's just—

VIVIAN. No. I know. But if I know he's talking about me, then I'll speculate, then I'll get all preoccupied and nostalgic and maybe a little obsessive, so. No. I'll just pretend you didn't say anything at all.

JESSICA. Okay.

VIVIAN. Because I really don't want to know.

ALLIE. Neither do I. I mean, unless he said something I should really know about—

JORDAN. Or like, if he mentioned me in passing or something—

ALLIE. Or wondered what I was up to—

VIVIAN. Ladies. This isn't about us. It's about Jessica, right? It's about you.

JESSICA. Me?

ALLIE. Jessica, how long have you been dating him?

JESSICA. Oh, we're not dating.

JORDAN. Right. But how long have you seeing each other?

JESSICA. We're not seeing each other.

VIVIAN. Okay, sure, but how long have you been together?

JESSICA. We're not / together—

ALLIE. Jessica! Jessie.

VIVIAN. Honestly.

JESSICA. Really. We're not together anymore. We spend a lot of *time* together, if that's what you mean.

VIVIAN. I see. And what do you do when you're together?

JESSICA. I don't know. We watch movies or talk or have a beer or. And we have the same taste in books and we both like poetry and. Our politics are really similar, so there's that and.

VIVIAN. But when he's having a bad day—

ALLIE. When he's just too tired or upset or bedraggled to talk about books or movies or politics—

JORDAN. And all he needs is a woman in his arms—

VIVIAN. When that happens?

JESSICA. We. I mean, yes, sometimes, but it's not. We have an understanding.

VIVIAN. I thought so.

JESSICA. He struggles with intimacy.

VIVIAN.	**ALLIE.**	**JORDAN.**
Oh, the struggle!	Mmmm.	Intimacy!

ALLIE. So you're just friends.

JESSICA. Right.

ALLIE. Friends who sleep together.

JESSICA. Right.

ALLIE. And who take care of each other.

JESSICA. I don't need to be taken care of.

ALLIE. We know that. But he does. Right? He needs to be taken care of.

VIVIAN. …Right?

JORDAN. Your tea's ready. Do you take sugar? Cream?

JESSICA. Do you have soy milk?

JORDAN. We sure do.

(They sip their tea.)

ALLIE. You know what I miss? The neck kissing. He was really good at that.

EVERYBODY ELSE. Yeeahh.

ALLIE. The way he'd move in with the lust of a thousand soldiers coming home from war. The hunger in his eyes. The steadiness of his breath. That furtive limp smacking of countless romantic possibilities.

JORDAN. Maybe it was an accident. Some near-death episode resulting in shattered knee caps and broken dreams.

ALLIE. Maybe it was congenital. A family secret. An evolutionary glitch.

JORDAN. Maybe it was a knife fight. Knives are unbearably sexy.

VIVIAN. Or maybe it's something horribly prosaic. But I really hope not.

ALLIE. His enthusiasm was uncanny, wasn't it? You can't find that kind of enthusiasm in most men. The sheer passion for contact.

VIVIAN. It was like adolescence. It was like living out a sex scene from the Judy Blume novels you'd pass around your sixth grade classroom. Everything about it—the breath, the smell, the touch…everything was so…fictional.

EVERYBODY ELSE. Yeeaahhh.

VIVIAN. And of course you assume it's different with you. That somehow *you're* the cause of his staggering enthusiasm.

ALLIE. But no.

JORDAN. Turns out he's just an enthusiastic sort of guy.

ALLIE. With an intimacy problem.

JORDAN. And a penchant for blowjobs.

VIVIAN. And the sad truth of it is, we fell for it. He swaggered up to us, smiled, and we fell for it.

JESSICA. I should get going.

VIVIAN. You're meeting him. Aren't you.

JESSICA. We had plans.

VIVIAN. Dollar fifty Busch Light night?

JESSICA. How'd you know?

VIVIAN. It's so endearing, right? His love of cheap beer? The way he discusses it like a fine wine, affecting that agile combination of irony and reverence?

JORDAN. And his three dollar tips?

ALLIE. The waitresses would swoon over those tips.

VIVIAN. You know, Jessica, we thought about going straight to him. Directly to the source. But what good would that do? Female attention? A veritable buffet of scolding and coddling and armchair psychology. No. He'd love that. He loves to be scolded and coddled and psychologized.

And in the end, let's face it, he'd probably convince us all to sleep with him anyway.

JORDAN. He's very good at that.

ALLIE. Isn't he?

VIVIAN. So we came to you, Jessica. Or rather, we brought you to us.

JESSICA. So what do I do?

ALLIE. Break it off.

JESSICA. But he's just a friend. I can't break up with someone I'm not dating.

VIVIAN. Exactly. You see how he operates?

JORDAN. You'll have to start dating someone else.

JESSICA. But everyone thinks I'm dating him.

ALLIE. You could always move. Leave the city? The state? That's a proven method of detachment.

JORDAN. No, moving doesn't work. He sends emails. He writes dazzling emails.

JESSICA. He does. He really does.

JORDAN. You see?

JESSICA. But what if I don't want to leave him? What if we're meant to be?

ALLIE. Oh Jessica. *We* were meant to be.

JORDAN. We were meant to be.

VIVIAN. We were meant to be.

JESSICA. I can't just stand him up, you know.
I mean, we'd planned to meet before this, this—

ALLIE. Chat?

JORDAN. Confab?

ALLIE. Afternoon tea?

(JESSICA *tries to open the door. It's locked.*)

JESSICA. It's locked.

JORDAN. It sticks sometimes. Old house. Very old. Ancient.

VIVIAN. Actually, Jessica, I'd like you to think of our time here as a retreat. A detox period. A little respite from the outside world.

ALLIE. Have another cup of tea, won't you?

JORDAN. We have plenty.

(JORDAN *reveals a year's supply of tea.*)

A year's supply.

JESSICA. A year?

JORDAN. It'll be over before you know it.

ALLIE. And we'll have so much to talk about in the meantime!

JORDAN. We do have a lot in common after all.

JESSICA. A year, you said?

VIVIAN. Time flies when you're in the company of friends.

JESSICA. But what will we do? For a year?

JORDAN. We could have sex with each other. It'll be just like the 70s.

ALLIE. Too old-school. We should bake things and learn how to knit. Ironic domesticity is the new bra-burning.

VIVIAN. Wait!
Eyelash.
Make a wish.

JESSICA. (*Blows.*)

VIVIAN. Wish for something good?

JORDAN. I hope so.

ALLIE. So what do you think, Jess? About our little plan?

JESSICA. I think.
I think.
You don't happen to have Earl Grey, do you?

ALLIE. As a matter of fact, he's the only boy allowed.

(*The ladies drink their tea.*)

End of Play

AN EXAMINATION OF THE WHOLE PLAYWRIGHT/ACTOR RELATIONSHIP PRESENTED AS SOME KIND OF COP SHOW PARODY

by Greg Kotis

BIOGRAPHY

Greg Kotis is the author of many plays and musicals including *Yeast Nation* (Book/Lyrics), *The Truth About Santa*, *Pig Farm*, *Eat the Taste*, *Urinetown* (Book/ Lyrics, for which he won an Obie Award and two Tony® Awards), and *Jobey and Katherine*. His work has been produced and developed in theatres across the country and around the world, including Actors Theatre of Louisville, American Conservatory Theater, American Theater Company, Henry Miller's Theatre, The Lark Play Development Center, Manhattan Theatre Club, New York Stage and Film, Perseverance Theatre, Roundabout Theatre Company, Soho Rep, South Coast Repertory, and The Old Globe, among others. Greg is a member of the Neo-Futurists, the Cardiff Giant Theater Company, ASCAP, and the Dramatists Guild. He grew up in Wellfleet, Massachusetts, and now lives in Brooklyn with his wife Ayun Halliday, his daughter India, and his son Milo.

ACKNOWLEDGMENTS

An Examination of the Whole Playwright/Actor Relationship Presented As Some Kind of Cop Show Parody premiered at the Humana Festival of New American Plays in March 2010. It was directed by Sean Daniels with the following cast:

DETECTIVE CHASTEN .... Gamal Abdel Chasten
GREG .... Greg Kotis
DETECTIVE MAUPIN .... Gregory Maupin

and the following production staff:

Scenic Designer .... Brenda Ellis
Costume Designer...................................... Lindsay Chamberlin
Lighting Designer.. Nick Dent
Sound Designer .... Benjamin Marcum
Properties Designer.. Doc Manning
Fight Director .... Drew Fracher
Production Stage Manager............................Paul Mills Holmes
Dramaturg ....Sarah Lunnie

Stage Management Intern .... Nick Bussett

CHARACTERS

DETECTIVE CHASTEN
GREG
DETECTIVE MAUPIN

SETTING

An interrogation room.

Gamal Abdel Chasten, Greg Kotis (on floor)
and Gregory Maupin
in *An Examination of the Whole Playwright/Actor Relationship
Presented As Some Kind of Cop Show Parody*

34th Annual Humana Festival of New American Plays
Actors Theatre of Louisville, 2010
Photo by Harlan Taylor

AN EXAMINATION OF THE WHOLE PLAYWRIGHT/ACTOR RELATIONSHIP PRESENTED AS SOME KIND OF COP SHOW PARODY

An interrogation scene. Detectives CHASTEN *and* MAUPIN *are grilling* GREG. *It's late, the questioning has gone on too long. Detective* CHASTEN *looks over the script to this play.*

CHASTEN. Is this supposed to be funny?

(*Pause, no response.*)

What do you think, Greg, is this supposed to be a funny play?

GREG. Who says it's a play at all?

MAUPIN. Just answer the God damned question.

GREG. You answer it.

CHASTEN. He's not the playwright, Greg. You're the playwright, so you tell us. Is this supposed to be a funny play, an examination of the whole actor/playwright relationship presented as some kind of cop show parody? Or is there something else going on here?

MAUPIN. Or maybe it's just a funny play that turns out to be not that funny.

(*Pause.*)

GREG. I don't have to tell you a God damned thing.

(MAUPIN *moves in close, becoming threatening.*)

MAUPIN. You think we're fooling around here?! Huh?!! You think we're just going to stand around here, doing a whole good cop/bad cop routine for about seven minutes without having even a basic understanding of the intentions of the piece?! I'll tell you one thing, pal, I've been in plenty of plays in my time. Good plays. Short plays. And one way or the other I always find out if they're funny or not!

(CHASTEN *pulls* MAUPIN *off* GREG.)

CHASTEN. Okay, Maupin, take it easy.

MAUPIN. Yeah, I'll take it easy.

CHASTEN. How about you just pretend to smoke a cigarette over there or something.

MAUPIN. Yeah, I'll pretend to smoke a cigarette over there. Or something.

(MAUPIN *finds a spot to pretend to smoke a cigarette.* CHASTEN *takes out a cigarette, offers one to* GREG *who refuses. He takes one for himself, pretends to light it, then takes a few imaginary puffs.*)

CHASTEN. You'll have to forgive my friend over there. He has trouble acting in plays he doesn't understand.

GREG. Looks like he has trouble acting in plays period.

CHASTEN. Listen, Greg, I don't like sitting here asking you questions that never get answered any more than you do. But a whole bunch of people have come together for one night to see some theater, to do some theater. So the least you can do is to let them know what kind of play they're watching.

GREG. Let them know or let you know?

CHASTEN. Let us both know, Greg. Let everybody know. Maybe even let yourself know.

MAUPIN. Aw, what are we wasting our time for? He doesn't understand his own work any better then we do

(MAUPIN *grabs the script from* CHASTEN *and rifles through it.*)

I mean look at these lines, "I was just trying to mix it up a little. You know, good cop bad cop, that's the routine, right?" I mean, how are you supposed to play lines like these?

GREG. It comes later in the play.

MAUPIN. Oh, I know it comes later in the play, Greg. I'm holding the script; I know what's in it. I just don't understand why what's in it is in it.

GREG. Seems like there's a lot of things you don't understand.

(*Pause.* MAUPIN *grabs* GREG *by the collar.*)

MAUPIN. How about this, Greg, how about me grabbing you by the shirt, is this beyond my understanding? A little raising of the stakes, maybe? A little dramatic tension. Or how about *this.*

(*On "This"* MAUPIN *stage-knees* GREG, *who slumps to the floor.*)

A little physical comedy, perhaps? A little stage brutality for entertainment's sake?

(MAUPIN *lifts* GREG *up again.*)

Oh, but I don't want to say physical "comedy" now do I? I don't want to call it a comedy, because we're not supposed to know if it's funny or not!

(MAUPIN *swings* GREG *around and throws him into a wall.*)

CHASTEN. Okay, that's enough!

(CHASTEN *moves to pull* MAUPIN *off* GREG.)

MAUPIN. I mean, is *this* funny, Greg?!

(*On each "This"* MAUPIN *stage-kicks* GREG.)

How about this?! Or this?! Huh?!! You tell me, Greg, because at this point I really can't tell!

CHASTEN. I said that's enough!

(CHASTEN *pulls* MAUPIN *off* GREG *and shoves him away.*)

What's the matter with you?

MAUPIN. What? I was just trying to mix it up a little. You know, good cop bad cop, that's the routine, right?

CHASTEN. Yeah, that's the routine.

> (CHASTEN *moves to help* GREG.)

You okay?

GREG. Yeah, I think so.

MAUPIN. Aw, come on, they were just stage kicks.

CHASTEN. Just stage kicks?! He had to double over and fall on the floor, Maupin! He had to pretend he was in pain, so don't give me "just stage kicks."

MAUPIN. What is this, you get to be angry now?! You get to be the bad cop?!

CHASTEN. Maybe. And maybe I just need to be distracted long enough for Greg to make a grab for my—

> (*As the two argue,* GREG *grabs* CHASTEN*'s prop gun.*)

GREG. Okay, now, both of you, BACK OFF!

> (CHASTEN *and* MAUPIN *raise their hands and back off.*)

CHASTEN. Easy, now.

GREG. I said BACK OFF!

CHASTEN. Easy, Greg, we're backing off.

MAUPIN. Just don't do anything stupid, okay?

GREG. You're the one who's stupid! Not me! You!

CHASTEN. Unsympathetic, Greg. You wrote him as unsympathetic, not stupid.

GREG. Yeah, looks like I wrote a whole bunch of stuff, now didn't I.

CHASTEN. Good stuff, Greg. A whole lot of really good stuff. So don't end it like this, not with a lot of gun play in the last few minutes of the piece.

MAUPIN. There's a better ending than this, Greg. I know there is.

GREG. Oh, you do, do you?!

CHASTEN. Think about it, Greg? This play is supposed to be about the whole actor/playwright relationship. Don't ruin all that.

GREG. You wanna know about the whole actor/playwright relationship?! Huh?! Do ya?! 'Cause I wrote a whole *monologue* about it!

> (*On "monologue,"* GREG *pulls a sheaf of papers from his back pocket. It's quite substantial.* CHASTEN *and* MAUPIN *back off some more, equally threatened by the gun and the new pages.*)

MAUPIN. Whoa!

CHASTEN. Easy, now!

GREG. (*Crazed.*) That's right, a whole freakin' monologue about hoping, praying that the words you got in your head somehow made it to the page, and that those words somehow made it into the minds of the actors, and those actors somehow made the words coming out of their mouths sound like the words you got in your head! What can you say to them, you know?! How you gonna make those actors say those words just so. And move around the stage just so. Whaddaya call that?

MAUPIN. Blocking.

CHASTEN. We call it blocking, Greg. Or staging.

GREG. Yeah. I wrote a whole monologue about it. About twenty-six pages. It's got a lot of theory. Meisner. Brustein. You wanna learn this monologue?

MAUPIN. No.

GREG. You wanna memorize this monologue, make it work as a performance piece?!

CHASTEN. That's a whole other play, Greg! Come on!

GREG. Yeah. So we're not going to end this play with any monologue. It's about a forty-five minute monologue. No, what's going to happen now is I'm going to pretend to make a break for it, see? I'm going to pretend to make a break for it, then we're all going to start moving in slow motion!

MAUPIN. You gotta be outta your freakin' mind!

GREG. In slow motion, I said! So once I start moving slow, you start moving slow, too?!

CHASTEN. For Christ's sake, Greg, no!

GREG. Then we'll see what kind of ending I wrote! Then we'll see a whole bunch—!

> (*Slow motion mayhem!* GREG *makes a run for it!* MAUPIN *pulls his gun! Shots are exchanged!* MAUPIN *plugs* GREG *full of holes!* GREG *dies!* MAUPIN *and* CHASTEN *resume regular motion.*)

CHASTEN. God damned stupid playwright.

MAUPIN. Stupid play. Thought he could end it all with a bunch of slow-motion blocking.

CHASTEN. Looks like he got what he wanted.

MAUPIN. What now?

CHASTEN. Now? Now we'll just stand here and look a little haunted while the lights fade to black. Is that funny? Does that have anything to say about the whole actor/playwright relationship—about how we're all ultimately mysteries to each other, each locked up in the solitary confinement cells of our own psyches, and how even the elaborate ritual of writing and doing plays most often doesn't add up to a whole lot more than tapping on the cell block wall, trying to send a message that might never be heard let alone understood? I don't know. But what I do know is the script says we need to look haunted now, and maybe even a little fed up. So that's what we'll do, Maupin. That's exactly what we'll do.

MAUPIN. God damned stupid playwright.

CHASTEN. God damned stupid, stupid, stupid play.

End of Play

SIRENS
by Deborah Zoe Laufer

ABOUT *SIRENS*

This article first ran in the January/February 2010 issue of Inside Actors, *and is based on conversations with the playwright before rehearsals for the* Humana Festival *production began.*

"What if you wrote one song and you lived off it your whole life, and you lived well, but you couldn't write another one?" Deborah Zoe Laufer wondered. In Laufer's comedy *Sirens*, Sam's wife Rose was the inspiration for the passionate love song, "Rose Adelle"—maybe you've heard it? (You know, the one that was recorded by Willie Nelson, the Pogues *and* Billy Joel.) He wrote it back when they were dating to impress her. Twenty-five years later, Sam has another hit in his head, but he's struggling to write it down. He's in trouble.

Instead of turning to Rose for inspiration, Sam tries to grab onto a wisp of a memory of a fervent romance he had long ago. And then he turns to Facebook, wiling away the days playing Lexulous with younger women while searching for the pretty girl he knew a thousand years ago in high school, the one who made him feel the kind of giddy emotions that must be expressed in song. This, as you might imagine, is not good news for Rose. The song "Rose Adelle" is always on the radio, in the elevator, ringing as a cell phone tone, on her mind. It's a time capsule, a hermetically sealed and captured moment, a perfect recollection of the time in which Sam was most in love with her. The song is a source of comfort that what she and Sam once had was real, but it is also disheartening proof that what they have now is, well, maybe not enough.

When you spend a lifetime with someone, you amass a shared store of memories, and those memories can get confused. As Laufer says about her own husband, "There are stories that I think I was there for when in fact I wasn't. At a certain point, his history is my history, because I've spent more years with him than without him." With *Sirens*, Laufer looks into a marriage that has lasted over a long period of time. She imagines an amazingly vibrant and funny world in which a serious question can be asked: When the past is longer than the future and when ardor turns to comfort, how can you find a way to be happy with what you have? Eternity sounds really great in principle, but it might be just interminable.

Now that Rose and Sam's son has left for college, they are lurching toward their empty-nested future. A mother herself, Laufer empathizes with their predicament. "In some ways you're desperate for your kids to grow up and be independent and all that," she explains, "And in some ways you can't even remember what it was like before they were here. I just haven't seen a lot of plays that really deal with 'What Now?' after the kids move out. Not just the pain of the kid moving out, but the 'Then What?'" Both Sam and Rose want to recapture a sense of the romance they had back when they were younger, but they seem to be going about it separately. It's entirely possible Sam and Rose might crash onto the rocks if they can't find a way to come back together.

And "Rose Adelle" is always playing somewhere, reminding all who hear it of those love-struck, early times in a romance when everything is new. Those feelings of infatuation and obsession are, as yet, uncluttered by the detritus of real life, and are therefore the perfect feelings to capture in a pop song. After those feelings have mellowed, to write a new song involves remembering, living in the past for awhile. The lure of the past, the memories of youth, are so tempting. Seriously, those memories never get a little pudgy in the middle or lose their hair. Those lost loves can be mythologized so much more easily than a spouse. Music is second only to smells for triggering memory; many scientists even put it first. We all have those songs in the backs of our heads. The ones that remind us of our giddy young loves—requited or not. With some songs every lyric and chord change and whispered aside unintentionally caught by a microphone is burned into memory. And then there are those songs where the words and the melodies may be mystically lost to the ages, but we grasp for them. That's the siren call of nostalgia.

Too often, we lose sight of the people who matter most, those who stand right next to us, simply because it seems they've always been there. We forget to watch them change, and therefore can't change with them as we all grow older. In *Sirens*, Laufer dares us to remember our past while finding a way to embrace the future—and to live in the present.

—Julie Felise Dubiner

BIOGRAPHY

Deborah Zoe Laufer is a 2009 recipient of the Helen Merrill Playwriting Award, a 2010 recipient of a Lilly Award, and a two-time recipient of the LeCompte du Nouy grant from The Lincoln Center Foundation. *Sirens* premiered at Actors Theatre of Louisville in February 2010. Previously for Actors Theatre, she co-wrote *BRINK!* for production with the Acting Apprentice Company in 2009. Deborah's *End Days* was awarded the American Theatre Critics Association Steinberg Citation, and received its Off-Broadway premiere at Ensemble Studio Theatre in March 2009 through an Alfred P. Sloan Foundation Grant. It debuted at Florida Stage and has received over fifteen productions. *End Days* is listed in *The Burns Mantle Yearbook* as one of the best regional plays of 2008, and is published by Smith and Kraus in *The Best Plays of 2008*. *Out of Sterno* premiered at Portland Stage in March 2009 with grants from the Edgerton Foundation and the National Endowment for the Arts. *Fortune* premiered at Marin Theatre Company in January 2005. Her newest play, *Games*, was workshopped at The Missoula Colony in July 2010. *The Last Schwartz* was published by Smith and Kraus in *Women Playwrights: The Best Plays of 2003*. It premiered at Florida Stage and enjoyed a six-month run at the Zephyr Theatre in Los Angeles. Deborah is a graduate of The Juilliard School and a member of The Dramatists Guild. In addition to *Sirens*, the acting editions of *End Days, The Last Schwartz,* and *Out of Sterno* are published by Samuel French. More information about her work can be found at www. deborahzoelaufer.com.

ACKNOWLEDGMENTS

Sirens premiered at the Humana Festival of New American Plays in February 2010. It was directed by Casey Stangl with the following cast:

SAM ABRAMS...Brian Russell
ROSE ADELLE ABRAMS ....Mimi Lieber
LEAH / SIREN / WAITRESS.....................Lindsey Wochley
RICHARD MILLER...................................... Ben Hollandsworth

and the following production staff:

Scenic Designer ....Michael B. Raiford
Costume Designer...Sonya Berlovitz
Lighting Designer..Jeff Nellis
Sound Designer/Composer................................... Matt Callahan
Properties Designer.. Mark Walston
Wig/Makeup Designer ....Heather Fleming
Stage Manager..Stephen Horton
Dramaturg ....Julie Felise Dubiner
Casting................................Emily Ruddock, Zan Sawyer-Dailey

Directing Assistant...Gretchen Wright
Scenic Design Assistant.....................................Ryan Wineinger
Costume Design Assistant.................................... Jordan Bivens
Lighting Design Assistant ....Paola Rodriguez
Production Assistant ....Melissa Blair
Assistant Dramaturg .... Zach Chotzen-Freund

Developed at Geva Theatre Center, Rochester, New York; and Florida Stage's 1st Stage New Works Festival, Manalapan, Florida.

CHARACTERS

SAM ABRAMS, 40s-50s

ROSE ADELLE ABRAMS, 40s-50s, Sam's wife

SIREN, sublimely lovely. Early 20s

       Also plays: LEAH, WAITRESS

RICHARD MILLER, 40s-50s, Played by an actor in his early 20s

Mimi Lieber and Brian Russell
in *Sirens*

34th Annual Humana Festival of New American Plays
Actors Theatre of Louisville, 2010
Photo by Harlan Taylor

SIRENS

At the top of the play, as the audience is settling, we should hear three different versions of SAM's song, "Rose Adelle." And then, with each scene break we should hear another version. Perhaps Billy Joel. Mel Tormé. A Japanese version. A cell phone ring tone. Musak. Captain and Tennille. The song is ubiquitous. SAM can't escape it.

"Rose Adelle"

Rose Adelle, Rose Adelle
looked my way and how I fell
But just one kiss from your sweet lips and how I rose rose rose
Rose Adelle

Come down come down come down to me baby
Come down come down come down to me baby

Come down from your sweet pink bedroom
Drive down to the lake with me
Down where your parents can't see us baby
We'll uncover some mystery
I'm burning up when I think of you baby
It's driving me insane.
Come to the lake to cool my fire
Or set us both aflame.

Rose Adelle, Rose Adelle
looked my way and how I fell
But just one kiss from your sweet lips and how I rose rose rose
Rose Adelle

Scene 1

SAM *and* ROSE ADELLE *are at a travel agency. The backdrop is saturated with bright island scenes, while they seem small and gray.* ROSE *is constantly knitting. It is a long train, narrower than a scarf, so long that it winds around and around her.*

Note: SAM *and* ROSE *speak over each other in the way long-married couples might. The slashes (/) reflect when the next character begins speaking.*

SAM. What if Barry decides to come home?

ROSE. I told you, he's going to Courtney's house. Her parents.

SAM. But what if he changes his mind? And then we're away.

ROSE. You're hilarious. We should just wait home by the phone for the next thirty years? I told you she makes the decisions/ now.

SAM. It's nice that he's got a girl Hon. When we were in college, remember how great it was/ when we…

ROSE. All those years of late nights and fevers and term papers and bullies and all the things we worried ourselves sick over. Now "Courtney" decides where he goes.

> (*During this,* LEAH *walks past, perhaps pausing to look through some papers. She is tall and willowy and lovely. There is a faint wisp of music heard. Maybe a harp.* SAM *is transfixed by the sight of her. He is quietly humming to himself, trying to remember… Everything else disappears.*)

I said, "Didn't you go to Courtney's parents' for winter break? Don't you think it would be nice to come see your parents this time, let us get to know her?" "Maybe next break," he says.

LEAH. (*On her way out.*) I'll be with you folks in just a moment!

> (SAM *watches her leave, still humming, hungrily, longingly.*)

ROSE. Sam.

> (*Pause.*)

Sam!

SAM. Right! So…

ROSE. Am I here?

SAM. Huh?

ROSE. Do you see me here? Do you hear me when I talk?

SAM. …So maybe he'll come next break!

ROSE. Sure.

SAM. She sounds nice. On the phone.

ROSE. How is she going to sound? She's going to say, "Hello Barry's father— piss off"?

SAM. (*Looking around self-consciously.*) Rose…shhhh.

ROSE. He'll see. He likes the soft part of the bread, so I ate the crusts. You think she'll eat the crusts?

SAM. They can throw away the crusts.

ROSE. You think she'll get him a cup of water in the middle of the night? Rub his cheek when he has a bad dream?

SAM. That was when he was four,/ Hon.

ROSE. He'll wake up from his bad dream and we'll be on vacation.

SAM. Yeah. Then, maybe we shouldn't/ go.

ROSE. It's fine. It'll be fine.

SAM. Why don't we just drive to the Jersey Shore again? Remember?

ROSE. That's hilarious.

SAM. When we did that?

ROSE. I did not put up with you for twenty-five years to go to the Jersey/ Shore.

SAM. Maybe Maine? Or D.C. We could drive to D.C.

ROSE. I'm taking three weeks vacation. Peggy's covering/ for me.

SAM. Three weeks? Oh my God.

ROSE. We're going…far. We're doing something special.

> (LEAH *reenters. Maybe a harp is heard again.*)

LEAH. Hi. I'm Leah Peters.

ROSE. Hello.

SAM. Leah Peters.

LEAH. What can I help you with today?

SAM. What a beautiful name.

LEAH. You looking for a vacation package?

SAM. You look like you should be in high school.

ROSE. (*Sighs, annoyed.*) Sam.

LEAH. I assure you, Sir. I'm a qualified travel agent.

ROSE. He didn't mean that, Sweetheart.

LEAH. I've been working professionally for several months.

ROSE. He's flirting with you. Just ignore him. We're looking for something special. For our twenty-fifth wedding anniversary.

LEAH. Twenty-five years! Wow.

ROSE. You're telling me.

LEAH. That's quite an accomplishment.

ROSE. You have no idea.

> (*Both women laugh at this.*)

LEAH. I have a fantastic cruise package to the Mediterranean that might interest you. It's really special.

ROSE. We want something special.

LEAH. (*Reading off her clipboard.*) Let's see…explore the Greek Isles. Chart the journey of Odysseus.

SAM. A cruise?

LEAH. I just got this in. You're the first clients I'm offering this to.

SAM. Aren't there stories…about/ cruises…

ROSE. Nothing. There's nothing. It's fine.

SAM. There was an article. About these cruise ships. Disappearing.

(*There is a pause and then both women burst out laughing.*)

ROSE. Disappearing?! Like…*Brigadoon?*

LEAH. You're so cute! He's so cute.

ROSE. He's hilarious.

SAM. There were stories. Recently. Online.

ROSE. No, that sounds perfect. The Greek Isles.

LEAH. Okay. So! Let me get some of your information, and then I'll find those brochures. And we'll just agree that you're mine, I mean, my clients, so if you come back in you just ask for Leah Peters, okay?

SAM. Absolutely.

LEAH. Here's my card.

(SAM *reaches for it.* ROSE *grabs it first.*)

Okay! So…your names are…

SAM. Sam and Rose Abrams.

ROSE. Rose Adelle.

LEAH. Oh! Like the song.

ROSE. Exactly like the song.

SAM. Honey…

(*He sighs, embarrassed already.*)

LEAH. My parents loved that old song. Were you named after it?

ROSE. Actually, it was named after me.

LEAH. What?

ROSE. He—Sam wrote the song. About me.

LEAH. O.M.G.!

ROSE. So I would marry him.

LEAH. Get out of here, you wrote that song? My parents love that song! How awesome! You wrote that song?

ROSE. About me. All those things in that song, about how beautiful the girl was, with the sweet lips…

LEAH. That was some hot love song.

ROSE. That was me.

LEAH. (*Calling to a coworker:*) Joey, you won't believe who this is.

SAM. No. No, no, no, no. Please. That's all right. That's okay, Joey.

LEAH. And you're so modest.

SAM. (*Modestly.*) Oh. Well…

ROSE. He's embarrassed. He hasn't written anything since.

SAM. I have so. Written other songs.

ROSE. Hits. Hit songs.

LEAH. Well, I guess if you wrote a song like that, that's enough. Right?

SAM. Thank you, Leah. You're very sweet.

ROSE. Still, twenty-five years. You know. Not to have another song…

SAM. I wrote "Brunch at Katz's."

ROSE. I mean, for me, it's enough.

SAM. "Lady Liberty."

ROSE. We lived very well off that song for twenty-five years. Very well.

SAM. "Sunset on the Hudson."

ROSE. But Sam, he's embarrassed.

SAM. I'm not embarrassed, unless you embarrass me.

LEAH. My parents will totally freak when I tell them I met you.

ROSE. Did you know Mel Tormé sang that song? Earth, Wind and Fire?

LEAH. Ludacris!

ROSE. No really. But lately…he sits at the computer and tries to remember some other song he wrote a million years ago.

LEAH. You know what? I'm/ gonna just…

SAM. Rose. This young lady, Leah doesn't need/ to hear…

ROSE. I say, "Forget it! Forget that old song!" But no. He sits there, night and day…

LEAH. Cool!

ROSE. Or that's what he says he's doing, but who really knows, right?

LEAH. So, let me get you those brochures.

ROSE. Do you have a boyfriend, Leah?

LEAH. Um, yeah?

ROSE. What do you think he's doing right now?

LEAH. He works for Virgin Airlines. We actually met when I was…

ROSE. That's what he told you, right? That he was going to work today?

SAM. Rose, what are you doing?

(*There is an uncomfortable beat.*)

LEAH. You know what? I'm going to let you fill this out while I go find those brochures.

SAM. Thanks, Leah.

LEAH. I think you're going to love this package.

SAM. That sounds great.

LEAH. Great!

(*She hurries off. SAM watches her leave.*)

ROSE. Pretty girl.

SAM. (*Annoyed.*) What the hell, Rose?

ROSE. Don't you think she's pretty?

SAM. What's with you today?

ROSE. She has nice teeth.

SAM. I've written other songs.

ROSE. 'Course she has one of those long thin necks. Makes her look a little pin-headish.

SAM. "Throw Your Arms Around the Moon."

ROSE. You know who she reminds me of?

SAM. No.

ROSE. Guess. Guess who she reminds me of.

SAM. No!

ROSE. Allyson Mendelson.

(*Long, stunned pause.*)

She reminds me a bit of Allyson Mendelson.

(*Pause.*)

SAM. How do you know Allyson Mendelson?

ROSE. How do *you* know Allyson Mendelson?

(*Pause.*)

SAM. You've been looking at my computer?

ROSE. Facebook. What are you, twelve?

SAM. Rose. That's private./ I mean…

ROSE. Really? It doesn't seem private. You have one hundred thirty-two friends…

SAM. Oh God.

ROSE. Who seem to know everything about you. Your minute-by-minute change of status all through each day while I think you're working on your song. Sam Abrams is eating a pastrami sandwich is somehow worthy of note.

SAM. I don't look through any/ of your…

ROSE. You know everything about me, Sam. I have nothing to hide.

(*Silence.*)

Nice picture.

SAM. (*Deeply embarrassed.*) Oh God.

ROSE. Isn't that one of our wedding photos?

SAM. Yeah.

ROSE. With me cut out.

SAM. Well, it's you know, *my* profile picture, so…

ROSE. From twenty-five years ago.

SAM. (*Sigh.*) I can't believe you were spying on me. Looking through my…things.

ROSE. Lot of friends you have.

SAM. Well…

ROSE. All women.

SAM. Derek is my friend.

ROSE. All women and your brother. Who are those women Sam?

SAM. Mostly they're just people I play Scrabulous with. Well, it's called Lexulous now. It's Scrabble really. But there was this copyright lawsuit and…

ROSE. All these young women you met playing Scrabble?

SAM. Yeah, we just play Scrabble. Mostly. I mean, we don't even chat really. Most of them. I just friended them.

ROSE. Friended them.

SAM. Silly stuff. You know. I might poke them or throw a snowball or a groundhog or something…

ROSE. Poke them.

SAM. But we don't even talk. Really. Just on Scrabble. Chat. It's just a game. Really. It's…

ROSE. You play Scrabble with Allyson Mendelson?

SAM. No! No.

ROSE. Because you can't find her.

SAM. I don't… I don't even know… If she plays Scrabble.

ROSE. Who is she?

SAM. She's just this/ girl…

ROSE. Why are you trying to find her?

SAM. I went to high school with. It was…

ROSE. Hundreds of messages.

SAM. Nothing…really.

ROSE. "Arc you the Allyson Mendelson from Jefferson High?"

SAM. Yeah. Aw jeez.

ROSE. You never mentioned her.

SAM. It was…you know. We were teenagers.

ROSE. Did you love her?

SAM. We were kids! She broke my heart. She hurt me. I wrote her this song…

ROSE. Oh my God.

SAM. I'm trying to remember this song I'd written…

ROSE. It was her song?

SAM. Yeah. I thought maybe if I wrote to her…

ROSE. It's her song you've been trying to remember?

SAM. Rose. It was high school. This is thirty years ago/ we're talking. It was nothing.

ROSE. One hundred and eight messages. Asking about her. Looking for her. Is not nothing. Sam.

SAM. Yeah.

> (*Pause. Admitting:*)

Yeah.

ROSE. Are you going to meet up with her?

SAM. I can't find her.

ROSE. But if you found her. What would you do?

SAM. I don't know.

ROSE. You don't know?

SAM. Rose. Come on. Look, let's go home. Let's talk about this at home.

> (*He takes her arm.*)

ROSE. Don't touch me.

SAM. Rose. It's just… It's research.

ROSE. That's hilarious. I'm off at the shop, I think you're working on your damn song…

SAM. I am working on the song. This is part of it.

ROSE. Boy, am I an idiot. You're playing games.

SAM. No.

ROSE. Writing to girls.

SAM. No. No, I'm just… I'm trying…

ROSE. What?

SAM. I'm stuck. Rose. I'm stuck.

Everything I write now… It's bullshit. I can't write anything…true anymore. I can't feel anything true.

> (*He sighs deeply.*)

I'm trying to remember…what I was like…what it felt like…

ROSE. To be hurt?

SAM. To be…

ROSE. I'll hurt you with that lamp.

SAM. Come on, Honey.

ROSE. Why can't you remember what it's like with me?

SAM. We're been together for so long.

ROSE. Twenty-five years.

SAM. It's not the same now. Of course it isn't.

ROSE. It's the same for me.

SAM. As when we first met? Come on.

ROSE. I still love you as much as when we first met. More. I love you more.

SAM. I love you. Honey. It's just…that huge feeling… I'm trying to remember that huge painful, frantic…

ROSE. Lust. What you feel for Allyson Mendelson. For all these young women. They're everywhere. I'm hate them. All these/ stupid young…

SAM. It's not about the women! Rose. I'm trying to wake up.

ROSE. Oh. So playing scrabble,/ on Facebook…

SAM. It's all…deadened. Don't you feel that? Like we're under water. I go to sleep deadened every night. And I wake up with my heart pounding, that it's all behind us. That it's all over. Every great, thrilling thing that was going to happen to me, to us, every surprise, has happened already.

ROSE. That's nuts. You *make* thrilling things happen.

SAM. I have to do this Rose. Somehow. I have to make something. Feel something. Big. Before it's all gone. I have to find this song. Write this song.

ROSE. Why don't you just get a red convertible? Why don't you ride around in a leather jacket with the top down? Pretend you're young again.

SAM. Don't make fun of me.

(*Long pause.*)

ROSE. I could have married Richard Miller you know.

SAM. (*Sigh.*) I know.

ROSE. He was nuts about me. Lusted after me. Big time. I didn't have to marry you, you know.

SAM. I know.

ROSE. There were plenty of guys.

SAM. Richard Miller.

ROSE. And others. He was a looker. He had a nice head of hair. Richard Miller.

SAM. I had a nice head of hair twenty-five years ago too.

ROSE. I remember once he took me to the park. We rented one of those boats in the park. I was wearing this/ little pink skirt.

SAM. (*Said in unison with her.*) Little pink skirt.

ROSE. So romantic. He was crazy about me.

SAM. I was crazy about you…am.

ROSE. When we broke up he moved to Italy. Can you imagine? How heartbroken he must have been? To have to move that far away?

SAM. I thought he had a job there…

ROSE. To have to move so far away to try to forget the pain? Everything he saw must have hurt him—reminded him of the times we'd spent together. And now he had to go on without me.

SAM. You told me that he got a/ job in…

ROSE. I could have been living in Italy if I'd stayed with him. I could be sitting in a travel agency in Rome right now. Who knows where I could have gone. What I would have done with my life if I'd stayed with him. (*With growing fury.*) But you wrote that damn song! You tricked me into marrying you!

SAM. I tricked you? Rose…

ROSE. If I'd known what would happen. If I'd known you'd be writing to other girls. Allyson Mendelson…

SAM. Rosie.

ROSE. I would have told you where to put that song.

> (*During this* LEAH *starts toward them, hears the discussion and slinks back away.*)

SAM. (*Looking around. Everyone is watching them.*) Let's go home.

> (*Pause.*)

ROSE. Maybe I'll go on Facebook. How about that? Maybe I'll do a My Space. How would you like that? If you looked at my computer and I was poking Richard Miller?

SAM. I would think you were trying to remember what it was like to be eighteen again. And that that was your…touchstone to remember it.

ROSE. My ass. You'd be worried sick.

SAM. Okay.

ROSE. Jealous sick.

SAM. Okay.

> (*Pause.*)

ROSE. Or you wouldn't. That's how bad it is. You wouldn't.

> (*They sit in silence for a moment.*)

I want you to give it up.

SAM. What?

ROSE. All of it. Facebook. Scrabble. Allyson Mendelson.

SAM. Well… I'm in the middle of games. I can't just…

ROSE. You are out of your mind!!! When we get home I want you to delete it from your computer.

SAM. I will. Once I… I'm trying to write the song. It's helping Rose. It's helping me remember.

ROSE. No. Forget the damn song. Forget it. Delete them.

SAM. I…will. You just have to give me…a little time. To…

ROSE. To what?
Time to what, Sam?

SAM. To say goodbye. OK? Just let me…tell them goodbye.

(*Pause. LEAH returns cautiously and sits across from them again.*)

LEAH. So… I found those brochures.

SAM. (*Can't even look at her.*) Yeah. You know, maybe this isn't a good time.

ROSE. The hell it isn't. Give me those brochures. We're going on that fucking cruise.

Scene 2

The ship. ROSE and SAM are standing at the ship railing, looking out on the Mediterranean. Everything is a brilliant blue. But somehow they still seem small and gray. SAM is trying very hard.

ROSE. Isn't it gorgeous? It's so blue.

SAM. It is…incredibly blue.

ROSE. It's blue like in the brochures.

SAM. You're right Rosie. It really is. It's very, very…blue.

ROSE. Aren't you glad we came?

SAM. Of course. This was a great idea. I'm really glad we did this. Really glad.

(*He puts his arm around her and gives her a kiss on the cheek. She is delighted.*)

ROSE. This is so great! Here! Together!

SAM. (*Happy for her happiness.*) It is honey. It's great.

ROSE. Maybe I'll sell the shop!

SAM. What??

ROSE. Maybe I'll sell it. And then we'll be completely free. To…you know…

SAM. But…

ROSE. Travel, or…

SAM. But you…

ROSE. We could travel and…do whatever. Whatever we want.

SAM. …you love the shop.

ROSE. Well, it was good because I could be home with Barry. When he was little.

SAM. But… But…

ROSE. Make my own hours.

SAM. But you…you love…

ROSE. I love to travel!

SAM. The shop…   .

ROSE. Nobody really knits anymore. It's a generation of/ non-knitters.

SAM. That's not true. You were telling me the other day…about/ that group of…

ROSE. I'm going to do it.

SAM. Girls. Young girls who came in.

ROSE. I'm going to do it Sam.

SAM. To learn…to…

ROSE. I'm going to sell the shop.

SAM. …to…knit.

ROSE. I am. And then we can be free.

>   (*Beat.*)

SAM. Okay, Honey. Whatever you want.

>   (*We hear a thread of music.* SAM *is distracted away by a bikini-clad woman passing by them. He begins humming to himself, a little desperately.*
>   ROSE *takes this in. Determined:*)

ROSE. We've got the late seating tonight.

SAM. Oh?

ROSE. I thought, for our celebration, tonight it would be nice to have the late seating.

SAM. Good thinking.

ROSE. And there will probably be a cake, though I'm not saying for sure.

SAM. That's nice.

ROSE. I switched with the Morganthals. That was nice of them, don't you think? To switch with us?

SAM. Very nice.

>   (*Pause.*)

ROSE. You wish you were home.

SAM. No!

ROSE. You wish you were back at your computer. Talking with other people. People you don't even know. You're trapped here with me. And three thousand other people. But really you're trapped here with me.

SAM. Honey, what are you talking about?

ROSE. I love you Sam. I never stopped loving you.

SAM. I love you too.

ROSE. But, I don't want to just be tolerated for the next…however many years I've got left. I deserve better than that.

SAM. Rose, I don't just tolerate you. You're my best friend.

ROSE. I'm your *only* friend. That you actually *know*.

SAM. I came here. Because you wanted me to. I'm here. I'm here with you.

ROSE. No you're not. I'm alone. Like always.

SAM. What are you talking about, Rosie?

ROSE. Since Barry left. It's just me.

SAM. I'm with you all the time. When you're not working, we're constantly together.

ROSE. That's what it feels like. To you.

SAM. That's what it is.

ROSE. What am I supposed to do now? I did it. He's grown up. He's a nice boy. He's off on his own.

SAM. He'll be back. For visits.

ROSE. I don't have a song that I have to write. Barry. He was my song. Done.
> (*Silence.*)

SAM. So keep the shop.

ROSE. No!

SAM. Okay! Then you could take an art class. Or…scrapbooking? Wasn't that what Peggy was doing?

ROSE. Glue things into a book. That's what you think I should be doing. For the next forty years.

SAM. Peggy seems happy.

ROSE. You don't know me at all. Do you?

SAM. Sure I do.

ROSE. Forty years. If we're lucky. Forty years left.

SAM. God.

ROSE. Forty years gluing things into a book so that I remember them. And then what?
> (*Silence.*)

I want to be adored. Like my song.

SAM. Well…

ROSE. Why don't you adore me any more? Why don't you look at me and want to write your song?

SAM. I don't know. I'm sorry. I don't know how to feel that way any more.

ROSE. I would be a lot of things for you Sam, I would. But I can't be twenty-five again.

SAM. I don't want you to be.

ROSE. And you're not either you know. If those women you played Scrabble with…they think you look like your wedding picture.

SAM. No. I know. Believe me. They take one look at me, and they're horrified.

ROSE. What?

SAM. What?

ROSE. They take one look at you?

SAM. Oh. Well…

ROSE. You've met them?

SAM. No, but that's what I'm saying. No.

ROSE. What?

SAM. I mean…just for coffee.

ROSE. WHAT???

SAM. Just a few of them. Who live in New York. I'd just… You know…we'd meet for coffee.

ROSE. Oh my God.

SAM. But…like you said. I mean, they're expecting the Facebook guy to show up. They take one look at me…

ROSE. You've been meeting with these women?

SAM. No! No, not at all. Not, not any more Rose. I mean…it was nothing. Coffee. That's all.

ROSE. That's it.

SAM. Rosie. No.

ROSE. That's IT!

SAM. Nothing ever…

ROSE. I don't want to know. I don't want to know what you did. I don't want to hear what you hoped might happen with these women.

    (Beat.)

WHAT DID YOU HOPE MIGHT HAPPEN WITH THESE WOMEN??? No. I don't even want to know. It's over. You've flushed twenty-five years down the toilet.

SAM. Rosie. Don't say that.

ROSE. I mean it. I'm through. You have betrayed me.

SAM. I didn't. This is what I'm saying. I never did. Anything. I wouldn't have done…

(*Suddenly, there is the most beautiful music ever played, heard only by* SAM. *It is his song. It may be singing. It may be a harp. It may be the eerie, sad sound of the theremin.* SAM *is completely enthralled.* ROSE *continues to yell at him but he can't even hear her now.*)

ROSE. I'll never be able to look at you the same way again.

(*But he can hear nothing but the music. It fills him with all the longing and feeling he's been searching for. And she is so caught up in what she's saying that she doesn't notice he is gone.*)

You have your faults, Sam. God knows. God KNOWS you have your faults. But I hold my tongue. I'm not one to count grievances. Even though you're self-centered, and moody, and helpless around the house and…

(*The music swells, and we can only hear bits of what she says, while* SAM *hears none of it. He is trying to hum along.*)

…you have to be told to put your clothes in the hamper after twenty-five fucking years. What the hell! PUT YOUR FUCKING CLOTHES IN THE HAMPER! But this? Forget it. It's over.

(*The music fades out.*)

The marriage is over.

SAM. (*Coming back.*) Did you hear that?

ROSE. What?

SAM. That was it. That was my song. Oh my God.

(ROSE *stares at him stunned.*
He tries to hum it but it's already lost to him.)

How did it go, Rose? Oh shit—it's already gone…
Do you remember how it went?

ROSE. Oh. My. God.

SAM. What?

ROSE. (*Furious.*) Oh my God! I cannot believe…

SAM. Rose, don't you understand? That was my song. Didn't you hear it?

ROSE. Did you hear ME? CAN you hear me??? I said I'm through! Our marriage is over.

(*The music swells up again and* SAM *is again transported by it.*)

I gave up all my good years on you. My attractive years. The years I might have had a chance to find someone else. Someone to really love me.

(SAM *is completely swept away. He begins to climb up the railing.*)

What are you doing? Sam? Don't be an idiot. Get down from there.

SAM. I have to remember. Help me. Help me remember.

ROSE. Get down off there.

SAM. That's the most… Oh God. That's the most beautiful…

(*And he jumps overboard.*)

ROSE. SAM!!!

(*Blackout. We hear the splash.*)

HELP!!! Someone… Help! Man… Man overboard!!! HELP!

(*We hear* ROSE *continue to call for help. And the commotion that that creates.*)

Scene 3

Lights up on a small island in the Mediterranean. Saturated with brilliant light and color. SAM *is lying where he was beached, on a rock, unconscious, drying in the sun. There are bones and fragments of clothes along the shore. Also bits of luggage and small treasures—the debris of thousands of years of mortality.*

On another rock sits the SIREN. *She is sublimely lovely. She sits madly playing a hand-held solitaire game, frantically pushing the buttons.*

SAM *stirs. Looks around. Disoriented.*

SAM. (*Coughing.*) Ooof. My back. Ow.

Where am I?

(*The* SIREN *shushes him, sharply.*)

Oh my God!!! Allyson?

SIREN. Zeus Almighty.

SAM. Allyson, you're here. What are you…?

(*Suddenly disoriented.*)

Wait…where are we? Am I…dead?

SIREN. Are you? You were supposed to perish. Did you perish?

SAM. Did I…?

SIREN. You're not allowed to talk if you're dead.

SAM. Uhhhh…

SIREN. You're not dead.

(*To the Gods.*)

Was he sent by Zeus? Hades? Where did you come from?

SAM. …The Carnival Cruise?

SIREN. Ughh. Another jumper. I hate when this happens. It's so off-story.

SAM. Wait… Are you Allyson Mendelson?

SIREN. Is she a great and powerful emissary of the Gods?

SAM. No. She's a girl from Teaneck.

SIREN. Then, no.

SAM. You look so much like her. It's unbelievable.

SIREN. Yeah, well…you want me to look like her.

SAM. What is this place?

SIREN. Anthemusa.

SAM. I don't think that was on the itinerary.

SIREN. It's my island. You're *on* my island.

SAM. Oh God. I jumped, right? Overboard? And swam here?

SIREN. You were supposed to perish.

> (*Indicating the bones and human remains.*)

SAM. (*Horrified.*) All those people died here?

SIREN. (*Looking at him sternly.*) No, most of them washed up dead like the story says. Come on, try again. Go back out, and this time, don't make it.

SAM. I'm sorry, Miss. I'm very confused.

SIREN. Well, you could just wait here and languish. But that would be long and awful. If you choose, you can touch me…

> (*She plucks a flower near her rock and all the leaves fall off, or it wilts away.*)

And we can get it over with quickly. But it has to be your choice.

SAM. I think I've been out in the sun too long. I don't feel so well. Is there anything to drink?

> (*She indicates the ocean.*)

That's ocean water. That would kill me.

SIREN. Okay.

SAM. (*Standing stiffly.*) Oof. I must have swum for hours. What was I thinking?

SIREN. You followed the song.

SAM. The song! Yes! You heard it too?
Do you remember? How it goes?

SIREN. Yes.

SAM. You do? Can you sing it?

SIREN. No.

SAM. Can you… Can you hum it? Anything?

SIREN. No.

SAM. Come on. Please?

SIREN. No. Look, are you going to touch me and get this over with? Or do you want a slow painful death?

SAM. I don't want any death. I want to remember.

SIREN. Slow and painful then. Suit yourself.

> (*He stares at her for a moment.*)

SAM. You're so beautiful…it hurts.

SIREN. Yeah. That's my thing.

(She goes back to madly pushing the buttons.
He tries to hum. Starting to get it.)

SAM. I'm remembering. Here with you… It'll come back.

(She wins her game. The horn sounds and applause from the little box.)

What are you doing? What is that?

SIREN. *(Finally enjoying the conversation.)* This is my magic box. It was a gift from the Gods! It washed up on shore one day. There are all these numbered boxes, see? And if you put them in just the right order, you triumph.

SAM. It's solitaire.

SIREN. I'm very good. I always triumph. Always. And when I do the Gods rejoice —a little horn sounds and the boxes jump all over the square. It's wonderfully diverting. I can't seem to do it enough. It's just so wonderfully diverting.

(There is the sound of a ship's horn in the distance. She sighs.)

Oh. Wait.

(The SIREN *sings the eerie, beautiful song of the Siren. It is breathtaking.* SAM *rises in awe. She sings for a moment and then there is the sound of a ship crashing in the distance. Distant screams. She stops singing and goes back to her solitaire game.)*

You probably wonder if every game is winnable. It seems like it would all depend on the layout of the little numbered boxes. But now that I've become an expert…

(She holds up the game for a moment.)

Right here. See? It says I'm an expert. Now I always triumph.

SAM. *(Stunned.)* That was it—my song for Allyson. How do you know that song?

SIREN. Sorry, but that's my song.

SAM. No, no, no. That was it. Sing it again.

SIREN. I sing it when the boats come.

SAM. It's…it's the most…

SIREN. …beautiful thing you've ever heard. Yeah.
Here—see my stats? They're very high. I am very very good.

SAM. Oh God. I felt it. When you sang. Young. Like I could write again.

(He tries humming it, but again, can't remember the song.)

Why can't I get it? What's wrong with me?

SIREN. It's not your song. It's been my song for like, thousands of years. I came with that song.

SAM. Thousands of…

SIREN. When the boat comes I sing that song, and then the men steer the boat into those jagged rocks where it's torn asunder and they perish.

SAM. Oh no! Did the boat I was on—did that boat crash?

SIREN. When you jumped off they must have been distracted. I want to make that clear.

(*To the Gods.*)

They did not resist me. He distracted them.

SAM. It didn't crash?

SIREN. No. That was very bad of you.

SAM. Thank God! Rose is on that boat.
Ohhhh. Rose. She's gotta be pretty pissed.

SIREN. Why, did she want the boat to crash?

SAM. No. We were on our anniversary cruise. She was talking to me, and I jumped. Overboard. And swam away. From her. That's not good.

SIREN. You chose the song.

SAM. No. I just… I lost my head for a minute.
I… I love my wife.

SIREN. Uh-huh.

SAM. I do. I love her. But passion…

SIREN. Yeah?

SAM. That kind of passion, doesn't last.

SIREN. What does it do?

SAM. It fades. It turns into something…else.

SIREN. What does it turn into?

SAM. Comfort, I guess.

SIREN. And that's bad.

SAM. No. Unless you want passion. You're young. You don't know about all that yet.

SIREN. I know that passion crashes the boats.

SAM. Why do you sing to crash the boats?

SIREN. It's my part of the story.

SAM. What story?

SIREN. (*Exasperated sigh.*) My boss, Demeter? Her daughter, Persephone was stolen by Hades.

SAM. Wait, this sounds very familiar.

SIREN. We were sent to rescue her but there were…complications. Long story short, my boss is seeking revenge on man.

SAM. And now you just stay here and lure people to their deaths?

SIREN. Men. They can't resist me. They can tie themselves to the mast, or they can put wax in their ears, but if they hear one note, they go mad with passion.

SAM. That's terrible. Sing it again.

SIREN. No.

SAM. Please.

SIREN. Nope.

SAM. I… I need to hear it. And then I'll remember. Just once more.

SIREN. Uh uh.

SAM. I'll do…whatever. I'll give you…whatever. Whatever you ask.

SIREN. Your life?

SAM. What?

SIREN. Will you give up your life?

SAM. Of course not!

SIREN. Come on. And then I get my kill before the sun sets.

SAM. No!

SIREN. Look at me.

SAM. No!

SIREN. I am Allyson! You can touch me. Have me. However you want.

SAM. I can?

SIREN. Yes. And then you die!

SAM. I don't want to die.

SIREN. OH MY ZEUS! CAN YOU HEAR ME?? YOU ARE GOING TO DIE. DO YOU WANT TO DIE IN ECSTASY OR DO YOU WANT TO DIE IN AGONY???

SAM. You sound a lot more like Rose than Allyson.

SIREN. Look. We're way off story. You were supposed to die at sea. I'm offering you one great moment of passion. Okay? It's like…a bonus game! Come. Sweetheart. Did she call you Sweetheart?

SAM. No.

SIREN. What did she call you?

SAM. …Sam?

SIREN. Sam. Come to me Sam. Touch me.

SAM. How can I touch you?

SIREN. Any way you want.

SAM. All over?

SIREN. Sure.

SAM. How long before I die?

SIREN. You'll have enough time. Don't worry.

SAM. (*He looks at the skeletons along the shore.*) All these men chose that? They gave up everything for that one moment?

SIREN. (*Seductively.*) It was worth it. I'll make it worth it.

SAM. You look so much like her. Your hair, your lips, your arms, your…

SIREN. (*Trying various seductive poses.*) Come here.

SAM. What would Rose think?

SIREN. She'll never know. Come.

SAM. But I'll know.

SIREN. Come here. Sam.

SAM. Ohhh…

SIREN. Touch me.

SAM. You're so beautiful.

SIREN. Yes.

SAM. I do want you.

SIREN. Of course you do. Give in.

SAM. Yes.

SIREN. Come to me.

SAM. Is this what I want?

SIREN. Of course it is. Touch me.

SAM. Oooo.

SIREN. I'm Allyson.

SAM. I want… I want to write my song. How often do the boats come?

SIREN. What??

SAM. When the next boat comes, you'll sing again?

SIREN. Yes…

SAM. I'll just wait. Thanks. For you to sing again. Okay? I'll just wait.
> (*He curls up to fall asleep.*)

SIREN. (*Disgusted, to the Gods.*) That's a new one.
> (*She returns to her game.*)
>
> *The lights shift. The sun sets and rises. The* SIREN *continues playing her game.* SAM *wakens. Groans.*)

SAM. Ohhh. I'm so thirsty.

SIREN. You're *still* alive?

SAM. I'm going to die if I don't get water.

SIREN. Okay.
> (*He groans.*)

You haven't even looked for some. You're not very resourceful.

SAM. No. You're right.

> (*He groans.*)

SIREN. Do you always do this? Lie around and groan when you want something?

SAM. (*Getting up, painfully.*) I guess I do.

> (*He begins walking around the island.*)

I guess Rose just gets it for me.

SIREN. She must be having the time of her life right now. Without you groaning nearby.

SAM. I imagine she's heartbroken.

SIREN. Heartbroken. You're hilarious.

SAM. That's what Rose always says! She says I'm hilarious. But really she means I'm annoying.

SIREN. Yeah? That's what I mean too.
How does she bear it? Does she put wax in her ears?

SAM. No.

SIREN. She can probably leave for big blocks of time. I imagine that helps.

SAM. She doesn't want to though. She wants to be with me. All the time.

SIREN. Is she simple-minded?

SAM. No. She loves me.

SIREN. Why?

SAM. I don't know.

SIREN. Is it passion?

SAM. It's a good question really. She just always wants me around.

SIREN. She needs a box with numbers.

SAM. Why does she love me?

SIREN. It's a mystery.

SAM. It really takes very little to make her happy. She wants me to put my clothes in the laundry basket. She wants to travel. She wants me to stop looking away. Look at her.

> (*Having walked all the way around and back again.*)

This is a very small island. There's nothing. No water.

SIREN. Yeah. I didn't think so.

SAM. I'm going to die.

SIREN. You think?

SAM. Oh my God. I'm going to die. I am. I'm really going to die.

SIREN. I thought we had established that!

SAM. I can't die here.

Help me. Come back to New York with me.

SIREN. New York?

SAM. My island. If you came to New York, if you sang our song, we would be a massive big deal.

SIREN. I'm a massive big deal here.

SAM. Well, here. Yeah. But—big fish, little pond, you know?

SIREN. It's the Mediterranean.

SAM. But, with our song, and your voice…

SIREN. Yeah. See, that's not what I do. I sing my song and the boats crash. That's what I do.

>   (*Beat.*)

And now I honor the Gods with my triumph on the magic box.

SAM. That's all you want out of life? That's what you want your legacy to be?

SIREN. Legacy…

SAM. What you leave behind.

SIREN. What do you do that's so important?

SAM. (*A little embarrassed.*) I'm a…songwriter.

SIREN. What's that?

SAM. I write songs. That people sing. I write some songs that people sing. I wrote one song that people sing. "Rose Adelle"?

SIREN. Never heard of it.

SAM. It's very famous. I mean, most people…

SIREN. I never heard of it.

SAM. So anyway, that's what I do.

SIREN. So… I guess that's way more important than what I do.

SAM. No.

SIREN. I can see why you'd swim to my island and judge how what I do is so much less important than what you do on your island.

SAM. I didn't mean that.

SIREN. That's a huge—what did you call it? Legacy? That's a huge legacy you made. Very impressive legacy.

SAM. No. I know.

SIREN. You're a big fish I guess. In your big pond.

SAM. No. I'm nothing. You're right. I'm leaving nothing behind when I die. A song? A son who doesn't want to visit me? A wife…a wife that I've hurt.

SIREN. You jumped overboard.

SAM. I did.

(We hear a ship's horn in the distance.)

SIREN. Wait.

> *(She sings again. Again we hear a ship crash off in the distance. The screams are a bit louder this time. The SIREN goes back to her game.)*

SAM. *(He tries, unsuccessfully, to hum it. Miserable.)* It's gone. And those screams. You just killed all those people.

SIREN. Uh-huh.

> *(She is back to frantically moving the cards. Then there is the sound of a trumpet and applause from the box. The SIREN looks up triumphantly.)*

See? Told you. I won. I always win.

> *(To the Gods.)*

That one was for you!

SAM. Oh God. I'm a fool. I'm going to die here. I'm such a fool.

> *(SAM crumples into a ball. The sun sets. And rises.*
> *SAM is mumbling in his sleep. Singing pieces of "Rose Adelle.")*

Rose… Rosie.

> *(SAM wakens, dazed, and looks to the rock, but now it is ROSE sitting there instead of the SIREN. ROSE is in her seventies and is knitting.)*

SAM. Rose!

ROSE. Is that how you say it? Epiphone? You know—the fancy guitar he's been wanting?

SAM. The what?

ROSE. *(Exasperated.)* Oh my God. Have you been listening to me? Sam?

SAM. Rose. I'm so happy to see you.

> *(He goes to her and is about to throw his arms around her.)*

Can I touch you?

ROSE. Can you what?

SAM. Oh, I don't even care.

> *(He throws his arms around her.)*

ROSE. *(She is surprised but pleased.)* Crazy. Look, I know it's expensive and Stephanie will throw a fit.

SAM. Stephanie…

ROSE. But she won't be happy whatever we do. And how often does a boy turn sixteen.

SAM. Sixteen?

ROSE. *(Loudly.)* Do you have your hearing aids in?

SAM. What?

ROSE. (*Even louder and exasperated.*) Sam. For God's sakes, GO PUT IN YOUR HEARING AIDS.

SAM. You're so old. But you're Rose.

ROSE. Great. Thanks.

SAM. You're wonderful.

ROSE. (*Very pleased.*) Yeah? You think it's a good idea?

SAM. You always have good ideas. If I just listen to you.

ROSE. Stephanie wants Tom to earn the money himself if he wants a fancy guitar.

SAM. Tom.

ROSE. I told Barry, "Look. This is the grandparents' prerogative. To spoil the grandchildren. My parents did it. You'll do it."

SAM. Grandparents…

ROSE. That's what I told him.

SAM. We're grandparents.

ROSE. Are you following what I'm saying, Sam???

SAM. Yes, Sweetheart. So we'll get the guitar.

ROSE. He has that concert coming up. Or gig. He loves to say gig. He's adorable.

SAM. Yes.

ROSE. I think we give it to him there. Have the band play "Happy Birthday." We present it to him. And then he plays the new guitar—at the gig!

SAM. That seems a little overboard.

ROSE. It's not.

SAM. To make such a big show in front of…

ROSE. It's good. It'll be fine. It's his sixteenth birthday. It's special.

SAM. You have to *make* thrilling things happen.

ROSE. You only live once.

SAM. Hey, I'm going to write a song! For Tom! For his birthday!

ROSE. That's a great idea!

SAM. Tell me about him. Tom.

ROSE. Tell you about him? What are you, nuts?

SAM. You know, describe him. For the song, I mean.

ROSE. Well, Stephanie says he's just like you.

SAM. She does?

ROSE. Of course she does! And she's none too happy about it!

SAM. He's just like me. Tom. My grandson.
I love you Rose.

ROSE. Good.

SAM. I want to get old with you.

ROSE. Too late.

> *(They both laugh again.*
> *There is the sound of a boat off in the distance.)*

Oh. Wait.

> *(And* ROSE *sings her song. "Rose Adelle." SAM enjoys it. And the boat doesn't crash. He sits back and closes his eyes and listens to her sing. And she slowly walks off, and is replaced by the* SIREN. SAM *is quite hallucinatory by now.)*

SAM. Rose?

SIREN. Nope.

SAM. Rose, is that you?

SIREN. No.

SAM. Are you sure…

SIREN. Go back to sleep.

SAM. I remember when we met, Rose. You were wearing that pink skirt. We went on a little boat. In Central Park. No. Wait. That was Allyson. In the pink skirt? No. That was you, Rose. But it wasn't me. Who was it?

> *(Very frightened.)*

I can't remember. Which one were you? Which one was I?

SIREN. Wow. You're really losing it.

> *(To the Gods.)*

Not long now I'd say.

SAM. Rose. You were the one.

> *(Starting to weep.)*

Why did I jump? You were so beautiful in your pink skirt Rose. Why didn't I kiss you?

> *(Three little beeps come from the square box.)*

SIREN. What was that?

SAM. What was that?

SIREN. Are you talking to me little box? What are you saying?

SAM. *(Coming out of it, seeing the* SIREN.*)* Oh, it's you.

SIREN. Shhh. My box from the Gods is talking to me.

SAM. You don't look like Allyson any more.

SIREN. I don't?

> *(The box beeps again.)*

What does it mean?

(*To the Gods.*)

What does it mean?

SAM. The batteries are running out.

SIREN. What are the batteries?

SAM. They're little cylinders full of power. But you have to change them. Or recharge them.

SIREN. I do?

SAM. Yeah, they don't last forever.

SIREN. Oh no. The game will stop playing?

SAM. You're going to need more batteries.

SIREN. (*Thoroughly frantic.*) What will I do? I can't just wait for the boats anymore! I got used to the game. It's so diverting! I need the game!

SAM. Look, I need to get back. Back to my wife.

SIREN. What do I do?

SAM. Let me get to the next boat and if I survive, I'll bring you back some batteries.

SIREN. How will you get to a boat?

SAM. Just don't sing. Once.

SIREN. I can't do that.

SAM. Just once. Break the rules.

SIREN. You're just trying to trick me.

SAM. Please let me go.

SIREN. Hey. Why can't you just change your batteries. Recharge your batteries?

SAM. Recharge my batteries. People can't…

SIREN. Hah! I knew you were lying. The Gods would not give me a box that died.

> (*It beeps three times again. The sound of bwa bwa bwa bwa as it dies. Its light goes out. The* SIREN *stares at it in terror. Presses the buttons. Nothing happens. The game has died.*
> *Greek tragedy:*)

Noooooooooooooooooooooooo!

> (*The* SIREN *madly presses the buttons. Shakes the machine. Rattles it against her ear.*)

NO NO NO NO! It is dead. Noooooooooooooo.

> (*She hits it.*)

Stop it! Stop being dead.

> (*There is a boat horn off in the distance.*)

Oh no. No no no. I cannot sing. But I must sing.

(And she does. The eerie, beautiful song. But now it has a heartbreaking minor key. It is the saddest sound ever heard. But still it works. We hear the ship crash in the distance. The screams are painfully loud this time.)

SAM. *(Covering his ears.)* Stop. Stop!

(She has stopped. She is softly weeping to herself.)

SIREN. No more little numbered boxes. No more stats. No more triumph. This is what death is? Death is terrible.

You spoke the truth. You see the future.

SAM. I do.

Let me get to the ship.

SIREN. It's not in the story.

SAM. The story isn't over. We can change the story.

SIREN. Change the story?

SAM. I can see it. This is the next part.

SIREN. You'll get me batteries?

SAM. Yeah. Look. See this little compartment here? This is where you put them. The plus goes this way and the minus goes that way.

SIREN. And the game will live again?

SAM. Yes. The game will live.

(There is a ship's horn.)

Don't sing, all right? Let me get to the boat. And I'll get you the batteries.

(He dives into the water.)

SIREN. Go forth. Do not die. Get me the batteries!

(Lights fade.)

Scene 4

Lights up on ROSE, *in her apartment. She is dressed in black. She is holding the phone and pacing. All the time, knitting and knitting. Finally she consults a scrap of paper and dials.*

ROSE. Richard? Oh my God. It's Rosie! Rosie Abrams…or Jacobs. Was. Rosie Jacobs. Hi.

Yeah. I know. How are you?

Wow, how exciting. What's her name?

Caroline. Nice. Where was the wedding?

Oh, you live on Long Island? No, I know you live on Long Island. I called Long Island. I'm sorry. I'm a little nervous. So was it beautiful? Did you walk her down the aisle?

Ah. Our son, Barry…yeah, I married Sam. Sam Abrams? He was in your dorm? Yeah…so, did you marry an Italian girl?

Oh. I'm so sorry. How awful. Yeah…I…umm…lost…Sam…too.

No, no. It was a boating…thing. An incident, a boating…incident. Yeah. Actually, it was recent. I'm…it's terrible, I'm sure it looks terrible, me calling you…it was very recent, very very recent, and I was, I mean, I'm in… mourning, or…but I was thinking about you. I mean before this happened and… Well, that sounds awful too, right? God.

I found you on Facebook. You know, I was checking Sam's accounts to make sure…anyway, Mimi Glazer is a friend of his and a friend of yours, so I could see your info as a…friend of a friend. It's all so weird. God what a world, right. Richard. It's really good to talk to you. I kind of can't believe it. I really needed to hear…an old friend. I've been so…

Friday? I would like that, I would. But I think it's too soon. I'm still so…

> (*The doorbell rings.*)

Oh, could you hold on a sec

> (*She opens the door.* SAM *stands there, disheveled but grinning.*)

SAM. Honey, I'm home!

> (ROSE *stands with the phone, paralyzed.*)

I survived!

> (*She doesn't respond.*)

I made it back! To you!!

> (*Still nothing.*)

I'm so sorry. I realized. I've been an idiot. I've been a complete fool. I want to be with you. I do. I want to write my song for you. I want to be here for you.

> (*He goes to her, to hug her, but she backs away, stunned.*)

Rosie?

> (*She remembers the phone.*)

ROSE. Ummm…someone's at the door. So… You know what? Friday would be great. Seven. Great. I'll see you then Richard. Miller.

> (*She hangs up. Blackout.*)

Scene 5

> *Friday night.* ROSE *is getting ready for her date. She stands in her slip, pinning up her hair as* SAM *watches. She is nervous and having difficulty getting it right.*

SAM. So did the girl come? What was her name? Stephanie?

ROSE. Courtney.

SAM. Right. She came? That's nice. What was she like?

ROSE. It wasn't really the occasion. To get to know her.

SAM. No. Right. How did he look?

ROSE. Well…his father had just committed suicide by jumping off a cruise ship in order to escape his mother…so…let's see…he looked…traumatized. He looked a lot like me.

SAM. I'm so sorry, Rose.

ROSE. Yeah.

SAM. It was nice that he came back. Right?

ROSE. You were dead. What do you think he'd do? Send a postcard?

SAM. Right.

ROSE. Of course, now I know you have to die for him to come home…

> (*She looks at him evilly.*)

SAM. Did they seem good together? Is she good to him?

ROSE. She doesn't cut off his crusts.

SAM. No?

ROSE. He says he makes his own sandwiches. Apparently women don't make men sandwiches any more. Apparently we're throwbacks. Apparently men of your generation make their own damn sandwiches.

SAM. I could do that. Make sandwiches.

> (ROSE *laughs bitterly.*)

I could. I will. You just always did it so well that…but I will.
So, what do you think you'll have?

ROSE. What?

SAM. Tonight. They have good eggplant parmesan there. Remember? When we had the eggplant parmesan?

ROSE. No.

SAM. Last time we were there… Didn't we have the…

ROSE. You had the eggplant parmesan. I had the gnocchi.

SAM. Oh. Right.

> (*Pause.*)

So, you could have the gnocchi. Again.

ROSE. I'll see.

SAM. Was it good?

ROSE. What?

SAM. The gnocchi.

ROSE. Oh, God Sam. I don't remember, all right?

SAM. So, you'll see what the specials are. They usually have specials.

ROSE. I think I'll manage. Thanks.

> (*She fusses for a while as he watches.*)

SAM. Do you want me to hold the pins?

ROSE. I'm trying to put my hair up. Why would I want you to hold the pins?

SAM. I meant, I could hand them to you. One at a time.

ROSE. No. Thanks.

(*She looks at him. He is so desperate to help. She hands him the hairpins.*)

Okay. Thanks.

SAM. No problemo!

(*Pause.*)

So, Richard Miller. How about that.

ROSE. Mmhmm.

SAM. What does he do now, did you say?

ROSE. I don't know.

SAM. He didn't mention what he did? For a living?

ROSE. I imagine I'll find out tonight.

SAM. So what did you talk about?

ROSE. His daughter just got married. Caroline.

SAM. He has a daughter?

ROSE. Well, obviously, if she just got married. Could you hand me a pin? I mean, if you're going to hold them…

SAM. So, he's married.

ROSE. His wife died.

SAM. Oh. That's terrible.

ROSE. I mean, she didn't jump off a boat or anything.

SAM. Your hair looks nice like that. Up, like that. I always liked it like that.

ROSE. Don't you have something to do? You really don't have to stand over me while I get ready.

SAM. I like to watch you.

ROSE. Oh please.

SAM. What?

ROSE. You like to watch me.

SAM. I do.

ROSE. You like to watch me because I'm going out with another man tonight. For twenty-five years you didn't like to watch me.

SAM. Yeah. I don't know. I guess you're right.

ROSE. Yeah.

SAM. So stupid. It's so great to watch you. Why didn't I want to watch you?

ROSE. This is really exhausting, Sam. I'm very nervous. This is my first date in a long time. I don't have the energy to give you right now, okay?

SAM. Because you're going out on a date.

ROSE. That's right.

SAM. With another man.

ROSE. Yes.

SAM. While your husband stays home. And eats a sandwich in front of the TV. Because I will. Make a sandwich. I can make a sandwich.

ROSE. You could go out. Call Allyson Mendelson.

SAM. You don't want me to do that.

ROSE. Do whatever you want.

SAM. I don't want to do it Rose. I don't. Want to do that. Any more.

ROSE. It's up to you.

SAM. I can't really catch up with this. I don't understand. The rules. I don't…

ROSE. Look. I thought you were dead. What was I supposed to think? I had to move on.

SAM. It's only been a week.

ROSE. You left me.

SAM. I told you. I wasn't leaving you. I heard this beautiful…

ROSE. Yeah yeah yeah. Please don't tell me that again, okay? I was saying that I felt I couldn't live with you—with you not caring for me any more and you jumped overboard. I don't know what your version is but that's my version. You jumped overboard. Rather than even respond to me, rather than try to dissuade me, you jumped overboard. And swam away!

SAM. I was following…

ROSE. Stop! As far as I'm concerned we're…separated. You can do whatever you want.

SAM. Separated.

ROSE. Yes.

> (*She considers her hair done. She puts on her top. It is loud and skimpy—the sort of thing one would find at Mandy's or another teen shop.* SAM *automatically zips it up in the back.*)

SAM. What am I supposed to do now? Do you want me to move out?

> (ROSE *has never considered this.*)

ROSE. What would you eat?

SAM. I don't know.

ROSE. You've never even made the coffee.

SAM. I guess I could learn. If that's what you wanted.

ROSE. Who would do your wash?

SAM. I should learn how to do these things. Anyway. Right? So that you don't have to do them. Right? I mean, all the time? So that you don't have to do them all the time?

ROSE. Do you want to move out?

SAM. No!

ROSE. You sound like you want to move out.

SAM. Of course I don't.

ROSE. Then why don't you say that!? Why don't you put up a fight? Why don't you say, "We are not separated. We are married. You shouldn't be going out with another man and I'm not going to move out and you're going to make the coffee." Why don't you say that?

SAM. Is that what you want me to say?

ROSE. God. Forget it.

> (*She puts on her skirt. It is tight and far too short. Clearly from the same shop. She looks in the mirror and takes herself in.*)

How do I look?

SAM. That's…that's not how you usually dress.

ROSE. So?

SAM. So… I'm just…surprised.

ROSE. Does it look good?

SAM. Yeah…where did you get it?

ROSE. At a store Sam. Where am I going to get it? I wove it out of flax.

SAM. They look…young.

ROSE. So? Why shouldn't I look young?

SAM. No. It's good. It's good.

ROSE. (*Putting on thigh-high spiky boots.*) Why shouldn't I show off what I've got? I see you staring at the girls, the girls who dress like this. So why shouldn't I wear it.

SAM. You look good. Richard's lucky. You look nice.

ROSE. Nice?

SAM. One piece of hair isn't up.

ROSE. Where?

SAM. In the back.

ROSE. Where?

SAM. Here.

> (*He takes a pin and tries to put it up, but can't manage.*)

ROSE. Oh, for Christ's sake.

(*She takes the pin from him and fixes her hair.*)

Okay. I guess I'm ready.

SAM. Don't go out with another man. You're married to me. We're not separated. You make the coffee.

ROSE. Don't wait up.

(*Blackout.*)

Scene 6

ROSE *is at a table at the restaurant waiting. She is nursing a glass of wine. The* WAITRESS, *played by the* SIREN, *approaches the table.*

WAITRESS. Can I get you another?

ROSE. No, I'm sure he'll be here any minute.

WAITRESS. Yeah… Do you want to order an appetizer, and then…

ROSE. You asked me that. I'll wait.

WAITRESS. The thing is, we have a second seating at nine. So…

ROSE. We'll eat fast. Once he comes.

WAITRESS. I mean, I don't want to be rude…

ROSE. Oh, good! I thought you did want to be rude.

WAITRESS. Huh?

ROSE. I'm sorry. I'm kind of nervous.

WAITRESS. Okay.

(*She starts to leave.*)

ROSE. Do I look…

WAITRESS. Yeah?

ROSE. How do I look?

WAITRESS. Well…

ROSE. Do I look…old?

WAITRESS. You look about my mother's age. Why, how old are you?

ROSE. Never mind.

(*The* WAITRESS *looks at her.*)

WAITRESS. My sister has that same outfit. In blue.

ROSE. Yeah? So…is it… You like it?

WAITRESS. She's like sixteen.

ROSE. Oh God. I will take another wine. Wait.

(*She tosses back the rest of the glass and hands it to the* WAITRESS.)

WAITRESS. Will do.

(ROSE's *cell phone rings. The ringtone is her song— "Rose Adelle." She gropes through her bag to find it.*)

See. That's probably him. I'm sure he's on his way.

WAITRESS. Okay.

(*She leaves. ROSE finds and answers her phone.*)

ROSE. Hello?

What are you doing calling me? Well, you are interrupting.

I don't know. I haven't ordered yet.

He isn't here…yet. No, it's still early.

Don't, all right? I'm not interested.

So write it. But don't write it for me. I don't want any more songs.

(*She sees RICHARD. Stunned.*)

Oh my God.

(*She hangs up.*
RICHARD *enters. He is played by an actor in his early twenties. He looks great. Thin, full head of hair. But he walks stiffly.*)

RICHARD. Rose?

ROSE. Richard.

RICHARD. *Ciao Bella!* I'm so sorry! We should have exchanged cell numbers! I couldn't reach you.

ROSE. Oh my God.

RICHARD. I threw my back out. I got this back thing. I'm really sorry. I called your house to say I'd be late and this dude answered. Said you'd already left. He sounded…

ROSE. You haven't…you look just the same.

RICHARD. You too. You look just the same. I would know you anywhere.

ROSE. No. But you…haven't changed at *all*.

RICHARD. You too.

ROSE. You look twenty to me.

RICHARD. You too.

(*She goes to hug him.*)

ROSE. It's so good to see you Richard. I can't get over…

RICHARD. Oy… Oh, careful. Sorry to be such an old fart. But when my back goes…

ROSE. No, I know. Here. Let me help you sit down. Here.

(*He sits, like an old man. They pause and look at each other.*)

RICHARD. So…you look great. *La molto bella signora.*

ROSE. Yeah? You look…unbelievably great.

RICHARD. You were always a hottie.

ROSE. A hottie?

RICHARD. That's what they say now. The kids. Someone they like is a hottie.

ROSE. Yeah. No, I know. My son is…

RICHARD. I remember that little pink skirt—the day we went out on that boat in Central Park.

ROSE. Me too! I remember that too! I was just telling Sam…

RICHARD. Sam?

ROSE. That was such a wonderful day.

RICHARD. You were hot. I wanted to have you right then and there.

ROSE. You did?

RICHARD. I would have taken you. Right there in that boat. In front of everyone.

ROSE. Really?

RICHARD. Oh yeah. You were wearing that little pink skirt.

ROSE. Yeah?

RICHARD. *Ho voluto prendere sotto che trafora poco la gonna.*

ROSE. That's beautiful. What does that mean?

RICHARD. I wanted to get under that little pink skirt.

ROSE. Oh.

RICHARD. You betcha. You were the bomb.

ROSE. Huh.

> (*Beat.*)

You never even kissed me.

RICHARD. Sure I did.

ROSE. No. I thought… I thought you weren't that interested in me. That way. I mean, it was very romantic, but you didn't even…

RICHARD. Are you sure? I thought I got to second base that day.

ROSE. What?

RICHARD. I remember telling my buddy Mike. I got to second base that day.

ROSE. You told your friend Mike.

RICHARD. Sorry. Shouldn't kiss and tell.

ROSE. You never even kissed me. You never held my hand.

> (*He reaches across the table and takes her hand.*)

RICHARD. I'm holding your hand now.

ROSE. (*Very flushed.*) Oh. Yes.

> (*He kisses each of her fingers.*)

RICHARD. I kissed you this time.

>   (ROSE *sits flustered.*)

ROSE. So... Richard...

RICHARD. Rosie.

ROSE. Does...does your daughter live in Long Island too? Where does...

RICHARD. Let's talk about us.

ROSE. Our son, Barry...he's in school in Vermont...

>   (*Her cell phone rings. She hesitates, then answers it.*)

What? No, I'm fine. He's here.

I'm sorry, Richard.

RICHARD. No. That's okay. You're a popular lady.

ROSE. Okay. I'm going now. I don't know yet. Look, I'm going to go. Don't. Don't sing it. I don't want to hear it. No. Okay 'bye. I'm hanging up! 'Bye. Sorry about that.

RICHARD. Rose. Rosie. I was sorry to hear about your loss.

ROSE. Yes. You too.

RICHARD. What was his name... I'm sorry.

ROSE. Sam Abrams.

RICHARD. Sam Abrams...

ROSE. You were in the same dorm. Remember?

RICHARD. I only remember you Rosie. *Ho avuto solo degli occhi per lei.*

ROSE. But don't you remember when Sam asked me out and...

RICHARD. I was crazy about you.

ROSE. You were, right?

RICHARD. Sure.

ROSE. That's what I told him.

RICHARD. Who?

ROSE. And do you think... I mean, if we'd gotten together. Or...

RICHARD. I think there would have been fireworks.

ROSE. No. I mean, if we'd stayed together. If we'd...wound up together...

RICHARD. Well, it really hadn't gotten to that stage.

ROSE. Right.

RICHARD. You've got gorgeous eyes, Rose.

ROSE. Thanks. But if we had. I mean, if you hadn't left... If I hadn't gone out with Sam...

RICHARD. Well, I got that job.

ROSE. Right.

RICHARD. In Roma.

ROSE. Right. I just think about…how great we were. Together.

RICHARD. It was magic.

ROSE. Yeah? For me too. If Sam hadn't written me that song… I always thought you and I…

RICHARD. Yes. So…have you seen many men since your husband passed?

>   (*Pause.*)

ROSE. Ummm, I need to tell you about that.

>   (*The* WAITRESS *comes over with* ROSE*'s wine.*)

WAITRESS. Ah…he showed up!

RICHARD. Hello.

ROSE. How old does he look to you?

WAITRESS. Uh…he looks about my father's age. Do you want to hear the specials, or do you know what you'd like.

RICHARD. (*Reaching for* ROSE*'s hand.*) I've already got something special.

WAITRESS. So…no then.

>   (RICHARD *just stares at* ROSE.)

See, your reservation was for seven? So…if you would like to order your dinner now…

RICHARD. Get me a bottle of your finest wine.

WAITRESS. There's a wide variety. Do you want the wine list?

RICHARD. Surprise me.

WAITRESS. Red or white?

RICHARD. Surprise me. I like to be surprised.

WAITRESS. Got it.

>   (*She leaves.*)

RICHARD. Where were we?

ROSE. The thing is…when I called you, Sam had had this boating incident?

RICHARD. You said. So tragic. When was that?

ROSE. Yeah. That's the thing. That was last week.

RICHARD. Last week?

ROSE. I…I thought he was gone. Or…he was gone. I mean, they couldn't find him. They just thought…we all thought he was gone. Dead.

RICHARD. Right…

ROSE. And then he turned up.

RICHARD. His body? Wait, did he turn up last week, or he went missing last week?

ROSE. It all happened last week.

RICHARD. Interesting.

ROSE. And he turned up...alive. Actually. Yes.

RICHARD. Oh! Well...wonderful. Right?

ROSE. But...when I called you, I thought I was a...a widow. When actually...

RICHARD. So that was him on the phone? When I called your house?

ROSE. Yes.

RICHARD. I hope I didn't make things uncomfortable. I mean, was our tryst supposed to remain secret or...

ROSE. No! No. He knows. He knows I'm out. With you.

RICHARD. Oh! So, you have one of those open marriages.

ROSE. We're separated.

RICHARD. You just get more and more intriguing to me.

ROSE. I do?

RICHARD. You smell good. It's intoxicating.

ROSE. Thanks.

RICHARD. Rose. Rose Jacobs.

ROSE. Ummmm.

RICHARD. Have you dated much? Since you were...separated?

ROSE. It's only been...a few days.

RICHARD. So... No?

ROSE. No! Of course not.

RICHARD. So, I will be the first man you've been with in...how many years have you been married?

ROSE. How do you mean been with?

RICHARD. Twenty? Twenty-five?

ROSE. We just celebrated our twenty-fifth wedding anniversary. In fact, we were on a cruise for our twenty-fifth...

(*Her cell phone rings. She decides to ignore it.*)

RICHARD. What if we take our dinner to go?

ROSE. What? Why would we...

RICHARD. Do you need to get that?

ROSE. No. No, I don't.

(*She flips the phone open and closes it so that the ringing stops.*)

RICHARD. Let's tell the waitress we're going to take it to go.

ROSE. We just ordered wine. I don't... This is all so bizarre. Richard. I feel like...you haven't changed at all, but then you're completely...

RICHARD. Different? The years have mellowed me. Like a fine wine.

    (*At that moment the* WAITRESS *comes back with the bottle of wine.*)

Speaking of which.

    (*To the* WAITRESS.)

You must have supernatural, telepathic powers.

WAITRESS. Okay.

    (*Holding up the bottle.*)

I surprised you. With our most expensive bottle.

    (*She pours a glass.*)

Do you need to smell it and taste it or can I just pour?

    (*He sloshes it around and smells it and tastes it.*)

RICHARD. *Magnifico.* We would like two orders of the fillet mignon, and we would like to have it to go. Is that possible?

ROSE. No. Wait.

WAITRESS. That would be great actually.

ROSE. Why don't we just eat here…

RICHARD. Wonderful. We'll drink this wine while we wait.

WAITRESS. Sounds good. Cheers.

    (*She takes the menus and leaves.*)

ROSE. No no no!

Richard. Where are we going?

RICHARD. Have you ever been to *Long Island*?

    (*Whenever he says "Long Island" it sounds like a distant, exotic place.*)

ROSE. Of course I've been to Long Island. But why don't we just eat our…

RICHARD. You've never been to this part of *Long Island.* You're in for a special treat.

    (*He raises his glass to her.*)

To us.

ROSE. Richard, I'm not… I need some time.

RICHARD. You can take all the time you want.

ROSE. Maybe I should just go home. I'm feeling very…

RICHARD. You're not feeling well?

ROSE. …sad.

RICHARD. No! No, don't feel sad. Sweetheart.

    (*Her phone rings again.*)

ROSE. (*Answering it.*) Don't call me any more! That's it. Or I'm turning the phone off! I mean it.

(*She hangs up.*)

RICHARD. Why don't you just turn it off?

ROSE. Well, if there's an emergency... I want him to be able to...
No. You're right. I'm turning it off.

(*She does.*)

RICHARD. Good *bella*. Now it's just us. Let's drink up this wine. Mmmm.
It's very nice.

ROSE. I can't go home. Till much later. Sam can't think this didn't go well.

RICHARD. Isn't this going well? I think it could go very, very well.

ROSE. I have to come in late. He needs to worry. A fraction of the amount
he made me worry. He made me sick. I thought my life was over. It's been a
terrible week.

RICHARD. He doesn't deserve you.

ROSE. Maybe. Probably he does.

(*She starts crying.*)

I probably deserve him.

RICHARD. No. Sweetheart. Don't cry. Come now. Drink your wine. We
have a whole bottle to drink. And then we'll have a nice dinner on *Long Island*.

ROSE. Do you have a guest room? Or...your daughter's room...

RICHARD. Let's see how we feel. Come. To us.

(SAM *enters, looking around wildly. Maybe he has a guitar around his neck.*)

SAM. Rose!

ROSE. Sam. What are you doing here?

SAM. Rose. What the hell. Have you been crying?

ROSE. No.

SAM. Did he make you cry?

ROSE. I'm fine. You remember Richard? Richard, Sam.

RICHARD. No. I don't think so.

SAM. Yeah. I remember you.

ROSE. Isn't it amazing? How little he's changed? It's unbelievable, isn't it?

SAM. No. He looks...old.

ROSE. Really? He looks twenty to me.

RICHARD. And you look twenty to me Rose.

(*To* SAM.)

Would you care to join us for a drink?

SAM. No.

RICHARD. Before we go?

SAM. Where are we going?

RICHARD. Rose and I. To my place. On *Long Island*.

SAM. No you're not.

ROSE. Sam. You should leave.

SAM. She's not going anywhere with you. She's coming home with me. Right now. I'm going to make us both…sandwiches.

RICHARD. We've ordered the fillet mignon.

SAM. She doesn't like that.

RICHARD. I think you're mistaken.

SAM. If you'd spent twenty-five years with her you'd know she likes the gnocchi here.

RICHARD. Well, anything you like. Anything on the menu. Or anywhere really. Anywhere in town. Or *Long Island*. I will get you whatever suits your fancy.

(*The* WAITRESS *approaches with the to-go bags.*)

WAITRESS. Here you go. And here's the check. Thanks for coming!

(*Seeing* SAM.)

Hi! Do you have a…reservation?

SAM. Come on Rose. We're going home.

WAITRESS. Wait. Don't I know you?

SAM. I don't think so.
Where's your coat, Sweetheart?

WAITRESS. Scrabulous!

SAM. Oh my God.

ROSE. Oh my God.

WAITRESS. We met for coffee! Remember? Sam, right? You were so funny!

ROSE. He's hilarious.

SAM. Rose.

WAITRESS. You never called. Do you still have my number?

RICHARD. You really have an interesting marriage Rosie.

SAM. I'm not doing that. I'm sorry. I'm not doing that any more.

WAITRESS. What?

SAM. Scrabble…coffee. Any more. I'm…this is my wife. Rose.

WAITRESS. Oh.

ROSE. Come on Richard.

RICHARD. (*Pulling out his credit card and giving it to the* WAITRESS.) Settle us up please.

SAM. Rose. Listen.

RICHARD. I think she doesn't want to listen to you. I think she's made it clear.

SAM. Let me sing you the song Rosie. Please.

ROSE. I've heard enough.

SAM. I think you'll like it. I wrote it without even trying. All that feeling. It's back. It's about you, Rose.

RICHARD. Why don't you record it and send it to her?

SAM. Why don't you step outside.

ROSE. What?

RICHARD. What?

WAITRESS. What?

SAM. I'll fight you, you bastard.

ROSE. Oh my God, Sam. What are you doing?

SAM. Get up. I'll pound you right here.

WAITRESS. Well, no. Not in the restaurant.

RICHARD. You mean boxing?

ROSE. He's lost his mind. Sam, please.

RICHARD. I have a bad back…

>(SAM *sings the song here. It is not the* SIREN'*s song. It is a new song. Maybe he plays the guitar and accompanies himself with it. If not, maybe he has brought a cassette recorder with a piano accompaniment that he sings to.*)

SAM. (*Singing.*) Richard Miller's not that great.

RICHARD. Hey!

SAM. Richard Miller's not that great.

ROSE. Sam!

SAM. Richard Miller is not that great.

WAITRESS. (*Taking the credit card.*) I'll ring this up. I'll just include the tip to save time.

>(*She hurries off.*)

SAM. Oh I know I'm disappointing in most every single way.
And I know you could do better. You remind me every day.

RICHARD. You can do better Rose.

SAM. But I realize that the life I live is empty for me Rose.
If you're not there right beside me yelling "Sam pick up your clothes."

ROSE. Oh my God Sam. Not here.

SAM. Richard Miller's not that great.

ROSE. I'm sorry Richard.

SAM. Richard Miller's not that great.
Richard Miller is not that great.

My batteries are running down, and yours are too I know.
But even though the charge is dim, you haven't lost your glow.
There are billions of other people on this little spinning ball.
But if you're the one I die with Rose, It's not so bad at all.

Richard Miller's not that great.
Richard Miller's not that great.
Richard Miller is not that great.

SAM. Rose. I would choose you. If we met today. Would you choose me?

ROSE. If we met today…probably not.

SAM. Oh.

ROSE. But twenty-five years ago I chose you Sam. And…that's always been enough for me.

SAM. Thank you Rose.

RICHARD. Wait… Does that mean you're not coming to *Long Island*?

ROSE. No, Richard. I'm sorry.

> (*He kisses her hand.*)

SAM. Thank you Rose. You won't be sorry. I'll make sure every day that you won't be sorry.

ROSE. Oh, Sam. I'm already sorry. But let's go home.

> (*He grabs her and gives her a long passionate kiss.*)

Huh. Let's go home.

> (*The* WAITRESS *returns and hands* RICHARD *back his card and the bill, which he signs.*)

WAITRESS. Thanks for the generous tip.

RICHARD. *Prego, bella ragazza.*

WAITRESS. Wow. Cool.

Scene 7

> *Lights shift.* SAM *and* ROSE *are on a small boat in the Mediterranean. Everything is awash with blue.*

SAM. This is amazing. It's so blue.

ROSE. Yes.

SAM. And that breeze. Feels so good. Doesn't it?

ROSE. Mmhm.

SAM. I love the way the ocean smells. Particularly here. It's like perfume. There's something about…

ROSE. (*Laughing.*) You're impossible.

SAM. I know you think this is nuts Rose. That I have to do this. That I have to pay her back.

ROSE. It is nuts.

SAM. But you came anyway.

ROSE. Of course I came.

(*A long beat.*)

SAM. (*Taking it all in again. Filled with joy.*) My God. It's so beautiful.

ROSE. (*Looking all the way around her. They are in a tiny boat on a huge sea.*) Who would have thought we'd wind up here?

SAM. So lucky.

ROSE. We were Barry's age when we met. Decided to spend the next sixty, seventy years together. We were kids.

ROSE. It's crazy, right? We were idiots. What did we know?

SAM. Nothing.

ROSE. And nobody says—what the hell are you doing? They throw you a party.

SAM. Crazy.

ROSE. And here we are, twenty-five years later./ And we still know nothing.

SAM. And we still know nothing.
I don't even know who I'd be if I hadn't spent my life with you. I mean, the me I am, it's from being with the you you are because you were with me.

ROSE. Okay…

SAM. Ah! This is the place. You got the package?

ROSE. (*Sigh.*) Sure. Let me tie you to the mast.

SAM. I really don't think you need to Rosie. I won't jump ship again.

ROSE. That's great, Hon. Now go stand against the mast.

SAM. Okay.

ROSE. Here. Hold this.

(*She takes her knitting which is now absurdly long and wraps it around* SAM.)

SAM. Good. Now get the batteries.

(*She gets a large package covered in bubble wrap and plastic.*)

ROSE. This is hilarious.

SAM. Yeah.

(*Distantly at first and then louder and louder, we hear the beautiful and now heartbreakingly sad song of the* SIREN. *It is a wail. Long and plaintive and aching. Only* SAM *can hear it.*)

ROSE. You hear it.

SAM. Throw it in Honey.

(She hurls the package overboard. We hear a splash. They both stand watching it float away for a moment.

And then the SIREN's *song goes from its mournful minor key, back to its original lovely melody.* SAM *is filled with feeling. He reaches for* ROSE.)

ROSE. What does it sound like?

SAM. *(Filled with emotion.)* It sounds like…you.

(She goes to him. He wraps the remaining scarf around her and they stand together.)

ROSE. She's going to need more batteries.

SAM. We'll have to come back. Every five years.

ROSE. No. Every year.

(They kiss.)

SAM. I choose you Rose Adelle Abrams.

ROSE. Yeah. Crazy. I choose you too.

(They stand, tied together as the lights swell to brilliant color, the music swells and then…

Blackout.)

End of Play

THE METHOD GUN
Written by Kirk Lynn
Created by Rude Mechs

ABOUT *THE METHOD GUN*

This article first ran in the January/February 2010 issue of Inside Actors, *and is based on conversations with the creators before rehearsals for the Humana Festival production began.*

Thomas Graves welcomes the audience to the theatre. He asks the audience to reach beneath their seats where they will find an envelope containing a piece of paper and a pencil.

Then he asks the audience to close their eyes and think of the teacher who influenced them more than any other living human, whether for good or ill. Thomas asks the audience to generate an image of this person, whom he describes as their "guru."

Then he asks the audience to open their eyes and write their guru's name on the piece of paper. We will collect the names in a bowl which he will pass through the audience.

He suggests that if anyone can't think of a name to write down, he or she could write the name "Stella Burden."

So begins *The Method Gun*, a play created by Rude Mechs to investigate the alchemy of performance—what actors will do in pursuit of a truthful moment on stage and the toll that pursuit takes on their lives, relationships and sanity. In typical Mechs style, *The Method Gun* does so with a rigor and eccentricity that convey both the absurdity of the single-minded pursuit of stage truth, as well as the moments of fleeting, breathtaking beauty that actors can create.

Stella Burden is purported to have been a mid-century actor training guru, who left the country without explanation in the mid-1970s. *The Method Gun* is Rude Mechs' examination of Burden and her company, who continued rehearsing her last project—a production of *A Streetcar Named Desire* without any of its major characters—for nine years, before giving a single performance. Burden's training technique, "The Approach," has echoes of the Method acting technique popularized by Lee Strasberg, Stella Adler and others in mid-twentieth century America. The Method trained actors to forge personal connections to their characters in order to produce emotionally honest performances. Burden's Approach added actual physical risk to the practice of emotional recall, and she was as revered by her students as she was ridiculed by others.

The play began in an acting exercise that playwright (and Mechs Co-Producing Artistic Director or "Copad") Kirk Lynn drafted as a way to consider the nature of actors' risk and sacrifice. "I knew it would be life-threatening, and I thought actors would actually try it," Lynn says. "They'd be willing to risk their lives to get to a place of honesty and present-ness. Because actors risk all sort of things: they're willing to embarrass themselves, to risk their livelihood and relationships, as well as depression or addiction, whatever it takes.

They're amazing. This exercise encapsulated that risk in a single moment, as a metaphor for what they actually do every night."

Lynn took this exercise—a kind of Russian roulette where actors risk a real bullet—to the rest of Rude Mechs, which began the company's investigations of Stella Burden, dangerous training and performing techniques, and the dynamics of working in a company. In one experiment, Copad Thomas Graves led a series of exercises about working with a guru. "The guru breakthrough was huge," says Copad Madge Darlington. "Thomas lectured and then we all took turns being a guru, thinking about what it is to be in a guru's presence. At one point, a company member said, 'This is bullshit,' and left. We were 80% sure she was just going to pick up her kids. But we were 20% sure that she'd really left us for good." Adds Lynn, "We found that ambiguity really pleasurable. 80/20 became a central principle for putting together the show— we want the audience to be 80% sure that parts of it are a kind of put-on, and 20% undecided."

The company also continued to explore Burden's training techniques. "Stella's acting exercises were like Indiana Jones," says Thomas Graves. "You have to be really precise. We imagined boulders rolling by and knives being thrown through the space while we're acting." The technique they developed culminates in an awe-inspiring feat of meticulous focus towards the end of *The Method Gun*. It's simpler than synchronized boulders but just as dangerous, and evokes the peril and thrill of an adventure movie in the confines of the Victor Jory Theatre.

Ultimately *The Method Gun* is its own nightly experiment: Can real threat evoke an honest performance? Is a life that's 80% ridiculous actor ritual and 20% honesty worthwhile? Is theatre an act of fruitless, self-indulgent stupidity or an act of truth? As Copad and *The Method Gun* director Shawn Sides puts it, "Did this company succeed or fail? They went through all of this—clinging to rituals and techniques that weren't fruitful anymore, digging into Stella's texts, fighting over whether they're straying from the Approach, working and bonding and failing daily. And then they make one beautiful thing. Do all the little failures add up to make the whole thing a disaster, or does the love along the way and the one beautiful thing make it a success?"

> *Thomas explains that at the beginning of a new rehearsal process Stella Burden made it a ritual to write down the names of their most important teachers and collect the names in a bowl. After the first performance, she would burn the names as a way of honoring and destroying the lessons they had learned.*

—Adrien-Alice Hansel

BIOGRAPHIES

Since 1995, **Rude Mechs** has created a mercurial slate of original theatrical productions that represents a genre-defying cocktail of big ideas, cheap laughs, and dizzying spectacle. What these works hold in common is the use of play to make performance, the use of theaters as meeting places for audiences and artists, and the use of humor as a tool for intellectual investigation. Rude Mechs is an ensemble-based theatre company that operates with a full company of 28 members. We create original plays that we produce in Austin, TX, and tour nationally and internationally. Our touring productions include *The Method Gun*, *Get Your War On*, *How Late It Was, How Late*, *Cherrywood*, and *Lipstick Traces*. Our Off-Broadway productions include *Get Your War On* and *Lipstick Traces*.

Rude Mechs has received over 170 local and national awards and nominations for our work, including several MAP Fund Awards and frequent support from the National Endowment for the Arts. We've enjoyed two Off-Broadway premieres and toured to top national venues such as The Walker Arts Center (Minneapolis, MN), The Wexner Center (Columbus, OH), and Woolly Mammoth Theatre Company (Washington, DC). We seek to participate in the international community of artists by contributing to festivals such Austria's SommerSzene, the Galway Arts Festival, the Edinburgh Fringe Festival, the Kiasma Festival, the Philadelphia Live Arts Festival, and the Under the Radar Festival in New York City.

Kirk Lynn lives in Austin, Texas with his wife, Carrie Fountain and their daughter Olive Lynn Fountain. He makes most of this theater with the Rude Mechs. He hopes by the time you read this bio, his first novel will be under contract. He teaches playwriting at the University of Texas. He likes deer hunting, canoeing and reading the short stories of Anton Chekhov.

ACKNOWLEDGMENTS

The Method Gun premiered at the Humana Festival of New American Plays in March 2010. It was directed by Shawn Sides with the following cast (in alphabetical order):

CARL REYHOLT as Pablo/Paper Boy/
Tamale Vender/Doctor ....Thomas Graves
CONNIE TORREY as Colored Woman/
Mexican Woman ....Hannah Kenah
KOKO BOND as Negro Woman/
Nurse..Lana Lesley
ROBERT "HOPS" GILBERT as Steve......E. Jason Liebrecht
ELIZABETH JOHNS as Eunice...........................Shawn Sides

and the following production staff:

Production Manager/ Technical Director	Madge Darlington
Scenic Designer	Leilah Stewart
Costume Designer	Katey Gilligan
Lighting Designer	Brian Scott
Sound Designer/Composer	Graham Reynolds
Properties Designer	Doc Manning
Projection Designers	Lowell Bartholomee, Michael Mergen
Video Technician	Philip Allgeier
Stage Manager	Lowell Bartholomee
Production Assistant	Zachary Krohn
Dramaturg	Adrien-Alice Hansel
Directing Assistant	Gretchen Wright
Costume Design Assistant	Christy Smith
Assistant Dramaturg	Zach Chotzen-Freund

The Method Gun is a project of Creative Capital and has received creation support from the Multi-Arts Production (MAP) Fund, The Orchard Project, the National Endowment for the Arts, the University of Texas Humanities Institute, The Harry Ransom Center, and The Long Center for the Performing Arts. Rude Mechs is supported by the Texas Commission on the Arts and the City of Austin through the Cultural Arts Division.

CHARACTERS

Thomas as Carl Reyholt as Pablo / Paper Boy / Tamale Vender/ Doctor

Hannah as Connie Torrey as Colored Woman / Mexican Woman

Lana as Koko Bond as Negro Woman / Nurse

Jason as Robert "Hops" Gilbert as Steve

Shawn as Elizabeth Johns as Eunice

SETTING

A theatre and rehearsal space.

"—use your imagination! You've got mermaid's blood in your veins, so be a mermaid! Let yourself go at least once in your life, fall head over heels in love with a merman, dive in with a big splash, and leave the Herr Professor and the rest of us standing on the shore, helplessly waving our arms!"

—Act III, *Uncle Vanya*, Anton Chekhov, translated by Paul Schmidt

Thomas Graves
in *The Method Gun*

34th Annual Humana Festival of New American Plays
Actors Theatre of Louisville, 2010
Photo by Alan Simons

THE METHOD GUN

INTRODUCTION

The floor is covered in spike tape of all different colors
marking the positions of stairs, columns, furniture placement and camera angles
from the various set designs used throughout the nine years of rehearsal process
for the Stella Burden Company's production of A Streetcar Named Desire.

On stage is an Equity cot covered with an old quilt,
a metal ice chest,
a window shade hung from steel frames,
an ornate footed bowl,
an upright piano of questionable tuning,
a Shinto shrine containing a tiger carved from soap,
a rolling tamale cart,
a chair and a reading lamp,
a folding paper screen,
a kitchen table covered in poker chips, cards and a near-empty whiskey bottle,
an A/V cart which holds an overhead projector, a filmstrip projector, and a
record player,
and a birdcage containing a loaded Colt revolver
hanging from the perch.

As the audience enters
LANA LESLEY *plays piano.*
The other actors, THOMAS GRAVES, SHAWN SIDES, JASON
LIEBRECHT *and* HANNAH KENAH
check their props,
warm up,
and talk to each other and any friends in the audience.
The idea is to make the room feel warm and relaxed.

When it's time to get started, the actors prepare to perform a re-creation of a rehearsal
of the Stella Burden Company,
including placing an overhead on the projector
which reads: **REHEARSAL**
> **8/26/73**
> **One Year Since Stella Left**

ELIZABETH *stands at the doorway.*
CONNIE *and* CARL *gather around some chairs.*
ROBERT *does exercises on the floor.*
And KOKO *sits at the piano.*

ELIZABETH. I think we're starting to stray from the Approach.

    (CONNIE *hits a chair as hard as she can.*)

CONNIE. Listen, let's just do the scene, or don't, but let's not do this again.

ELIZABETH. If Stella were to walk through that door right now
how would you want her to see us acting?
Like this, like him, like you?

CARL. Will you please stop talking?!
Do you notice how much I don't talk?
I don't talk all the time. But you?
Just watch the difference between me and you.

ROBERT. I have a blister!

    (*The re-creation ends.*
    And THOMAS *says—*)

THOMAS. Howdy, everybody.
My name's Thomas.
I'm one of the Rude Mechs.
That was a brief reenactment from the show
we're going to do for you tonight, *The Method Gun.*

We want to welcome you to this, the Actors Theatre of Louisville.
And thank you for joining us for the 34th Humana Festival of New American Plays.

We're grateful to The Humana Foundation
for making this festival possible
and for their continued support.

Now:
Turn off your cell phones
unwrap your candy
don't record anything
please fill out surveys; the ushers will give you a flier
there's no reentry to the theatre if you leave.

All right. Thank you for joining us this evening {afternoon}.
Now before we take over the show
we want to give you a chance to do just a tiny bit of audience participation.
Everybody crack your knuckles. Good.

Now everybody reach beneath your seat
where you'll find an envelope
containing a pencil and a piece of paper.

Once you've got your hands on those
I want you to close your eyes.

I want you to think of somebody who taught you something.
I want you to recall the teacher who influenced you more than any other living
      human.
Whether for good or for ill.
I want you to generate an image of this person,
who I would describe as your guru.
Think of his or her facial expressions.
Think of his or her hair.
There's nothing more personal than hair.
Now, when you have a good image.
Open your eyes
and use your pencil to write your guru's name on the piece of paper.
Please, really do write someone's name down.
We want to collect these names
as a way of gathering the energy of everything we've all been taught
and inviting into the room the spirit of what we've all learned
and what it was like to be a student at any point in your life
in need of guidance and discipline and encouragement
from anyone.
If you can't think of someone to write down,
you can write the name: Stella Burden.

> (*A transparency of Stella Burden is placed on the overhead projector
> and projected onto one of the rolling blinds.*
>
> *Bowls are passed through the audience
> to collect the names they've written down.
> When all of the names are collected*
> THOMAS *continues*—)

Stella Burden is the woman to whom tonight's show is dedicated.
Ms. Burden taught and directed in the American theatre in the 1960s and 70s,
before walking out on her company and emigrating to South America,
never to be heard from again.
But her students carried on her traditions
even after she disappeared,
completing the company's nine-year-long rehearsal process
and presenting one final public performance.

> (HANNAH *takes over the pre-show speech.*
> LANA *comes to take the bowls from her.*
> THOMAS, JASON, *and* SHAWN *gather upstage right.*)

HANNAH. The show the students presented was Tennessee Williams' *A
Streetcar Named Desire*, but not as you and I know it—
the company performed the show without the characters:

Stanley, Stella, Mitch or Blanche.

>   (THOMAS, JASON, *and* SHAWN *break to gather artifacts.*)

That's the performance we're going to recreate for you tonight.
We'll present *Streetcar* in its entirety,
performing every line, every action, every stage direction
that does not involve one of the main characters.
In order to help with this task we'll be relying on these—what I would call—
"artifacts," I guess
which belonged to Ms. Burden.

>   (*Actors bring the following forward*
>   *to show the audience*
>   *as* HANNAH *names the artifacts.*)

We have an unopened letter
written by Stella herself,
written to one of her students
and kept in this locked box.
We have a soap statue of a tiger
that Stella considered a good luck charm.
And we have Stella's gun
which was loaded when they found it
and we're not going to say how it is now.

But I can tell you
parts of the show are quite dangerous
so we'll ask you to remain in your seats
especially during our re-creation of the final performance of the Stella Burden
        Company
which happens toward the end of the show.

Along the way we'll also be re-imagining the rehearsals
and performing experiments
with Stella Burden's actor training technique: the Approach.

In fact, we've completed one just now.
At the beginning of a new rehearsal process
Stella Burden made it a ritual
to ask her company to write down the names of their most important teachers,
including her own name,
if she was it for them
and she collected the names in a bowl.

Then after the first performance,
she would burn the names

as a way of honoring
and destroying
the lessons they had learned.

    (LANA *takes the names that have been collected from the audience
and pours them into the footed bowl.*)

SHAWN. Now we're going to get started
with another exercise used by Stella Burden's company of actors:
Crying Practice.

TRAINING TECHNIQUE: Crying Practice

*The actors place an overhead on the projector
which reads—*
TRAINING TECHNIQUE: Crying Practice.

They gather in a line downstage facing the audience.

One of them takes a simple kitchen timer and sets it for three minutes.

Then the actors begin crying.

*When the timer goes off
the company stops crying.*

REHEARSAL
8/26/73
One Year Since Stella Left

*The actors prepare to perform a re-creation of a rehearsal
of the Stella Burden Company,
including placing an overhead on the projector
which reads:* **REHEARSAL**
8/26/73
One Year Since Stella Left

Exactly as before—
ELIZABETH *stands at the doorway.*
CONNIE *and* CARL *gather around some chairs.*
ROBERT *does exercises on the floor.*
And KOKO *sits at the piano.*

ELIZABETH. I think we're starting to stray from the Approach.

    (CONNIE *hits a chair as hard as she can.*)

CONNIE. Listen, let's just do the scene, or don't, but let's not do this again.

ELIZABETH. If Stella were to walk through that door right now
how would you want her to see us acting?

Like this, like him, like you?

CARL. Will you please stop talking?!

Do you notice how much I don't talk?

I don't talk all the time. But you?

Just watch the difference between me and you.

ROBERT. I have a blister!

> (KOKO *grabs a mic from the piano and stands in the light of the overhead projector to pray.*)

KOKO. God,

please allow a couple of your rougher angels

to rip a little hole in heaven

and you use it to shit Tennessee Williams' ghost directly into our presence

as we perform the story of *A Streetcar Named Desire*

without the characters of Stanley, Stella, Mitch, or Blanche.

Help us do this idea

even if it turns out to be something stupid

or embarrassing, or impossible.

Help us to be emotionally honest,

at least in little bursts

for as long as we can handle it.

Please guide our company

as we try to find our way without Stella.

Amen.

ELIZABETH. Okay, now let's start.

A STREETCAR NAMED DESIRE
Scene One

The cast performs Scene One of A Streetcar Named Desire—
always without the characters of Stella, Stanley, Mitch and Blanche.

When it's time for an absent character to speak—
in this case Blanche—
the actors treat the audience as the absent character,
looking to the audience and leaving a silence where their lines would be.

The scene begins with Blanche's unexpected arrival at Elysian Fields
and continues up through the point when EUNICE, *Stella's upstairs neighbor,*
leaves Blanche alone in Stella's apartment.

The performance is punctuated by strange laughter—
a part of Stella Burden's Approach to Acting.

CARL REYHOLT AUDITION
10/22/66
Six Years Before Stella Left

THOMAS *enters and introduces his monologue.*

THOMAS. Thanks, Lana.

All right everybody,

I want to give y'all a little background

about how we got here.

Why we're focusing on this part of Stella Burden's life.

Especially since we know so little about it.

But what happened was, in 2007, our company, the Rude Mechs

received support from the Creative Capital Foundation

the MAP Fund and The University of Texas Harry Ransom Center

to travel to South America and do some research

into what became of Stella Burden after she left the U.S.

But when we got back we decided the more interesting story

wasn't what we discovered in Ecuador and Peru.

We thought we could say the most about Stella Burden

by focusing on the people she left behind,

the company who continued working without their guru—

actors who had each been handpicked by Stella herself

through a series of bizarre interviews and auditions like this.

>(*An overhead is placed on the projector which reads:*
>**Carl Reyholt's Audition**
>**10/22/66**
>**Six Years Before Stella Left**

THOMAS *carries a chair to center-stage to reenact* CARL's *audition.*)

CARL. My name is Carl Reyholt.

I'll be performing a monologue of self-composition.

>(CARL *then crawls under the chair to begin balled up on the ground.*
>*As he speaks he grows like a flower.*
>*It is intensely odd.*)

I am dirt.

I'm nothing but mud and sticks.

I'm not even a kind of person yet.

I need you to make me, Stella.

Make me into an actor.

I wanna be a great actor.

>(CARL *knocks the chair over and his audition is interrupted.*)

I thought I would already be fantastic by now—

I thought I would hear more applause if I stood on stage this long by now—

not free applause/cheap applause
but sweat applause/hard work applause—
I wanna deserve that effort—
I wanna deserve everything!
I'm looking for a new way.
I'm not just talking about my character.
I'm asking: how does one become oneself?
That's what I'm hoping you can do for me, Stella Burden.
That's what I'm hoping you can do for me, the Method Gun.

I know one thing, if you say, "go there,"
I swear, I will go all the way there,
whether you mean out there, go there

> (*And* CARL *performs a singular physical feat.*)

or go there, in here.

> (*And* CARL *disappears into his own heart.*)

REHEARSAL
3/18/74
One Year Until Opening Night

Projection: **REHEARSAL**
> **3/18/74**
> **One Year Until Opening Night**

KOKO *practices a riff on the piano.*
ELIZABETH *enters with a script to give notes.*
The others gather around on the floor.
CONNIE *brings a beer to* CARL
and noticeably does not bring a beer to ELIZABETH.

ELIZABETH. All right. Here are my notes on the first *Streetcar* scene.
Nothing new happened.
Nothing happened at all.
It's the same as it always is.

CARL. So I guess the question is
are we trying to find new stuff
or are we trying to make what we have perfect?

CONNIE. Stop it.

> (KOKO *bangs on the piano and crosses to the others.*)

KOKO. We have to start rehearsing harder.
We have to start believing what we do.
We have to watch out for one another
and trust that someone's watching out for you.

That way we don't have to watch out for ourselves
which you can never really do anyway.
We have to start assuming what we believe
we want
has already happened
in the future.

> (KOKO *exits and then after a moment re-enters.*)

But God, no, I agree with what I think you're saying.
I wish Stella was back already.
Amen.

CONNIE. Stop praying.

ROBERT. What do you care?!

CONNIE. I'm an atheist.

ROBERT. What you are is a fucking mystery to me
and I hope it stays that way, forever.
And if I do start to understand you,
I would rather a plane crash through the ceiling
and land on my face.

ELIZABETH. But I do think I'm panicking.
I think I'm panicking.
I think I'm having a panic attack.

CONNIE. That isn't how we're gonna perform it.
That's just rehearsal.
The performance will be full of risk and tension.
Tension and risk.

ELIZABETH. What should I do?

> (CARL *goes to the Shinto shrine and gets the soap tiger.*)

CARL. Maybe we should ask the tiger?

> (ELIZABETH *shakes her head in frustration.*)

ROBERT. Let me hold you for a second.
Come on.
Just for a second.
Let me hold you.

ELIZABETH. Is this a good idea?

> (ROBERT *crosses the stage and holds* ELIZABETH.
> *When he lets her go*
> *everyone is clearly uncomfortable—*
> CARL *approaches to hug* ELIZABETH *as well*
> *but his affections are unwanted*
> *and the gesture dissolves into an awkward conversation.*)

CARL. Is it hot outside?

ELIZABETH. It's the same as it always is.

A DRAMATURGICAL LIST
OF ALL THE THINGS IN THE WORLD
THAT A PLAY WOULD BE BETTER
IF IT HAD AT LEAST ONE OF

A TIGER *runs onstage and hops on the back of the piano.*

The TIGER *is performed by one of the actors in a tiger costume
and given voice by* JASON
who sits in the chair with the reading lamp on and speaks into a mic.

TIGER. Hi everybody! Hello. Hello. I am a tiger!

Is there a John in the house tonight?

Is there a Lizabeth or a Liz or a Beth?

Hello, Elizabeth. Hello, John.

I want to be personal to each one of you.

I am the only tiger in this play.

I arrive to deliver a serious dramaturgical list

of all the things in the world

that a play would be better if it had at least one of.

Okay. Numero Uno. A tiger.

And that's it. That's the end of the list.

I think we all can agree

that given a choice between *Death of a Salesman*

and *Death of a Salesman From a Tiger*

that the second one just seems more exciting!

But what in particular, you wonder, makes tigers so well suited for the modern
   drama?

That's a good question, Lizabeth.

I am glad you asked, John.

Tigers are good for plays because of the simple fact that we are a symbol.

It turns out tigers are both extremely dangerous and extremely beautiful—

Tigers represent both life on this planet and death—

so I'm surprised there are not a lot more plays with tigers in them.

I mean let's have some different kinds of plays! Am I right!?

You know Freud said, blah blah blah bullshit fuck

I don't give a fuck what Freud said.

This play has a tiger! And I am this play's tiger! Your tiger! For you!

So if you have trouble for a scene

or don't want to follow all the exposition stuff—

just remember, any moment, any moment

I could run through and eat the person you are most bored with
or the person you are most interested in
or the person you are sitting next to. Be careful.
Now, tiger, goodbye!
Bongos!

A STREETCAR NAMED DESIRE
Scene One (continued)

The actors continue with their Streetcar *rehearsals.*
STEVE *and* PABLO *enter laughing.*
STEVE *is telling* PABLO *a joke.*
Their revelry is interrupted when STEVE*'s wife,* EUNICE, *begins screaming that he's late for dinner.*
STEVE *yells to* PABLO *to get beer for the poker game later.*
The scene breaks down when EUNICE *tells* STEVE—

EUNICE. Well, never mind about that.
You just get yourself home here once in a while.

> (*The actress playing* EUNICE *breaks character, noticing and disdaining her own voice.*)

ELIZABETH. Whiiiile. Whiiiiiiiiile.
I hate the sound of my own voice.

REHEARSAL
1/16/75
Six Months Until Opening Night

SHAWN *introduces the next rehearsal—*
SHAWN. The Rude Mechs' interest in the Stella Burden Company
began with the question: Why?
Did they stay together
strictly for the sake of the show?
Or did they get so used to rehearsing
they couldn't function in a world in which things actually happen?
Couldn't hold down jobs teaching theatre
in small liberal arts colleges around the country?
Where you can't just make things up
and then ask for a do-over when things go wrong.
You have to remember this is before any of 'em know
what kind of influence they're gonna have.

> (ROBERT *crosses to* KOKO *with an ice pack and apologizes.*)

ROBERT. I'm sorry.
SHAWN. They have no idea what happens on opening night.

At this point they don't even know if they're ever gonna actually perform the show for an audience.

> (*A slide is placed on the overhead which reads—*
> **REHEARSAL**
> **1/16/75**
> **Six Months Until Opening Night**
>
> KOKO *places an ice pack on her arm and begins crying.*
> CARL *uses the soap tiger to voice opinions.*
> *All the others leave the stage.*)

CARL. You have to have faith in the final production.

KOKO. I don't.

CARL. No, no, no.—
You have to.

KOKO. I don't.

CARL. I don't believe you.

KOKO. I don't have faith in anything anymore.
The play.
The technique.
Nothing.
I'll be better in a little while.
I'll get it back.
Just let's do something besides *Streetcar* for a while.

> (CARL, *trying to hide his excitement, runs to the overhead projector to place the slide and call out the next scene.*)

TRAINING TECHNIQUE: Kissing Practice

The overhead CARL *places on the projector*
reads: **TRAINING TECHNIQUE: Kissing Practice.**

CARL. KISSING PRACTICE!

> (*They gather in a line downstage facing the audience.*
>
> *One of them puts a record on the record player.*
>
> *Then the actors begin kissing.*
>
> *They do it rhythmically based on the following text from*
> Theatre: Art in Action © *Glencoe/McGraw Hill.*)

>> "*Romantic scenes require careful rehearsal. They should be rehearsed privately with the director before they are attempted in rehearsals with the entire cast.*
>> "*There are four key parts to a successful stage kiss: (1) proper foot position; (2) correct body position; (3) exact time count; and (4) a*

smooth break. The script or the director will tell you what kind of kiss is needed in the scene—a motherly peck or a romantic embrace. The first part is getting into the embrace. The woman usually faces the audience with her feet about six inches apart. The man then steps toward the woman on the foot closet to her, puts that foot between her feet and swings around so that they end up facing each other.

"Body position is the second part of a stage kiss. For most romantic kisses little or no light should be seen between the couple. The woman should be facing the audience, and the man should be facing her, his back squarely toward the audience. The couple should decide ahead of time which way they will tilt their heads—to the right or to the left. The couple does not have to make any actual physical contact at all; many professional actors do not. Correct foot and body position give the illusion of a real kiss.

"The third and most important part of the kiss is the count. A sweet romantic kiss lasts one second; a reasonably romantic kiss lasts two seconds; and a very romantic kiss lasts from three to five seconds. Anything over five seconds will usually cause the wrong audience response.

"Perhaps the most difficult part of the stage embrace is the parting or separation of the couple. First, it must be done with the same emotional value as the kiss established, usually a smooth slow release. Second, it is important for the couple to maintain physical contact with the hands until the "break"—the actual separation. To do this, the couple slowly pulls apart while sliding their hands down each other's arms. The break may occur at the forearms, or the couple may continue until they are holding hands. Then they may step away from each other, gently releasing their hands."

(The actors continue practicing until the record runs out.)

CONNIE TORREY
TELEVISION INTERVIEW, *STAGE FOCUS!*
HOSTED BY CONRAD RILKE
1972
The Year Stella Left

The actors arrange the chairs and the birdcage in the center of the room.
HANNAH *is being interviewed by* THOMAS.
*The rest of the cast uses the available A/V equipment
to simulate filming.*
For instance a filmstrip projector held on the shoulder is a projector.
The mic stand is used as a boom.

Projection: **CONNIE TORREY**
                TELEVISION INTERVIEW, *STAGE FOCUS!*
                HOSTED BY CONRAD RILKE
                1972
                The Year Stella Left

HANNAH. This next scene is complete bullshit.
It's not based on an interview or a re-creation.
What it says on the overhead—that's a lie.
This scene is from an old version of the play,
an early version,
in which everything was just made up—
because none of the members of the Stella Burden Company
ever wrote down exactly which exercises were
and which exercises were not part of the Approach.
But the reason we kept this scene in the show is because
when Connie Torrey, the member of Stella's company who I play—
when we were asking her if she would help us—
she was hesitant and wanted to see what we had so far
and when she read that old draft of the play
for some reason she said this scene was so true.

CONRAD. Why did Stella Burden quit working?

CONNIE. Stella didn't quit working.
She quit getting hired.
Who can afford nine years of rehearsal anymore?
You see?

CONRAD. Not sure I do.

CONNIE. Stella's ideas became beyond understanding.
That's the point of her Approach to acting.
Not to explain "how to" in a word-for-word way
but to escape explanation
so the only map is in if you follow her.

CONRAD. What did Stella mean when she said she wanted to, quote,
"eat beauty and shit truth."

> (*On the word "shit"* LANA *makes a beeping sound
> to simulate the censoring of curse words on television.*)

CONNIE. Did Stella say that?
Of course she did.
But not to be taken seriously word for word—
she just wanted to be taken seriously as a woman who has ideas.
When you hire Stella you hire her ideas.

CONRAD. And this so-called performance she had planned for the Pentagon—

to wander thru with nothing but balloons tied to her breasts—
What is that in protest to?

CONNIE. Boredom it sounds like.
Stella wanted to use her life as a stage
for the performance of all her desires.

CONRAD. And did she happen to mention what those desires were?

> (CONNIE *might choose to act some of the following desires out.*)

CONNIE. She taught them to us, one by one.
To kiss strangers who look good to us.
To laugh louder than most people can yell.
And to use real beer in every rehearsal
no matter how early or what brand.

CONRAD. Doesn't that get expensive?

CONNIE. We will run out of money eventually.
Until then we'll keep going.

CONRAD. All right.
Let's talk about these rehearsals of *A Streetcar Named Desire*.

> (CONNIE *is looking at the camera man.*)

CONNIE. I'm sorry.
I got distracted.

CONRAD. I asked how rehearsal was going.

CONNIE. On TV there's only what you're supposed to see
but the theatre's full of everything else.

> (CONNIE *hops up and begins running in a circle around the room*
> *calling out things she likes,*
> *for instance: a man's sweater, a woman's haircut, or a nice pair of shoes.*)

That's what I like to look at.

CONRAD. Does the company miss Stella?

> (CONNIE *sadly comes back to the interview.*)

CONNIE. She was a fantastic resource to have on our side.
Not only did she know how to—
It's hard to describe.
She gave us ourselves.
And now we don't even have that.

CONRAD. You've been left to your own devices.

CONNIE. No. We have a couple old high school acting textbooks
we look at when we have a question.
And there's a filmstrip entitled what "Makes an Actor"
that was left in the machine by someone who used to use our rehearsal room.
And of course we still have exercises from Stella Burden's Approach.

CONRAD. Aren't you afraid that observers will confuse
one with the other
and we'll lose what Stella intended.

CONNIE. I think Stella intended to confuse observers
from time to time.
We don't even know why she left
and we're the closest thing she has to family.

CONRAD. You don't think she's coming back?

CONNIE. She left her gun.

CONRAD. What does that mean?

CONNIE. She always keeps a loaded gun in the rehearsal room,
to remind us we can kill each other,
or her,
or ourselves, I guess.
It's right here in this birdcage.

> (*One of the "cameramen" points his filmstrip projector
> at the birdcage and makes a beautiful shadow of the gun on the back wall.*)

CONRAD. Is it real?

CONNIE. You wanna find out?

CONRAD. How do you mean?

CONNIE. That's what our work is!
The acting approach Stella teaches isn't a way of getting to something,
it's a way of deserving what you get.
How much did you pay for that camera?

CONRAD. It belongs to the studio.

> (CONNIE *reaches out to touch the camera.*)

You're supposed to act like it's not there.

CONNIE. See? You know how I'm supposed to act.
That's why it's your show.

CONRAD. You're right.
It is my show.
and I think we've got enough.

CONNIE. But who's gonna watch it?
Who's gonna be the audience
if everyone has something burning
to be made, or done, or written, or shot?

> (CONNIE *steals the mic from* CONRAD.)

We can't all be the star.
Someone has to play the small roles.

CONRAD. So that's why Stella Burden left the theater?

(CONRAD *exits without waiting for a reply.*)

CONNIE. She only left the country.

The theater is bigger than that.

She went to the jungle so you and I would have more room here.

The last thing she said to me was,

"watch out,"

so that's my advice to you.

A STREETCAR NAMED DESIRE
Scene Two

The actors continue with their Streetcar *rehearsals.*

THOMAS *is a* TAMALE VENDOR.

He pushes a tamale cart with an umbrella across the stage calling out—

VENDOR'S VOICE. Red-hot!

Red-hot!

THOMAS *exits as the* TAMALE VENDOR.

ROBERT "HOPS" GILBERT
AS TOLD TO CARL REYHOLT
Approx. 5/12/75
Two Months Until Opening Night

An overhead is placed on the projector which reads:

ROBERT "HOPS" GILBERT
AS TOLD TO CARL REYHOLT
Approx. 5/12/75
Two Months Until Opening Night

Throughout, ROBERT *gets a beer from the ice chest and drinks it.*

ROBERT. You know, what I think's wrong—

The gods—they're tired of us

They think our stories are boring.

They think our theater stinks.

It really gets to you after a while.

(CARL *crosses,* ROBERT *points him out.*)

And actors are freaks, you know?

You spend all your time with a bunch of actors

and before you know it, you're a freak yourself.

Can't avoid it.

I got a tattoo, see?

(ROBERT *shows off his tattoo.*
The audience's reaction is discouraging.)

Looks stupid, doesn't it?
That's it. I'm getting to be a freak, too.
I'm not a complete idiot, yet,
I can still use my head, but my heart…
I don't have any passion for anything anymore.
I don't want anything.
I don't need anything.
I don't love anybody—
No, that's not right.
I do love you, Stella Burden.
She found me and gave me work
and now the work I get is based on that work—

I got time off from rehearsal a couple weeks ago to teach that fight choreography
workshop in Cleveland
with a bunch of college kids. Now *they're* passionate.
So many signed up I had to do two sessions, four hours each.
It was very successful.
But I just couldn't get the spirit of the thing.
Hour after hour showing kids how to fake a fight.
I kept having this dumb fantasy that when I turned my back
they were gonna rush me all at once and tear me apart, limb from limb,
but as long as they kept coming up one at a time
I could keep teaching them into submission.

Finally, after eight hours
I was locking the classroom door behind me
and this one last little freak scared the shit out of me
asking a question about how he should "disengage."

I said "show me" and his lunge was so earnest
he stepped on my toe
and then I was filled passion.
A blind rage came over me
and I actually cocked my fist like I was gonna hit him
and he cowered.

I mean, we're supposed to be paving the way for a new generation of artists…
You think in a hundred years artists are going to admire us for the way we
live now?
They won't.

A STREETCAR NAMED DESIRE
Scene Three

The actors continue with their Streetcar *rehearsals.*
STEVE *and* PABLO *sit at the kitchen table and play poker.*

STEVE *tells another off-color joke.*
The pauses for the absent Mitch's speech are elongated
as Mitch is distracted.

Suddenly STEVE *and* PABLO *throw their cards in the air*
and rush forward…grappling and cursing.
Something is overturned with a crash.

The men wrestle until things get out of hand.
They run off as STEVE *yells—*

STEVE. Let's get quick out of here.

MY BIG PLAN FOR THE SHOW

The TIGER *is pushed on inside the metal ice chest,*
growling
and swinging at the actors.

TIGER. Oh dammit! Dammit. Dammit. Dammit.
Did I just miss them? That sucks. That sucks so hard.
But you keep watching.
Eventually I will catch an actor
and eat it. That's my big plan for the show.

This, also, reminds me of a joke:
Two tigers are eating a clown
and one of them turns to the other and says,
"Does this taste funny to you?"

It's so strange to want to eat somebody.
I'm not even hungry most of the time.
Usually I'm just bored.

I used to love birds. I used to have a rule
I would never eat a bird.
Then one day I broke the rule.
I don't know why.
I wish I never did it.
But we have a saying in Tigersville—
"You can't uneat a bird."
And all I can tell you about that is this:

It's so fucking true you don't even know it.
That's what it's like to want to eat somebody—
Not hunger so much as the feeling
that a part of you is missing
then you start to think
maybe the missing part is shaped like that bird there
and so you do what a tiger does
but the empty feeling doesn't go away—
you feel as empty as the sky—
then you know what they mean when they say,
you can't uneat a bird,
or an Elizabeth, for that matter, or a John.
Bongos!

A STREETCAR NAMED DESIRE
Plot Summary

LANA *sits at the piano and recaps* A Streetcar Named Desire
as she plays "Paper Moon."
SHAWN, HANNAH, *and* THOMAS
come out and mop up the beer from the previous scene
by standing on towels and scooting around
in a kind of cleaning-up soft-shoe.

JASON *shows overheads from the* Streetcar *movie.*

LANA. Alright! So we weren't sure how familiar you all are with *A Streetcar Named Desire*. Or, if you are familiar with it, really how long has it been since you last read the play or saw a production? As we started researching and re-creating Burden's work on it, we were reminded how much we love it. So now, I'm going to very briefly recap the entire play to reignite your own memories and affection for it. And I'm going to accompany myself.

Scene One. Blanche arrives in New Orleans seeking refuge at her sister, Stella's house. Blanche tells Stella their home place, Belle Reve, has been lost. Stanley, Stella's husband, comes home and the conversation becomes awkward.

Scene Two. Stanley looks through Blanche's trunk for the deed of sale to her family's home. Blanche gets upset when he grabs a box of love letters from her dead husband. Stanley lets slip that Stella is pregnant.

Scene Three. Stanley and his friends play poker. Blanche meets Stanley's sensitive friend, Mitch. Stanley is drunk and he hits Stella. Stella runs upstairs to the neighbors, Stanley runs out into the street bellowing his wife's name and ripping off his shirt.

Scene Four. Blanche tries to convince Stella to leave Stanley. Stanley overhears.

Scene Five. Three months have passed. Stanley insinuates that he's heard shameful stories about Blanche's past, then leaves her alone to wonder what he knows. When a young man arrives collecting for the newspaper, Blanche lures him inside and kisses him.

Scene Six. Blanche goes on a date with Mitch. She tells him the story of how her husband died, how she found him in bed with a man, how she told her husband that he disgusted her, and how he shot himself for shame. After years of suffering, Blanche finds comfort with Mitch.

Scene Seven. Stella prepares for a birthday party for Blanche. Stanley tells Stella about Blanche's past. He's found out she's not so innocent or pure or young as she says. Blanche bathes and sings "Paper Moon."

Scene Eight. Blanche has a birthday party. Stanley gives her a bus ticket. Mitch stands her up. Stella goes into labor.

Scene Nine. Mitch comes over and refuses to marry Blanche. Outside, a Mexican woman sells flowers for the dead.

Scene Ten. Stella is in the hospital having their baby. Stanley comes home, puts on his silk pajamas and then rapes Blanche.

Scene Eleven. Blanche tells what Stanley did. Stella doesn't believe her. It drives Blanche crazy. The men play poker as a doctor and a nurse from the sanitarium come to take Blanche away. Upstairs, the baby sleeps like an angel.

CARL REYHOLT
University of Texas
Lecture Demonstration
12/01/77
Five Years After Stella Left

CARL *rolls on a lectern*
and delivers the following lecture.
Projection:
CARL REYHOLT
University of Texas
Lecture Demonstration
12/01/77
Five Years After Stella Left

CARL. Fact: you can't do your best everyday.
That's something Stella understood.
There was this *one day* when I was terrible on stage. Terrible.
Maybe like today. NO! Let's make this a good day.
I'm trying! But effort isn't everything.

At the last few weeks of rehearsal with the company
there was a bad energy.
Everybody was always fighting.
Before she left
when we got that way, Stella used to say, "forget it."
It always hurt my feelings.
But she only ever meant forget it for that night.
We should have tried something else,
something different.
For instance, right now, I wanna dance.

How many of you either work in an office of any kind
or think you might work in an office one day?
Raise your hands. Errrrr. Good.
I guess there's not gonna be a lot of farmers anymore.
But you all *know*—
you can't just stop in the middle of a quarterly sales review that's going terrible
and decide to do something else/something different.
But we can. That's what Stella taught us!
Or we can quit! We can go our separate ways whenever we want!
Or go get tocktails! Fuck it.

This dance is called:
The night rehearsal was terrible.
It felt like the play would never be good in a hundred years.
All our work is wasted.
I feel stupid for even hoping I could make something good.
I wish god would kill me by throwing me between a drunk driver's Chevy Nova
and a baby
who's going to grow up to be a real artist.
Amen.
Now dance!

> (*And then* CARL *dances.*
> *It begins strangely and becomes ecstatic.*
> *At the height of its frenzy*
> CARL *invites you to join him.*)

Everybody do it.

> (*The dance ends and* CARL *is happy, at first.*)

It was fun. It was good. I felt like, YES!
But it probably wouldn't have worked.
They probably wouldn't have joined me.
We would have just kept fighting.

I don't think any of us ever learned a single thing Stella was trying to teach and that's probably why she left.

(CARL *leaves.*)

REHEARSAL
7/6/75
Three Weeks Until Opening Night

ELIZABETH *pursues* ROBERT *onto the stage.*

Projection: **REHEARSAL**
7/6/75
Three Weeks Until Opening Night

ELIZABETH. You're drunk. Aren't you?

ROBERT. No.

ELIZABETH. Don't lie. I can tell.
It wouldn't even matter if you knew your part,
but you're always messing up.

ROBERT. I've never messed up in performance.

ELIZABETH. You hit Koko during the stoop scene.
I'm gonna tell the company.

ROBERT. Don't you pin that on me.

ELIZABETH. You were drunk.
I'm gonna tell the company.
Tell the company.
I'm gonna tell the company.

> (*Then the actors repeat the blocking
> but speak the lines from* Streetcar, *Scene Five,
> between* EUNICE *and* STEVE,
> *as* EUNICE *confronts* STEVE *about his whoring.*)

> (*The projection is changed to read:*
> ***Streetcar* Scene Five**
> *The* Streetcar *re-creation ends.*
> SHAWN *and* JASON *walk through blocking again,
> this time with no text at all.*)

> (*The projection is changed to read:*
> **REHEARSAL**
> **7/14/75**
> **Two Weeks Until Opening Night.**
> JASON *leaves the stage.*
> SHAWN *morphs her blocking into a solo dance.*)

(The projection is changed to read:
REHEARSAL
7/19/75
Twelve Days Until Opening Night

"Dancing in the Moonlight" begins playing.

HANNAH *and* LANA *enter and dance on their chairs.*

SHAWN *goes to play maracas.*

THOMAS *and* JASON *walk through*
completely naked
with balloons tied to their penises.
They linger on the stage experiencing the buoyancy
and trying to make something happen.

HANNAH *and* LANA *watch from their bench.*
They smoke a joint.

Everyone is happy.)

<u>WHAT MAKES AN ACTOR</u>

The actors gather around the projector
and watch a filmstrip we found entitled
"What Makes an Actor?"
After the first nine or ten frames
ELIZABETH *stands up and says—*

ELIZABETH. I hate my voice.
I hate the way my voice sounds.
I hate the way my voice sounds when I'm inside the theater building.
I hate the way my voice feels in my throat.
I hate the way my voice feels in my throat when I project.
I hate the way my voice makes my body jiggle like jello.
I hate my ears.
I hate my odd-shaped ears.
I hate it when he hugs me and his face is right beside one of my ears.
I hate my face.
I hate the way my face looks in stage make-up.
I hate the way my face looks when I laugh.
I hate laughing onstage.
Hahahahahahahahahaha.
I never know what to do with my hands.
I hate my hair.
One day rehearsal was nothing but noticing how often I blink.

I'm surprised I see anything.
I like dancing.
I like to sit and listen to music on stage.
You can hear a song one hundred times in your apartment
but on stage everything is completely transformed.
You take a normal woman from my hometown
put her on stage and play her a song
and if she listens closely
that song will be transformed into the most beautiful song in the world.
And the woman will be transformed, too.
Her ears will grow huge
and her face will contort
and her hands will fly around her body like wounded birds.
I asked Stella why it doesn't happen the other way
Why doesn't the woman grow perfect and live forever?
And Stella wrote out an explanation for me
and put it in this box and locked it
and gave me the key
and told me that whenever I wanted to know the answer
I should unlock the box and open it
and take out the letter
and light it on fire
and read as much of it as I can before it burns out.

TRAINING TECHNIQUE: Rasa Boxes
7/21/75
One Week Until Opening Night
Projection: **TRAINING TECHNIQUE: Rasa Boxes**

The rest of the company gathers around ELIZABETH
at the box that contains the letter.

CARL. Maybe that's what Stella's doing in South America.
Maybe she's writing a book.
Explaining all this.
And she's in South America to get perspective on it.

> *(The company sets about using chalk*
> *to turn the stage into a 3 x 3 grid.*
> *In each box they write:*
> *Kissing, Despair, Fight*
> *Joy, Horse, Madness*
> *Confrontational Vulgarity, Stanley, Foreign Repose.*

As they draw on the stage
ROBERT *stands in the middle of the stage*
just talking.)

ROBERT. That's all we need is another book about theater.
We don't understand the ones we have.
They shouldn't publish any more books for ten years.
Let us catch up.
They should shoot authors on sight.
People publish and publish, but what?
For 25 years Stella's been lecturing and writing
about shit smart people already know
and stupid people have no interest in.

> *(The others continue working*
> *even as they respond to* ROBERT.)

KOKO. You've changed.

ROBERT. Because I'm alive.
I'm fucking growing.
I know you liked me better when I was an acorn,
but I'm an oak tree.
I'M AN OAK TREE.

KOKO. You act like a fucking oak tree.

ROBERT. What does that mean?

KOKO. You said it. How should I know?

ROBERT. Well if I do it's because you did it to me.

KOKO. Don't blame the company.
Every second of your life.
Every inch.
That's you choosing.
I can't wait 'til we finish this play
and I can be done with you.

CARL. I just want to point out I'm not talking.

CONNIE. Okay, now let's start.

ROBERT. I'm sorry.
I won't say another word except, I'm sorry.
I'm sorry.

> *(The company does an exercise based on Rasa Boxes.*
> *It looks like people running to different parts of the stage*
> *and performing in a style associated with the physical space.*
> *So in "Fight" the actors perform the fight from* Streetcar.
> *Joy is joyous, Madness is crazy, Foreign Language in repose*

is the actors speaking the lines below in a foreign language while lying down.
Despair is depressing. Romantic is the actors moving through the steps of Kissing
Practice.
The Stanley is the actors pretending to rip their shirts while screaming the lines below.
And Confrontational Vulgarity involves the actors making the most reprehensible
gestures.

When compelled to speak the actors use the following lines from Streetcar:)

EUNICE. I heard about you and that blonde!

STEVE. That's a damn lie!

NTU THEATRE CONFERENCE
BIRMINGHAM, AL ARTIST PANEL
3/6/2007
35 Years After Stella Left

The actors gather downstage and sit as at a panel.

An overhead projects **NTU Theatre Conference**
Birmingham, AL Artist Panel
3/6/2007
35 Years After Stella Left

LANA. We would like to take a moment
to thank the people who taught us this—
the Stella Burden Company.
They meant so much to our company
so it was a dream come true to meet them
and they all were so generous with information
about the Approach
and Stella Burden
and even their personal lives—
with the possible exception of Carl
who anytime we asked him something personal would say—

THOMAS. "Can we talk about something else?"

LANA. But it was Carl who arranged a lot of the interviews for us—
and who put together this sort of a reunion panel
at which someone from an audience very much like this
asked Koko Bond:

> (LANA *hands an index card to an audience member that says*
> *"How did you become a part of the company?"*)

KOKO. That's a good question.
I'm glad you asked!
My audition for Stella Burden consisted of one question.

She asked me to choose: Truth or Beauty?

      (KOKO *surveys the audience: Truth or Beauty?*)

I didn't know what to choose.
I didn't even know what part I was trying out for.

CARL. Me too.

KOKO. I always thought
if I ever got cast in a production of *A Streetcar Named Desire*
it would be to play the part of Blanche DuBois—

CONNIE. She didn't know yet.

      (KOKO *as Blanche*—)

KOKO. —she walks through the door of this strange place
and meets all these freaks with no manners,
always yelling at one another—

ROBERT. I NEVER YELLED!

KOKO. and because it's New Orleans—
you can imagine everyone smelled
like smoke and booze and sweat and sex—

CARL. Can we talk about something else.

KOKO. —which is how I felt
the first time I walked into that rehearsal room.

CONNIE. I remember you only watched at first.

KOKO. The company went to work
and I became Stanley—

ROBERT. How?

      (KOKO *as Stanley*—)

KOKO. They were all so refined.

CARL. Not all of us.

CONNIE. What we seemed like.

KOKO. The way you spoke to one another.
Your vocabularies.
Saying all this about risk and truth—
stage left is on your right—

ROBERT. I still don't know that.

KOKO. And when someone in a theatre says "heads"
you never look up
so whatever's falling doesn't mess up your pretty face.

CONNIE. —those lucky enough.

KOKO. They all knew stuff,
simple stuff it seems like now—

CARL. I'm still trying to forget—

KOKO. but *then* it seemed like you were refined
and I was just some kind of bum.

CONNIE. No.

KOKO. Yeah.

CONNIE. No. You were refined.
You dressed nice.
I always liked that blue dress you wore.

KOKO. Yeah. No. I know.
I wore it because you told me.

CARL. See?

KOKO. I started acting like Mitch around you.

CONNIE. No.

(KOKO *as Mitch*—)

KOKO. Yeah. All of you.
But you especially,
I had such a crush.
I was older
but I was your puppy dog
—I would do whatever they wanted.

ROBERT. Seriously, she would.

KOKO. I chose truth.
I chose to believe what they told me.

CONNIE. (*Giggling.*) Shit.

KOKO. I believed them
when they told me Sunday rehearsals started at six in the morning
so they could see the sunrise.
Which I did see and it was beautiful.

CARL. See?

KOKO. They heard me praying once
and told me Stella couldn't stand any secrets.
If I had something to say
I had to grab a mic
and say it to the whole group.

CONNIE. I'm so sorry.

KOKO. And I believed we would never do anything
that would ever actually get anyone hurt.
I mean, we were pushing boundaries
but within limits
I thought.

But it didn't matter.
I would have kept going no matter.

CARL. We couldn't.

KOKO. So it turns out, of course,
the perfect part for me would have been Stella.

ROBERT. Not Burden.

> (KOKO *as Stella*—)

KOKO. Right.
I mean, Stella Kowalski.
'Cause, no matter how small the house is.
Or how little money there is.
No matter who gets drunk.
No matter how much yelling there is.
I'm the true believer.
You know, Blanche is the one who goes crazy in that play
but Stella's the one who keeps coming back for more.

> (KOKO *off mic, pleading with her old company members.*)

We should of kept going.
I'd do it again today.
Or start a new show.
Or we could just start over.
I want to.
Just to stand next to you
and know you're there—
know—
you'll always be there.
'Cause I'll always be there for you.
You know what I mean?
You know?
I don't know if you can understand me.
I don't know if you ever did.
…
I would give my life's savings
if I could make myself understood to you after all these years.

> (CONNIE *rises and goes to* KOKO *and hugs her.*
> *After a moment* KOKO *breaks the embrace to explain to* CONNIE—)

It's not much.
I haven't managed to save hardly anything at all.
In fact I probably owe more in credit cards than I have in savings.

CONNIE. I know. Me too.

> (ROBERT *gets up and joins the hug.*)

ROBERT. Yeah. Me too.

> (CARL *approaches awkwardly*
> *as he did* ELIZABETH *earlier in the play*
> *only this time he is accepted into the hug.*)

REHEARSAL
7/24/75
Six Days Until Opening Night

The group hug breaks up
and all exit the stage except ROBERT.

An overhead is projected which reads:
REHEARSAL
7/24/75
Six Days Until Opening Night

ELIZABETH *enters and says—*

ELIZABETH. I don't want you to be angry anymore.

ROBERT. Why not?

ELIZABETH. It's so wrong for you.
You're a happy person,
you have a nice voice,
you know what to do with your hands,
and more than that, you're…you're a pretty man.
People pay money just to look at you.
But you're so angry all the time.

ROBERT. I'm angry because we're always fighting.
I guess I just won't fight anymore.

ELIZABETH. Promise me?

ROBERT. I promise.

> (ROBERT *hugs* ELIZABETH.)

I'm completely and totally at peace.
See?
I'm totally at peace and I'll stay that way for the rest of my life.

> (*The two sit together and watch the following* Streetcar *reenactments.*)

A STREETCAR NAMED DESIRE
Scene Five (continued)

CARL *enters as the* PAPER BOY
collecting for the Evening Star—
He allows himself to be lured inside by the absent Blanche.

He takes out his lighter and sparks it
and holds it aloft for her absent cigarette—
and then he leans forward to kiss her absent lips.

A STREETCAR NAMED DESIRE
Scene Nine

CONNIE *enters with a basket of flowers*
and performs the MEXICAN WOMAN.

She is at the door and offers Blanche some of her flowers.

Blanche darts back into the apartment slamming the door.
The MEXICAN WOMAN *turns away and starts to move down the street.*

The MEXICAN WOMAN *turns slowly and drifts back off with her soft*
mournful cries.

The Streetcar *re-creation ends.*

REHEARSAL
7/26/75
Four Days Until Opening Night

ELIZABETH, ROBERT *and* CARL *gather at the table to drink shots.*

Projection: **REHEARSAL**
            7/26/75
            Four Days Until Opening Night

ELIZABETH. Stella isn't coming back.
Think about it.
Would you?

CARL. I would come back.

ELIZABETH. I disagree.

ROBERT. You don't know what he would do.

ELIZABETH. I'm not asking what he would do.
I'm asking what he would do if he was Stella.
It's different.
We know what he would do.
He's doing it.
He's done it.
Did you know he proposed to me once?
Remember?

CARL. I remember.

ELIZABETH. It was the worst proposal ever.

CARL. I guess you could of said yes.

ROBERT. Then you would really be miserable.

ELIZABETH. In your mind it was going to be good, right?

CARL. Oh yeah. In my mind I was going to sweep you off my/off of your feet.

ELIZABETH. Well, you didn't. It didn't work.
It was just another question somebody asked me that I had to say no to.
I didn't want you to marry me and I still don't.
I think I would make the worst wife in the world.
You're lucky I'm so smart.

ROBERT. You really are.

CARL. Can we talk about something else?

ELIZABETH. Sure.

ROBERT. What?

ELIZABETH. Is it hot outside?

CARL. It's the same as it always is.

> (CARL *exits broken-hearted.*
> ELIZABETH *and* ROBERT *begin the final* Streetcar *scene.*)

A STREETCAR NAMED DESIRE
Final Scene

STEVE *sits alone with a bottle of whiskey*
and a handful of playing cards.
He is playing poker with the absent Stanley and Mitch.

ELIZABETH *portrays his wife,* EUNICE—
She talks to the absent Blanche.
Telling Blanche how wonderful she looks.
But EUNICE *ends up standing alone crying*
as in Crying Practice.

CARL *and* KOKO *enter as a* DOCTOR *and a* MATRON.
The gravity of their profession is exaggerated—
The DOCTOR *rings the doorbell.*
EUNICE *opens the door for them.*

The absent Blanche suddenly gasps
and rushes past the DOCTOR *into the bedroom.*
The MATRON *advances*
catching hold of the absent Blanche's wrist.

EUNICE *takes the absent Stella into her arms.*
The DOCTOR *takes off his hat and he becomes personalized.*
He tells the absent Blanche to let go.
She does.

And the DOCTOR *and the* MATRON *exit with the absent Blanche.*

The men continue playing poker.

OPENING NIGHT
7/29/75

The full company enters and begins setting up for the final scene.

Projection: **OPENING NIGHT**
7/29/75

ROBERT. All right. Now we all know it—
so I think the question becomes
are we still gonna perform this with all the risk and tension
the way Stella had planned?
Or have any of us changed our minds about that?

ELIZABETH. What are you pissed off about?

ROBERT. Why are you doing this?

ELIZABETH. We can't live on ticket sales and teaching.
So, I thought of this plan.
This is just the rough, stupid version, okay?
I formally propose we cancel the show and sell all the equipment.
We then invest the capital in a no-load municipal bond fund,
earn four or five per cent,
and use it to get a little cottage in Mexico and continue our studies.

CARL. Say that again?

ELIZABETH. I said we would invest the money in a no-load municipal
bond fund
and get a little place in Mexico, together.

CARL. Not Mexico—you said something else.

ELIZABETH. I propose to cancel the show and sell all the equipment.

CARL. Aha! That was it!
So you are going to dissolve the company?
Perfect. Great idea.
And what do you propose to do with us?

ELIZABETH. I can't solve everything with one sentence.
I think we have to figure this out as we go.

CARL. Oh my god.
I never understood a single thing until now.
I was stupid, so I thought the company belonged to all of us.
And because one stupid thought leads to another
I thought the equipment also belonged to all of us.

KOKO. It does. It's all of ours.

ELIZABETH. I didn't say it wasn't.

ROBERT. But you're going to sell it anyway.

CONNIE. None of this makes any sense to me.

ELIZABETH. I can't figure out why you're so upset.
I'm not pretending my little scheme is perfect or anything,
and if you all don't like it
I'm not going to insist on it. (*A pause.*)
I'm sorry I ever started this conversation.

CONNIE. Why don't we just go get the gun
and then do a little research
and find a bad business
or a bad person
and take all their money?
Because I know if we put as much time
and energy into that as we do into this
we could do it right
and no one would get hurt
and everyone would end up happy in the end.

CARL. Who gets to hold the gun?

ELIZABETH. You're so fucking stupid.
Both of you.

KOKO. Stella saw potential in us.
She started working with us because we each had potential in different things.
But we haven't done it.
Our potential is still waiting for us to come get it.
It's just waiting in our hearts or our heads or our bodies,
wherever we each have it—
our potential is just waiting and wondering why the fuck we haven't shown
up yet.
When will we get there? It's getting late.

ELIZABETH. Can't anyone make her stop?

CARL. YOU SHUT UP!
I want to have my say too.

CONNIE. You already had your say.

CARL. You all wrecked my life.
I never lived.
You're all old,
but I'm still young,
but just barely.
My best young years are totally cashed.
There's a great big chunk of my life that's in total defeasance.

ROBERT. What's defeasance?
Where do you get that word?

CARL. You're still young, too.
Run away with me. Please.

CONNIE. No way.

CARL. I'm brave. I'm smart.
I could be a Schopenhauer
or the Dostoyevsky of acting.
Whatever that means.
Holy shit. I've lost it.
I'm totally nuts!
Stella!

       (CARL *goes and gets the gun.*)

KOKO. God.
Rip the hole now.
Reach down and choose me.
Pick me up
and carry me away.

CONNIE. Stop praying.
Whatever you pray
I pray the exact opposite.
Silently to myself.
I've been doing it for years.

       (CARL *shoots at* ELIZABETH.)

ELIZABETH. What the fuck is wrong with you?!
Take that thing away from him.
He's fucking shooting that thing at me!

CARL. Why won't she die?
Am I missing?
Oh, fuck me!

ROBERT. (*Quietly.*) It's a prop gun.
It fires blanks.

ELIZABETH. I quit.
That's what happens next.
My name is Elizabeth Johns and I quit.
You know, it just gets to be too much
and the woman that I play,
Elizabeth Johns, turns to her friends
and she tells them:
No more.
No more.

Not because of the fighting.
Or because he pointed Stella's gun at me.
Or because, of course, it's fake.
But just everything.
The small things.
The beer.
You never bring me a beer.
And I don't want to hear about family anymore.
And no one ever says "good work" anymore.
And I hate you.
We're not bringing honor to Stella's name.
We're not.
So after the one and only performance of this stupid version of Streetcar
she's done.
She's leaving.
And she's never coming back.
This is bullshit.
The Approach is bullshit.
And Stella is bullshit.
And everything we've done is nothing.

7/30/75
THE FINAL PERFORMANCE OF
THE STELLA BURDEN COMPANY

*Lights swing down on the end of ten-foot steel poles
and continue swinging as we work through the whole of* Streetcar
*doing all of the blocking among the pendulums without any text.
It is beautiful and dangerous.*

BAD NEWS

*As the pendulums slowly stop swinging
the actors all sort of fade away leaving* ELIZABETH *alone on stage.*
ELIZABETH *gets Stella's letter and carries it to the table
but before she can read it
the* TIGER *enters to take* ELIZABETH JOHNS *away.*

TIGER. Okay, I've got some bad news for you—
Elizabeth Johns.
I am your tiger.
All your screaming and waving your hands—
it attracted my attention
And now I've got you.
You're going to have to come with me.

(*Nothing for a second.*)

ELIZABETH. Where are we going?

TIGER. I don't know, but you can't stay here.
You're no longer a part of this.

ELIZABETH. Wait a minute, Tiger.
I need to read the letter.
I mean, she wrote it to me.

TIGER. Are you sure you want to do that?

> (ELIZABETH *answers by lighting the letter on fire and reading what she can—*
> *it will read something like—*)

ELIZABETH. "If you ever believed something stupid—If you ever accepted something as true just because it was beautiful—you get another chance…"

> (*The letter burns out.*
> *The* TIGER *gives* ELIZABETH *its arm*
> *and as the two of them exit…*)

TIGER. You gonna be all right?

> (SHAWN *answers yes or no.*)

Where are you gonna go?

> (SHAWN *answers a place.*)

You think we'll fit in there?

> (SHAWN *answers yes or no.*)

I wonder. I wonder.

CRYING PRACTICE

The actors gather at the front for Crying Practice.

They leave a space where ELIZABETH *used to stand.*

After about a minute of crying the footed bowl bursts into flames burning up all the names which the audience wrote down.

Then the names the audience wrote down scroll across the screen as if projected from the film projector.

*When the names finish scrolling by
the egg timer goes off
and the lights go out.*

End of Play

THE CHERRY SISTERS REVISITED
by Dan O'Brien
music by Michael Friedman

ABOUT *THE CHERRY SISTERS REVISITED*

This article first ran in the January/February 2010 issue of Inside Actors, *and is based on conversations with the creators before rehearsals for the Humana Festival production began.*

"The vaudeville is both familiar and strange, which makes it uncanny, even haunting," says playwright Dan O'Brien. *The Cherry Sisters Revisited* takes us to a ghostly realm, where vaudeville and contemporary theatre, past and present, collide and coexist. The Cherry Sisters were five motherless girls-of-a-certain-age on the cold, windswept Iowa prairie who thought they could be as good as those big-city vaudeville stars who came through a few times a year. They fell prey to the dream of fame. They worked together in their barn to come up with an act which, by all accounts, was so terrible that it was hilarious. Like all performers, the sisters took to the stage with a desire to be liked, or even loved. Does it matter why they were popular? Does it matter that the audience's enjoyment came at the sisters' expense? As their agent Pops says, "There's only one thing Americans love more than success—and that's failure."

The real Cherries found themselves confronted at first by simple verbal vitriol, but it escalated into an almost all-out war between them and the audience. Night after night, from their start in the Midwest to their ascendance to the World's Fair and ultimately Broadway, they were pelted by "fruit and veg," but they just kept singing and dancing and speechifying. At the heart of the mystery surrounding them is whether or not they knew how awful they were, if they were in on the joke. According to legend, they thought they were terrific, but that seems unlikely. "I have trouble believing that they never had any idea, that they were happily ridiculed by everyone," says O'Brien. "Because it's impressive the amount of longevity they had, how they made money for a fair amount of time, especially for women who were never ingénues to begin with; they really had a remarkable amount of control over their dubious act. I like the idea that they began naively, believing that what they were doing was kind of perfect, but that their act became something else, some kind of mysterious self-exploitation." In a historical footnote, it was their lawsuit against a particularly nasty critic that established the precedent of fair comment—it's your opinion, and you're entitled to it.

In *The Cherry Sisters Revisited*, O'Brien has drawn from the remnants left to us of the true story of the Cherry Sisters and the vaudeville, and added his own inventions. Their act has been revived for the audience's viewing pleasure, but much of it springs from O'Brien's rich imagination. He and composer Michael Friedman (whose Humana Festival work includes *Uncle Sam's Satiric Spectacular*, 2005; and *This Beautiful City*, 2008) are recreating songs for which only titles survived. "I wanted to keep fragments of what was real in the story, and that's how we're approaching the music as well, O'Brien says. "The challenge with the music is similar to the challenge in the entire play, in that we want to evoke the vaudeville while letting it become something more personal, idiosyncratic, perhaps anachronistic at times and therefore more contemporary."

The Cherries seem like an extreme, if nearly forgotten, example of the same craving for fame that seems to live in the back (or front...) of all of our psyches. Sadly, it's not hard to imagine those girls being laughed at on the vaudeville stage as contestants dying to be America's idol or next top model or chef or survivor. "I think there's something specific to our culture here, in how we focus so much on self-invention and individualism, the idea that if you just try hard enough, if you believe, you will be hugely successful somehow," O'Brien says. But this idea of self-invention comes with a shadow side of humiliation. "We can tell ourselves that it's all about who the best fashion designer is, or who the next top model is, but it's also about watching these aspirants be judged and disparaged. That's what makes it dangerous and meaningful and entertaining."

Dangerous it is and was—in a real sense of dodging cabbages, tomatoes and kitchen sinks, as well as the view it gives us of ourselves. We sit in front of our televisions, or in a darkened theatre, laughing at the people performing for us, whether they know they're being funny or not. We forget that they are real...or ghosts...or both. Our joy comes from laughing at others, and in *The Cherry Sisters Revisited*, O'Brien leaves us wondering about our culpability in the abuse suffered by these wannabes—whenever and wherever they are. The American landscape is littered with the broken dreams of old vaudeville houses and abandoned barns. If you listen closely, maybe you'll hear the old ghosts within, desperate to entertain you.

—Julie Felise Dubiner

BIOGRAPHIES

Dan O'Brien's play *The Cherry Sisters Revisited* premiered at Actors Theatre of Louisville's Humana Festival in 2010. His other plays include *The Dear Boy* (Second Stage), *The Voyage of the Carcass* (Page 73 Productions; Stage 13/SoHo Playhouse), *Moving Picture* (Williamstown Theatre Festival), *The Angel in the Trees* (Production Company), *The House in Hydesville* (Geva Theatre Center), *Key West* (Geva), *Am Lit* (Ensemble Studio Theatre), *Lamarck* (Perishable Theatre), and *The Three Christs of Ypsilanti*, which will premiere at Black Dahlia Theatre in Los Angeles in 2011. His new play *The Body of an American*, the 2009-2010 McKnight National Residency and Commission from The Playwrights' Center, has received a Sundance Institute Time Warner Storytelling Fellowship, a TCG Future Collaborations Grant, and a residency at the Rockefeller Foundation's Bellagio Center in Bellagio, Italy. Awards include the American Theatre Critics Association's Osborn Award, and residencies from Yaddo, the O'Neill

Playwrights Conference, and the New Harmony Project. His plays have been commissioned by Manhattan Theatre Club, Ensemble Studio Theatre, Geva Theatre Center, and Williamstown Theatre Festival. He has served as a Hodder Fellow at Princeton University, the inaugural Djerassi Fellow in Playwriting at the University of Wisconsin in Madison, and the Tennessee Williams Fellow in Playwriting at The University of the South (Sewanee) in 2002-2003, and in 2005. O'Brien is also a poet, and his work has appeared in many literary magazines. His song cycle *Theotokia (Hymn to the Mother of God),* with composer Jonathan Berger, premiered at the 2010 Spoleto Festival USA. O'Brien is a Core Writer at The Playwrights' Center. www.danobrien.org.

Michael Friedman wrote the music and lyrics for *Bloody Bloody Andrew Jackson,* which recently completed its Broadway run, following a run at the Public Theater. He is a founding Associate Artist of The Civilians, and has been the Composer/Lyricist for the company's *This Beautiful City, [I Am] Nobody's Lunch, Gone Missing, Brooklyn at Eye Level,* and *Canard, Canard, Goose?* and the upcoming *Great Immensity* and *Pretty Filthy.* He also wrote music and lyrics for *Saved, In the Bubble, The Brand New Kid, God's Ear,* and *The Blue Demon.* With Steve Cosson, he is the co-author of *Paris Commune.* His music has been heard at New York Theatre Workshop, Playwrights Horizons, The Roundabout Theatre Company, Second Stage, Soho Rep, Theater for a New Audience, Signature, and The Acting Company, regionally at the ART, Huntington, Mark Taper Forum, Guthrie, Kennedy Center, Hartford Stage, Humana Festival, Berkeley Repertory, Dallas Theatre Center, Williamstown Theatre Festival, Portland Center Stage, and internationally at London's Soho and Gate Theatres, and the Edinburgh Festival. Film/TV work includes *Coach, On Common Ground, Beloved, Emile Norman: By His Own Design, Floaters* and *Affair Game.* He was also the dramaturg for the recent Broadway revival of *A Raisin in the Sun,* directed by Kenny Leon. He is an Artistic Associate at New York Theatre Workshop, and a recipient of a MacDowell Fellowship, a Meet the Composer Fellowship, and a Princeton University Hodder Fellowship. He received a 2007 Obie Award for sustained excellence.

ACKNOWLEDGMENTS

The Cherry Sisters Revisited premiered at the Humana Festival of New American Plays in March 2010. It was directed by Andrew Leynse with the following cast:

EFFIE CHERRY .... Renata Friedman
ADDIE CHERRY .... Katie Kreisler
LIZZIE CHERRY .... Kate Gersten
ELLA CHERRY.. Cassie Beck
JESSIE CHERRY .... Donna Lynne Champlin
POPS .... John Hickok

and the following production staff:

Music Director/Pianist...................................... Stephen Malone
Scenic Designer .... Scott Bradley
Costume Designer.. Lorraine Venberg
Lighting Designer.. Brian J. Lilienthal
Sound Designer .... Matt Callahan
Properties Designer.. Mark Walston
Wig/Makeup Designer .... Heather Fleming
Movement Director .... Delilah Smyth
Production Stage Manager............................ Paul Mills Holmes
Dialect Coach.. Rocco Dal Vera
Production Assistant.. Cadi Thomas
Dramaturg .... Julie Felise Dubiner
Casting.. Stephanie Klapper

Directing Assistant.. Jay Briggs
Scenic Design Assistant....................................... Ryan Wineinger
Lighting Design Assistants........ John Burkland, Andrew Cissna
Stage Management Intern .... Nick Bussett
Assistant Dramaturg .... Emily Feldman

Music commissioned by Actors Theatre of Louisville with the support of the Harold and Mimi Steinberg Charitable Trust.

Developed for the Humana Festival by Actors Theatre of Louisville through a partnership with Louisiana State University.

The Cherry Sisters Revisited was aided in its artistic development by a residency at Yaddo, the 2006 New Harmony Project, the Hodder Fellowship at Princeton University, and the Tennessee Williams Fellowship at The University of the South (Sewanee), and staged readings with Primary Stages, Stage 13, The Actors Company Theatre, and the Perry-Mansfield New Works Festival.

CHARACTERS

EFFIE, the youngest, the smartest.

ADDIE, the next youngest, the funniest.

LIZZIE, the middle one, the prettiest.

ELLA, the next-to-eldest. Slow, prophetic.

JESSIE, the eldest.

POPS, their father; and also their agent.

TIME

1892–1935, and the present.

PLACE

Various. The stage is fluid but in its foundation looks like the husk of an old, decrepit barn in Iowa, a wintry landscape outside.

NOTES

While many scenes are meant to take place somewhere specific, usually marked in the script by a scene title, much of the play takes place in a kind of limbo outside time and space: at once the theater itself, and the memory of a ghost inside an old, decrepit barn, heartless plains wind howling through the boards.

Regarding the ages of the various Cherry Sisters: ideally all of the actors will be in their 20s and 30s or thereabouts, playing a little younger and then older as the play progresses. As the play is meant to be a vaudeville and a fable, and happens in the theatrical present tense, the age of the actors doesn't really matter so much as the dynamic between them.

Concerning the "true story" of the Cherry Sisters, I am indebted to Avery Hale's 1944 article for *Coronet*, "So Bad They Were Good," as well as Anthony Slide's *Selected Vaudeville Criticism* (Rowman & Littlefield, 1988).

The mouths of their rancid features opened like caverns,
and sounds like the wailing of damned souls issued therefrom…

—W.E. "Billy" Hamilton in the *Odebolt Chronicle*
February 17, 1898

(back) Renata Friedman, Donna Lynne Champlin, Kate Gersten
(front) Cassie Beck and Lynne Champlin
in *The Cherry Sisters Revisited*

34th Annual Humana Festival of New American Plays
Actors Theatre of Louisville, 2010
Photo by Harlan Taylor

THE CHERRY SISTERS REVISITED

ACT ONE

EFFIE. Do you believe in ghosts?

You, in the audience. Think about that. (*Pause.*) 'Cause you're looking at one.

> (*She points a finger.*)

—You did this to us.

> (*Iris-light widens on the sisters in the world....*)

1: Cedar Rapids, Iowa. Outside the theater.

EFFIE. Let's see it again.

JESSIE. You say that every time we see it, Effie...

EFFIE. And every time it's beautiful. —A miracle!

ADDIE. I'll go back inside the theater with you, Effie. If you want.

> (ADDIE *takes* EFFIE's *hand.*)

JESSIE. Lizzie, stop looking at yourself in that mirror, it's vain!

LIZZIE. It's not a mirror, it's a shop window, that dress is pretty—where's Pops?

> (*They all look for him.*)

JESSIE. I'm beginning to get worried.... He should've been here by now...

> (ELLA *points. The others look to where she's pointing.*
> JESSIE *takes* ELLA's *hand in hers.*)

That's not Pops, dear, that's a pile of dead leaves.

EFFIE. Let's see the show again! Can we? Please? —Just one more time—

LIZZIE. You can't spend all day inside a theater, Effie.

ELLA. Effie can.

> (*They're all a bit startled, but only a bit, by what* ELLA's *said.*)

EFFIE. Thank you, Ella.

ELLA. Don't mention it.

EFFIE. I only like it in there because it's not like at home. It's the opposite of home. It's profound! in there...

LIZZIE. "Profound," Effie?

ADDIE. It means very much.

LIZZIE. I know what profound means. I'm not stupid, like Ella is...

JESSIE. It's too crowded in there. It's raucous, and it smells like sin.

You mark my words: in the Twentieth Century, there will be no such thing as the vaudeville!

213

EFFIE. You say that every week, Jessie. And every week we come back.

JESSIE. We have to—someone has to make sure Pops gets home…

(ELLA *points to the pile of dead leaves again.* JESSIE *takes her hand once more.*)
Stop pointing at nothing, dear, that's rude.

EFFIE. We've never seen some of them before. Some of them were famous—

ADDIE. They're on jump-break from New York City—

JESSIE. You don't even know what "jump-break" means.

ADDIE. Do you?

(LIZZIE *starts singing to herself, absentmindedly beneath the ensuing dialogue.*)

LIZZIE. (*Wistfully.*) I'm so lonely for Old Broadway,
  I'm so bored by these cornfields and hay…

EFFIE. Then came the Spanish gypsies! Remember? That daring young girl in her pink underwear—

JESSIE. Pull your skirts down now, Effie—

EFFIE. —holding onto that long, thick rope with just her long, strong teeth. She clenched herself, spinning there, like a great, pink, blurred abstraction… She can't be much older than we are!

JESSIE. Get down off that post, Effie Cherry—you're going to fall down—!

EFFIE. Then she falls! like an angel on a pin, upon a prancing pony's jouncing spine—

JESSIE. Oh, Effie, stop! Please! —People are *looking* at us!

EFFIE. That's the point!
—Then on one leg she poses (*She poses.*), the daintiest ballerina—better than that, because she's balanced on a gosh darned moving horse!

ADDIE. Hurrah! Huzzah! "Gosh darn"!

JESSIE. Such language—!

(JESSIE *covers* ELLA's *ears.*)

EFFIE. She *leaps!*

(EFFIE *leaps, and lands—or falls, rather, ungracefully, possibly painfully. The others look on, concernedly…*
JESSIE *runs to her, kneels, gathers* EFFIE *into her prodigious bosoms.*)

JESSIE. Oh Effie dear, are you all right…?

(EFFIE *stands, a bit shaken: she's fine. She smiles at her sister* JESSIE. *A moment.*)

ADDIE. Then her sister bounds onstage—

(ADDIE *bounds in the dirt and dust.*)

JESSIE. Oh no, I'm not playing—

ADDIE. I'm talking about myself.

LIZZIE. That's funny, that misunderstanding.

ADDIE. In her pink underwear also—

JESSIE. Pull your skirts down, girls! Now you both look like whores!

ADDIE. —Jessie!

JESSIE. What?

ADDIE. "Such language"!

JESSIE. "Whores" is in the Bible, my dear Addison—all the time.

EFFIE. —They defy gravity! They shimmy upside down! They shift from palm to palm as graceful as any two Orientals do!

> (ADDIE *and* EFFIE *attempt some approximation of the above, failing badly at it but who cares?*
> LIZZIE *giggles,* JESSIE *disapproves;* ELLA *might smile, then yawn, or drool.*)

LIZZIE. Then a handsome young man *erupts* on the scene—like a gazelle—

> (*She prances herself—a gazelle, but a clumsy one.*)

EFFIE. A gazelle?

ADDIE. "Erupts"?

EFFIE. There were others—Ella, come here.

JESSIE. Don't you involve her in this—

ELLA. (*To* JESSIE.) I want to—let me go!

> (JESSIE *does let her go.*
> *The four sisters have formed a kind of human pyramid around* JESSIE, *as if their older sister is in on the act.*)

EFFIE. An entire family of Spanish gypsies balanced there, one beside—

ADDIE. —on top of!

EFFIE. —the other! A structure of un-heretofore-dreamt-of perfection...!

> (*The five of them: a very imperfect pyramid.*
> *Another pause.*)

I want to go into show business.

> (*They all come tumbling down.*)

JESSIE. Don't joke like that.

EFFIE. I want to write acts. And perform them. I want to make costumes. And wear them. I want to rehearse in our own little barn, during long winter months, while the snow piles four fathoms deep on the prairie outside. I want to travel out ahead of ourselves in time and space on the steam of our own imaginative locomotion—leave Pops behind, leave Iowa behind, and journey—to New York City!

> (*As before,* LIZZIE *sings to herself while* EFFIE *goes on talking.*)

LIZZIE. I'm so homesick for Broadway's crowds,

    I'm so sick of these donkeys and plows.

    The something, something, something else…

EFFIE. New York City, which might as well be Rome for all I care, for New York's so far away and full of fast-talking wisenheimers, immigrants and sons-of-immigrants who'll swindle you within a dime of your life—oh, New York City! (*She swoons, a little.*) where the banks are like churches, and the people all live in coffins so close to one another you can reach out your hand, out your window, and boil your tea right off your neighbor's stove. And all the streets are numbered because nobody knows how to read—who's got the time? and time's money, in New York City. And the only livestock to be found are pigeons, and roaches, and rats… Oh, the manifold lovelinesses of New York! We'll tour, the old world, to Europe—and Spain! Somewhere brown and papery —I love paper—where it never snows, and corn is an alien commodity… A land full of gypsy girls, just like us, who wear kerchiefs round their heads to keep the robust lice in, and squat round fires on their wide, mannish haunches, singing and joking their rough gay lives away…

And men too!—of course there'll be men there… Brown gypsy-types with wavy black hair and dark eyes set in a face of tan wrinkles, like the lines in a leather-bound book…

    (*She gasps, an epiphany of some kind.*

    The others look at her as if they're looking in a mirror—and liking what they see.

    Except JESSIE, *who looks disturbed.*

    A long pause here. They wait to see what JESSIE *will say.*)

JESSIE. What about Pops?

    (*A long, long pause here.*)

ADDIE. What about him…?

JESSIE. He needs us… He'll fall apart without us.

ADDIE. Good.

LIZZIE. Oh, Addie…

JESSIE. Remember that time we found him in the barn, with a rope in his hand, standing on a chair…?

    (*Pause.*)

LIZZIE. He said he was about to hang something.

ADDIE. He was.

    (*Another pause.*)

EFFIE. Well we'll have to leave him one day…won't we?

JESSIE. We will. When we get married.

LIZZIE. Someone has to ask us first.

(*Another pause. They look each other up and down.*)

EFFIE. Jessie's right: we can't leave him, ever. Poor Pops…where do you think he's gone?

> (*Slowly, again,* ELLA *points to the pile of dead leaves downstage.*
> *A cold wind blows.*
> *This time no one scolds her.*
> *Pause.*
> EFFIE *moves downstage first.*
> *She pulls away the blanket of leaves to reveal:*
> POPS Cherry.
> *Curled up like a fetus.*
> *Hugging whiskey bottles to his chest. A stub of wet cigar bit tightly in his teeth…*
> *His face is deathly pale.*
> *He looks dead*
> *He is.*
> *After a short beat of horror, and then a mysterious, long exhalation of something like relief…*EFFIE *speaks to us.*)

You saw it coming, didn't you.

You're used to such surprises, in "the theatre."

As my slow sister Ella had discovered, I know not wherefrom—from the ether, perhaps?—our father died that day. While we were inside at the show… How—providential, you might say…

Because our father, Pops Cherry—"Pops" is just a nickname, by the way, and he's only a Cherry by way of corruption from the Irish—O'Chernussy, probably, originally, though who can be sure of anything he's ever told us?

Our father had not been well since the death of our mother, now many, many years ago. Nineteen years ago, in fact. My age, to the day. And since that day he'd been drunk. Sometimes worse.

> (POPS *jumps to his feet, his whiskey bottles stuck to him. As if he's wearing a suit made of whiskey bottles.*)

POPS. You always were unlucky!

EFFIE. I love you, Pops. I miss you.

POPS. Ech?

EFFIE. I said I—

POPS. Everything you touch turns to pewter!

EFFIE. "Pewter"?

POPS. I ought to say manure, but this is a family crowd.

EFFIE. (*Looking out.*) It is?

POPS. —Like your mother was, bedad!

EFFIE. (*Excited.*) In what ways am I like Momma, Pops?

POPS. You're too smart for your own good, that's what. Look at that great big horse's head of yours. Like a great big horse's skull! all long in front and fat in back. It's what killed your mother before the start of it all, that great big horse's nut of yours...

> (EFFIE *touches her head, with fear and wonder.*)

You took what it was your mother had.

EFFIE. What did she have, Pops?

POPS. Babies. One Cherry right after the other—pop, pop, pop, pop, pop. And heaving one last long sigh she took a great big soaring lep' out of that writhing birdlike body of hers up into the basin of sky and out of the throes of trying to bring you and that monstrously fat head of yours out into the world of men. (*He inhales extravagantly, staggers.*)

Poor girl, poor wife, poor me.

> (*He tries to rip one of the bottles off his clothes. But they're empty now anyway.*)

Damn it all to Hell! (*He tries to smoke his cigar. He asks the audience.*) D'you got a match?

EFFIE. We're going into showbiz, Pops.

POPS. —*Shoe*-biz? what for? Do you know what that's like, handling feet all day...?

EFFIE. Show biz, Pops, the vaudeville.

POPS. Oh. Och no.

EFFIE. What's wrong?

POPS. You're not whores now, are you?

EFFIE. Not all prostitutes are actresses, Pops.

POPS. Name one. —And you can't do nothing, neither!

EFFIE. Like what?

POPS. —Like talent!

EFFIE. How do you know that? You don't know that yet—we're good! You'll see!

POPS. Will I? I don't think I will...

EFFIE. Why not?

POPS. You see, because I've died...

EFFIE. Oh, I forgot...

POPS. And so have you, died, too... You're a ghost now too, you know.

EFFIE. Am I?

POPS. Don't forget that now.

EFFIE. I always do...

POPS. Don't we all?

EFFIE. Where am I then?

POPS. In the ether.

EFFIE. Where's that?

POPS. In the theater.

EFFIE. Which theater?

POPS. In the barn, back in Iowa. In a way. In the future. Or no-time at all… You're haunted, me girl. Ghosts can be haunted too, you know.

> (*Pause. She pushes him offstage.*)

EFFIE. Get offstage now, Pops. —Go!

POPS. If you're ever famous, remember—you got your talent from me!

> (*He sings, as he goes.*)

Me bodice, neat an' modest, O, is slippin', sir
  Be careful, sir, be careful, please!
The silken thread that holds it up is rippin', sir
—O, do be careful! —O, do be careful!
There now, it's down about me waist,
Me pearly goods are all uncased,
I hope they're temper'd to your taste
—St. Patrick's Day in the morning!

> (*He disappears, singing, bottles tinkling into the wings.*)

Fiddle-dee-dee, fiddle-dee-die…

> (*Emphasis on the "die"…*
> EFFIE *doesn't want to cry.*
> *Wind and snow.*)

2: The Barn in Marion. Rehearsal. Winter.

ELLA's *not here.*
LIZZIE's *wiping the dirt on her skirt…*

LIZZIE. He looked so sad in that pinewood box, as they lowered him into the ground…

ADDIE. You couldn't see his face. The lid was screwed on.

> (JESSIE *eats some cheese, and sighs.*)

JESSIE. Sad…

EFFIE. Here's what I envision:
Numerous acts, some funny, some sad. Some songs, Lizzie, you'll sing a few pretty ditties. Something sentimental of the euphemistic school. You know the score. I have the titles, you can fill in the rest.
One: "I Ain't Never Been Kissed." Two: "Let's Canoodle in the Doodle-ee-doo." And three—"Corn Juice!" Exclamation point. Naturally.

Let me write this all down:

> (*She does, in a little brown book that seems to appear in the ether.*)

ADDIE. Where'd you find that?

EFFIE. In the ether.

JESSIE. (*Eating cheese.*) You're nuts, Effie Cherry…

EFFIE. What's nuts? to dream? —Perchance to dream, Jessie!

LIZZIE. Who said that?

ADDIE. Walt Whitman.

LIZZIE. Who's he?

ADDIE. Some nurse.

LIZZIE. How's this sound?

> (LIZZIE *sings, with her ukulele.*)

Let's canoodle in the doodle-ee-doo
And foodle with the poodle-ee-pee.
I'll piddle your diddle
If you fiddle my middle,
Canoodling in the doodle-ee-doodle-ee-doodle-ee-
Dum-m-m!

EFFIE. Keep working on that one.
We'll need some playlets—

LIZZIE. What's a "playlet"?

ADDIE. Like a play, but suckling.

LIZZIE. —That's a good one, Addie!

ADDIE. Is it? I don't know about that one yet…

EFFIE. And some comic monologuing. Addie, that's your forte, make it fresh, make it funny.

JESSIE. —What about me?

EFFIE. What about you, Jessie.

JESSIE. What do I do?

EFFIE. Well, so far. I've got you down for the…"heavy lifting." Jessie.

> (*Pause.*)

JESSIE. Lifting what?

EFFIE. Props and scenery, mostly.

LIZZIE. You're the most athletic, Jessie. Everyone knows that…

JESSIE. What about Addie?—she's got man-hands!

> (ADDIE *examines her hands.*)

LIZZIE. It's true…

JESSIE. I'm heavy…if that's what you mean. I don't eat much. Lord knows we don't *ever* eat much, any of us, except maybe cheese, on a good day… Corn… It's a mystery to me.
I'm just naturally matronly…

> (JESSIE *eats some more cheese.*)

—But I can't lift much! My heart's not strong. Like Momma's wasn't…

> (*A deep pause, surprisingly felt.*
> *They all glance at, or away from, or just think about* EFFIE *and her very large head…*
> EFFIE *touches said head, without noticing what she's doing…*
> ADDIE *changes the subject.*)

ADDIE. So I'm reading this book:

> (*Shows the cover.*)

LIZZIE. *So You Want to Live in Vaudeville?* (*Pause.*)
Well do you?

ADDIE. It's a rhetorical question. It's got killer Brooklynese.

EFFIE. Definitions?

ADDIE. You betcha.

EFFIE. Phonetic?

ADDIE. No, English.

LIZZIE. Where is Phoenicia, anyway?

EFFIE. Let me hear some please:

ADDIE. "Take my seat, young goil! I'm only goin' so far as Yahnkers!"

> (*Pause.* EFFIE *savors.*)

EFFIE. That's beautiful.

ADDIE. Isn't it?

LIZZIE. Where is Yonkers anyway?

ADDIE. Brooklyn, I guess.

JESSIE. That's crude. I think such speech is vulgar.

LIZZIE. What about a Negro song? some kind of sassy soft-shoeing? some blackface maybe? Addie would make a very convincing coon, I think.

JESSIE. That is also in poor taste.

LIZZIE. Whose taste? I find their music stirring.

JESSIE. In the Twentieth Century no one will laugh at Negroes.

LIZZIE. Why not? Where will they have all gone?

ADDIE. The Twentieth Century is eight years from now, Jessie…

JESSIE. I know that. —This is *America*, Addie!

EFFIE. And when our act is strong and tight we'll do a show, at home, at the Marion Grange Hall. We'll hone our craft on friendly turf, then raise enough in capital to take our show all the way to Cedar Rapids—

(*LIZZIE gasps.*)

Don't gasp, it's true—it's within our reach, our grasp. Every day, a great actress dries up onstage, like a prune, and every day another one *blooms!*

JESSIE. But what if we're not good enough…?

(*A sudden, long pause ensues… JESSIE eats some more cheese, morosely. EFFIE's about to touch her head again, but ADDIE takes her hand and holds it.*)

LIZZIE. He looked so sad in that coffin, the earth was frozen six feet down…

(*JESSIE eats more cheese.*)

EFFIE. We'll need a name.

ADDIE. We have one already, don't we?

LIZZIE. Do we? Which one?

JESSIE. The name God gave us.

ADDIE. You mean Pops gave us…

LIZZIE. "The Cherries."

(*It just sits there in the barn.*)

ADDIE. We'll be popular with the men.

LIZZIE. Why?

JESSIE. Yes, why, Addie?

ADDIE. Where's Ella with our lunch?

LIZZIE. I'm hungry now too…

JESSIE. Have my cheese.

(*She offers LIZZIE some.*)

LIZZIE. I've got to watch my figure. (*Pause.*) We all do.

JESSIE. (*Eating more cheese.*) We all do what?

EFFIE. What's wrong with our figures, Lizzie?

LIZZIE. Well. With the possible exception of you, Effie, who's already bone-thin, like a thin old swayback mule—

EFFIE. Like a what?

LIZZIE. —the rest of us are far too…matronly. (*Pause.*) Like Jessie said.

EFFIE. How can we be matronly? We're not even married—

LIZZIE. That's my point exactly.

It hardly matters much for you, Addie—you're the funny one, all that matters is your wits. If you get fat you'll be *more* funny, probably, because fat people are mostly jolly, except when they're mean, and then they're positively evil…

And as for Effie it's her brains inside that great big head of hers… And Jessie here is for the heavy lifting, as we've discussed, despite the danger to her heart. No: I'm the one who must stay pretty, Pops would always say.

ADDIE. Where's Ella with our gosh-darned lunch!

JESSIE. —Such language!

EFFIE. She's inside sewing our new leotards.

JESSIE. Are you sure that's such a good idea?

ADDIE. Some of history's best seamstresses have been mentally impaired.

LIZZIE. Really?

ADDIE. No, I was just trying out a joke—does it work?

JESSIE. I don't think she should be let loose out there, what with all this wind and driving snow…

EFFIE. She's not a cat.

ADDIE. It *is* snowing fiercely out there, Effie…

EFFIE. It's always snowing here.

LIZZIE. I know. Why *is* that?

EFFIE. —We need to focus, girls! —Focus! We've got so much more work to do!

LIZZIE. I think I see her coming now…

JESSIE. That's her outside in the wind and driving snow—keep walking, Ella! You can make it!

LIZZIE. Are you sure that's Ella out there in the wind and…?

JESSIE. Driving snow.

LIZZIE. Driving snow?

JESSIE. Who else could she be?

LIZZIE. I don't know, a ghost maybe?

ADDIE. Whose ghost?

LIZZIE. She looks a lot like Momma did…

JESSIE. Do you remember when Momma would take the washing from the line, in the snow? The temperature would drop, and the snow would sweep in… The sheets would be frozen, they'd crack like boards when she folded them in front of the fire.

EFFIE. —What about: "The Beautiful Cherry Sisters"?

(*They look each other up and down.*)

No.

ADDIE. That won't work.

LIZZIE. —*I'm* not ugly!

ADDIE. That's mostly true.

EFFIE. "The Four Cherry Sisters" simply?

LIZZIE. "The Four Cherry Sisters Simply" is far too modest.

JESSIE. Five. With Ella.

> (*Another pause.*)

Well we have to, don't we?

We can't leave her alone out here, surely…

ADDIE. Can she sing and dance?

JESSIE. She's one of us, Addie, she's a Cherry!

ADDIE. She's an idiot, Jessie. (*Short pause.*) I mean that in the clinical sense.

JESSIE. So?

EFFIE. People are going to laugh at her…

LIZZIE. But that's the point, isn't it?

JESSIE. —Come on, Ella! You can make it!

LIZZIE. She's teetering in the wind!

JESSIE. She's wandered off the trail!

LIZZIE. She's carrying our new leotards—they're pretty! They're bunched before her face!

JESSIE. Look—one's flown away!

LIZZIE. Like a flamingo!

JESSIE. Do you remember how silent mother was? how graceful and composed…?

LIZZIE. Like Ella, though not as dumb…

JESSIE. I remember her standing at the stove, with baby Addie in her arms, rocking her to sleep and singing… She had such a pretty voice, like you do, Lizzie…with her breast in Addie's mouth…

ADDIE. I wish I could remember that.

EFFIE. —You were too young when she died, Addie.

ADDIE. What do you know—you weren't even fully born yet!

> (ADDIE *immediately regrets what she's said.*)

JESSIE. —Keep walking, Ella, you're almost here!

LIZZIE. Oh look—she's fallen in a drift—

ADDIE. Oh now she's up again! Here she comes!

EFFIE. —"The Musical Cherries"?

LIZZIE. Redundant.

EFFIE. "Cherries A-Poppin'!"

JESSIE. Been done before.

EFFIE. "The Five Ripe Cherries"?

ADDIE. That sounds like we smell bad.

LIZZIE. Or taste good.

ADDIE. That's filthy!

JESSIE. —It doesn't matter what we're called, girls! No one's going to care! No one's going to believe us, when they see us up there on that stage at the Marion Grange Hall. They'll say, Who do these girls think they are? We knew their poor mother, we knew Pops—we know what *he* was like...
No, they won't believe us for a minute.

EFFIE. Then we'll have to believe it first. (*Pause.*) If we believe it, then they will.

JESSIE. Is that how it works...?

EFFIE. What do you say, girls? Can you believe it?

> (*No one answers.*
> *The answer would seem to be "maybe?"*)

That's it: "The Unbelievable Cherry Sisters!" (*Pause.*) Exclamation point!

JESSIE. Well it's accurate, anyway...

> (*Enter* ELLA, *all covered in snow.*
> *She carries a great big bass drum, strapped vertically to her chest.*
> *She bangs the drum slowly, loudly, with a dirty wooden spoon...*
> *She stops drumming. Turns slowly to reveal that one side of the drum reads:*
> *"The Unbelievable Cherry Sisters!"*)

ELLA. I believe in *you,* Effie.

> (*All look to* EFFIE.)

EFFIE. How did you know that, Ella? were you listening outside...?

3: Marion Grange Hall. Night.

> ELLA *continues to beat her drum occasionally, throughout the following.*

ADDIE. Good evening, ladies and Germans! (*Silence.*) That was supposed to be—just a bit of bidness. (*Pause.*) Because there's a lot of folks here of German extraction, in Marion, Iowa, you see. Immigrants, via Ellis Island, etcetera. Well—(*To herself.*) "don't explain your jokes," Chapter Twelve...

Welcome, everyone, to *le premier* performance of what everyone's just dying to pop inside their mouths: The Cherries! (*Silence.*) That's right, "The Unbelievable Cherry Sisters!" Exclamation! Point!

> (*Much more silence.* JESSIE *steps forward.*)

JESSIE. You can clap, you know. It's considered polite.

> (*A few hands applaud.*
> *The sisters sing the following song together, to the tune of* "Ta-ra-ra boom-dee-ay."
> ELLA *is beating the rhythm out on her giant bass drum. She is not very rhythmical.*)

ALL. Cherries ripe, boom-dee-ay!
   Cherries red, boom-dee-ay!
   The Cherry Sisters
   Are here today!
   Cherries sweet, boom-dee-ay!
   Cherries wet, boom-dee-ay!
   The Cherry Sisters
   Came all this way!
   Cherries fat, boom-dee-ay!
   Cherries tart, boom-dee-ay!
   The Cherry Sisters
   —*Won't go away!*
      (*Big finish, big drumming: no clapping.*)

ADDIE. So what is it about these Iowa winters? I mean, come on—we get it already!
      (*Silence. ELLA bangs the drum: a rim shot, of sorts.*)
Have you heard the one about why the cow jumped over the moon? The farmer's hands were cold! (*Pause.*) On her udders. (*Pause.*) Because udders are kind of like nipples…on a cow.
      (ELLA's *rim shot.*)
What do you call a very clean Norwegian? —German!
      (ELLA's *rim shot. Silence.*)
Tough crowd…
      (ELLA's *rim shot.*)
That's not a joke, Ella.
And now for a pretty little ditty from our pretty little Lizzie…!
      (LIZZIE *takes the fore, singing.*)

LIZZIE. I ain't never been kissed,
   I ain't never been kissed.
   I ain't talking cheeks, I'm talking hot lips!
   No matter how hard I swing these hips,
   I ain't never had no lover's kiss.
   I ain't never been a dish,
   I ain't never been a dish
   For a boy, a goy or an Amish.
   No matter how many frogs I kiss,
   Not *one* becomes my prince!
   What do you think, fellas?
   What do you say, dames?
   Ain't I got the goods?
   Ain't I got good gams—?

(*Awkward finish. This question hangs lewdly in the air.*)

EFFIE. (*To us.*) It was a magical moment…
Everything could have changed. They could clap, or they could not…
They is you now: what will *you* do?

(*Pause.*)

Then it happened—a smattering, a spattering of applause.
We went on, holding them, or so we thought, enthralled, through the comic bits, played by Addie, and then Addie and me together. More songs from Lizzie, including her newest, "The Spaniard That Marked My Wife."

LIZZIE. (*Correcting.*) "My Life!"

EFFIE. My life, my life…
And Jessie providing a cautionary tale of lost virtue entitled,

JESSIE. "My First Cigar"!

EFFIE. And then we rounded out the evening with the five of us in leotards in what was fast becoming our signature spectacle: all the way from the banks of the River Denial…the Human Pyramid!

(*They've shucked their calico dresses. They're in their pyramid now, in leotards that look homemade, more like long underwear, dyed imperfectly pink, threadbare and puckered at the knees and elbows.*)

EFFIE. If only Pops could see us now.

(*He appears.*)

POPS. You look like fat whores, bedad.

EFFIE. Pops—

(*She tumbles down out of the pyramid.*)

POPS. The five of yous wailing and shrieking, squealing and wailing, leaping about in just your undert'ings like a horde of sex-starved banshees—

EFFIE. Pops!

POPS. There's nothing special about you! —The five of yous are nothing—you're *nothing!*

EFFIE. The audience is clapping, Pops, they're loving us—

POPS. That's not love…

EFFIE. They're clapping for us—what do you think that means?

POPS. —They know who you are!

(*Pause.*)

It's a very small town, bedad… This is the Midwest, me girl: they're clapping because they're *trying to be nice!*

(EFFIE *is shaken.*
POPS *tries to detach a whiskey bottle from his clothing: it's stuck. And it's empty anyway.*)

POPS. Damn it all to Hell! (*He tries to smoke his cigar, calls offstage.*) I need a match—

    (*He's gone.*)

EFFIE. Our hands were laced together…as we bowed our heads…

And for a moment, for no reason I could figure…I imagined that this little stage we stood upon had become a kind of gallows.

    (ELLA *begins beating her drum again.*)

ADDIE. Who are you talking to, Effie?

EFFIE. We're a hit. (*Pause.*) Aren't we?

    (*Backstage.*)

ADDIE. What did you expect?

LIZZIE. A boy just asked me for my autograph. He said, "You girls really *are* unbelievable!"

JESSIE. Did you hear that applause? So well-mannered.

EFFIE. —Ella, stop beating that drum!

    (ELLA *stops for a minute. Then starts again, a little more quietly.*
    EFFIE *is counting the money.*)

(*Astounded.*) One hundred dollars…

LIZZIE. That's more than Mr. Vlanck makes all year!

JESSIE. —So generous of them!

LIZZIE. Mr. Vlanck asked me in the wings, he said, "Ven are you goink to Cedar Vapids?"

ADDIE. That's good, Lizzie—"Cedar Vapids"!

JESSIE. Why do you know so much about Mr. Vlanck, Lizzie?

LIZZIE. He said we should just hurry up and get to Cedar Vapids right away: "Do not vaste anozher day—get out of zees town. Please!"

EFFIE. We're not ready.

LIZZIE. That's what he said, Effie, and he's a teacher. And German. And Germans never lie!

EFFIE. Cedar Rapids is the city, Lizzie.

LIZZIE. So? I know that…

EFFIE. They're cosmopolitan there, they're savvy. They're used to the best entertainment the corn-belt has to offer. These people out there tonight, they're just—rubes.

JESSIE. Effie!

    (*Pause. Even* ELLA *pauses.*)

We're rubes too…

EFFIE. They *had* to be nice, that's all I mean to say… They know who we are. How do we know they're not lying when they clap?

JESSIE. Oh, Effie… That's the saddest thing you've ever said.

EFFIE. —Ella! Stop beating that drum!

(ELLA *stops.*)

ELLA. What's the matter, Effie? Don't you love us too?

(*Pause.*)

EFFIE. …How do we get to Cedar Rapids, girls?

LIZZIE. By boat?

EFFIE. No, we practice.

LIZZIE. Practice what? swimming?

EFFIE. (*To us.*) We went home and polished our routines. Pyramids grew taller, arms and thighs grew lither beneath pink underthings…
And the songs—the songs needed no work at all. A beautiful little ballad entitled "Why Speak of Love When the Rent Is So High?" promised to bring Cedar Vapids to its knees.

LIZZIE. Why speak of love when the rent is so high?
    Why talk of spring when winter is nigh?
    Why give a darn about nothin' at all
    If I can't have you?
    Why speak of lunch when your stomach's upset—?

EFFIE. Thank you, Lizzie.

ADDIE. Thank you, Lizzie.

LIZZIE. There's more.

EFFIE. No, there's not.

LIZZIE. It's a much longer song—

EFFIE. We've heard it already. Several times.

ADDIE. Today.

(*Pause.*)

LIZZIE. —Where's Ella with our gosh-darned lunch!

JESSIE. Such language!

LIZZIE. Darn my language all to heck I'm wasting away to nothing!

EFFIE. (*To us.*) And the jokes were flying fast, especially in Brooklynese, which came out thick and spicy these days:

ADDIE. (*As a man.*) "Take my seat, young goil! I'm only goin' so far as Yahnkers!"

EFFIE. "Oh no! I can't take your seat, sir!"

ADDIE. "Yes you can. And I'll take yours!"

(*"He" pinches her.*)

EFFIE. "Ooo!" —That's too hard, Addie, don't pinch me so hard.

ADDIE. That's how men are…

EFFIE. How would you know?

ADDIE. (*Prompting.*) "My dear sir—"

EFFIE. "My dear sir, I think you're fresh!"

ADDIE. "I think *you're* fresh! Like a summer rain!"

EFFIE. "And you're like a winter drizzle."

ADDIE. "I can't help it! You make me feel damp!" —Damp?

EFFIE. "Fresh!"

> (EFFIE *slaps* ADDIE.)

ADDIE. Ow, Effie. That hurt

EFFIE. That's how women are. You have to pay attention.

—Say your rhyming couplet now, Addie: not to me but to them.

ADDIE. "A woman is a fragile beast! She needs a man to give her peace!" That's not funny at all.

EFFIE. I know. It's cow shit. (*To us.*) We were ready for Cedar Vapids!

4: Cedar Rapids. Night.

EFFIE. The stage there was so immense…like the surface of some enormous grand piano…

And midway through our first comic sketch, the rehearsal of which you were just a party to…what should happen but a horn should toot?

> (*A horn toots.*
> ELLA *enters, covered in snow again.*
> *More importantly, perhaps, she clenches a cardboard horn tight in her teeth.*
> *She toots again and again, etc.*)

And another. And another…

And soon that entire theater in Cedar Rapids was clogged with such a cacophony of cardboard horns, like a flock of captive geese—no, like the Israelites at the walls of Jericho—no, as if we'd found ourselves suddenly at the center of some hive of demonically possessed bees—*shut up, Ella, please!*

> (ELLA *toots her horn.*
> *They're smiling at the audience, terrified.*)

LIZZIE. What's going on out there…?

ADDIE. They're blowing horns at us…

LIZZIE. I can hear that—

JESSIE. How rude!

EFFIE. What's going on out there…?

LIZZIE. They're blowing horns at us!

EFFIE. I know but what does it all *mean?*

ADDIE. —Let me see that horn.

> (ADDIE *takes the horn from* ELLA, *examines it.*)

There was a rally here last night. See? Political. That's what it says on the horn: "Up With Greevey!" Exclamation point.

JESSIE. Who's "Greevey"?

LIZZIE. What's going up him?

EFFIE. (*To us.*) It *was* strange. Not a boo, not applause…neither cheers nor jeers nor silence… A horn.
But if applause can be a lie…then maybe a horn might mean applause?

> (*Pause.*)

ADDIE. Effie, are you listening to us?

EFFIE. They're so grateful for our performance here tonight, girls…that mere clapping will not do.

> (*Pause. She tries again.*)

In Cedar Rapids, if you love an act so much and mere clapping will not suffice—you blow! Your horn!

JESSIE. It's a theory…

> (ELLA *takes her horn back from* ADDIE, *starts tooting again.*)

LIZZIE. What should we do now?

EFFIE. —Give them more, girls! More!

ADDIE. "You say you're going downtown, doll, well I've been there before!"

EFFIE. (*To us.*) We finished our euphemistic comic interlude, and sang a song or two. Jessie came out alone and spun her speech on—

JESSIE. "Marriage and the Advantages of Male Chastity in the Twentieth Century!"

EFFIE. Exclamation point, naturally. —She was so obsessed with this coming century!

ADDIE. What did the corn cob say to the corn stalk? You leaf around here?

> (ELLA's *rim shot.*)

Two cows in a field: one cow says moo. The other says, You readin' my mind?

> (*Rim shot.*)

What do you call a lonely bull in a pasture all alone? —Beef stroganoff!

> (*A very long, confused rim shot.*)

LIZZIE. What does that one even mean, Addie?

ADDIE. I don't know but Pops used to say it…

EFFIE. (*To us.*) And gradually, horn by horn, the tooting died away.

Silence returned. No laughter, no applause. Nothing. Just one long, unbroken hush…

We can't see a thing, with the lights in our eyes. We know you're out there. Breathing. Watching. Listening…as if concentrating, mightily…trying to figure something out…

What are you trying to figure out?

> (*Silence.*)

Then something even stranger occurred:

ALL. We are all five yerrow queens.
> Some are fat and some are rean.
> Prease to take a rook at us
> Whire we dance our fine loutine!

> (*They're all dancing, in a line:*
> ELLA *looks Chinese, in a "coolie" hat;* LIZZIE *is dressed like a Japanese geisha;* EFFIE *has a Hindu dot on her forehead, and a sari; and* ADDIE *wears Eskimo furs and brandishes a spear with a fish on it.*
> JESSIE, *the Hawaiian Queen, wears a grass skirt and lei.*)

JESSIE. I am Queen Lili'uokalani,
> I am queen of all Hawai'i.
> From O'ahu to green Maui
> I enjoy the mahi-mahi.
> At every royal luau
> I will eat my Pig Kalua.
> Then some mangos and papaya,
> And then something called hapia.
> Mai Tai cocktails, lomi salmon,
> Coconut sure cures your famine!
> And don't forget the Pupu platter—
> Avoid the poi or you'll grow fatter.
> Some have said that I too heavy
> But I think they simply jeal-y.
> Watch my sister's ukulele
> While I dance my hula-hula.
> Wiki! wiki! wiki! wiki! wiki!

EFFIE. (*Whispering.*) Jessie!

JESSIE. What?

EFFIE. Move over that way—

JESSIE. There's a footlight over there—

ADDIE. Move your feet!

LIZZIE. —Keep smiling, girls! Move those hips like you mean it!

JESSIE. Don't you push me please missie—!

ADDIE. Jessie—

JESSIE. What—

EFFIE. Jessie!

LIZZIE. —You're going to catch on fire!

> (*And* LIZZIE *screams, as:*
> JESSIE *catches fire.*
> *Or, rather,* JESSIE's *skirt goes up in flames. Or up in smoke, as the case may be. Now* JESSIE *screams.*
> *The others scream now too. Pandemonium, Pan-Asian style.*
> *They try to put it out, blowing, screaming, waving their hands, swatting her skirt with their skirts.*
> *But* ELLA, *somehow, has been quickest. Here she comes running back onstage with a fire extinguisher.*
> *She sprays it all up and down* JESSIE's *front. She sprays her sister's face too, a lot, just to be safe.*
> JESSIE's *skirts smolder, her face drips: a tableau vivant, with a touch of presentiment, perhaps…*
> *Pause.*
> *A seismic eruption of laughter in the audience now, rolling on beneath the following.*)

EFFIE. They could not stop laughing…

> (*More laughter. The girls are in ecstasy, bewildered.*)

Is this what love feels like?

POPS. (*Appearing.*) Hear that?

EFFIE. —Do *you* hear that?

POPS. They're laughing at you, Effie…

EFFIE. They're laughing *with* me, Pops. With us. We made them laugh, it's beautiful—!

POPS. You made them laugh because you caught yourselves on fire! (*Pause.*) Jessie did. At least she's got *some* talent… They wish you'd all catch fire, that way they'd be sure to get their money's worth.

EFFIE. —Liar!

POPS. When have I ever?

EFFIE. What you've seen tonight is the mark of true genius. We encounter accident and we subsume—we spin it into gold!

POPS. You're mixing up your metaphors now, me girl.

EFFIE. Why don't you just go back to Hell—that's not a metaphor, that's where you *live!*

POPS. Your sister went up in flames. Does that mean nothing to you at all?

(*Pause.*)

I need a match…

> (*He walks over to* JESSIE's *still smoldering skirt, lights his brand new cigar off it.*)

EFFIE. Where'd you get that?

POPS. Me stogie?

EFFIE. Where are your bottles?

POPS. Me drink?

EFFIE. Your whiskey. You've always got them, hanging off your person like cowbells so I can hear you coming…

Why are you wearing that suit? You've changed, you're changing now…

POPS. Listen, sweetheart—

EFFIE. Your brogue—

POPS. This is where we say goodbye for now.

EFFIE. Your hair's not even white anymore… That mustache—

POPS. You're getting ahead of me now, Effie. Watch it.

> (POPS *finishes wiping the death-pallor from his face with his handkerchief. He affixes a mustache.*
> *He pushes her out of the way.*)

EFFIE. —Pops!

5: Backstage, Cedar Rapids, moments after the show.

POPS. Pops is my name, talent agentry's my game.

> (*He doffs his hat.* EFFIE *is suddenly quite shy.* ADDIE *is folding her arms.*)

ADDIE. We knew a Pops once…

POPS. It's a popular name these days, Pops, in the voe-dee-veal at least, 'specially 'mongst us men. Managers and agents mostly—"of course," you say!—whose job it is to fan the flames of the artist's soul into a more mature, that is, profit-making, conflagration. A veritable forest fire of profit, if you will. Smell that smoke? (*He inhales his cigar.*)

I've got a real name, of course, one my mother gave, but I'm not about to give that to you…

> (*He laughs. A pause, then to* LIZZIE.)

Except you, maybe you, you I might tell one day.

> (*He touches* LIZZIE *on the chin: she swoons.*)

LIZZIE. —Oh!

JESSIE. May we help you with something, "Pops"?

POPS. Who's this, your spinster aunt, visiting from England?

JESSIE. —Oh!

POPS. Please, do not become affronted. I mean merely to be familiar with you girls. A real confidante.

ADDIE. We've already got confidantes, Pops: each other.

LIZZIE. We can always use more confidence, Pops—we're *so* insecure!

POPS. You girls really are something, you know that?

I was out there tonight, watching the show, as is my wont, whenever I'm on jump-break from Chicago—

LIZZIE. "Jump-break"!

JESSIE. "Wont"?

ADDIE. You don't sound Chicago, you sound Brooklynese.

POPS. —I always make a point of slowing myself down here, in Cedar Rapids, of all places, to peruse the local talent.

LIZZIE. You think we've got talent? —*I* do.

POPS. Who cares what I think? The audience loved you! You killed them! You slaughtered them! They're decimated! Massacred! —It's beautiful!

ADDIE. (*To Jessie.*) He's spitting on you—

POPS. Only in America… I mean, I'm a patriot. And only in this country, in this day and age, could five motherless girls from Wherever-The-Fuck-You're-From-Iowa—

JESSIE. Oh-h!

> (JESSIE *almost faints—at the language.*)

POPS. —find stardom on the voe-dee-veal stage!

ADDIE. Why do you keep saying it like that, the "voe-dee-veal"?

POPS. It's French. Don't you girls know any French?

LIZZIE. You mean like kissing?

EFFIE. How do you know we're motherless?

POPS. Well that's obvious, isn't it?

> (*Pause. Is that compassion in his eyes?*
> *Then, to* ELLA.)

Fatherless too?

> (ELLA *shakes her head, "No."*
> *She points at him.*)

What's wrong with her, she dumb?

ADDIE. She's an idiot.

POPS. I can see that.

JESSIE. She means that in the clinical sense, Pops.

LIZZIE. She got kicked in the head by a mule when she was five. It wasn't all her fault.

(ELLA *smiles, and nods, and holds up four fingers.*)

POPS. Testy beast, the mule. It's because they're so sterile.

No, I mean is she dumb in the sense of speechlessness? Can she talk?

JESSIE. She can talk if she wants to. Say something, Ella.

ELLA. You're the very bad man.

(*Pause.*)

POPS. She's perfect, don't ever change.

Who's in charge here?

LIZZIE. Jessie's the eldest.

JESSIE. I'm only twenty-nine. —And I've never even *been* to England!

POPS. No no, who's the brains, the *artiste.* Who's got the vision here?

(*Another pause.*
EFFIE *shyly replies.*)

EFFIE. That would be me. The *artiste*…Effie Cherry.

(*He sizes her up and down. She lowers her gaze some more.*)

POPS. Beauty and brains. It just isn't fair.

EFFIE. (*Blushes crimson.*) Lizzie's the pretty one.

POPS. Oh no, you're pretty also. 'Cause you got prettiness…in here.

(*He taps her big fat head. She smiles widely, though she's trying not to.*)

Want my opinion though?

EFFIE. Of course!

POPS. You're gonna be stars.

(*He re-lights his cigar.*)

LIZZIE. We are?

POPS. Aren't we?

ADDIE. Who's we?

LIZZIE. Even Ella is?

POPS. Especially Ella! Audiences love retarded gals—

JESSIE. We prefer "idiot," if you don't mind.

POPS. —so long as you keep their noses clean.

(*He gives* ELLA *a handkerchief: she uses it, a lot.*)

Keep it.

I'm gonna take you fours to Chicago. What do you think of that idea?

JESSIE. Five.

LIZZIE. What's in Chicago, Pops?

POPS. The Chicago World's Fair's in Chicago next year, that's what.

EFFIE. You want to take us to the World's Fair?

POPS. That's the next step in this story of ours, the story of your lives, and you are writing it, I'm just proofreading and there ain't no type-o's I can see: Chicago World's Fair, 1893. It's your destiny!

EFFIE. He's a philosopher…

POPS. I don't like books much, they make me suspicious of my fellow man. —But trust me: you four girls are one of a kind—

JESSIE. Five.

POPS. —and I'm not the only one who's gonna think so!

(*He takes out another handkerchief to mop his brow.*)

JESSIE. He's sweating so much…

LIZZIE. He can't help it. He's Latin.

ADDIE. I don't trust him at all…

EFFIE. What's not to trust?

JESSIE. The slicked-back hair…

LIZZIE. (*She sighs.*) His slicked-back hair…

ADDIE. The olive skin…

EFFIE. Such olive skin!

JESSIE. His waxed-up mustache.

LIZZIE. —Let me stroke your waxed-up mustache!

(*Pause.*)

POPS. I'm sorry, doll. You say something?

LIZZIE. Did I?

EFFIE. Are you originally from Spain?

POPS. What's that?

EFFIE. A country near France. —Don't you have some Spanish blood in you somewhere?

POPS. As a matter of fact, I do… Let me see here, I'm part Spanish-Dutch-Welsh-French-Slovakian-Sioux. If you go back a generation or—ten. How'd you know all that?

LIZZIE. It's your mustache.

POPS. You're observant. You both are.

EFFIE. And your skin—like a leather-bound book…

(*Pause. Both* LIZZIE *and* EFFIE *are batting their eyes, blushing fiercely.*)

POPS. You girls sure know how to flatter a man.

But listen: there's one thing you gotta do if you want to go all the way with me.

(JESSIE *gasps, maybe gags a little.*)

EFFIE & LIZZIE. —What?

POPS. Write…a one-act play!

LIZZIE. Ew. Why?

POPS. You're darling because you're so dim.

(*He touches* LIZZIE *on the chin, again. She swoons—again.*)

Everyone knows that every multilayered, multifaceted vaudeville show needs a stirring one-act play—a "short dramatic thunderbolt!" as they say, within the machinery of variety—a diamond, if you will, set upon the ring of the revue…

EFFIE. He's poetic, too…

LIZZIE. I love diamond rings!

POPS. And, as a short, dramatic thunderwork, it must contain some deep human truth.

LIZZIE. What's a human truth?

POPS. You're the ingénue: thinking gives you wrinkles. (*Her chin, again: swoons.*) It's good business sense, girls: if you want to reach the top of your profession you'll have to write a short, sharp one-act play with deep, human truth.

EFFIE. I've been working on that.

(*Pause.*)

ADDIE. No you haven't, Effie—ow.

POPS. Oh yeah?

EFFIE. "Yeah."

POPS. Well you work on it some more, doll. And you work hard. Till your hand cramps. Then longer.

And when you're done working you send it on to me, via U.S. parcel post. On my dime.

(POPS *gives* EFFIE *a shiny, sparkling dime.*)

There's plenty more where that came from…

And if your one-act play is any good, I promise you girls we'll go all the way together…to the Chicago World's Fair! —In Chicago!

(*He reaches into his pants pocket again, pulls out a chocolate bar, offers to* LIZZIE.)

LIZZIE. What's that.

POPS. Milk chocolate.

LIZZIE. I can't, I'm matronly.

POPS. Who ever told you such a thing? You're as skinny as an aborigine! As your agent, I am telling you, in the next few months you must *all* gain at least thirty to forty pounds per female person. (*To Effie.*) Maybe more, in your case.

LIZZIE. —Oh!

(LIZZIE *takes the chocolate bar, begins eating ravenously.*)

POPS. Here's my card.

(POPS *reaches into his pants pocket again, pulls out his business card.*)

LIZZIE. —There's so much in your pocket!

POPS. What's your name again?

EFFIE. Effie. It's short for Iphigenia.

ADDIE. No it's not, Effie—stop touching me!

POPS. No, I'm talking about your show.

LIZZIE. (*Mouth full.*) "Unbelievable Cherry Sisters"!

POPS. That's the name of your act. You're going to have many more shows, I promise you, for years to come… Let's name your first show…something special…

EFFIE. (*Thinking.*) Let me think—

POPS. How's about: "The Unbelievable Cherry Sisters in: Seeing Is Believing!"

(*He gives* EFFIE *his card.*

She takes it.)

Because you girls need to be seen to be believed.

6: The barn. Winter again. Is it ever not winter?

EFFIE's *alone this time.*

She speaks to us.

EFFIE. I know what you're thinking…

But I'd never known men could be beautiful before.

I didn't even know you could use that word, "beauty," with men…

And I don't think he's handsome in the conventional sense. He is a touch… mature.

—But he said I was an artist.

He touched my big fat head.

He told me to write a one-act play—for him…with deep, human truth…

ELLA. (*Appearing.*) How can a face be like a book?

EFFIE. —Ella! You scared me.

(ELLA's *carrying a basket of supplies. She has some snow on her hair and shoulders.*)

ELLA. *Can* a face be like a book…?

EFFIE. Is that a riddle, Ella?

ELLA. Do you want to have a wedding one day?

EFFIE. Of course. Don't you?

ELLA. I won't have a wedding… I'm too slow… I'll never catch a man.

EFFIE. Maybe he'll catch you.

ELLA. Will it be beautiful?

EFFIE. My wedding? I hope so. One day.

ELLA. What will you wear?

(*Before* EFFIE *can answer.*)

I see you in a white dress, like snow...
A veil over your face...of snow...
Your wedding will take place out of doors, at night.

EFFIE. (*To us.*) Like Tiresias in the plays of William Shakespeare, Ella had the gift of second sight. Or future sight. As the Scots say. As you may have guessed already...
It could be unnerving sometimes.

ELLA. Let me stay and watch you write.

EFFIE. Okay. (*Time passes.*) It's boring. (*Time passes.*) Do you see anything happening yet...?

(ELLA *shakes her head "no."*)

ELLA. I'll be making your waxed-up mustache...

(*She pulls out some tarpaper, a scissors, a bottle of glue.*)

EFFIE. (*To us.*) How did she know I'd need a mustache for Addie...?
And why did she say I'd be married out of doors at night, with a veil of snow?

ELLA. (*Dreamily, quietly.*) How can a face be like a book?

EFFIE. (*To herself, as much as to us.*) How old am I now? I must be twenty-one, twenty-two... (*Time passes.*) What on earth should I be writing about?

(*Another pause.*)

If I close my eyes, weeks later, I can still hear his voice...

(*An idea. She writes.*)

LIZZIE. "Enter an innocent young gypsy girl."

(LIZZIE *enters, dressed innocently enough: something white, diaphanous; though dirty and ratty still, her nightgown maybe.*
She has a few pages of script in her hand. She shakes off some snow.)

EFFIE. What are you doing?

LIZZIE. I'm freezing!

(LIZZIE *grabs a "gypsy" shawl.*)

EFFIE. That's my part, I'm the innocent young gypsy girl.

LIZZIE. No you're not—you're writing.

EFFIE. I can both write and act.

LIZZIE. You can't—you have to *choose*—!

EFFIE. Why?

ELLA. (*As she works.*) How can a face be like a book?

EFFIE. —What does that even *mean*, Ella?

LIZZIE. Sounds like witchcraft to me…

EFFIE. You can play her for now, Lizzie. While we rehearse. But when I'm done writing *I* will play the innocent young gypsy girl—

LIZZIE. No!—why? I'm prettier than you are, I'm the (*Mispronouncing.*) ingénue—

EFFIE. "Ingénue."

LIZZIE. Who cares? —I hate French people!

JESSIE. (*Offstage.*) Hurry up, it's snowing outside!

LIZZIE. Again?

EFFIE. (*Writing.*) "Enter the innocent young gypsy girl's very matronly mother."

(JESSIE *enters, shaking off snow, script pages in hand also.*)

JESSIE. "I am the innocent young gypsy girl's very matronly mother. I wear a kerchief wrapped round my head to keep the robust lice in. I squat on wide mannish haunches and cook dinner out on open flames. I am rife with superstition. I fear no man, only Fate. Yes, Fate, and—the Spanish Cavalier!"

(*Enter* ADDIE, *with gusto, script pages too. In leather chaps.*)

ADDIE. "I am the Spanish Cavalier! A-ho! Hallo!"

(ADDIE's *"Spanish Cavalier" strongly resembles* POPS *the agent.*)

EFFIE. (*Murmuring, writing.*) "Spanish Cavalier, with olive skin, swaggered thighs…chest cocked out and mustache…"

ADDIE. Mustache.

LIZZIE. Mustache?

EFFIE. —Waxed-up mustache! —Ella!

(ELLA *has just finished crafting her tarpaper mustache.*
She moves to ADDIE, *daubs glue on her lip, sticks the mustache in place.*)

ADDIE. "A-ha! A-ho!" —A-choo. This itches, Ella.

EFFIE. (*Prompting.*) You are the Spanish Cavalier.

ADDIE. —I know who I am!

LIZZIE. Why can't you be the cavalier, Effie? if you have to act. Why does Addie always have to play the man?

ADDIE. "I am the Spanish Cavalier! Hallo! As I have already made mention! And my way is to be cavalier—with women!"

(*"He" does a little dance. Castanets.*)

ADDIE. List to me while I tell you
How much I enjoy your young women!
In some very naughty ways
I have been known to have my way
With them!
Because you see I am guapo,

Muy guapo,
Muy muy muy muy muy muy
Muy guapo,
And I nunca take nay for an answer!

LIZZIE. "Hello. I am the innocent young gypsy girl."

ADDIE. "You're squatting."

LIZZIE. "Yes. Do you like it?"

ADDIE. "Yes. —But also, you are squatting on my land."

LIZZIE. "I don't pretend to understand what it is you think you're saying, Señor Cavalier! We gypsies are like the Red Indian that way, like the mighty Sioux, or the wily—(*A la the French.*)—*Iroquois*, in that we know this land to be no man's land. It is God's land, and we are all but gypsies wandering God's frontier."

JESSIE. That's good, Effie. That's patriotic.

ADDIE. It's too wordy. As usual.

EFFIE. Don't make me self-conscious—it's flowing through me!

ADDIE. "Impertinent gypsy tramp! How dare you speak to me in such bald romantic platitudes. This is my land, not God's! (*"He" spits. Dances.*) I will punish you now, striking you once, no twice, firmly, upon your delicate soft bustle with my stiff riding crop—and yet, I won't. Why? Because I see something in you."

LIZZIE. "You see something…?"

ADDIE. "In you."

LIZZIE. "In me? Already?"

ADDIE. "Something… I've never seen before. Something quite like—"

LIZZIE. "What. Tell me. Oh do not be afraid, Monsieur Cavalier, to tell me what-all you are seeing inside of me already!"

(*A pause. The "Spanish Cavalier" turns away.*)

ADDIE. "I must go. (*"He" turns back.*)
But tonight: meet me here again, young buxom gypsy wench. And we shall wed. You and me. By the light of the full, full…full moon."

(ADDIE *exits the scene—but not the barn—singing.*)

Muy muy muy muy muy muy
Muy muy muy muy muy…

(ELLA *moves to* ADDIE, *gives her mustache a touch-up of glue.*)

EFFIE. (*To us.*) A wedding! Out of doors! at night! How do I come up with these things?

ELLA. How can a face be like a—?

EFFIE. Okay, we get it already, Ella.

(JESSIE *shuffles on.*)

Come on, Jessie, be quicker than that…

JESSIE. I'm old.

EFFIE. Then start sooner.

JESSIE. —My *character* is old!

LIZZIE. —"Mother!"

JESSIE. "There, there, my child. There, there. There. Now, rest your head, here, upon my pendulous breasts. These breasts are large with mother-feeling. As if bursting with the sweet milk of mother-love. Rest your head…and unburden your heart's woe to me."

LIZZIE. (*Smothered in* JESSIE's *breasts.*) "I met a man!"

JESSIE. …Hmn?

(LIZZIE *breaks free.*)

LIZZIE. —I said "I met a man!"

JESSIE. "O dear Lord! Undone!"

LIZZIE. "In the woods—"

JESSIE. "How often have I told you not to wander these woods alone? You may be nothing but an impertinent gypsy tramp, but you are virginal and therefore tasty as a cherry tart, and men will snap you up if they can."

LIZZIE. "He is a Spanish Cavalier—"

JESSIE. "O Lord! O Lord! Undone! Undone!"

LIZZIE. "His hair is dark, and his face is brown—like a book."

JESSIE. "A book?"

ELLA. A book.

LIZZIE. "And his mustache—"

ELLA. Is made of paper.

EFFIE. Ella! Be quiet!

LIZZIE. "He said I should meet him, in the woods again tonight. By moonlight we shall wed. In a wedding dress like snow. A veil of snow, also. And then…well, then—I know not what will become of me!"

(*She swoons. Falls down.*

JESSIE, *as the Gypsy Mother, seems to think long and hard about something.*)

JESSIE. "Here is what I think: I have thought long and hard about this…

"If you meet him tonight in the woods, he will only pretend to wed. One can not wed by moonlight without a priest. I learned that the hard way. Have you never wondered who your father is? Never mind. Because he won't bring a priest, your Spanish Cavalier. He hates God, and all that God stands for. (*She spits.*) It will be a *façade*. A *charade*. A *canard*. And he will fool you just to have his way!"

LIZZIE. (*Standing up.*) "His way with what?"

JESSIE. "Why—with whatever it is men do with women."

LIZZIE. "Which is what, exactly?"

JESSIE. "Which is what?"

LIZZIE. "Exactly."

JESSIE. "What do they *do?*"

LIZZIE. "Yes, tell me please, Mother, I've never understood!"

JESSIE. "Why—they *love* them!"

LIZZIE. "O!"

JESSIE. "Yes, over and over again—and not always in very nice ways."

LIZZIE. "O! O!"

JESSIE. "List to me while I tell you, young innocent gypsy girl tramp daughter: if you meet this Spanish Cavalier in the woods again by moonlight: you are lost! Forever! —Do not go, my girl, do not go!"

EFFIE. (*To us.*) She goes.

Just as we go, to the World's Fair, in Chicago, 1893…

It really is the World's Fair: the whole world's there… (*She sings softly, to herself.*)
    I'm so lonely for Old Broadway…

It's not New York…but we're getting closer…

In a dark room at the Palace of Fine Arts, Edison exhibits a moving picture machine. It will kill the vaudeville, someone whispers by my side… But when I turn to see who's speaking: I see Pops with his mouth next to *Lizzie's* ear…

> (*In tableau, in shadow,* POPS *is whispering to* LIZZIE, *who giggles…*
> *The sound of an audience laughing.*)

I let her keep her role, for the time being… She's right: you can't both write and act.

> (*On stage now,* ADDIE *and* LIZZIE *are off-book, more costumed: a cape and gleaming sword for* ADDIE.)

ADDIE. (*Swaggering.*) "You've come! My innocent young cherry-tart-like gypsy wench!"

LIZZIE. "Of course I've come—you *rake!*"

> (*"She" slaps "him."*)

ADDIE. "You love me!"

LIZZIE. "Of course I do! How could I *not* do? —But I know you not! I know not love. How could we two *but* love? You are a mystery to me, a buzzing hive of bees. You are the dark, sea-salty depths—"

ADDIE. "Take off your clothes."

LIZZIE. "Yes, right away."

> (LIZZIE *takes off her clothes, down to her pink leotard.*)

"What ho! Where is the priest?"

ADDIE. "Don't be so naïve. A *'padre'*? (*"He" spits.*) Do you see this sword that hangs from my belt? This is all the *padre* I need!"

LIZZIE. "I don't even understand the comparison!"

ADDIE. —"Take off *all* your clothes!"

> (*"He" draws his sword.*
> LIZZIE *screams, a long drawn out contralto scream…*
> *Lights out. Lights up again.*)

7: Backstage, World's Fair.

LIZZIE. I feel so different…

> (LIZZIE *sits. Her hands go to her stomach.*
> JESSIE *is reading a newspaper.*)

JESSIE. It makes no sense at all… It's like they saw some other show, someone else, not us. Some *imposters*…

ADDIE. Read it out loud to everyone.

JESSIE. "The Unbelievable Cherry Sisters in: Seeing is Believing!"— exclamation point—"wowed the audiences last night"—

LIZZIE. That's not bad.

JESSIE. —"with their awesome dearth of saving graces,"

> (*Pause.*)

ADDIE. That's bad.

LIZZIE. What's "dearth" mean? a little or a lot?

JESSIE. "with their alternately mewling and booming howls disguised as music,"

LIZZIE. I do not howl!

JESSIE. "their leotards like madhouse uniforms,"

ADDIE. Sorry, Ella.

> (ELLA *seems quite hurt by this.*)

JESSIE. "their disgraceful bovine leaping,"

LIZZIE. What's "bovine"?

ADDIE. Worse than matronly. But only just a little.

JESSIE. "and their one-act melodramatic play, *The Gypsy's Warning!*"— exclamation point—"which betrays an all-too-obvious spinsterish anxiety."

> (*A long pause.* JESSIE *puts the paper down.*)

LIZZIE. What's "spinsterish anxiety" mean?

> (EFFIE *sits down heavily.*)

EFFIE. It means I wrote it.

> (LIZZIE *is wearing the white dress.*)

LIZZIE. …Where's Pops?

JESSIE. He's dead, Lizzie. He's been dead these last few years…

ADDIE. She's talking about the other one, Jessie.

LIZZIE. Am I?

JESSIE. Oh.

ELLA. I'm going to be going away…

> (*She raises her hand and points spookily at:*
> POPS, *who's entered the scene, unseen. His new suit's newer, his slick hair's slicker. He's smoking a thicker, longer cigar.*
> *But he's sweating a lot more.*)

POPS. How's it feel to be famous?

ADDIE. —Infamous, more like it.

JESSIE. Have you read these reviews?

POPS. Who reads reviews? Sure, I read them…

JESSIE. The *New York Times* sent someone—

POPS. What's that, a weekly?

JESSIE. —and the headline reads simply: "Five Freaks From Iowa."

> (*Pause.*)

POPS. That depends on your interpretation.

ADDIE. Of Iowa?

POPS. We're sold out all week long, girls. Now tell me: would that happen if we were a flop?

LIZZIE. Maybe…

POPS. Lizzie! …I'm surprised at you.

> (*He goes to chuck her under the chin—she turns away this time.*)

LIZZIE. Sometimes I get the feeling…

POPS. What feeling?

LIZZIE. —I'm going to throw up.

> (*She exits to throw up.* POPS *takes out his handkerchief to mop his face. His handkerchief is getting bigger and bigger…*)

POPS. What's the matter with you gals? Didn't they laugh?

ADDIE. In all the wrong places.

POPS. *Ipso facto,* that's a contradiction in terms—!

JESSIE. What about Lizzie's songs? They laughed at the sweet ones, and they laughed most impertinently, I must say, at the comic…

POPS. Do not doubt, my girls! Do not give in! remember what Lincoln said.

ADDIE. What did he say?

POPS. "Don't worry about it!"

Look, you're green. It's sweet. I see this every day. You don't yet know how hard this business can be... But this is how they love you on stage!

Love is a mysterious thing, onstage...

It does not always come when you want it to. It does not always come from whom you would like it to come from. Sometimes people love people they're not supposed to love. Or they love you in a way you really wish they wouldn't—that's a crime, in certain states.

But love is love, like money's money, so please, girls—don't be so picky!

> (*The sisters look unconvinced.*)

ADDIE. You sure are sweating a lot, Pops...

POPS. Am I? I think I got a touch of whatever Lizzie's got...

> (LIZZIE *has returned, looking peaked.*
> POPS *reaches into his pants pocket.*)

Guess what I have for you here, girls...

LIZZIE. Please don't say chocolate.

> (*He pulls out a telegram.*)

POPS. It's a wire—

LIZZIE. That's a piece of yellow paper.

POPS. From Hammerstein.

JESSIE. Who's Hammerstein?

ADDIE. A kind of cow.

POPS. You're kidding me, right? Only the biggest producer on Broadway... And here it says, in regulation English, that you four gals have been invited to New York City...to play the Olympia Theatre on Broadway!

JESSIE. What do you mean four?

> (*Pause.*)

LIZZIE. You mean five of us, right Pops?

ELLA. I'm going to be going away...

POPS. Try to understand things, girls. Hammerstein runs a family establishment. He's cleaned up the vaudeville. He values, as do I, as does everyone who's ever seen your show, your...fidelity to one another.

But he knows you'll get more laughs without her.

And I have to say I agree. I was wrong about Ella. In a melodrama, she'd be fine. Drama's kind to imbeciles. But no one wants to laugh at a girl like this... it's *too* cruel.

> (*Pause.*)

Here's your advance: five hundred dollars. One for each of you—even Ella.

> (*He holds out a hundred-dollar bill to* ELLA.)

What do you say, Ella? You don't mind going home, do you girl? There's a good girl… I'll bet you miss it there, all that snow.

(ELLA *takes the bill. Puts a corner in her mouth, tastes it.*)

…So what's it gonna be, Effie? New York City, yes or no?

(*He's holding out the remaining cash to* EFFIE.
A quick beat; then EFFIE *takes the money, gives a hundred dollars to* ADDIE, *then to* LIZZIE.)

JESSIE. How could you…?

ADDIE. We'll send her more money, Jessie…

LIZZIE. She'll be happier at home—

JESSIE. Alone? —Have you all lost your minds?

ADDIE. It's for her own good, Jessie.

LIZZIE. She's ridiculed, I hear them sometimes.

JESSIE. —So are we!

EFFIE. We'll never get where we need to go if we keep her with us. She's holding us back.

JESSIE. She's our sister.

EFFIE. You can go home with her, if you want. We're going to New York City.

(ELLA *smiles mysteriously.*
EFFIE *holds the remaining hundred-dollar bill out to* JESSIE.)

…What's it gonna be, Jessie? Are you coming with us? Yes or no.

(JESSIE *looks away from* ELLA. *She looks away from all her sisters.*
After a pause, she takes the remaining hundred-dollar bill from EFFIE.)

(*To* POPS.) Wire Hammerstein we're coming.

(*Lights out. Or down to that sharp iris-light again, on:*
EFFIE, *to us.*)

And that's how we got to the top of our profession.

(*Iris-light shrinks to black.*
Intermission.)

ACT TWO

8: New York, Oscar Hammerstein's Olympia Theatre on Broadway.

All the sisters onstage, except ELLA.
JESSIE'S *banging the bass drum now, still with that old wooden spoon.
Bright lights, big show, big finish.*

ALL. Cherries ripe, boom-dee-ay!
Cherries red, boom-dee-ay!
The Cherry Sisters
—*Are on Broadway!*

EFFIE. —Oh!

(A small dense head of cabbage has come flying out of the darkened house and pegged EFFIE *in the back, or the front, or the side of her very large head. She's down.*

The other sisters rush to her aid, help her to stand, etc.)

JESSIE. *(To the audience, with fury.)* Who did that? *(No response.)*
Who threw that head of cabbage at my sister's head? You? fat man, fourth row, mustache, very sad-looking wife… Did you throw that cabbage at my sister?

(No response. Some titters. To another.)

You—you look like the sort of man who'd throw a vegetable at a girl… What do you have against women? You came from a woman, if I'm not mistaken, from her *womb*—

(Someone throws a rotten tomato at JESSIE—*it explodes off the wall.)*

EFFIE. Let's move on, Jessie.

JESSIE. Yes, let's.
Let's move on to the homily then, shall we? —Does everyone know what a "homily" is? Probably not. I'll let you in on a little secret here: a homily is "a tedious moral lecture," according to Dr. Webster. And let me *also* tell you, my homily's going to be *very* moral tonight, and exceedingly tedious! I can assure you… There's no reason why the theater can not be both tedious *and* educative, is there?

(EFFIE whispers in her ear.)

(To the audience.) Not tedious. —Not tedious at all! or tedious to you, perhaps, who have no moral compass…

VOICE. *(In the audience.)* Why don't you go back to Idaho!

JESSIE. "Idaho"? No, sir, I am no lowly spud-grubber… I am one proud Iowonian woman, of the golden-tasseled corn state. Though I doubt very much you'd be able to find either Iowa or Idaho on a color-coded map of the Union—with labels. —Can you even read?
No, I shall remain here on stage. Because my sisters and I have been engaged by one Mr. Oscar S. Hammerstein—the S. is for savings!—to perform for you

all here tonight. And we are at the top of that bill—for a reason: "The Cherry Sisters in: Something Good, Something Sad!" Exclamation point!

> (*Some lettuce lands limply onstage.*)

That's it. That's good. Get it out of your system. Any more fruit and veg'? Cough it up:

> (*Several more tomatoes hit the back of the stage; a sack of potatoes; some overripe melons; a chicken carcass.*
> *Silence.*
> JESSIE *steps into a special light.*)

Tonight's homily is entitled, "Manners in the Twentieth Century!" Exclamation point, naturally.

> (*Silence, as* JESSIE *arranges herself for oration.*
> *The other three sisters stand patiently upstage, listening, or pretending to listen.*
> EFFIE *is still rubbing her sore head.*
> JESSIE *speaks with the overblown gestures and rhetorical flourishes of a temperance crusader, or some other zealot.*)

"There are many things one must do, and many more things one must *never* do! These are the customs of a people…

"From sun-spangled Borneo, to the snow-swept Aleutians. From stone-strewn Tierra del Fuego, to the fish-friendly coasts of Nova Scotia. (*Pause.*) From Mohamed-loving Istanbul—"

VOICE. To your fat white ass!

JESSIE. (*Trying to ignore.*) "—every people have evolved their own especial manners, for good and for ill. Sometimes manners differ, from a people to a people, in their particular. But all good manners have one thing in common:"

VOICE. Shut your cake hole!

JESSIE. "—*kindness!*

"For what are good manners 'good' for? Well, as Dr. Darwin has suggested none too recently, nothing exists for no good reason at all—"

> (*Someone throws a cat on stage—*ADDIE *quickly hurls it off.*)

(*Flustered, heroic.*) "—Well. I don't know about you, but I believe that in the coming century Man's manners will have evolved to such dizzying heights of decency that wars shall have become uncouth. Gauche, if you will."

> (*Some offal, internal organs. A cascade of dubious condoms.*)

"—*Famine!* What well-bred man will withdraw his crust of bread from within the mouth of one starveling Swahili?

"Nay, as I have proved, and as Dr. Darwin has none too recently divulged, as I mentioned, we learn, and we learn. And then we learn some more. And as we learn we become much nicer mammals. —Ah! For we are mammals, are we not? Argue me that! What man amongst us here will argue with me that we are not mammals!"

(A kitchen sink.)

"And so I believe, in the very core of my being, nay, in the white-hot wet molten core of my most feminine parts *(She beats her chest.)*, that one hundred years from now we shall live together, every last one of us—even you, Mustache!—in a state of Edenic good manners.

"For who amongst us desires pain and cruelty before kindness and love? Who confounds the rose for the knife, the slap for the tickle, the—?"

> *(A watermelon is heaved out of the front row and hits her in the gut.*
> *She catches it, staggering back.)*

Oh dear God—

> *(An enormous wave of laughter.)*

EFFIE. *(Stepping forward, to us.)* There it is again. There you go…
I heard it this time, maybe for the first time…
I'm thinking…is this what laughter is?

LIZZIE. *(Gamely; jauntily.)* Corn juice!
> I'm so thirsty for corn juice!
> It's been so long
> Since I sang this song
> O, for corn juice!
> I've had the juice of *naranjas*,
> I've slurped the juice of the grape,
> I've sucked the nectar of the gods,
> But Iowa's juice is great!

EFFIE. I'm thinking of Jessie's Dr. Darwin. I'm thinking: you're an audience of baboons, of chimpanzees and apes in your tuxes and your gowns, or whatever it is you're wearing these days, sitting up on your hind legs, baring your yellow fangs…as you howl and shriek and gibber and drool…
I could've said something. I could've shut you up. I could have shut my sisters up. We could always just leave the stage. Can't we?
Why can't we—?

LIZZIE. O, corn juice!
> I'm addicted to corn juice!
> I've got the shakes
> And my stomach aches
> For some of your corn juice!
> I've sniffed the cocaine powder,
> I've smoked the marijuana leaf,
> I've jacked the morphine in my veins,
> But Iowa's juice is so cheap!

EFFIE. The fruit and veg' rained down…

> *(The fruit and veg' rains down.)*

(*A dumb-show of dodging:*
Every time a Cherry sister's hit, the audience erupts in an orgy of laughter and
applause.
LIZZIE begins to cry. Despite the assault, she finishes her song, tears and refuse
staining her face.)

LIZZIE. O corn juice!

I'll do anything for corn juice!

Just name your price

And I'll treat you nice

For some of your corn juice!

> (*Lights move in on* LIZZIE, *a grotesque mask, then out.*
> POPS *is waiting in the dressing room.*)

9: Backstage, Hammerstein's Olympia Theatre on Broadway.

POPS. Don't be so naïve. This is what happens in New York when they love you: they feed you!

It's like the zoo, girls. Consider it a compliment.

> (LIZZIE's *still crying.* JESSIE *tries to comfort her.*
> POPS *is drenched in sweat. He mops his face with a handkerchief throughout.*
> *This handkerchief is now really a towel.*)

ADDIE. Those weren't compliments they were throwing out there…

LIZZIE. Do they hate us? —They don't even *know* us!

POPS. They're jealous, I'm telling you.

JESSIE. Jealous of what?

ADDIE. Yes, what exactly are they jealous of, Pops?

POPS. Not the audience, girls. The stars!

LIZZIE. Stars get jealous?

JESSIE. Which ones?

LIZZIE. You mean like astrology?

POPS. The brightest in the firmament today: Dixey, Dockstader. That slut Lottie Collins. Sheldman's Educated Dogs. —They're all so jealous of you and your red-hot ascendancy. Face it, girls: you're hot. And what happens in New York City when you're hot is they hire some young gallery gods to pelt you with defunct fruit and veg'. And other things. Rubbers. —It's a time-honored Gothamist tradition!

ADDIE. Are *you* hot, Pops?

POPS. Just a little.

ADDIE. It's November.

POPS. Maybe I got T.B., I don't know.

LIZZIE. I don't find T.B. funny anymore…

POPS. I'm excited is all! It's obvious we got something going here, girls. Your talent, I dare say your genius, and of course your very popularity right now, are all so enormously immense that you're gonna have to expect fruit and veg' at every show!

LIZZIE. I had no idea that stars could be so cruel.

POPS. Believe it, doll, they're heartless.

> (POPS *touches* LIZZIE *on the chin: she turns away.*)

ADDIE. Should we do it back to them, then?

POPS. Do what, Butch.

ADDIE. Go to their shows and throw garbage at the stars.

POPS. No no no—

ADDIE. Why not?

JESSIE. Yes, why not, Pops?

POPS. We're better off being stoic. Like what's his name, Jesus. Or Joan of Arc—in your case.

There's only one thing Americans love more than success, and that's failure.

> (EFFIE *sits down, looking dejected and confused.*
> ADDIE *takes her hand.*)

(*To* EFFIE, *re: her head.*) You should ice that thing.
And now, ladies. For your own protection—

> (*A net rises up, or descends, between the audience and the actors.*
> EFFIE *talks to us through it.*)

EFFIE. We made the stars jealous, every time we stepped on stage…

> (EFFIE *starts to slowly undress, throughout the following.*)

LIZZIE. Did you see how much garbage I got during "Corn Juice!" tonight? A steady barrage, a constant volley, a deluge of rotten envy!

ADDIE. I got sprayed during my comic monologue: some joker threw diced carrots through the net.

JESSIE. That fellow with the melons was back again tonight. Thank goodness for our protective netting!

EFFIE. (*To us.*) I read the papers to myself instead. I don't know why I did it.

LIZZIE. Someone threw a bottle at me tonight!

EFFIE. "The most talentless act to hit Broadway since Poodles Malloy in '84"…

ADDIE. Someone threw their chair!

EFFIE. "Miss Lizzie Cherry narrowly escapes being pretty, but her sisters were never in any such danger"…

JESSIE. (*Pulling a gun out.*) Someone threw this gun at me during my homily—

(ADDIE *and* LIZZIE *duck for cover.*)

It's not loaded…but it's the thought that counts, right?

EFFIE. (*Reading, in her underwear.*) "Their long, skinny arms, equipped with talons at the extremities, swung mechanically, and anon were waved frantically at the suffering audience. The mouths of their rancid features opened like caverns, and sounds like the wailing of damned souls issued therefrom."

(EFFIE *puts the newspapers down. Looks out at us.*)

And every night: we sold out.

ADDIE. They hate us…

LIZZIE. They loathe us!

JESSIE. They absolutely despise us.

(EFFIE *joins in:*)

ALL. —We're the best act in New York City!

ADDIE. What's the matter, Effie. Aren't you coming with us?

(JESSIE *and* LIZZIE *and* ADDIE *disappear, leaving* EFFIE *alone, backstage, late at night, in her underwear.*
Her underwear is rather ornate, frilly, almost a bit tarty.)

POPS. (*Appearing.*) Baby doll.

EFFIE. You scared me.

POPS. Who'd you think I was?
You decent? I'll turn around.

EFFIE. No, I'm fine.

POPS. No you're not: you're in your underthings.

EFFIE. Am I? (*Coquettishly.*) I'm sure it's nothing *you've* seen before, Pops…

POPS. You mean it's nothing I've *never* seen before.

EFFIE. That's a double negative.

POPS. I know. Ergo I have seen women in their underwear before, Effie. All the time.

EFFIE. Have you? that's fresh… (*She flirts strenuously.*) I don't think you should be talking to me like this, Pops…

POPS. Abramowicz. Myron Abramowicz.

(*He sits down beside her.*)

That's my name… I ever tell you that?

EFFIE. Are you Jewish?

POPS. Is my fly open? Just kidding. I'm Episcopalian. You got a problem with the Jews?

EFFIE. No.

POPS. Good. 'Cause my father was Hasidic.

EFFIE. Is that near Spain?

POPS. Not in a very long time…

Where is everyone? You know, I thought you were Lizzie from behind.

EFFIE. —Oh!

(*She moves in for a coquettish slap.*)

POPS. What are you doing?

EFFIE. I wasn't going to do it hard…

POPS. Well don't do it at all, okay? —Where is she?

EFFIE. Home. At the boarding house… She's not feeling well, as usual.

POPS. What about you?

EFFIE. I feel—

POPS. Desperate? just kidding,

What do you think of New York City, Effie? Is it everything you ever dreamed it would be?

EFFIE. I don't know yet…

POPS. Well you should find out. Fast. You should go out sometime, on the town. Find a man. An accountant, maybe. Somebody with very poor eyesight. You like men, don't you?

EFFIE. Like them how?

POPS. You're not like that sister of yours, are you?

EFFIE. I get lonely sometimes…if that's what you mean… After the show.

POPS. Tell me about it…

(*He lays his head lightly on her shoulder.*)

EFFIE. You smell like my father.

POPS. That's probably just 'cause I'm drunk.

(*Pause.*)

—And shvitzing! Jesus! all the time… I keep sweating around you girls… It's disgusting—*I'm* disgusting, aren't I?

(*Pause.*)

It's so hard, Effie…

EFFIE. What's hard? —It is?

POPS. Performing, all the time. You know? Isn't it?

EFFIE. You're not performing.

POPS. I am! All the time! So are you…

Sometimes I get so, so tired…

(*He leans his head against her shoulder again.*
He closes his eyes.)

You're the smart one… You're so much smarter than the other girls… Why are they all so dumb?

Are they dumb? or do they just pretend? Maybe I'm the stupid one here. I mean, *you* knew what was going on the whole time, right?…you've always known what was *really* going on…

> (*With his eyes closed, slowly, his hand has begun moving up her body, to her breasts. He gropes her for a bit. She's frozen.*
> *After a beat:* EFFIE *tries to kiss him.*
> POPS *stands up.*)

Sorry, you're not my type.

EFFIE. But—

POPS. It's not personal—

EFFIE. You said my head was beautiful—!

POPS. Listen, Effie, I'm marrying your sister.

EFFIE. —Which one?

POPS. Which one? Are you crazy? We're doing it Monday morning. City Hall. Hot shit.

EFFIE. Why?

POPS. Monday? It's our day off.

EFFIE. Why are you getting married at all?

—Because she's pretty? She's not that pretty, she's prettier than me, but—

POPS. Effie—

EFFIE. Did you knock her up? You seduced her, right? —You forced yourself on her probably, backstage, in Chicago, I saw you whispering—

POPS. This isn't one of your one-act plays! …I love her. Simply put. In my way. More or less.

EFFIE. What about the show?

POPS. Show's over. Don't cry—New York City, at least. That's what I came back here to tell you girls. That's why I've been out celebrating… Hammerstein's cancelled our gig. Something about a joke getting old.

EFFIE. What about the money?

POPS. I'm keeping most of it. You'll understand…for Lizzie, the kids… It's the right thing to do.

You'll tell the other girls, okay? I can't face them all tonight…

> (*Pause.*)

Hey, don't look so sad… We had some fun, didn't we? —We were popular! Most people are *never* popular, even with their own families…

And remember, love's like money: every bit counts.

You'll get home okay?

(*She doesn't answer. He turns the lights out on* EFFIE *as he goes.*)

POPS. (*From off.*) So long!

LIZZIE. So long, everybody! Good bye!

(LIZZIE *appears in a wedding dress, bouquet in hand.*
Crowds, train whistles, shoes clacking on marble…)

JESSIE. Congratulations, Lizzie!

ADDIE. Congratulations, Lizzie…

(JESSIE *is crying.*)

LIZZIE. I only wish Ella could've come! What a hurry it's all been!

EFFIE. What do you expect from a shotgun wedding?

LIZZIE. What did you say, Effie…? I can't hear you so well anymore, what with all the crowds of Grand Central Station, and the whistles of the trains, and the sounds of shoes clacking on marble—

EFFIE. I said you got knocked up!

(*A train whistle shrieks.*)

POPS. (*Offstage.*) —Come on, Lizzie, train's leaving!

(LIZZIE *begins to cry now too.*)

LIZZIE. I'll write you from Saratoga Springs. We're going there for the horses, and the baths. And the horses. Everybody knows the only thing Pops loves more than a good horse race is taking a bath! (*She cries a lot.*) It'll be so lovely, you'll see.

And by the time I'm home again…I promise you all I'll be pregnant!

JESSIE. Where's home, Lizzie?

LIZZIE. What, Jessie?

JESSIE. Where are you going to live from now on?

LIZZIE. Flushing! —Isn't that the most beautiful name? So clean!

(LIZZIE *cries, a lot.*)

EFFIE. —Did you know his name is Myron?

LIZZIE. Of course, Effie! He told me that months ago…

What's wrong with you…? You look like you've seen a ghost.

POPS. (*Off.*) Lizzie! Train's leaving!

EFFIE. Goodbye, Lizzie.

LIZZIE. What did you say? I can't hear you… I can't hear you so well anymore…!

(LIZZIE *goes.*
But before going:
She turns and throws her bouquet up over her shoulder, into the air.
She's gone.
The bouquet lands onstage and breaks into many small pieces.)

EFFIE. (*To us.*) Five months later she died in childbirth. (*Pause.*) Unlike me, this baby died too.
We never heard from Pops again…

> (ADDIE *and* EFFIE *slowly pick up the pieces of* LIZZIE'*s bouquet while they quietly sing.*)

ADDIE. I ain't never been kissed…

EFFIE. (*To us.*) After Lizzie died, Addie and I sang her songs as duets. (*She sings.*)
I ain't talking cheeks, I'm talking hot lips.

ADDIE. No matter how hard I swing these hips…

EFFIE & ADDIE. I ain't never had no lover's kiss.

> (*Music continues, becomes a new song.*)

I wrote a new song. Something just for me to sing, alone:
Love's like money,
I ain't never got enough.
My wallet's always empty,
My heart's only full of fluff.
Love's like money,
Better squirrel it away.
Winter's gonna come, one day,
And steal your nuts away.
I used to dream that love was free
But now I see you earn it,
You sell it and you steal it
And in a pinch you burn it
—It's business and you're the boss!
Love's like money,
Even when you're rich
It could all just disappear,
And leave you sleeping in a ditch.
I used to dream that love was free
But now I see you earn it,
You sell it and you steal it
And in a pinch you burn it
—It's business and you're the boss!
Love's like money,
Doesn't matter what you're owed.
It's your job to make it
Out here on the open road…

> (*Train whistle blows.*
> ADDIE *and* JESSIE *appear, with luggage.*
> ADDIE *carries two suitcase—one for* EFFIE.*)

ADDIE. Let's go, Effie. Train's leaving.

    (EFFIE *takes her suitcase.*)

JESSIE. It'll be so nice to see Ella again…

EFFIE. We're not going home. We're going on tour.

JESSIE. How can we—?

ADDIE. We don't have any money left, Jessie…

JESSIE. We don't have a manager either!

EFFIE. I'll be our manager from now on.

JESSIE. That's absurd! A manager is a man—that's why it's spelled that way!

EFFIE. Not anymore, Jessie. It's the Twentieth Century now. Remember?

10: The Open Road.

EFFIE. Pick up the pace, girls! —Pick up those bags, Jessie, they won't carry themselves.

    (JESSIE *has several bags, in fact, like a pack mule.*)

JESSIE. Where are we now…?

ADDIE. In Cairo.

JESSIE. As in Egypt?

ADDIE. Illinois actually.

JESSIE. Where's my ticket? …Has anyone seen my other suitcase?

EFFIE. We'll need more light in here!

ADDIE. —Drop the net! —Raise the curtain!

EFFIE. That's not what the contract said, asshole.

JESSIE. Effie! …It's like I don't know you anymore…

    (EFFIE *runs into the arms of* JESSIE.)

EFFIE. "Mother!"

JESSIE. "There, there, my child. There, there. There. Now, rest your head, here, upon my pendulous breasts."

ADDIE. Ladies and—one gentlemen. —Is that a gentleman? I beg your pardon, Sister.
—The human pyramid!

    (*They do it*—JESSIE's *always on the bottom.*
    They break out of it.)

EFFIE. Let's go.

ADDIE. Look, there's a letter here from Ella—

    (ELLA *appears, wearing some kind of fancy headdress.*)

ELLA. Dear my three remaining sisters:

Snow is cold here; Iowa is cold here, in winter. And fall. And spring. Summer is just about right, don't you think?
Thanks for all that spare change you send…

EFFIE. (*To us.*) If you're surprised she can write like this, so are we.

ADDIE. Is that a semicolon?

JESSIE. Is she getting someone else to write these letters for her? Whom?

ADDIE. That's Ella's handwriting all right: enormous…

EFFIE. In red crayon.

ELLA. I've been working on my routine.

JESSIE. What routine?

ELLA. Because I know, if only I can get better, if I can find some more talent—*in* me, somewhere—then one day I'll be able to see you all again, to perform with you, out on the open road…
I miss you all…
I know I was not so good before. I don't blame you all that much.

     (*She starts to juggle, some old whiskey bottles.*)

Every day now I go out to the barn, and I practice my juggling—some of Pops' old bottles. The ones he kept hidden inside all that wet hay. There's so much wet hay—! Which is why it hardly matters when I break a few.

     (*She breaks all of them.*)

JESSIE. That sounds dangerous…

ELLA. (*Cuts her finger.*) Shit.

EFFIE. Let's go girls, train's leaving.

JESSIE. —Again?

ADDIE. Oskaloosa…

     (EFFIE's *scribbling in her little brown journal.*)

EFFIE. Thirteen dollars for deposit please…

ADDIE. Osceola…

EFFIE. Eight seventy-four, no make that -five.

ADDIE. Ottumwa…

JESSIE. Where's that? In Canada?

EFFIE. We're in Dubuque now.

JESSIE. Sioux City.

ADDIE. (*Fading away.*) Waterloooo…

JESSIE. As in France?

EFFIE. What difference does it make where we are, Jessie? We're on stage—we're all over the corn-belt these days!

JESSIE. "We're the best the corn-belt has to offer"…

EFFIE. We are!

JESSIE. I'm going to take a nap.

> (JESSIE *takes out a hip flask and swigs.*)

ADDIE. (*Prompting.*) "My dear sir—"

EFFIE. "My dear sir, I think you're fresh!"

ADDIE. "I think *you're* fresh! Like a summer rain!"

EFFIE. "And you're like a winter drizzle."

ADDIE. "I can't help it! You make me feel damp!"

EFFIE. —"Fresh!"

> (EFFIE *slaps* ADDIE *perfunctorily.*)

ADDIE. Ladies and—or should I say, nightwalkers and—gentleman farmers: —The human pyramid!

> (*They do it again:* JESSIE's *on the bottom again, of course.*)

ELLA. Dear Mis Hermanas:

> (*Enter* ELLA *again, with a unicycle, and wearing a dirty army helmet. She's got some mud on her face too.*)

Today is spring thaw. Mud is ubiquitous.

EFFIE. "Ubiquitous"?

ELLA. Meaning "everywhere," like God used to be. You should know that, Effie!

EFFIE. I *do* know that but—

ELLA. I've been learning to ride my unicycle.

> (ELLA *prepares to ride the unicycle.*)

JESSIE. Where'd she find a unicycle…?

ELLA. I made it. From an old bike with only one wheel left. Hence "uni."

EFFIE. We know what a unicycle is…

ADDIE. "Hence"?

ELLA. And it's difficult but I think I might learn how to do it well, one day. And juggle at the very same time.

> (*She tries to juggle and cycle at the same time: she fails.*
> *She falls.*)

—Damn! Damn it all to Hell I swear it is hard work!

JESSIE. Amen, sister…

ELLA. I think one day you will like my new act, girls. When you come home to visit, I'll show you.

When will you be coming home…?

JESSIE. When *will* we, Effie…?

EFFIE. (*Her book.*) Tulsa. Five flat for deposit please…

ADDIE. Amarillo.

EFFIE. Three dollars and thirteen cents.

JESSIE. Does anyone else have this rash?

ADDIE. That's not a rash, Jessie. Those are bedbug bites.

JESSIE. —Jesus!

EFFIE. —Jessie! Your language—

JESSIE. Oh, blow it out your ass.

>   (JESSIE *takes another swig.*)

ADDIE. Salt Lake City.

EFFIE. (*Journal.*) Two fifty: "house was small and mean."

JESSIE. These Mormons can be so touchy sometimes...

ADDIE. It's the polygamy. It makes you grouchy.

EFFIE. Manhattan.

JESSIE. Where?

ADDIE. Kansas.

JESSIE. Oh.

EFFIE. Bellevue.

JESSIE. Hospital?

ADDIE. Nebraska.

JESSIE. Right. —Are you going to eat that meatloaf?

ADDIE. That's not meatloaf, that's an old sponge.

JESSIE. ...It's raining so hard.

EFFIE. No that's hail.

ADDIE. And sleet.

JESSIE. It's snowing again...

EFFIE. Flood.

JESSIE. Lift up your skirts, girls—!

ADDIE. Drought.

JESSIE. —Has anyone seen my medicine?

ADDIE. You mean your corn juice?

EFFIE. Twister!

ADDIE. Dust bowl! —A-choo!

EFFIE. Locusts.

JESSIE. Are you going to eat that honey?

ADDIE. That's not honey, I just sneezed.

JESSIE. Is there a draft?

EFFIE. It's winter.

ADDIE. Summer.

JESSIE. Autumn.

EFFIE. Winter.

ADDIE. Winter.

JESSIE. When is it ever not winter?

EFFIE. These years are racing by—like a train—

ADDIE. Like we're *on* that train—

EFFIE. There's a cow. And another. And another.

ADDIE. It's all moving so fast—!

JESSIE. Is anyone else feeling nauseous?

EFFIE. Is this what life's like, getting old...?

ADDIE. Cabool, Missouri.

EFFIE. Twenty-four cents and (*Someone throws these onstage.*) two miniature chickens.

ADDIE. Thank you!

JESSIE. My corns...

ADDIE. Mansfield, Missouri.

EFFIE. One Canadian dime.

ADDIE. —Cheapskates!

JESSIE. Does this feel like a hernia to you...?

ADDIE. Licking, Missouri.

EFFIE. Nobody came. Nobody at all. Left Licking, all our bills unpaid.

ADDIE. Missouri...Missouri...

JESSIE. (*Sounding a lot like "misery."*) Missouri...

EFFIE. What's wrong with you this time, Jessie?

JESSIE. I'm sweating, all over. I'm hot, I'm tired—

EFFIE. Maybe you shouldn't carry that accordion around with you all the time.

JESSIE. My squeezebox? —I've got to practice.

ADDIE. Maybe it's the change of life.

JESSIE. What change of life?

ADDIE. You know...

EFFIE. Already?

ADDIE. It *is* getting a bit stale, Effie... Maybe we need a new act? Something a little more...contemporary?

> (JESSIE *plays her squeezebox.*
> As EFFIE *hooks on a very long thick black beard.*)

EFFIE. "K-nock, k-nock!"

JESSIE. "Who'sa dere?"

EFFIE. "It is I! The landlord, Tevieh Schmalzagazicht! —Oy gevalt!"

JESSIE. "—Oh sole mio!"

ADDIE. "Turn offa de light and shutupa de face!"

JESSIE. "—He wantsa de rent!"

ADDIE. "How cana we paya de renta! We can nota evena feed spaghetti to our own bambinos and bambinas!"

JESSIE. "We can nota feed our bambinitos because you nevera go to a worka!"

ADDIE. "How cana I go to a worka when I'm Italian? —Oh! I wish I wasa back at a home-a in Sicilia with Mama!"

EFFIE. (*Still Tevieh.*) "And for this I went to college? —You know what? forget about it…"

JESSIE. (*On her squeezebox.*) We can not pay the landlord
  When his hands go k-nock, k-nock, k-nock.

ADDIE. We can not pay the loan sharks
  With the meatballs that we hock.

JESSIE. We can not pay the doctor
  After a visit from the stork.

ADDIE. So we blow out all our candles,
  Not a flame and not a spark,

JESSIE. And we feed our children garlic
  So we can find them in the dark!

  (ELLA *appears in the barn loft above, wearing an aviator cap, goggles on her forehead.*)

ELLA. Dear Gals:
What a hot summer it's been. Jesus! —Jesus H. Christ! Our barn is falling down practically! The barn has become a bastion of broken bottles and rags—

EFFIE. "Bastion"? I know what that means, but—

ADDIE. Why is she yelling so much…?

JESSIE. She's been drinking. She sounds drunk.

ELLA. I am finally now so good at juggling whilst riding on this unicycle, that I have decided to string a rope from loft to rafter out here in the barn—

JESSIE. Oh sweet Jesus…

ELLA. And any moment now I promise you I'll be ready to wheel out across that empty space above our very hard barnyard floor—

JESSIE. She can't do that!

ELLA. —whilst juggling—

EFFIE. "Whilst"?

JESSIE. —She'll die!

ELLA. And yes, I am afraid that I might die…
So I have taken to fortifying myself with corn juice. I find it gives me strength.
No wonder Pops was so fond of the devil drink!—woops.

> (ELLA *has been climbing up onto the loft railing, reaching out for a piece of*
> *dangling rope…and she almost falls.*
> JESSIE *almost faints: she sits.*)

Effie…?
Remember that dream I told you about? Years ago? That you would get married,
out of doors, at night? With a dress like snow, and a veil of snow also…?
Well I was wrong about one thing: it's not a wedding. Not a wedding at all…

> (ELLA *disappears.*
> JESSIE, *below, picks up her suitcase.*)

JESSIE. I'm going home.

EFFIE. They paid to see a show, Jessie.

JESSIE. Who cares about them? —Our sister's about to kill herself!

ADDIE. We'll go home together, when the tour's over. Okay? Just for a rest.
—How's that sound, Effie? take a month off—

EFFIE. Whose side are you on?

> (*Pause. Now* ADDIE *is hurt.*)

JESSIE. We can sell the land, keep the house. Or get a house in town—

EFFIE. (*Disgusted.*) In Marion?

JESSIE. In Cedar Rapids, if we want. An apartment, in the city.

EFFIE. Cedar Rapids's not the city.

ADDIE. —What would we *do* all day, Jessie?

JESSIE. Nothing! Can you imagine how nice that would be?
We'd take care of Ella…listen to the radio, all of us together, to all the acts
coming straight to us from New York City. We'd make fun of them for
once—it'd be so nice to make fun of somebody else, for once, wouldn't it?
And we'd grow our own vegetables, and fruit. We wouldn't have to dodge them
anymore—we'd eat them! And we'd clean up all that mess that Ella's made.
We'd walk up and down that old house in Marion, remembering things how
they used to be.

EFFIE. Things were awful in that house.

JESSIE. Then we'd remember it better than it was…
Instead of living out here, on the open road all the time—

ADDIE. I like it out here, on the open road. We meet so many people—

JESSIE. Who we never see again.

ADDIE. Nobody ever tells us what to do—

JESSIE. Don't you want to fall in love? Don't you want a family?

ADDIE. Why?… I already have one.

EFFIE. She's lazy. That's all it is. —You've always been this way, Jessie. —*And* pessimistic. You've never *once* believed in us!

JESSIE. Oh, Effie. (*Pause.*) That was impolite.

> (*Another pause.*)

Tonight, Effie. Because you're my sister. Then I'm done.

ADDIE. —Inmates and guards of Leavenworth Prison—and Warden Johansen, of course:

The human pyramid!

> (*They do it one more time.*
> *This time* JESSIE *collapses under the weight of her sisters.*
> *She's squashed flat like a bug. They roll off her.*)

EFFIE. Jessie. —Jessie, get up.

> (*The sound of applause is deafening.*)

ADDIE. I'll get a doctor—

> (ADDIE *exits.*)

EFFIE. (*To us.*) It was her heart.

> (*As the protective netting rises up out of view…*
> *And* POPS *appears, looking like the old Pops again, whiskey bottles dangling off his ragged clothes, blasted wet cigar in his mouth.*)

POPS. There you've gone and killed another one, you murderous little girl. Wherefore all this rage, little Effie? Why?

> (EFFIE *runs at him, with a murderous rage.*
> POPS *evades gracefully—he's a ghost, he sings.*)

Your skirts are up above your knees, you're dancin', girl—
Be careful, girl, be careful, please;
Me eyes are like twin stars o' fire, advancin', girl
—O, do be careful! —O, do be careful!
There now, it's up above your waist,
Your pearly goods are all uncased,
They're surely temper'd to my taste
—St. Patrick's Day in the morning!

JESSIE. (*Pops up.*) Hi, Pops.

POPS. Hello, me dear.

JESSIE. Is Mother here?

POPS. You know, I haven't thought to ask.

JESSIE. Are we in Heaven, Pops, or Hell?

POPS. They won't tell me that one yet neither!

EFFIE. —How can you even *talk* to him?

JESSIE. He's dead. I'm dead. He's our father.

POPS. Have you not learned your lesson yet, Effie? Have you not figured out what went wrong?

EFFIE. What went wrong? —*You* went wrong! Momma *dying* went wrong—

POPS. (*Chuckling.*) Oh now, Effie… It's almost over now. Can't you see? It's the end of the road for you… It's time you went home.

JESSIE. I'd like to deliver a little homily before I go: it's called, "On The Importance of Manners in The Afterlife." No exclamation necessary now, naturally. You can chime in anytime you'd like, Pops.

POPS. I wouldn't dream.

JESSIE. (*In her usual style.*) "What will the coming life bring? Is there such a thing as life beyond the grave? Whom shall we meet—or meet again—in Heaven, Hell, or *Purgatorio*, as our dago brethren say.

"Well, I don't know about you, but I believe our after-lives will be better than our before-ones. Full of chit-chat and finger sandwiches.

"And we shall be kind to one another at last. Even unto family members, whom we may have hated in life, or felt betrayed or injured by…

"For if we can not forgive them now, then how shall we ever begin to forgive ourselves?"

> (*Someone in the audience throws* JESSIE *white roses.*)

EFFIE. —I'm so sorry, Jessie!

JESSIE. Why?

EFFIE. We're no good! I'm no good! —I'm horrible! I was horrible! Just like you were. We were all of us no good at all and I've known it for the longest time!

JESSIE. So have I… We've all known that, haven't we? The whole world's known that…

EFFIE. Why didn't you say something? why didn't we ever speak of it?

> (JESSIE *gives* EFFIE *one of her white roses.* JESSIE *disappears.*
> POPS *follows.*)

POPS. (*To Effie, as he goes.*) I'll see you soon, me girl.

EFFIE. I will never forgive you.

> (ADDIE *appears, carrying their two suitcases.*)

ADDIE. Let's go, Effie. Train's leaving, again…

11: That barn in Marion.

Train whistle becomes a heartless plains wind…
EFFIE *looks around her.* ADDIE *looks to* EFFIE.
EFFIE *turns to us, to say something—then forgets what she was about to say.*
How much time has passed?

Though the girls are elderly now, the tempo here is quick, fluid, a patter of senility. ADDIE *sniffs the air.*

ADDIE. Smells like snow.

EFFIE. It's winter…

ADDIE. Again? That's nice.

EFFIE. What is?

ADDIE. What?

EFFIE. Where are we now?

ADDIE. Back home, in Iowa.

EFFIE. It's like we never left…!

ADDIE. Did we?

EFFIE. What time is it now?

ADDIE. 1935.

EFFIE. Exactly?

ADDIE. Give or take.

EFFIE. That's late… This barn could use some work.

ADDIE. What?

EFFIE. —I said that's nice!

ADDIE. Where's Ella?

EFFIE. Oh, she's dead…

ADDIE. Did she die out here on that tightrope? Did she fall to her death from way up there?

EFFIE. Oh no.

ADDIE. That's nice.

EFFIE. —That *is* nice!

ADDIE. What is?

EFFIE. We moved home, when Jessie died. We lived with Ella, who died in her bed of old age…

ADDIE. Old age?

EFFIE. Old age.

ADDIE. That's nice.

EFFIE. —And easy!
We had to burn our furniture sometimes, for warmth…

ADDIE. (*Nostalgically.*) I remember warmth.
We still have our chickens though, don't we?

EFFIE. We ate them. Had to. The Depression.

ADDIE. Depression?

EFFIE. The Depression.

    (*They both sigh, depressed.*)

Why are we out here again?

ADDIE. You don't know?

EFFIE. Should I?

ADDIE. It was your idea.

EFFIE. Was it? Why?

ADDIE. To rehearse, I think…

EFFIE. Rehearsal is such a depressing word. Redundant.

ADDIE. What is?

EFFIE. We are.

ADDIE. What are we meant to be rehearsing again .?

EFFIE. A job, I think. For a show, in New York City.

    (*Short pause. Some magic.*)

ADDIE. What kind of show?

EFFIE. A nostalgic revue…

ADDIE. "Nostalgia is a useless emotion."

EFFIE. Who said that?

ADDIE. What?

EFFIE. Who?

ADDIE. —And I agree!

EFFIE. —Me too!

ADDIE. Whatever was I saying…?

EFFIE. Who invited us all the way to New York City?

ADDIE. You should know. Some guy.

EFFIE. Some man.

ADDIE. Some schmoe.

EFFIE. —What a timewaster!

ADDIE. I've got the letter here to prove it.

EFFIE. He wrote us a letter?

ADDIE. He phoned you.

EFFIE. What's a telephone?

ADDIE. Who knows?

EFFIE. Who knows?

ADDIE. Should we go?

EFFIE. Would you like to?

    (*Pause.*)

They'll be kinder to us this time, Addie. I think so…

ADDIE. How do you know that?

EFFIE. I don't.

ADDIE. Do we need the money? If we need the money…

EFFIE. Of course we need the money.

ADDIE. That's not why.

EFFIE. No, that's not why.

ADDIE. Will they laugh at us?

EFFIE. I think they will.

ADDIE. Will they cry?

EFFIE. I hope they don't.

ADDIE. —But we're so out of practice!

EFFIE. Are we? At what?

ADDIE. Remembering… How to sing, and dance. Tell our funny jokes…
(*Pause. Something happens.*) "I'm only goin' so far as Yahnkers!"

EFFIE. Where'd that come from?

ADDIE. I have no idea.

EFFIE. From the ether.

ADDIE. What do you call a cow with no milk?

EFFIE. Who knows?

ADDIE. Who knows?

EFFIE. —What the Hell?

ADDIE. Look at my fingers! —Like lizards!

EFFIE. That's why we're here? To remember?

ADDIE. What are we remembering again? Tell me one more time…

EFFIE. Our show. Don't you want to go?

ADDIE. To New York City?

EFFIE. New York City.

ADDIE. All right, Effie. I'll go if you will.

> (EFFIE *takes* ADDIE's *hand this time.*
> *They sing the song slowly, in a minor key.*)

EFFIE. I ain't never been kissed,

ADDIE. I ain't never been kissed.

EFFIE & ADDIE. We ain't talking cheeks, we're talking hot lips.
No matter how hard we swing these hips,
We ain't never had no lover's kiss.

> (*A pause.*)

(*To us.*) Not a missile was fired. Not a voice cried out in ridicule…
Some women wept softly. Men hid their eyes in their hands and were thankful for the dark.

ADDIE. Good night, Effie. This was fun.

> (*She kisses her sister. Lets go of her hand.*)

EFFIE. Addie passed away that year.
I moved to Cedar Rapids, where I opened up a bakery and sold only cherry tarts…and cherry pies… Anything with a cherry in it, really.
I never went to the theater, or (*With derision.*) the movies.
I ran for public office. I lost.
I grew fond of pasta, and ranting in public, often at the same time. I'd tell anyone who'd listen to me the world was going to Hell and here's why.
I kept on writing in this little brown book. A memoir of sorts, that remains unpublished to this day…in a drawer…in a desk somewhere in Iowa…
It hardly explains things anyway, so… So what?

> (*Her sisters appear one by one, with their lines.*)

ELLA. (*Pointing.*) It's snowing.

> (*It's true:*
> *Snowflakes are falling from the rafters, as if the roof has lifted off the barn.*
> *The snow will grow heavier, the lighting blue and wintry.*)

EFFIE. And then, one night, or early one winter's morning, as I lay in my bed above the bakery…I saw in my room a tall man, a Spaniard.
A cavalier, with his knife sheathed by his side…

ADDIE. I'm not a man, Effie. I'm your sister. Here I am again.

EFFIE. And in the street below I thought I heard his horse chuff and stamp its hooves in the snow.

JESSIE. It's me, Effie! It's freezing out here!

> (LIZZIE *begins to sing, softly beneath the scene.*)

LIZZIE. I'm so lonely for Old Broadway,
  I'm so bored by these cornfields and hay…

> (POPS—*as their father—appears, standing in the shadows.*)

EFFIE. I rose from my bed and followed my ears, out into the hallway and down the back stairs…

ADDIE. Watch your step—

EFFIE. Out into the street where the snow's falling fast…

JESSIE. Don't fall, Effie—

EFFIE. Not silently, the snow sounds like rain. —No, like applause, falling on rooftops, past darkened windowpanes… Steady clapping falling down from unseen hands.

ADDIE. Don't slip in the snow, Effie. Here, hold my hand.

    (ADDIE *and* EFFIE *join hands again.*)

EFFIE. I was wearing my white nightgown…

ELLA. Like a wedding dress.

    (*Pause.*)

Let's see it again.

ADDIE. It's all over now, Effie.

EFFIE. I want to see it—just once more, okay? Can we? Please? —We can.

JESSIE. If you don't come now then we can't go either.

LIZZIE. We won't go, Effie, if you won't come. Come on!

ADDIE. Please, Effie. Show's over…

EFFIE. Am I ready though?

JESSIE. Aren't you yet?

EFFIE. Have I figured it out this time? what went wrong?

ADDIE. What went wrong?

EFFIE. I don't know. Whose fault was it?

JESSIE. "Fault"?

EFFIE. Was it Pops?

JESSIE. Yes.

EFFIE. Was it the people in the audience?

LIZZIE. Yes.

EFFIE. Was it my fault…?

ADDIE. Was it worth it?

    (EFFIE *looks around her, at the snow; out to us.*
    Now she looks to her sisters.)

EFFIE. I want to see it again. Just one more time.

    (*Stage to black.*)

End of Play

PHOENIX
by Scott Organ

ABOUT *PHOENIX*

This article first ran in the January/February 2010 issue of Inside Actors, *and is based on conversations with the playwright before rehearsals for the Humana Festival production began.*

When Sue and Bruce meet for coffee in the first scene of *Phoenix*, they're practically strangers. A few weeks have passed since a chance meeting turned into a one-night stand, and Bruce was beginning to think he'd never hear from her again. He's hoping this time he'll get her phone number—maybe even a second date—but Sue has just three things to say:

Number one: *I like you.*
Number two: *I can't see you anymore.*
Number three: *I'm pregnant.*

Sue has no intention of keeping the baby. She barely knows Bruce. A traveling nurse, she has carefully organized her life to avoid the entanglements and complications of human relationships. But when she tells him she plans to terminate the pregnancy, Bruce throws her a curveball: he'd like to come with her. Not to try and stop her, he explains; he doesn't want children, either. But he feels a powerful, inarticulate need to be party to the experience. "I can't explain it," says Bruce. "All I know is I feel very compelled to be there. To… participate in it. To…live it." Cautiously, Sue agrees.

Thus begins a journey that spans seven weeks, 4,000 miles, and many cups of coffee, as Bruce and Sue question the calculated lives they lead and begin to contemplate the possibility of something different. Unfolding in a series of caffeine-fueled conversations between two strangers, *Phoenix* explores the fears and stubborn assumptions of its weather-worn heroes with compassion and sly humor.

Playwright Scott Organ is interested in inertia, in the deadening forces of habit and routine. "The older you get," Organ muses, "the more danger there is of closing yourself off to the unknown. It might be something as simple as, *How did I become a person who only sleeps on the left side of the bed?* When the hell did that happen?" But not all habits are so benign, and Organ believes following the path of least resistance holds its own dangers. "The more comfortable you become with a routine, the more difficult it can be to break out of it and try something new. You get older, you get cautious. If you're too cautious, you might miss out on the opportunity of a lifetime."

Despite the potentially controversial decision at the heart of the play, *Phoenix* isn't a story about right-to-life politics. "I'm not interested in exploring abortion as a political or ethical issue," Organ explains. "I'm interested in exploring abortion to the extent that it's a very real, difficult experience that people go through. And I think in many dramatic treatments I've seen, the human experience is eclipsed by the political overlay." Instead, *Phoenix* charts the subtle, tectonic shifts that sometimes occur when two strangers meet. "When you meet a stranger," Organ explains, "anything is possible. This person might hold the key to a door you didn't even know was there to be unlocked. I'm fascinated by the potential of the people you don't know."

Organ adds that an underlying secularism informs the play: "David Mamet said every play is in some way about the question, 'How do you live in a world in which you are doomed to die?' He believes that on some level, that's what all plays are kind of about. And I think that's a really interesting way to break it down. What do you do after you make the intellectual leap that there's really no master plan for the life you're living? How do you respond to the creeping feeling that maybe no one's in charge?"

If existential unease is *Phoenix*'s starting premise, the play argues for the possibility, maybe even the necessity, of connecting with another human being as a way to navigate the unknown and make it bearable. For Bruce and Sue, the possibility for redemption seems to lie, finally, in each other—if they're brave enough to take a chance.

—Sarah Lunnie

BIOGRAPHY

Scott Organ's play *Phoenix* had its world premiere at the 2010 Humana Festival of New American Plays and its New York premiere at The Barrow Group. As a playwright, Scott's work has been commissioned by the Atlantic Theater Company, developed by The New Group and The Barrow Group, and has been performed and workshopped throughout the United States. His full-length play *Fixed* premiered at the Hangar Theater in Ithaca, New York. His play *City* was produced at the Circle X Theater in Los Angeles, where it won the L.A. Drama-Logue Award for best new play. It was subsequently produced at the first New York International Fringe Festival, directed by Tony Award winner Michael Rupert, and at The Flea Theater in New York, directed by Kevin Moriarty. His short plays *China* and *The Mulligan* were published in *New American Short Plays 2005*, edited by Craig Lucas, and have been performed throughout the country. His one-act play *and everybody else* can be found in *Best American Short Plays 2002-2003*. His short play *Afraid. Yes. Of.* premiered Off-Broadway as a part of The Fear Project at The Barrow Group. Many other short plays have been performed at the Atlantic Theater Company's 453 New Works Series, which he helped create. Scott is also the author of the screenplays *Better Man, Ghostkeepers* and the original television pilots *The Powerball 7* and *The Pines*.

ACKNOWLEDGMENTS

Phoenix premiered at the Humana Festival of New American Plays in March 2010. It was directed by Aaron Posner with the following cast:

SUE ....Suli Holum
BRUCE ....Trey Lyford

and the following production staff:

Scenic Designer ....Michael B. Raiford
Costume Designer...Lorraine Venberg
Lighting Designer...Jeff Nellis
Sound Designer ....Benjamin Marcum
Properties Designer.. Mark Walston
Stage Manager...Kimberly J. First
Dramaturg ....Sarah Lunnie
Casting...............................Emily Ruddock, Zan Sawyer-Dailey

Directing Assistant.. Jeffrey Mosser
Scenic Design Assistant.....................................Ryan Wineinger
Lighting Design Assistant .... Paola Rodriguez
Stage Management Intern ....Katie Shade
Assistant Dramaturg .... Zach Chotzen-Freund

Phoenix benefitted from developmental readings in New York at The Barrow Group and The New Group.

CHARACTERS

SUE

BRUCE

Suli Holum and Trey Lyford
in *Phoenix*

34th Annual Humana Festival of New American Plays
Actors Theatre of Louisville, 2010
Photo by Harlan Taylor

PHOENIX

BRUCE *and* SUE, *in a coffee shop.*

SUE. Three things.

BRUCE. Oh, okay.

SUE. Yeah.

BRUCE. We're diving right in.

SUE. There's three things I want to say.

BRUCE. Okay. Good things come in threes, right? Isn't that what they say?

SUE. Deaths.

BRUCE. Sorry?

SUE. And deaths. Come in threes. Is what they say. And good things too.

BRUCE. Okay. Well. Before you start, let me just be the first to say welcome back.

SUE. Thank you.

BRUCE. What did that mean "Let me be the first to say"?

SUE. I don't know.

BRUCE. I'm the only one here.

SUE. No big deal.

BRUCE. How about this—welcome back.

SUE. Thanks again.

BRUCE. And how was it?

SUE. Uh, the trip? It was okay. It was business.

BRUCE. I wasn't sure I would hear from you.

SUE. You did. You are.

BRUCE. It's been a while. It's been…what? A month?

SUE. Four weeks.

BRUCE. A month, right?

SUE. No. Four weeks isn't really…

BRUCE. Okay, right. Four weeks.

SUE. I was away.

BRUCE. On business.

SUE. That's right.

BRUCE. Well. Welcome back.

SUE. Thank you.

BRUCE. A good trip?

SUE. I guess. Neither good nor bad.

BRUCE. Okay.

SUE. Yeah. No, it was fine.

BRUCE. All right. Number one.

SUE. What?

BRUCE. You had three things.

SUE. Oh. For a second I thought that was like a catch phrase or something…

BRUCE. Which?

SUE. You said "number one." Like "number one."

BRUCE. Meaning?

SUE. No. Let's just…

BRUCE. Right. The three. Let's hear it.

SUE. One.

BRUCE. (*Pretending it's his catch phrase—*) Number One.

SUE. What?

BRUCE. No, it's a… Go ahead.

SUE. The first thing I wanted to tell you. Before I left town.

BRUCE. Back then, yes… *Four* weeks ago.

SUE. Is I had a great time with you that night.

BRUCE. Me too.

SUE. I did. On that…you know, it didn't even qualify as a date…

BRUCE. Drinks, or…

SUE. Yeah.

BRUCE. Me too. I thought we really hit it off.

SUE. Yeah.

BRUCE. And the whole, crazy night, it was funny, it felt like we were stupid college kids or something.

SUE. We actually were kind of stupid.

BRUCE. But, yes, it was fun, the whole… I was going to say date.

SUE. Hook up, I guess.

BRUCE. Better than that. Drinks.

SUE. Well.

BRUCE. Just the hanging out, you know? Talking, and…as a team, you know, our silver medal performance in the trivia thing.

SUE. We were robbed.

BRUCE. My fault…

SUE. No…

BRUCE. It was…

SUE. Absolutely not. To say no one is buried in Grant's Tomb…

BRUCE. Yeah…

SUE. That he's "entombed—"

BRUCE. "Entombed."

SUE. Not buried. Is…

BRUCE. I agree.

SUE. We were robbed.

BRUCE. You are so good at trivia. You are. You're very trivial…minded… You're smart.

SUE. Well, it was fun.

BRUCE. And, you know, I hadn't planned on things going where they did. You know, later.

SUE. I thought they might.

BRUCE. And… You did?

SUE. Yes.

BRUCE. Oh. Well. I wasn't going to presume, or hope that… I just didn't really have a plan, per se, in my head.

SUE. I knew.

BRUCE. You did?

SUE. I know myself. And I liked you.

BRUCE. Liked me?

SUE. That night. You know, and still. You're a great guy.

BRUCE. Thanks.

SUE. You're a little weird.

BRUCE. Oh.

SUE. Yeah. You are.

BRUCE. Okay.

SUE. But I think that's okay. There's good weird and there's bad weird.

BRUCE. Right. Bad, like, come look at my homemade chain mail armor that I made with my own two hands…

SUE. You have chain mail armor?

BRUCE. No, I'm saying if…

SUE. Yes. And no. There's worse weird, believe me.

BRUCE. Or I'm in a barbershop quartet.

SUE. Depends. I feel like some guys could pull that off.

BRUCE. I'm not in one.

SUE. Depending on who you are.

BRUCE. I'm not in one.

SUE. That's fine.

BRUCE. Do you think that I should look into it?

SUE. A barbershop quartet?

BRUCE. Yes.

SUE. No.

BRUCE. Then we are agreed. See, I knew we get along.

SUE. Yeah. No, it was fun. That night.

BRUCE. Agreed once again.

SUE. Better than most.

BRUCE. Okay, I can live with that. "Better than most." I won't put it on my headstone, but…

SUE. Meaning. Meeting strangers. Your odds, you know. They suck.

BRUCE. Right.

SUE. Not better than most.

BRUCE. Okay.

SUE. As far as drinks with strangers go, that was my most enjoyable yet.

BRUCE. Number One!

SUE. I get it.

BRUCE. Sorry.

SUE. No, it's kind of funny, actually.

BRUCE. Most enjoyable yet for me too.

SUE. Okay.

BRUCE. Just handing out the superlatives now, aren't we?

SUE. Yes.

BRUCE. Bestest not-quite-date ever.

SUE. Yeah, and—

BRUCE. I'm just glad you called, and I'm glad to see you in person and it had been a while and I was holding out hope, but it had been a bit, so I was a little nervous I wouldn't hear from you, but here you are.

SUE. Here I am.

BRUCE. Yes. Time had passed. A month. Or, you know, nearly—

SUE. Right.

BRUCE. Which was enough time for me to think, "Okay, I get the point…"

SUE. Yeah, well…

BRUCE. And think, "Next time, Bruce, get the girl's number, too," you know?

SUE. Sure.

BRUCE. Don't just settle with handing yours over. It's fundamental. But, damn, that was fun, right, that night?

SUE. Yeah, it was.

BRUCE. Right? And here you are. You called.

SUE. Yeah.

BRUCE. Awesome.

SUE. And I should get to the second thing.

BRUCE. Let's do this.

SUE. Okay, then.

BRUCE. I like your style. It's very, you know…

SUE. Okay.

BRUCE. Hit me.

SUE. Bearing in mind all that I said…

BRUCE. (I'm) Bearing…

SUE. I can't see you anymore.

    (Pause. He begins waving in front of her face.)

BRUCE. I'm right here. Right here.

    (Pause.)

I didn't expect that.

SUE. Are you bearing in mind still?

BRUCE. Is that supposed to take the sting out?

SUE. I guess it is.

BRUCE. What? That you like hanging out with me but you don't want to see me anymore so, what? It kind of evens out?

SUE. Yes?

    (Pause.)

BRUCE. There's somebody else?

SUE. No.

BRUCE. You sure?

SUE. Yes.

BRUCE. Because then I would understand.

SUE. Then yes. Someone else. My husband, in fact.

BRUCE. No one else.

SUE. No.

BRUCE. You just prefer the company of say, no one, over, say, me.

SUE. I like you. I just don't want to be involved with anyone right now.

BRUCE. I hear you.

SUE. Good.

BRUCE. I mean, I hear you. Dinner for one, nothing like it.

SUE. Right…

BRUCE. You know. A can of soup is just the right size for… And sprawling all across the bed. The great long late nights alone with not a fucking soul to talk to except your two cats…

SUE. You should probably get out more.

BRUCE. You know what, Sue? I probably should.

> (*Pause.*)

SUE. How did you know I have two cats?

BRUCE. I didn't.

SUE. I do.

BRUCE. Congratulations.

SUE. Thank you.

BRUCE. Cats don't live forever, you know.

SUE. Yeah.

BRUCE. I'm sorry. That sounded mean.

SUE. It's just the truth.

BRUCE. Well. Just because it's the truth doesn't mean I have to spout it out all the time.

SUE. It's not a problem.

BRUCE. You know, "More than 25 million people have died of AIDS."

SUE. Really?

BRUCE. Just because it's true doesn't mean I have to spout it out.

SUE. Is anyone doing anything about AIDS, I mean, seriously…

BRUCE. Well. I won't lie to you…

SUE. Don't.

BRUCE. I am sorry you're not interested. I am.

SUE. It's not you. I just…it's not something I want to do right now. I was away and I was thinking about my life, about the world, and…

BRUCE. And what?

SUE. And I just thought…

BRUCE. What?

SUE. I don't know. I don't know.

BRUCE. You should figure that out.

SUE. Well, no, I don't really have to figure any fucking thing out.

BRUCE. Of course not. I'm sorry.

      (*Pause.*)

Yeah. Sorry.

SUE. Forget it.

BRUCE. Our first and last fight.

SUE. Yeah.

BRUCE. Not bad. Only one fight.

SUE. Not bad.

BRUCE. You keep the cats.

SUE. Thanks.

BRUCE. We'll split up the books later.

SUE. Yeah.

      (*Pause.*)

I should go. I need to go.

BRUCE. Okay.

SUE. I have to check in at work.

BRUCE. Okay.

SUE. Well, Bruce. It was nice to talk to you.

BRUCE. And you.

SUE. It was nice to see you and I wish you all the best.

      (*Pause.*)

In all your future endeavors. Whatever they may be.

BRUCE. Right back at you.

      (*She starts out.*)

Sue.

SUE. Yeah?

BRUCE. Three.

SUE. What?

BRUCE. Number three?

SUE. Oh.

BRUCE. Yeah.

SUE. Right. I said three.

BRUCE. You did.

SUE. Forget it.

BRUCE. No, no.

SUE. Uh…

BRUCE. Let's hear it.

SUE. Yeah…

BRUCE. So far it's—one, I like you. Two, let's never see each other again. I'm really looking forward to three. What could it be?

SUE. It's, uhh…

BRUCE. Come on. You said three.

SUE. Remember, of all the myriad things we discussed that night, and you said you couldn't have kids…

BRUCE. Yeah.

SUE. Yeah, well…

BRUCE. Great first date material. Genius.

SUE. Well—we were talking about everything.

BRUCE. Oh, fuck.

SUE. What?

BRUCE. That's why.

SUE. What?

BRUCE. You want children.

SUE. No.

BRUCE. Of course.

SUE. I told you I didn't. That's why it came up.

BRUCE. Of course you would say that now.

SUE. No, I said it first, I said I don't want kids and then you told me…

BRUCE. Stupid stupid me.

SUE. No, that's not it. Seriously.

BRUCE. What then?

SUE. Well.

BRUCE. Go ahead.

SUE. You can.

BRUCE. I can what?

SUE. You can have kids.

BRUCE. Why?

SUE. I don't really know why.

BRUCE. Well, no. How do you know?

SUE. Because I'm pregnant.

BRUCE. Right, right, right.

SUE. Yeah.

(*Pause.*)

BRUCE. With whose?

SUE. Whose?

BRUCE. Uh-huh…

SUE. With you.

BRUCE. Me.

SUE. Yeah. That's what I'm trying to tell you.

BRUCE. With me.

SUE. Yes.

BRUCE. Me.

SUE. Yes.

BRUCE. But I can't.

SUE. You can. You can. I thought you should know.

>   (*Pause.*)

So, you know, now you know something new about yourself.

BRUCE. Okay. We were careful still.

SUE. Not careful enough.

BRUCE. Right.

SUE. I thought this was something you should know.

BRUCE. Right.

SUE. That you deserved to know.

BRUCE. And there's been no one else.

SUE. No one else.

BRUCE. Really?

SUE. I would remember. I remember those things. Sex. With people.

BRUCE. Wow. I was told I couldn't.

SUE. I know.

BRUCE. That's what they told me. That's what the doctors told me.

SUE. Well. They were wrong. And no worries—I am going to take care of it.

BRUCE. Take care of the baby?

SUE. Take care of the situation.

BRUCE. Oh. Oh.

SUE. Yes. I'll take care of it. I don't need any help is what I'm saying.

BRUCE. Oh.

SUE. Financial, or otherwise. No worries.

BRUCE. No worries.

SUE. Yeah.

BRUCE. Holy shit.

SUE. What?

BRUCE. Really?

SUE. Yeah. I thought you should know.

BRUCE. Yeah.

SUE. It seemed the right thing to do.

BRUCE. Thank you.

SUE. I have to go now.

BRUCE. What?

SUE. So. Once again. Thanks for a fun night.

BRUCE. Really?

SUE. What?

BRUCE. And now you're just walking out the door?

SUE. I have work. I have to check in with them.

BRUCE. I feel like you've chucked a grenade on me and now you're permanently walking out forever.

SUE. I have to check in with work. I just got back into town last night.

BRUCE. Isn't there more that we need to talk about?

SUE. I don't think so, no. It's pretty straightforward.

BRUCE. Is it?

SUE. Yeah. For me, at least.

BRUCE. But we're, you know, even if it's…some weird…I mean, this is something we've shared, or…you've dropped this grenade on my lap. Because I was told that I couldn't.

SUE. Yes. They were wrong. And I really do apologize but I have to leave.

BRUCE. I feel—

SUE. I'm sorry.

BRUCE. I feel the least you could do is talk to me…

SUE. I can't.

BRUCE. For a few moments at least.

SUE. I can't.

BRUCE. A few minutes out of your entire life you could loan some out to me to let me register this, to talk about this with you, for whom without this would never be happening. Can you not give me that?

SUE. No.

BRUCE. Not even that? Not even that?

SUE. No.

> (*He looks shocked. Pause.*)

At least not now. Not now. Later maybe I can find a little time.

BRUCE. That would be nice.

SUE. We'll see.

BRUCE. Beyond nice, it would be a tremendous act of charity…

SUE. Can I call you later?

BRUCE. Will you?

SUE. I'll try.

BRUCE. If you try you will succeed.

SUE. Yeah.

BRUCE. Calling is easy. I can show you.

SUE. No.

BRUCE. I can even set you up so you press just one single number and it will call me.

SUE. Okay…

BRUCE. It's called speed dial.

SUE. I'll call you.

BRUCE. Okay, then.

     (*He sticks out his hand.*)

SUE. What is that?

BRUCE. A handshake. A deal.

     (*She hesitates.*)

I know it's one huge hell of a commitment thing, this having to place a phone call to me, but…

     (*She shakes his hand. Lights out.*)

Scene 2

     A phone ringing. BRUCE *and* SUE *on their phones, apart.*

BRUCE. (*Looking first at his phone—*) If it isn't my old friend "restricted caller."

SUE. Keeps the stalkers at bay.

BRUCE. Am I a stalker?

SUE. You have potential…

BRUCE. Someone who finally believes in me.

SUE. But to the point.

BRUCE. Right. Okay.

SUE. I don't have a lot of time…

BRUCE. Okay. My turn for three things.

SUE. Okay.

BRUCE. Maybe three. Depending on what you say.

SUE. Okay.

BRUCE. Seriously. Thank you for taking the time to call.

SUE. No problem.

BRUCE. I really appreciate it…

SUE. It's fine. Let's just go ahead.

BRUCE. Oh. Okay.

SUE. Yeah.

BRUCE. One is—have you…

SUE. Have I?

BRUCE. You know…

SUE. No, I don't.

BRUCE. What is it they say—terminated…the pregnancy?

SUE. Abortion is another term you may have heard.

BRUCE. Yeah.

SUE. Have I done that yet?

BRUCE. Yes.

SUE. No, I have not.

BRUCE. Oh.

SUE. Not yet.

BRUCE. Okay. Then two: When are you doing that?

SUE. Why?

BRUCE. I just wanted to know.

SUE. In a week or so.

BRUCE. Oh.

SUE. Yeah.

BRUCE. You have to wait? I mean, I don't even know…

SUE. It's a scheduling thing.

BRUCE. Oh.

SUE. I'm going to a facility—a place I'm very familiar with.

BRUCE. Okay.

SUE. It's a clinic that I know and trust.

BRUCE. You're a nurse.

SUE. That's right.

BRUCE. So you know people.

SUE. I do.

BRUCE. You're a…what are you…you're a traveling nurse?

SUE. That's right.

BRUCE. And what is that?

SUE. Well. It's a nurse. Who travels.

(*Pause.*)

BRUCE. Have I done something to piss you off?

SUE. You've impregnated me.

BRUCE. I didn't mean to.

SUE. I know.

BRUCE. Not only did I not mean to, I didn't think it was physically possible.

SUE. I know.

BRUCE. You were, as I recall, rather forthright in the removal of my pants.

SUE. On a side-note, you should, you know, consider rotating your stock.,.

BRUCE. What?

SUE. Your so-called "protection."

BRUCE. If you're implying that my condoms were somehow old as a result of a lack of sexual activity on my part in recent, what, years, then, you know, you're dead on.

SUE. I'm just saying, they have expiration dates.

BRUCE. Mine don't.

SUE. Because, I think, yours pre-date the modern practice of listing the expiration date.

BRUCE. Oh, man.

SUE. Look. It's just this whole thing is a bit of a pain in the ass, and I agreed to call and talk, briefly, with you, and you're not necessarily making anything easier with the...casual conversation...the "tell me about your job" blah blah blah...

(BRUCE *looks a little like he's been punched. A pause.*)

I signed up with an agency. I travel to different hospitals and facilities all over the country, sometimes outside the country, and I work for short periods of time, usually three months or so, and then I go somewhere else.

BRUCE. All the time.

SUE. Pretty much.

BRUCE. But you live here.

SUE. No. Not really.

BRUCE. Really?

SUE. Yeah.

BRUCE. You don't live here?

SUE. No.

BRUCE. This never came up that night.

SUE. I find it takes away from a first date, telling the other person you don't actually live here.

BRUCE. Wow.

SUE. My mother lives here. I come here a few times a year.

BRUCE. You didn't tell me this.

SUE. You know what, Bruce? Had I—we wouldn't have had such a good time.

BRUCE. And we wouldn't be pregnant.

SUE. *We* aren't pregnant.

BRUCE. Okay.

SUE. I'm sorry I didn't mention it that night.

BRUCE. So when you said you were going away on business, you weren't just going away on business?

SUE. No.

BRUCE. You were leaving for…what?

SUE. Three months.

BRUCE. So when you said you would call me when you got back?

SUE. I misrepresented when I would be getting back.

BRUCE. Misrepresented.

SUE. I lied.

BRUCE. So you did. And why are you back?

SUE. Nothing. Just coincidence. Job stuff.

BRUCE. Oh.

SUE. My job ran short and I'm being reassigned.

BRUCE. So I just got lucky then.

SUE. Depending on how you look at it.

BRUCE. That you happened to be back in town and happened to call.

SUE. I never would have even told you if you hadn't told me that you couldn't have kids.

BRUCE. I never would've heard from you.

SUE. Probably not.

BRUCE. No.

SUE. No. Definitely not.

BRUCE. Okay.

SUE. I don't want to be in a relationship.

BRUCE. I've gathered.

SUE. Yeah.

BRUCE. At least not with me.

SUE. No, that's not true. I liked you.

BRUCE. There you go again with the past tense…

SUE. Because, Bruce, and I am truly sorry if this sounds harsh, but you are past tense.

BRUCE. I already am.

SUE. I thought I made that clear. But you made me shake your hand. And here we are.

(*Pause.*)

So what's number three?

(*He says nothing.*)

I've upset you.

BRUCE. No.

SUE. I've called you past tense.

BRUCE. You did do that.

(*A beat.*)

SUE. Look. If I am short with you, it's because I have a whole army of brutal hormones fucking in a huge way with my body right now.

BRUCE. You do?

SUE. You know what? I knew we had conceived. I knew it when it happened.

BRUCE. How could you know something like that?

SUE. I felt it.

BRUCE. Really?

SUE. I know that seems crazy but it's true. And I ignored it because I thought we had been safe and remembered you telling me that you couldn't have kids. But I gotta tell you—the hormones kicked in right away. They're quite the tremendous force, let me tell you.

BRUCE. Thanks for telling me that.

SUE. I don't know what the fuck is going on, really. I don't recognize myself. I want to kill most people. I want to sleep. I want to eat all the time except when I want to throw up.

BRUCE. Sorry…

SUE. Would you like to know what I had for lunch?

BRUCE. Of course.

SUE. Two big disgusting bear claws. For lunch.

BRUCE. Yum.

SUE. I'm a healthy eater.

BRUCE. I like a bear claw.

SUE. Don't say that word.

BRUCE. Bear claw?

SUE. Stop.

BRUCE. Sorry. You said it.

SUE. Do you want me to vomit?

BRUCE. No, I don't.

SUE. You see? This is what I've been reduced to. And to top it all off, I have another week of this.

BRUCE. I'm sorry.

SUE. It's not your fault.

BRUCE. Nonetheless.

SUE. Or it is your fault.

BRUCE. I am so sick of you bad-mouthing my condoms.
> (*She smiles at this.*)

I didn't know you'd feel the pregnancy so soon.

SUE. You do. At least I do. Pretty damn soon. It's just a pain in the ass. And I am eager to have it done with. So if I seem to be…

BRUCE. No. It's okay.

SUE. You want to tell me your third thing?

BRUCE. Uh…

SUE. No, go ahead. The hormones have spiked or something. I won't snap at you. I promise.

BRUCE. You sure?

SUE. I promise.

BRUCE. Okay. The third thing—may I come with you.

SUE. Come with me where?

BRUCE. When you…terminate the pregnancy.

SUE. May you come with me?

BRUCE. Yes.

SUE. No.

BRUCE. No?

SUE. No. What the hell kind of question is that?

BRUCE. A stupid one, I guess.

SUE. Yes.

BRUCE. A stupid one.
> (*Pause.*)

SUE. Why? Why would you want to do that?

BRUCE. Because. I'm not exactly sure. Because I'm involved…

SUE. Nominally.

BRUCE. Biologically.

(*Pause.*)

Look. I'm not trying to insert my will into all of this. I realize that's not my place.

SUE. That's good.

BRUCE. And frankly it's not as if I want you to do anything different than what you want to.

SUE. Good. Because you would get nowhere with that.

BRUCE. No. I don't... I don't want kids. I really don't.

SUE. Okay.

BRUCE. I just want to be party to this thing that has happened...

SUE. Nothing has really happened.

BRUCE. No?

SUE. No. Nothing of consequence.

BRUCE. To you, perhaps.

SUE. Yes, to me.

BRUCE. I didn't even know that I could have kids.

SUE. And now you know. But that is unrelated to this. It's of no consequence.

BRUCE. I want to come along.

SUE. Why?

BRUCE. I can't explain it. All I know is I feel very compelled to be there. To...participate in it. To...live it.

SUE. You realize your "participation" would be sitting on a shitty couch reading an old copy of *Rolling Stone*?

BRUCE. That's fine.

SUE. It's a procedure. A relatively simple one at that. It's fucking outpatient.

BRUCE. I understand that.

SUE. And you still want to be there?

BRUCE. I do.

SUE. Well, no.

BRUCE. I insist.

SUE. You can't insist. You have no right to insist.

BRUCE. Okay, it seems you got me there.

SUE. Yeah, well...

BRUCE. Look. I just want to be there. I do. And though I may have no rights, per se, I ask you to let me do this. That, and then I leave you alone. I'll just meet you there—I'll read the *Rolling Stone*—you'll come out, we'll say hi, and then that's that.

SUE. That's that?

BRUCE. Yeah.

SUE. Why?

BRUCE. I don't exactly know. I don't.

SUE. You supply your own transportation?

BRUCE. Of course.

SUE. And afterwards, that's that?

BRUCE. My word.

SUE. Okay, then.

BRUCE. Really?

SUE. Yes. You want to meet me there, I won't stop you.

BRUCE. So that's a yes?

SUE. That is a yes.

BRUCE. Thank you.

SUE. No problem.

BRUCE. So when are you doing it?

SUE. Next Wednesday.

BRUCE. Okay, great. Where?

SUE. Phoenix.

BRUCE. Phoenix…? Is that the name of the facility?

SUE. That's the name of the city.

BRUCE. What city?

SUE. The city where the clinic is.

BRUCE. Phoenix, Arizona?

SUE. Yes.

BRUCE. Phoenix, Phoenix?

SUE. Yes. My next job. Phoenix.

BRUCE. Next Wednesday way the hell off in Phoenix. Arizona.

SUE. That's right.

      (Long pause.)

BRUCE. What time?

SUE. What?

BRUCE. What time is your appointment?

SUE. Oh, come on.

BRUCE. Come on what?

SUE. You're not coming to Phoenix.

BRUCE. Yes, I am.

SUE. Bruce…

BRUCE. I think so, yes. So, you know, where do I go? And what time?

SUE. I don't know. I haven't worked out all the details.

BRUCE. Okay. Well. Will you call me when you do?

> (*Beat.*)

You said yes.

SUE. Fine. I'll call you the night before.

BRUCE. That's the best you can do?

SUE. Do you want me to call?

BRUCE. Fine. Will you shake on that? Metaphorically speaking?

SUE. What's with you and shaking?

BRUCE. It used to mean something. It means something to me.

SUE. Okay, fine.

> (BRUCE *does a shaking motion.*)

BRUCE. Are you shaking?

> (*She isn't.*)

SUE. Yes.

BRUCE. You promise?

SUE. Yes.

> (*They shake.*)

BRUCE. Okay. See you Wednesday.

SUE. Right. Okay.

> (*Lights out.*)

Scene 3

> BRUCE *has two coffees—he holds one out to* SUE.

BRUCE. Cream, right?

SUE. Bruce.

BRUCE. No cream? I was sure it was cream. They were about to close so I had to make some executive decisions. Decaf, because of the hour, I hope that's okay.

SUE. Bruce.

BRUCE. They're closed. I thought we could walk or something.

SUE. What are you doing here? When I called you I fully expected to catch you at home…

BRUCE. I told you I would come.

SUE. I thought you might have a modicum of what some people call "common sense."

BRUCE. And thanks for meeting up with me tonight. I know we didn't phone-shake on that part.

SUE. You drove for like three days all the way out here. What was I supposed to do?

BRUCE. I wasn't expecting anything.

SUE. That's good.

BRUCE. I told you that. My arm is starting to hurt.

> (*She takes the coffee.*)

SUE. Bruce. It's certifiable. Really. Think about it. And yes, I take cream.

BRUCE. I have a backlog of vacation. Use it or lose it, you know? And I've always wanted to go to the Grand Canyon State.

SUE. They have flights, you know. They actually fly planes out here.

BRUCE. You haven't been?

SUE. Where? What are you talking about?

BRUCE. The Grand Canyon.

SUE. No.

BRUCE. It's, uh…worth seeing.

SUE. Okay.

BRUCE. That's a big understatement.

You're here for three months, right?

SUE. Roughly, yes.

BRUCE. You should go.

SUE. I probably should.

BRUCE. Definitely. Definitely.

SUE. You're insane.

BRUCE. It's like a four-hour drive from here. It's nothing. I'm telling you— It's, uhh…you can't perceive the depth of the thing. Or I couldn't. Because I have nothing to compare it to. I've never seen anything that deep, you know? It's uhh, really moving. Makes you really think.

SUE. About what?

BRUCE. I don't know. Time, you know. Time. The great tremendous past.

SUE. Yeah, well. I have a hard enough time with the present.

BRUCE. It makes you feel pretty insignificant.

SUE. Why would you intentionally choose to feel insignificant?

BRUCE. It's liberating in a way, don't you think?

SUE. No. I don't. Sounds like it sucks.

BRUCE. You know what?

SUE. What?

BRUCE. You seemed more fun on our date.

SUE. I am fun. I am.

BRUCE. Okay.

SUE. I am so much fun. That's a ridiculous thing to say about me.

BRUCE. Sorry.

SUE. You should see how much fun I am.

BRUCE. Okay.

SUE. Okay, what?

BRUCE. Let's see it.

SUE. It's not like I… I don't just do fun on command.

BRUCE. Okay.

SUE. I was fun on that date.

BRUCE. You were.

SUE. Right?

BRUCE. So much fun, we're in Phoenix.

SUE. Yeah, well.

BRUCE. No. That night was a lot of fun for me.

SUE. Okay, then. See?

BRUCE. Yes. I stand corrected. You're fun.

> (*Pause.*)

SUE. So. The Grand Canyon.

BRUCE. Yeah.

SUE. It's…what? How old? It's…what? The earth is billions of years old…?

BRUCE. 6,000.

SUE. What?

BRUCE. The earth is 6,000 years old. Roughly.

SUE. Uh.

BRUCE. Grand Canyon was created by the flood.

SUE. The flood.

BRUCE. Yeah.

SUE. The one with Noah.

BRUCE. Yep.

> (*Pause.*)

SUE. (*To no one in particular—*) Check.

BRUCE. It's a joke.

SUE. Oh. Well. I don't really know you, so…

BRUCE. It's a joke.

SUE. Okay.

BRUCE. I think the earth is four or five billion years old.

SUE. I thought I was old.

BRUCE. No. You're not old.

SUE. Four or five billion?

BRUCE. I think so.

> (SUE *ponders this.*)

SUE. Okay, then. But. Did you know?

BRUCE. What?

SUE. I read this thing—there are these scientists who say that the science is there or will be there to time travel.

BRUCE. Sounds good.

SUE. You'd think, yes. You'd think. But here's the thing.

BRUCE. What?

SUE. If that's true, which some very reputable people say is true, then where are the time travel tourists?

BRUCE. What are they?

SUE. Where are the people from the future who come back here?

BRUCE. Not here yet.

SUE. Why not?

BRUCE. I don't know.

SUE. Well, I do.

BRUCE. Tell me.

SUE. Because they aren't coming back. They haven't which means they won't. Because if they had we would know. Which could only mean one thing.

BRUCE. What?

SUE. It could only mean that this world, at least as we know it, will not be around for that much longer.

BRUCE. Really?

SUE. Yes. It's the only conclusion. In fact, there was a heavily-advertised time travelers convention—it was at MIT on May 7, 2005, designed for time travelers to all come back on that date…

BRUCE. No one showed.

SUE. A lot of people showed.

BRUCE. Oh. Really?

SUE. But none were from the future.

BRUCE. They didn't come back because the world as we know it isn't even going to be around for that much longer.

SUE. That's right.

BRUCE. Wow.

SUE. Yeah.

BRUCE. If that's true.

SUE. I think it is.

BRUCE. Then that sucks.

SUE. I thought you like feeling insignificant.

BRUCE. Not that insignificant.

SUE. I think it's about time, don't you?

BRUCE. For what?

SUE. Earth is old. Time to move on. Let 'er blow up.

BRUCE. You really believe that?

SUE. I do. Did you read what happened today?

BRUCE. No. What happened?

SUE. It doesn't even matter, really. Same old shit. Pick a day, read the paper. Doesn't matter.

BRUCE. What happened today?

SUE. Doesn't matter. It's just all very clear that we don't really learn a thing and we just play out the same shit over and over, over the millennia, and frankly, the sooner we fuck the planet, the better for the bacteria that are itching to take over.

BRUCE. Wow.

SUE. And you say I'm not fun.

BRUCE. I can't believe I'm about to do this…

SUE. What?

BRUCE. I shouldn't be bringing this up.

SUE. What?

BRUCE. But I feel given the depths of your morbidity, I have no choice.

SUE. What?

BRUCE. And I am breaking all sorts of rules here…

SUE. Just tell me.

BRUCE. I'm that guy.

SUE. What guy?

BRUCE. The guy…from the future.

SUE. You're that guy?

BRUCE. I am that guy. Hi there.

SUE. Well. Wow. Welcome to the past.

BRUCE. Thank you.

SUE. I'm honored. You've come out to me.

BRUCE. You gave me no choice.

SUE. So what's the future like?

BRUCE. It's a lot like *Battlestar Galactica*. The original one.

SUE. Nice.

BRUCE. Yeah. It's not bad.

SUE. I'm glad to hear it.

BRUCE. Did you ever consider that maybe people from the future don't tell the people in the past who they are?

SUE. Why wouldn't they? I would.

BRUCE. I'll tell you why—people can't handle it. People can't handle very much in the way of outright truth.

SUE. I agree with you there.

BRUCE. If I went public, I'd end up in some subterranean holding cell in Quantico, Virginia.

SUE. Possibly.

BRUCE. So we do it on the down low…

We just come in periodically to poke around, see what's going on.

SUE. Is that right? So why now?

BRUCE. Well. The truth?

SUE. Yeah.

BRUCE. Women from this era have a reputation for being kind of easy.

SUE. Oh yeah?

BRUCE. So guys come back looking for a little action.

SUE. A sex vacation in the past.

BRUCE. That's right. I hate to reduce it to this, but you're pretty much fish in a barrel.

SUE. Is that right?

BRUCE. In the future, men learn a great deal more about seduction which makes us so efficient in this era.

SUE. You didn't seduce me.

BRUCE. That's how good I am.

SUE. Yeah, right.

BRUCE. If you see it, it ain't seduction.

SUE. Is that right?

BRUCE. It's a saying we have in the future.

SUE. So what other advancements do we have to look forward to?

BRUCE. Better batteries. Like, way better batteries that last hundreds of times longer.

SUE. That's positive.

BRUCE. Yeah, you won't believe the batteries of the future.

SUE. What else?

BRUCE. Turns out the Mormons were right.

SUE. Really?

BRUCE. Yeah. It was a big surprise to everyone. Except the Mormons. Latter Day all the way. It's another saying we have in the future.

SUE. Wow.

BRUCE. I'm kidding.

SUE. About being from the future?

BRUCE. About the Mormons. No, so far no God has made him, her or itself known. The big stuff is still mostly orchestrated by mankind. Things got really warm for a while. The size of the population became a lot more reasonable. Then the cold comes. Comes and stays.

SUE. What happened?

BRUCE. A massive meteor, smashing into the earth. Knocked off our axis. The electromagnetic field permanently altered. Nothing worked anymore. Nothing. Just a planet of very cold people, wandering around in the dark looking for food. As you can imagine, things got ugly.

SUE. Were you around for this?

BRUCE. This was way before me. After some very brutal thousands of years…

SUE. Still no God?

BRUCE. No God. Nowhere.

SUE. And you're telling me this why? To cheer me up?

BRUCE. I'm not done. People started to organize again. They did. It took a long time of warring and slavery and general brutality, but our better instincts came to fore.

SUE. See, I don't believe you.

BRUCE. No?

SUE. Our better instincts are merely a by-product of living a lucky life.

BRUCE. You think?

SUE. I do. We are all a hair away from being the savages we are at our core.

BRUCE. History proves you wrong. Future history. They started over. From scratch, they started over. The good guys organized and made it happen. And they had absolutely everything to relearn. Everything. It had all been forgotten. And they didn't do too bad. So you can stop stressing that it's all going to end.

SUE. Thanks. That's a load off.

BRUCE. Right? There is a reason to stick around.

SUE. I guess I have to take your word for it, being that I am merely from the present.

BRUCE. You do.

SUE. Okay. There's no Grand Canyon in the future?

BRUCE. I'm sad to say that there is not.

SUE. What happened to it?

BRUCE. It filled with sediment.

SUE. So you came all the way back here to see the Grand Canyon?

BRUCE. No.

SUE. Then what for?

BRUCE. To see you.

SUE. To see me.

BRUCE. Yeah.

SUE. Why me?

BRUCE. You seemed nice. At least on paper.
          (*Pause.*)

SUE. Maybe you are bad weird.

BRUCE. Oh—I joined a barbershop quartet. I would sing for you but it kind of defeats the purpose without my guys here.

SUE. No worries.
          (*Pause.*)

BRUCE. It's getting late.

SUE. Yeah.

BRUCE. We have to get up early.

SUE. Yeah. Where are you staying?

BRUCE. The Taurus.

SUE. Is that a hotel?

BRUCE. My car.

SUE. Oh. You don't have a room?

BRUCE. No.

SUE. Oh. How come?

BRUCE. I don't know. There's some sort of convention in town.

SUE. Time Travelers?

BRUCE. Yep. I really have no excuse for not having gone further back into the past to book my room…

SUE. Stay at my place.

BRUCE. No, look, I told you I wouldn't bother you any more than briefly tomorrow.

SUE. Wait. You're actually going to say no to the Long Term Slash Short Term Inn & Lodge.

BRUCE. It does sound rather enchanting.

SUE. Right? They have a continental breakfast.

BRUCE. Hmm… Maybe if it were inter-continental.

SUE. Oh. It is. Muffins from the English.

BRUCE. Oh. Well. Toast from the French?

SUE. *Absolutement.*

BRUCE. Wow.

SUE. So…is that a *oui*?

BRUCE. For the Long Term Slash…

SUE. Short Term Inn & Lodge.

BRUCE. Inns I can do without. Hard to say no to a lodge though.

SUE. You are preaching to the choir.

BRUCE. Do they have hot chocolate?

SUE. No.

BRUCE. Okay, it's a deal.

SUE. Just don't try any of that sophisticated future seduction.

BRUCE. You got it.

SUE. Okay. You have to use your powers with a certain amount of responsibility.

BRUCE. Of course.

(*Lights out.*)

Scene 4

SUE*'s housing. They are half dressed. No one is saying anything.*

BRUCE. It's just second nature, the whole seduction thing…

SUE. Of course.

BRUCE. Yeah. I can't really help it.

SUE. Right. At least we know I didn't get pregnant.

BRUCE. True.

SUE. I hope you understand that this is merely because I am lonely and in a new city.

BRUCE. Got it. Lonely. New city.

SUE. Or alone, rather. Which I don't mind.

BRUCE. Okay.

SUE. I'm alone. A little lonely. It breaks up the day.

BRUCE. Of course.

SUE. And nothing more.

BRUCE. It's okay—I'm on a sex vacation.

SUE. I forgot. Happy sex vacation.

BRUCE. Thank you. And thank you for participating.

SUE. Always eager to help a tourist.

BRUCE. So. Where are the cats?

SUE. With my mother. They're mine. But they live with my mother.

BRUCE. Can't even commit to the cats.

SUE. No.

BRUCE. Thanks for letting me stay.

SUE. It's no problem.

BRUCE. And you were right.

SUE. About what?

BRUCE. You are fun.

SUE. See?

BRUCE. You are.

SUE. I tried to tell you.

BRUCE. When you're not forecasting doom, you're okay.

SUE. Thanks.

BRUCE. You know. You and I, we're two for two.

SUE. How do you mean?

BRUCE. I mean, we've hung out a couple of times, and it's been fun.

SUE. Yeah. Tomorrow might put a dent in our numbers.

BRUCE. Doesn't it…

> (*But he trails off.*)

SUE. Doesn't it what?

BRUCE. I don't know. We have a good time, you and I. Doesn't it seem to be a shame that we won't ever see each other again?

> (*A beat.*)

SUE. Let me ask you something.

BRUCE. Sure.

SUE. Are you just interested in me because I am being such a pain in the ass?

BRUCE. You mean, because you're playing hard to get?

SUE. You see, I'm not playing really.

BRUCE. You're just plain ole hard to get.

SUE. I suppose.

BRUCE. Well. That's a good question. Um. Probably partly.

SUE. You see?

BRUCE. But I think I would probably like you even if you weren't a pain in the ass, as much as I enjoy pains in the ass.

SUE. My point is, here we are in Phoenix, Arizona, and I have been explicit with you that I am not interested in any sort of a relationship. And I keep putting you off and…

BRUCE. Was all this tonight putting me off?

SUE. Beyond that. I have not encouraged you and, being human, you find that attractive, or a challenge.

BRUCE. Perhaps I do.

SUE. But I'm just trying to remind you—take the game out of it and it's just people. And people, meaning me, are boring and petty and selfish, and if I were to sit here now with you and suddenly start twinkling about the eyes and asking you your favorite poem and movie and recipe and hanging onto your words as if they were the cure to cancer, then you would feel amused and emboldened for a while, until it became clear to you that there is no game in it at which point you would marshal your forces on the next nice ass that walks by.

BRUCE. Wow. You are…

SUE. What?

BRUCE. What is it you hope to get out of life? Really. Because I'm having a hard time imagining what it could be.

SUE. As few problems as possible. I want things to go smoothly. I don't want disappointment. I don't want to get my hopes up.

BRUCE. It's not all disappointment, you know.

SUE. It is. It is. It ultimately always is. You see, you say that to me, and fact is, that's bullshit, because you're gonna die. And how is your endgame anything other than a disappointment? To the people who love you? And in the interim, everyone is a terrified asshole, who given a few minor adjustments to their life, would so easily cut your fucking head off with a machete…

BRUCE. You think that?

SUE. Of course I think that. Of course. Our baser nature is our base nature. What in the hell have we learned? Really. Tell me.

BRUCE. And this is how your interest in nursing began?

SUE. No.

BRUCE. I was wondering.

SUE. It began when I was young and I needed a job to get me out of the house fast and they were hiring and paying for schooling and otherwise I may not have even made it this far. Don't get me wrong. My job requires compassion and that is something I actually have, believe it or not. In fact, I have so much compassion, I'm trying to save both of us from having to go through the annoyance and potential pain of an inevitably doomed relationship.

BRUCE. I don't need you to look out for me.

SUE. I think you do. I think you don't know any better. That's what I think.

BRUCE. Tell me why it's doomed.

SUE. It's doomed because I doom it. That's why. I don't even live anywhere. I don't. That's how I actually like it. And that's just one of many many reasons why I preemptively doom our relationship.

BRUCE. Let me just say this, I don't need you making decisions for me, out of whatever it is you think you have over me, your omniscience or whatever the hell you think it is you own.

SUE. I'm trying to save you some time and effort.

BRUCE. And furthermore. I'm not looking to get married to you. As you may recall, all I really said was that I thought it was a shame that we won't see each other again. And though it is obvious that I have some interest in you…

SUE. You drove to Phoenix to join me for my abortion.

BRUCE. Which is actually not really about you.

SUE. Fine.

BRUCE. And all I was saying was that it would be a shame. And I get you, I really do, and I get that you are trying to put me off, and I will confess to you that I may not be as incorrigible as you think, and that you are starting to have some success…

SUE. What do you mean?

BRUCE. That you are beginning to succeed in putting me off. You are winning that battle.

SUE. Okay, then.

BRUCE. It's working.

SUE. Okay.

BRUCE. I feel that I am beginning to like you less.

SUE. Great.

BRUCE. So—well done.

SUE. Thank you.

(*Pause. She begins to re-dress.*)

BRUCE. Yes. Let's do that.

(*He puts on his other clothes—they do this in silence. They finish. Long pause.*)

SUE. I'm sorry.

BRUCE. For what?

SUE. I'm just…sorry.

BRUCE. Okay.

SUE. Fact is.

BRUCE. What?

SUE. Fact is—I don't entirely dislike you.

BRUCE. I'm turning red from your effusions.

SUE. Will you let me talk in the way I would like to talk?

BRUCE. Okay.

SUE. I wouldn't be this stand-offish if it weren't for the fact that I like you too.

BRUCE. So this is what it feels like to be liked by you?

(*A beat.*)

All I was saying was—maybe next time you come see your mom or something, we could have a beer or something. Go bowling. That's really all I was saying.

(*A beat.*)

SUE. I like bowling.

BRUCE. I do too.

SUE. Me too.

BRUCE. That's all I'm saying. I just didn't want to drive out of here tomorrow without saying that maybe there could be a way to see each other again.

SUE. Okay.

BRUCE. And not will you marry me now.

SUE. Okay.

(*Beat.*)

Are you going to make me shake on something?

BRUCE. No.

SUE. Okay. Good.

BRUCE. I'm saying the equivalent of "call me next time you are in town and perhaps we could go bowling."

SUE. Okay. That's fine.

BRUCE. Okay then.

SUE. I'm not a very good bowler.

BRUCE. Well. You don't have to be.

SUE. Are you?

BRUCE. Not particularly.

SUE. Good.

BRUCE. I get lucky sometimes.

SUE. I don't.

BRUCE. And that's the crux of it.

SUE. The crux of what?

BRUCE. Bowling. Sometimes you get lucky, sometimes you don't.

SUE. I guess so. Why are we still up? We have to get up early.

BRUCE. It's already early. Look outside.

> (*She does.*)

SUE. What should we do? We'd sleep for what—an hour?

BRUCE. I can't do that.

SUE. Me neither. Maybe we should just clean up and go out and get some coffee or something.

BRUCE. Catch the sunrise.

SUE. Yeah, okay.

BRUCE. Okay.

> (*Pause.*)

Now?

SUE. Not just yet, no.

BRUCE. What are you doing?

SUE. Nothing.

BRUCE. Okay.

> (*They both are still for a moment. Lights out.*)

Scene 5

> *The clinic.* SUE *and* BRUCE.

BRUCE. Damn.

SUE. What?

BRUCE. You promised.

SUE. I promised what?

BRUCE. No *Rolling Stone* anywhere.

SUE. Oh, sorry.

BRUCE. I'll survive. How are you feeling?

SUE. Tired.

BRUCE. Me too. Nice place. Empty.

SUE. I know the nurses. The clinic doesn't actually open for an hour.

BRUCE. Aren't you fancy?

SUE. I am fancy. So is this worth the three-day drive?

BRUCE. I think so, yeah.

    (*Pause.*)

In the future, having a child, you know, is so much easier.

SUE. Why is that?

BRUCE. Because most people travel back in time to take care of themselves as babies.

SUE. Really?

BRUCE. What better caretaker?

SUE. I guess so. Did you do that too?

BRUCE. I did. It's hard work.

SUE. I'll bet.

BRUCE. I was a big crier from day one.

SUE. You turned out okay.

BRUCE. Thanks.

SUE. Not too bad.

    (*Pause.*)

I certainly admire anyone who has the balls to raise a child.

BRUCE. Me too.

SUE. And I'll tell you what would keep me from doing it.

BRUCE. What?

SUE. The simple fact that they could die before you.

BRUCE. Oh.

SUE. And therefore what is the fucking point? Because that is a storm I could not weather.

BRUCE. Wow.

SUE. I guess it doesn't happen a lot but it does happen. I work in hospitals, I can tell you. And you think it won't happen to you, but I can tell you this with one hundred percent certainty—everyone thinks that until it happens to them. Doesn't matter. No one is safe. I know. I've seen it.

BRUCE. I agree.

SUE. You do?

BRUCE. I do.

SUE. I thought you were my counterpoint on these issues.

BRUCE. You're right. No one is safe. No one.

SUE. That's right.

BRUCE. When I went to the movies with my wife years ago I certainly didn't think I would be the only one eventually coming home.

SUE. You're married.

BRUCE. I was.

SUE. Oh. What happened?

BRUCE. An accident. You know, you talk of our base natures and machetes and all that, but when it comes down to it most people are just getting hit by cars. Nearly 50,000 people last year died in auto accidents just here in this country.

SUE. I'm sorry.

BRUCE. Thanks.

SUE. When was this?

BRUCE. Years ago.

SUE. You never mentioned it.

BRUCE. There never seems to be the perfect moment for such a conversational tidbit.

SUE. And you thought, why not the abortion clinic?

BRUCE. Exactly. What else to do in the abortion clinic? When there's no *Rolling Stone.*

SUE. I'm sorry.

BRUCE. That's when I was told that having children would be an impossibility.

SUE. Oh, wow.

BRUCE. To which, I thought, well, as I have no wife to speak of, I don't think that's a big problem.

SUE. Right.

BRUCE. So I get you. No one is safe.

SUE. No.

BRUCE. And yet we have our lives to lead, don't we?

SUE. I guess so.

      (*A pause. They are both alone in their thoughts for a long moment.*)

BRUCE. It's kind of cowardly, really, when you think about it.

SUE. What is?

BRUCE. You know, cowering in the corner because of what might happen.

SUE. And what will happen.

BRUCE. Yeah, and what will happen.

SUE. If you're trying to get me riled up, it's not working. Because I'll agree with you on that point. I believe it is very definitely cowardly.

BRUCE. And that's okay by you?

SUE. It'll have to be.

BRUCE. It's not that I'm so brazen.

SUE. No?

BRUCE. No. Not brazen at all for a while. After the accident. No.

SUE. Of course not.

BRUCE. What does one do with that sort of information, you know?

SUE. A godless wilderness.

BRUCE. Well. Perhaps, yes.

SUE. It's hard not to come to that conclusion.

BRUCE. If God can't wake a sleeping truck driver, then what fucking good is he really?

SUE. Yeah.

BRUCE. Just a little tap on the shoulder. "Hey you, wake up…"

(*Pause.*)

But, you know, what are you gonna do? Not drive?

SUE. I try not to.

BRUCE. You still have to drive. And driving, despite it all, is a goddamn fun thing to do.

SUE. I don't know.

BRUCE. It is. It is. My trip out here. Was amazing.

SUE. I guess so.

BRUCE. I get it, Sue. I get it. Not much is safe. I get that. I definitely learned that little tidbit.

SUE. I'm sorry that you did.

BRUCE. But I get you. It's a terrifying prospect, having a child, isn't it?

SUE. I think so.

BRUCE. My wife and I had been deliberating about it.

SUE. Really?

BRUCE. Yeah. And, uh, after the accident. I just knew I didn't want to have kids anymore.

SUE. Yeah.

(BRUCE *is lost in thought for a moment.*)

BRUCE. But I don't know. I really don't know. I'm just thinking about all this… What if I was just…wrong…about myself?

SUE. What do you mean?

BRUCE. And like I was saying, you have to live your life, you know?

SUE. That's what they say on the TV.

BRUCE. You have to drive a car to get where you want...

SUE. Trains are pretty safe.

BRUCE. It's so fuckin'... Here we are all alone at an abortion clinic in Phoenix, Arizona. Think about this.

SUE. Think about what?

BRUCE. What brought us together, you know?

SUE. We like the same bar?

BRUCE. No. I don't think so, no.

SUE. What else could it be?

BRUCE. Because I don't know. I mean, what are we doing here?

SUE. Abortion. Remember?

BRUCE. No. Bigger than that. What got us here?

SUE. The Taurus.

BRUCE. Do you see this?

SUE. See what?

BRUCE. What am I doing here? I came all the way here. I drove here. Here we are.

SUE. I didn't ask you to come.

BRUCE. You see this, right?

SUE. What are you talking about?

BRUCE. What I'm saying to you, Sue, is that perhaps what has happened... is something extraordinary.

SUE. Nothing has happened.

BRUCE. They tell me I can't have kids. Suddenly, what? I don't want them? Of course I don't. Because I can't have them. And then...

SUE. So what are you saying? You're saying now you do? You want children now?

BRUCE. Uh, you know...

SUE. What?

BRUCE. Yeah.

SUE. Okay. That's your prerogative.

BRUCE. Do you see what I'm saying?

SUE. Your life, Bruce.

BRUCE. Maybe there are gifts, you know? Sometimes? Maybe there are.

SUE. What are you talking about?

BRUCE. You.

    (He points to her belly.)

Both of you.

SUE. Funny.

BRUCE. You know, if I suddenly did believe in miracles then this is one.

SUE. All right, Bruce. I get the joke.

BRUCE. I'm not joking. Look at me. I'm not.

> (*Pause.*)

SUE. You want what? That we...

BRUCE. I don't know.

SUE. What? What?

BRUCE. Okay. That we walk out of here...

SUE. Wait...that we walk out of here?

BRUCE. And we go get a cup of coffee, of decaf coffee, and have a conversation.

SUE. A conversation?

BRUCE. Yes. A conversation. Yes. About this situation. About us.

> (*Pause.*)

SUE. Bruce.

BRUCE. What?

SUE. And I am serious about this.

BRUCE. Okay.

SUE. Get the fuck out of here.

BRUCE. No. Why?

SUE. Get the fuck out. I am done with you.

BRUCE. No. Listen, all I'm saying is we talk...

SUE. As I'm sure you noted, there is security here, and as I am sure you will intuit, they will be siding with me the minute I start screaming for you to get the fuck out.

BRUCE. Just come with me so we can talk about the future.

SUE. There is no future. No future.

BRUCE. But, okay, if you don't want to be involved, maybe, I don't know, maybe I could take this child and raise him or her.

SUE. You're insane.

BRUCE. And can we go have this discussion somewhere other than an abortion clinic?

SUE. No. We need to be in the abortion clinic in order to get the abortion. I don't believe Starbucks offers abortions.

BRUCE. Because we kind of have to have it now. And I think we've been given this chance—this exceptional thing has happened...

SUE. No discussion.

BRUCE. Please. I need you to hear me out. Just hear me out…

SUE. …No…

BRUCE. …Let's just put the appointment off perhaps, for a day or two, let's just do that, okay?

SUE. No.

BRUCE. And let's just go outside, right now…

SUE. Stop. Bruce.

BRUCE. What?

SUE. You and I are done. With this conversation. With each other. For good. How do I know this? Because unless you walk out right now I'm going to scream…

BRUCE. Please don't.

SUE. Out.

BRUCE. Please.

SUE. (*Loud*—) Leave me alone.

BRUCE. (*Quiet.*) Please.

SUE. (*Louder.*) Leave me alone.

> (*Pause.*)

BRUCE. Sue.

SUE. (*Cutting him off—loud—*) Get out!

> (*Lights out.*)

Scene 6

> BRUCE*'s apartment.* SUE *is at the door, in her coat. Uncomfortable.*
> *A long beat.*

SUE. I came back for the cats.

BRUCE. Okay.

SUE. Yeah.

BRUCE. Okay.

> (*Pause.*)

SUE. And…I wanted to stop by.

BRUCE. I just…never thought I would hear from you again. A restraining order, maybe.

SUE. Yeah, well. Here I am.

BRUCE. Here you are.

SUE. Hi there.

BRUCE. Hi.

(*She fishes around for something.*)

SUE. Let me get that restraining order.

(*Beat.*)

I'm kidding.

BRUCE. I wouldn't blame you if you did.

(*A beat.*)

Come in, I guess. Do you want to come in?

SUE. Okay. I guess for a minute. Do you have a minute?

BRUCE. Yeah.

SUE. Or is this a bad time?

BRUCE. No.

SUE. Okay. You're not busy?

BRUCE. I'm just... Nevermind.

SUE. What?

BRUCE. No. It sounds stupid.

SUE. What?

BRUCE. I'm making a casserole.

SUE. That's not stupid.

BRUCE. Who makes casseroles?

SUE. You.

BRUCE. Me. For one. Come in.

(*She walks into the apartment. A beat.*)

Do we...? Can I take your coat? Is it...?

SUE. No, that's okay. We can keep it brief.

BRUCE. Coffee, or...

SUE. No. Thanks. Look. Let me just get to it.

BRUCE. You do like to do that.

SUE. What happened a couple of weeks ago. That was fucked up of you.

BRUCE. I know.

SUE. It really was.

BRUCE. I know it was.

SUE. I didn't begin to expect that from you and I was taken aback and reacted the only way I felt I could. I wish it hadn't come to that, but it did. You are hard to deal with sometimes. You are hard to say no to. And I needed to say no to you.

BRUCE. I know you did.

SUE. Yeah. You don't just spring that on someone at an abortion clinic. You just don't do that, Bruce.

BRUCE. Look. Whatever you need to dish out, dish it out. You want contrition, I offer you contrition.

SUE. I'm not trying to punish you.

BRUCE. It's fine if you are.

SUE. And I know it was not an ordinary situation. We hadn't slept.

BRUCE. So what? It's no excuse.

SUE. I don't know.

(*Beat.*)

BRUCE. You know what? I left that place just angry. But, you know, I had a three-day drive coming back here, so…

SUE. So…

BRUCE. So I had time to think. And get a little sleep, you know?

SUE. Yeah.

BRUCE. And truth is, I was a lunatic out there, you're right. We hadn't slept. If I had had that thought any earlier than when I did, there in the clinic, I would've told you.

SUE. Yeah.

BRUCE. But I didn't. I, uhh, I'm sitting there and all of the sudden I have this bright idea, you know…

SUE. Yeah.

BRUCE. Which was not so bright…

SUE. Yeah.

BRUCE. It's just funny, really…

SUE. What?

BRUCE. How you have a whole life of knowledge and experience behind you, and suddenly you're willing to just drop it all. It's crazy.

SUE. No, I know.

BRUCE. I'm that much of a sucker? There's what? Suddenly miraculous events? A guiding hand out there? A greater meaning? I mean, there are just mounds of evidence in my life to suggest otherwise and there I am suddenly a sucker…

SUE. Don't be so hard on yourself.

BRUCE. I need to be hard on myself. Keep myself in check. I do. You know, it's simple, really, there are no miracles.

SUE. I guess not.

BRUCE. You know, and really, I wouldn't want there to be.

SUE. Why not?

BRUCE. Because the implications are just too terrible.

    (*Pause.*)

So you know, I am very glad you are here...

SUE. You are?

BRUCE. I am. These past couple of weeks—I've been thinking about you...

SUE. Why?

BRUCE. Thinking I just wish I had the chance to tell you in person that I am very sorry for my behavior. But the dumbass that I am, you know, I still don't have a number for you, do you realize that?

SUE. I wasn't sure.

BRUCE. That's how ridiculous I am.

SUE. You're not ridiculous.

BRUCE. Saying that shit to you in the clinic. I'm standing there, saying let's talk about having a kid and I don't even have your phone number.

SUE. It's not important.

BRUCE. No. There are no miracles. Just the stupid shit that befalls us.

SUE. Yeah.

BRUCE. And so, I am so sorry.

SUE. It's okay. Me too. I'm sorry.

BRUCE. Let's just...can we just call this thing even...

SUE. Okay...

BRUCE. ...and move on.

SUE. What do you mean?

BRUCE. Everything cancels out. We're even. Here we are, no better, no worse.

SUE. Okay.

BRUCE. Which is better than so many run-ins you have with people.

SUE. Yeah.

BRUCE. You see what I mean?

SUE. I guess.

BRUCE. And really, seriously, beyond apologizing to you I should thank you.

SUE. For what?

BRUCE. For actually being a grounding force for me.

SUE. Me being a grounding force for you?

BRUCE. That's right. I can be a victim of my own enthusiasm if I'm not careful.

SUE. I don't think that's necessarily a bad thing.

BRUCE. It can be. It absolutely can. For me. You know, if I don't keep my feet on the ground, I… I what?

SUE. You fall down?

BRUCE. Yeah. I fall down on my ass. Which hurts. And looks stupid to onlookers.

SUE. Yeah.

BRUCE. So thank you.

SUE. Okay.

BRUCE. So maybe not even even. I came out a little better in the end.
　　　　(*Sticks his hand out—*)
Shall we shake on it for poetry's sake?
　　　　(*Pause. She shakes.*)

SUE. Okay.
　　　　(*A beat.*)

BRUCE. Thanks for coming by.

SUE. Yeah. Okay.
　　　　(*But she doesn't go. A long pause. Nothing is said.*)

BRUCE. How did it go?

SUE. How did what go?

BRUCE. After I left the other day.

SUE. Oh.

BRUCE. Yeah. How did it go? Did it go okay?

SUE. Oh. Well. It didn't go.

BRUCE. Oh. What do you mean?

SUE. You had me very upset.

BRUCE. No, I know. I'm sorry again.

SUE. I know.

BRUCE. You didn't have the abortion?

SUE. That day.
　　　　(*Beat.*)
Not that day.

BRUCE. Oh. Yeah. Right.
　　　　(*Beat.*)

SUE. Did you think otherwise?

BRUCE. When I saw you here, maybe for a moment, I thought…

SUE. Does that upset you?

BRUCE. That you had the abortion?

SUE. Yes?

BRUCE. It upsets me…

SUE. It does?

BRUCE. …in that I'm guessing it's a sucky thing to have to do.

SUE. Yeah. Well, it is.

BRUCE. But if what you mean is am I regretful, then no.

SUE. Yeah. Okay. Me too.

BRUCE. Yeah?

SUE. Yeah.

> (*Pause.*)

BRUCE. But it went okay?

SUE. It did, yeah.

BRUCE. Good.

SUE. Yeah.

> (*Pause.*)

BRUCE. Seemed like a good clinic.

SUE. Yeah.

BRUCE. Good security.

SUE. Yeah, well. Yeah.

BRUCE. Clean. It's a clean… All right, I'm just rambling.

SUE. Yeah.

BRUCE. Okay. I guess this is it, then.

SUE. Yeah?

BRUCE. Yeah. Nothing really tying us together anymore.

SUE. No?

BRUCE. I guess not.

> (*A long pause. Again, nothing is said. And* SUE *is not leaving.*)

You're still here.

SUE. Yeah.

BRUCE. Do you need more contrition? I have more. I can bring it on if you want.

SUE. I don't want any more contrition.

BRUCE. Then what else?

> (*She doesn't answer.*)

Am I missing something here?

SUE. You're content to just call it even, or whatever the hell you call it, and do your stupid handshake, which, incidentally I am so sick of, and go back to your casserole? Is that it?

BRUCE. Well. Sue. I guess.

SUE. You guess?

BRUCE. Are there other options?

SUE. I don't know. I guess not. Now that your feet are firmly concreted to the fucking earth…

BRUCE. You confuse me.

SUE. You think I confuse you? You should see what I do to myself.

BRUCE. What am I missing here? I was a stalker who got stupid. I am sorry. We shook and agreed to cut our losses. Right?

SUE. That's what this is, cutting our losses?

BRUCE. Don't you think we should? Since our third date involved an abortion clinic, screaming, and a scuffle with security?

SUE. I should've figured…

BRUCE. Sue.

SUE. Yeah?

BRUCE. We barely know each other.

SUE. So?

BRUCE. I don't even know your last name.

SUE. You don't know my last name?

BRUCE. No. I don't. I know you told it to me. But, no, I don't know it, okay?

SUE. That's just…fucking priceless.

BRUCE. Look. I don't know what's going on here. The last I saw of you, you were screaming at me. And here you are…

SUE. Here I am.

BRUCE. And so what it is you want?

SUE. To…to… I wanted to see you. To talk to you. You know, we met…

BRUCE. People meet all the time.

SUE. We've gone through all this craziness.

BRUCE. These things happen.

SUE. I know they do.

BRUCE. They just happen. All the time, in fact.

SUE. No, I know.

BRUCE. It's not extraordinary.

SUE. I know.

BRUCE. It never is. Anything that happens is not extraordinary.

SUE. I know. Just the, what do you call it, the stupid shit that befalls us.

BRUCE. Yeah…

SUE. But here it is. In our laps, nonetheless.

BRUCE. So what are you saying?

SUE. And maybe it's not extraordinary and it's certainly no miracle, but here we are, Bruce…

BRUCE. Yeah. Here we are. And…

SUE. I didn't come all the way here to get my cats…

(*A long pause.*)

BRUCE. You really think this might be a chance for us?

SUE. I don't know. Maybe. I don't know anymore. And why is it so hot in here?

BRUCE. I'm baking.

SUE. I know. Me too.

BRUCE. No, I'm actually baking. In the kitchen.

SUE. Right.

BRUCE. Should I…

SUE. What?

BRUCE. You must be getting warm in that coat.

SUE. So what are you saying?

BRUCE. I'm saying do you want me to take your coat?

SUE. No. No.

BRUCE. I know it's a little hot in here.

SUE. It's hot.

BRUCE. Do you want to take off your coat?

SUE. No.

BRUCE. Okay.

SUE. Do you want me to take off my coat?

BRUCE. If you're warm, yes.

SUE. I'm fine.

BRUCE. Or to stay for a little while. I can make coffee.

SUE. I like tea.

BRUCE. Okay. Me too.

SUE. You do?

BRUCE. Yeah.

SUE. Then why did we keep getting coffee?

BRUCE. I don't know.

SUE. It's stupid. I like tea.

BRUCE. Me too. I prefer it.

SUE. Me too. You ordered coffee.

BRUCE. Because we called it "meeting for coffee." So did you for that matter.

SUE. You were having coffee. So…

BRUCE. Do you want some tea?

SUE. No.

> (*Beat.*)

Are you having some?

BRUCE. No. Yes. I am.

SUE. I'm okay.

BRUCE. I'm making some anyhow. What type of tea do you like?

> (*He starts off but she stops him.*)

SUE. Bruce. You know, it was tremendously misguided, but you were really laying it all on the line out there.

BRUCE. It turned into lunacy.

SUE. I guess it did. But at least it was something, you know. And it got me thinking. And for whatever reason, I went against everything that makes sense and I came up here to see you. And I'm here. And I like you, Bruce. In as much as I know you. Which, admittedly, is not a lot.

BRUCE. We like tea. Who knew?

SUE. Exactly. And if you don't want to sit around here and have one more conversation in the abstract about things that we just don't get, then I agree with you. I'm tired of that too.

BRUCE. Okay.

SUE. I'm getting sick of my own voice.

BRUCE. Me too.

> (*A beat.*)

Sick of my own voice. Not yours. You actually have a very pretty voice.

SUE. But you've taken a couple of stands with me and maybe it's time for me to take one too. Which is this: Bruce. I'm taking off my coat.

> (*She does.*)

BRUCE. Okay.

> (*He takes her coat.*)

SUE. Thank you. I was dying.

BRUCE. Let me turn off the oven.

SUE. Wait. Bruce.

> (*He turns back to her.*)

Do you like me? Because I like you. I like you.

BRUCE. I like you, Sue. I've liked you since the minute I met you.

(A beat.)

Now what?

SUE. I don't know. What do we do?

BRUCE. I don't know.

(A pause.)

SUE. We could bowl.

BRUCE. Bowl?

SUE. Bowling. Go bowling.

BRUCE. Oh.

SUE. Remember? "Call me when you're back in town and maybe we can go bowling?"

BRUCE. Yeah. I do.

SUE. I'm sorry. It's a stupid idea.

BRUCE. I'll go bowling with you.

SUE. You will?

BRUCE. I like bowling.

SUE. I remember.

BRUCE. Yeah.

SUE. We haven't even been on a date.

BRUCE. I know.

SUE. Not really. We can just go bowl a game or two, right?

BRUCE. Why not? Why the hell not?

SUE. Okay, then.

BRUCE. Okay. When?

SUE. I don't know. Now? Is now too soon?

BRUCE. Now?

SUE. Is that too soon? Tomorrow? The next day?

BRUCE. No. Now is good. Now is okay.

SUE. Okay, good. Good.

(Pause.)

Shall we just…

BRUCE. Yeah, no. We can just go.

SUE. Okay.

BRUCE. Let me, umm… I was going to say get my things, but one doesn't really need anything to bowl, do they?

SUE. Just ourselves.

BRUCE. Okay, then. Let me turn off my oven. And off to the bowling alley.

(*He steps out for a moment.*

She pulls out a scrap of paper and a pen, and is writing something down as he returns.)

Are we ready?

SUE. Before I forget.

(*She hands him the piece of paper.*)

My number.

BRUCE. Oh, thanks. Right.

(*Beat—he looks at it.*)

Holmes?

SUE. Sorry?

BRUCE. Your last name. It's Holmes.

SUE. Yeah. It is.

BRUCE. Sue Holmes.

SUE. And now I have to confess I don't know yours.

BRUCE. Really?

SUE. I don't know yours either, no.

BRUCE. After the shit you gave me.

SUE. Yeah.

BRUCE. It's James.

SUE. James.

BRUCE. Yeah.

SUE. Well, then.

BRUCE. Yeah.

SUE. Nice to meet you.

BRUCE. Nice to meet you too…

(SUE *sticks her hand out—they shake hands.*

Lights out.)

End of Play

HEIST!

Conceived and created by
Sean Daniels and Deborah Stein
Written by Deborah Stein
Created in collaboration with
Actors Theatre of Louisville's
2009-2010 Acting Apprentice Company

ABOUT *HEIST!*

This article first ran in the January/February 2010 issue of Inside Actors, *and is based on conversations with the creators before rehearsals for the Humana Festival production began.*

When audiences step into the world of *HEIST!*, Deborah Stein and Sean Daniels' amusing and audacious theatrical caper, they'll find themselves at a party celebrating the unveiling of a priceless painting. Archie Pellago, reclusive genius of the contemporary art scene, is permitting his latest work to be revealed at 21c Museum Hotel, North America's one-of-a-kind exhibition space for 21st century art, and the whole town is abuzz over this curatorial coup. In fact, a wealthy Louisville socialite is hosting the festivities, which are populated by an assortment of other colorful characters, from a fervent protester to a magician to a snooty art critic.

But some of the guests have even more exciting plans for the evening—and this party is about to go delightfully awry, thanks to a team of slippery art thieves determined to make off with the prize exhibit. The museum staff is on alert, and law enforcement (local, national *and* international!) has beefed up security. But can they stop the dashing Paul Vista and his team of schemers—or, for that matter, the Russian mobsters obsessed with snatching 21c's emblematic Red Penguin? As the audience travels through the museum galleries, they'll meet an array of supervillains and intrepid thieves, eccentric locals and lawmen in this performance event starring all 22 members of the 2009-2010 Acting Apprentice Company.

"The kind of theatre that I'm most excited about is highly theatrical, event-based, immersive, experiential theatre," says Stein, recalling the conversation during which she and Daniels dreamed up the project while developing another play in San Francisco last summer. "We were in a bar, and Deborah pointed out two people having an animated conversation in the corner," remembers Daniels. "She said, 'What if they were characters in a play that was suddenly happening around us?'" Soon, the writer-director duo were concocting the premise for a party/performance that would unfold at 21c Museum Hotel, a fixture of Louisville's downtown art scene. "It's such a unique, inspiring space with so much possibility, and so much already going on," says Stein. Daniels continues: "We thought, wouldn't it be fun to try and pull off an *Ocean's Eleven*-esque art heist?"

In addition to finding inspiration in its museum environment, *HEIST!* is also a madcap riff on the conventions and enduring pleasures of a genre. "There's a reason why this kind of story has been a staple of pop culture for the last fifty years. And I love the challenge of executing all these layers of plot that are happening at the same time," Stein explains. "The heist is a genre that you never see explored in theatre," Daniels adds, pointing out why it's a perfect match for a site-specific play: "The audience can instantly recognize certain character archetypes: the evil mobsters, the charming con men."

These familiarities became foundations for lively invention as the writer and director began using a highly collaborative process to develop characters with the Acting Apprentice Company. Starting with a list of character types from heist storylines and personalities who might attend a Louisville art opening, the team used guided improvisations to build the characters' specific quirks and preoccupations. "I think we're creating roles that will be very tailored to the performers," notes Stein. "It's an amazing opportunity to work with 22 actors who are totally game, creative and funny, and to have the muscle of an enormous cast in the space."

Just as actors influence the creation of characters, space and traffic patterns are wedded to story structure. Drawing on their backgrounds with non-traditional, ensemble-based play development, Daniels and Stein have fostered a spirit of groupthink with their *HEIST!* creative team in order to imagine and problem-solve, even keeping a huge storyboard in the rehearsal room— an evolving brainstorm from which Stein can draw to write her text. They also brought two Atlanta-based artists on board: animator Adam Pinney and his collaborator, René Dellefont. Their cartoon creations, playing at various points during the show, help to establish character histories and deliver some of the action-infused visuals that are staples of the genre. "Some of the most exciting work happens when you bring together really smart artists from different media," says Daniels.

Of course, seeing theatre in the context of groundbreaking visual art is another of the play's thrills. "I'm star-struck by the strength of 21c's collection, and can't get over how generous they've been, allowing us to work in some really interesting spaces," Stein marvels. "There's an attitude at 21c that art is meant to be experienced and lived with, not behind a velvet rope, which is very much in keeping with the original impulses for this piece." And this ideal of "living with" art goes to the heart of the team's pursuit. "Theatre is most exciting when you're aware of the liveness of it, that something is happening in real time, and you're part of a group experiencing it together," Stein explains. "There's something about site-specific, event-based theatre that really puts those aspects of playmaking at the forefront."

—Amy Wegener

BIOGRAPHY

Deborah Stein's plays include *God Save Gertrude*, *Wallflower*, *Bone Portraits*, and *Natasha And The Coat*. Her work has been produced and developed nationally at Actors Theatre of Louisville, The Theatre @ Boston Court, the Guthrie Theater, Seattle Repertory Theatre, Stages Repertory Theatre, Women's Project and Productions, The Wilma Theater, Live Girls! Theater, Bay Area Playwrights Festival, and Theater Artaud; in New York at the Public Theater, Dance Theatre Workshop, and Ars Nova; and internationally in Poland, Ireland, Edinburgh (the Traverse) and Prague. She has created original ensemble works with a number of collaborators, including Joseph Chaikin, Dominique Serrand, Lear deBessonet, and most frequently the Pig Iron Theatre Company, with whom she has collaborated since 2000. Her writing is published in *TheatreForum, Play: A Journal of Plays,* and *The Best American Poetry of 1996*. She has been a resident artist at Hedgebrook, Swarthmore College, Princeton University, and the Tofte Lake Center, and has taught writing at New York University, Northeastern University, St. Olaf College, Parsons School of Design, and Brown University, where she received her M.F.A. Deborah is the recipient of the 2010-2011 McKnight Advancement Grant at The Playwrights' Center in Minneapolis, where she was also a two-time Jerome Fellow and co-producing director of the Workhaus Collective. Currently, she is a resident artist at HERE, the recipient of a 2009-2011 Bush Artist Fellowship, and a resident playwright at New Dramatists.

ACKNOWLEDGMENTS

HEIST! premiered in the Humana Festival of New American Plays in March 2010. It was directed by Sean Daniels, featured animation by Adam Pinney in collaboration with René Dellefont, and was line produced by Emily Ruddock, with the following cast:

The Heist Team
PAUL VISTA	Tyler Jacob Rollinson
DUSTY PRESS	Courtney Moors
Q	Erin Adams
JUSTICE	Brittany Parker
VICTOR	Shayan Jazy Shojaee
CLARENCE FRANKLIN	Dan Applegate
ANDY POOLE (a.k.a. Archie Pellago)	Zane Johnston

The Law
JEFFERSON	
WASHINGTON FRANKLIN	Robbie Tann
KATE SHAPIRO	Alexis Bronkovic
PENELOPE FRANCIS	Patricia Cancio
CARL WEATHERS	Matt Whitfield

The Mysterious Party Crashers
BORIS PENGUROVICH.................................... David Darrow
TATIANA PENGUROVICH.......................... Kara Davidson
HANS H.H.G. SCHMIDT.................................... Michael Cox

The Art World
ALICE WEATHERS .... Gwen Ellis
TIMOTHY WYATT II.. York Walker
DIANE WORTHINGBOTTOM .... Natalie Allen
TANYA FELDMAN .... Jessica Rice

The Locals
CHELSEA COOLEY........................... Brett Ashley Robinson
DEVIN... Daniel Conway
LUKE MICHAEL
CHRISTIANSON .... Brandon T. Chinn
CLARISSA .... Erin Fried
COPS and MORE............... Jay Briggs, Leslie Cobb, Lizzy Lee,
                                        Jessica Potter, Katie Shade,
                                        Gretchen Wright

and the following production staff:
Costume Designer...................................... Lindsay Chamberlin
Lighting Designer... Brian J. Lilienthal
Sound Designer/Technical Coordinator .... Jason Czaja
Properties Designer... Joe Cunningham
Wig/Makeup Designer .... Heather Fleming
Animator.. Adam Pinney
Animation Collaborator .... René Dellefont
Fight Director .... Drew Fracher
Magic Consultant.. Jack Strauss
Video Technician.. Philip Allgeier
Stage Manager.. Leslie Cobb
Dramaturg .... Amy Wegener
Directing Assistants .... Jay Briggs, Gretchen Wright
Stage Management Interns .... Lizzy Lee, Jessica Potter,
                                        Katie Shade
Assistant Dramaturgs............................ Zach Chotzen-Freund,
                                        Emily Feldman

Commissioned and developed by Actors Theatre of Louisville.

Developed for the Humana Festival by Actors Theatre of Louisville through a partnership with Florida State University, Cameron Jackson, School of Theatre Producing Artistic Director.

Performances were held at 21c Museum Hotel, 700 West Main Street, with scenes at The St. Charles Building, Brown-Forman Corporation; and the Museum Plaza Design and Sales Offices.

SPECIAL THANKS

Special thanks to 21c Museum Hotel, the International Contemporary Art Foundation, Proof on Main, Laura Lee Brown, Steve Wilson, William Morrow, Molly Swyers and Kent Getsinger; AT&T; Brown-Forman Corporation, Shawn Hadley and Melanie Veleta; Matthew Meagher; and Casanova Lounge.

CHARACTER LIST

The Heist Team:
PAUL VISTA, a dashing international art thief
DUSTY PRESS, the brains behind the operation
Q, an art forger
JUSTICE, the grease girl
VICTOR KUSIK, an inside man
CLARENCE FRANKLIN, the Commissioner's son
ANDY POOLE, an artist in disguise

The Law:
JEFFERSON WASHINGTON FRANKLIN, Police Commissioner
KATE SHAPIRO, of Scotland Yard/Interpol
PENELOPE FRANCIS, of the FBI
CARL WEATHERS, a rookie cop, no relation to Alice

The Mysterious Party Crashers:
BORIS PENGUROVICH, a Russian with a plan
TATIANA PENGUROVICH, his sister, a sharpshooter and Olympian
HANS H.H.G. SCHMIDT, a German magician

The Art World:
ALICE WEATHERS, the museum curator, no relation to Carl
TIMOTHY WYATT II, an art critic
DIANE WORTHINGBOTTOM, the assistant curator
TANYA FELDMAN, a docent

The Locals:
CHELSEA COOLEY, our hostess for the evening
DEVIN, a performance artist
LUKE MICHAEL CHRISTIANSON, a believer

CLARISSA, a video blogger
LOUISA, the mute personal assistant

Additional characters include COPS and GALLERY INTERNS, who are actually the stage management team (and, in our production, the assistant directors). By costuming the crew, we were able to have them on the floor, giving actors cues, calling the show, and containing the mayhem without breaking the illusion of the party.

INTRODUCTION FROM THE AUTHOR

In April, 2010, the Actors Theatre Apprentice Company took over 21c Museum Hotel in Louisville, Kentucky for a one-of-a-kind theatrical event. *HEIST!* took place in eight rooms across two buildings, as well as on the street around the hotel. Characters mingled with audience members, audience members turned out to be characters, and everyone got swept up in the adventure of the performance, which was part action movie, part spoof, and part carnival ride.

This script is a record of that event.

I've described the show as it was performed at 21c, as best I can—given the interactive and improvisational nature of certain parts of the show, it was different every night. The goal of this script is, in part, to provide a framework for improvisation and playfulness—the more chaotic it seemed on the ground, the more carefully calibrated and structured it was in the script.

It was written and designed specifically for the 21c spaces, so future productions are encouraged to reconceive and reconfigure as needed.

NOTE ABOUT 21c

Excerpted from the 21c website:

"21c Museum Hotel holds within its walls over 9,000 square feet of exhibition space, exhibiting living artists from all over the world. The museum is North America's first museum dedicated solely to collecting and exhibiting contemporary art of the 21st century. It was founded in 2006 by Laura Lee Brown and Steve Wilson, philanthropists and arts patrons with a vision for supporting the revitalization of Louisville's downtown and engaging the public with contemporary art in a new way. *Art is in every corner at 21c Museum Hotel—in the elevators, courtyards, hallways, landings, public restrooms, roof, floor, and in the Proof restaurant and bar.*" (*Emphasis mine.*)

The main exhibition spaces are an upstairs gallery, just off of the hotel lobby, and a large, airy atrium gallery on the lower level. The chic art opening that begins the *HEIST!* adventure was set up as a party in this main atrium gallery, and party guests (our audience) also met characters in the lobby gallery and in four smaller galleries off of the main exhibits.

In March 2010, the main gallery show was called "Creating Identity: Portraits Today," a group show which included works by Chuck Close, Vic Muniz, Mickalene Thomas, Catherine Opie, Jock Sturges, Carrie Mae Weems, and many others. Each of the smaller galleries were dedicated to the work of individual artists: Kara Walker, Lindsay Cameron, Leslie Lyons, and Russel Hulsey.

And 21c isn't joking when they say that there is art everywhere: just as museum patrons encounter art in the bathrooms and hallways, characters from *HEIST!* were encountered in every nook and cranny. As our audience toured the space, they were as likely to meet a character in the workout room or sauna as in the main atrium gallery.

21c is located on 7th and Main Streets in downtown Louisville, four blocks from Actors Theatre and two blocks away from the Ohio River—and across the river from Indiana.

NOTE ABOUT THE STAGING

Every bit of stage direction herein is tailored for the specifics of the 21c space, which will need to be adapted for each production. Please feel free to adapt as needed. Some basics of our space:

- To enter the performance, you walk down a large staircase, into a gala party. When you arrive, the party has already started (and therefore, so has the play).
- The party is held in a tall, bright white atrium space with contemporary art on the walls; there is a skylight above the room, which feels airy even when packed with people.
- When characters enter the party, they also enter from the upstairs lobby, so the effect is that they are on a balcony looking down.
- There is a small stage with a podium and microphone set up at the far end of the atrium, for speeches.
- Off the main atrium are three smaller galleries, as well as two labyrinthine hallways which are full of art, and which take you to the bathroom, the sauna, the exercise room, and other hidden spaces where characters might be lurking.
- The other main playing space is across the street, in a building called the Museum Plaza Design and Sales Offices, which is a showroom of luxury apartments.

NOTE ABOUT GEOGRAPHICAL SPECIFICITY

This script is littered with specific geographical and cultural landmarks of Louisville, Kentucky: bourbon, horse racing, etc. Future productions should feel free to adapt these references to their present locations: in other words, part of the joy of this play is making sure that it's happening right here, right now (wherever that may be).

NOTE ABOUT THE RED PENGUIN

A major plot thread concerns a pair of possibly evil Russian siblings and their hunt for their family mascot, the Red Penguin (or, in the pidgin Russian favored by Boris and Tatiana, the *Krasny Pengvin*). This storyline was inspired by an actual work of art in the 21c permanent collection. The Red Penguin was created and designed by the Cracking Art Group, in an edition of 200 molded plastic figures measuring about 4 feet tall. While Boris and Tatiana insist that there is one "real" Penguin, this was an invention of the ensemble. The Red Penguin sculptures are also 21c's mascot, and are displayed throughout the building, in the entrance hall, and on the roof.

NOTE ABOUT THE CHARACTERS

Each character in *HEIST!* was invented by and created for a specific actor in the 2009-2010 Apprentice Company. Much of the detail of characterization in this script is a result of their wild, creative imaginations and the incredible energy each of them devoted to this project. For a play like this to work, every actor needs to know their character inside and out, to be quick on their toes, to be game for anything. I am enormously grateful to and proud of the original company for their hard work, brave risk-taking, and mind-bending talent.

In future productions, we hope that you invest as much in creating your own world, characters and inhabitants. Mainly, just make sure you have a tremendous amount of fun making it happen.

Matt Whitfield and Kara Davidson
in *HEIST!*

34th Annual Humana Festival of New American Plays
Actors Theatre of Louisville, 2010
Photo by Frankie Steel

HEIST!

ACT 1: The Party.

The audience enters 21c either through the hotel lobby entrance or through a bar. Once they are through the doors, the show has already begun: PAUL VISTA *and* DUSTY PRESS *sit at the bar, sipping cocktails, checking out the patrons, and looking generally fabulous. They are a pair of glamorous international art thieves: he in a smart suit with a sparkle in his eye; she's got killer heels to go with her blood-red lipstick. Not a hair out of place on either of them. They are the coolest people in the room.* PAUL *is always winking at you.* DUSTY *is always eating.*

Also noticeable right away, when entering 21c, is their logo and mascot: a four-foot Red Penguin, crafted out of plastic. The Red Penguins are among the first things that anyone notices when entering 21c: they are everywhere. Lined up on the roof, greeting you at the door, peppering the hallways and galleries: they are impossible to miss.

In the hotel lobby, audience members are welcomed to a big party, an art opening celebrating the newest work by ARCHIE PELLAGO. *On the check-in table are copies of the invitation, which reads:*

"You Are Invited To
Art > Fear
21c in partnership with Chelsea Cooley
(and the Cooley Series of Contemporary Art Happenings)
Present a New Work by
Archie Pellago
March 11-28, 2010

Archie Pellago's work challenges the viewer to interrogate his/her perceptions of what is art and what is life. By considering the breakdown of traditional venues for pedestrian imagination, the viewer is compelled to look at everyday happenings in a new way, and to reckon with the breakdown of traditional distinctions between good and bad, happy and sad, art and life."

The invitation also includes the address of 21c and its world-famous logo: the Red Penguin.

As you enter, you might be greeted by CHELSEA COOLEY, *an overly excitable debutante whose father has funded her expensive art habit;* ALICE WEATHERS, *the uptight and painfully fashionable head curator, who has organized the evening; and/or* CARL WEATHERS *(no relation), a local police officer, charged with conducting "random" security checks.*

You're probably waiting in the ticket line with some characters from the show. Some of them probably get frisked, or display press credentials, or ask to speak to ALICE. *When this happens,* CHELSEA *calls out loudly across the entire atrium—"Alice! Alice! Aaaaallll-iiiiiiiiiccce!" until the curator comes scurrying up the stairs.*

Once through the gauntlet of CHELSEA, ALICE, *and* CARL, *you descend the stairs to 21c's wide open atrium space, where a party is in full swing, with flattering light, jazzy music, and plentiful drinks.*

The centerpiece of the party is a small painting, veiled by a red curtain and secured behind an elaborate security setup involving lasers and steel bars. This is the newest work by the world-famous artist ARCHIE PELLAGO—*a notorious hermit and recluse. His last exhibited work, the Pellago Prism, was the last work of art that the Vista Seven attempted to steal…so security is tight. (Also, exhibiting as important and reclusive an artist as Pellago is a career-making opportunity for* ALICE WEATHERS…*which is why she's a little high-strung tonight.)*

As you go through the party, looking at art, you might be approached by one or more characters. Some examples:

- DIANE WORTHINGBOTTOM, the ambitious assistant curator, offers tours of the 21c exhibit. She is an efficient and knowledgeable docent, and has strong opinions about Alice's selection of the art. TANYA STEIMER FELDMAN, a young docent, also leads tours. She was late to work today, and lives in fear of being yelled at by DIANE. Her tours are more focused on pieces in the collection to which she responds emotionally.

- CHELSEA COOLEY, our generous and over-excited hostess, makes the rounds, makes sure that y'all are having a good time. She's often accompanied by DEVIN, her performance artist boyfriend, and LOUISA, her mute personal assistant. She's thrilled to introduce them to you, and thrilled that you're here.

- LUKE MICHAEL CHRISTIANSON tries to recruit volunteers for his Christian-themed tour of the art. If that fails, he offers a quick aerobics class in the exercise room.

- CLARISSA, a local arts and culture blogger, has a video camera and is interviewing various audience members about their impressions of the show. (If you ask her, she's thinks it's totally awesome.)

- HANS H.H.G. SCHMIDT, a menacing German magician, performs tricks with red foam balls and lengths of red string, telling stories about his childhood back in Berlin, and promising that his biggest trick is yet to come.

- CLARENCE FRANKLIN, computer nerd, tries to get the numbers of as many girls as possible. He's surprisingly successful, but not when his dad, COMMISSIONER FRANKLIN, comes by to kill his mojo.

- BORIS and TATIANA PENGUROVICH, a pair of Russian siblings who look like they just stepped off the set of a B-grade Cold War spy thriller, ask you if you have seen the Red Penguin. Since there are dozens of Red Penguins scattered throughout the building, you probably have.

- KATE SHAPIRO, from Scotland Yard, and PENELOPE FRANCIS, from the FBI, guard the perimeter. They do random ID checks and ask if anyone asked you to hold a bag. They also might frisk you to make sure you're not carrying any weapons, and warn you to back away from the Pellago.

- DEVIN also has his own opinions of the art, and sometimes would like to share these opinions with you. As you're shown around, you might stumble into a room in the back hallway...

- ...called the *Unterschlupf*. This is HANS SCHMIDT's secret lair; however, there's no way to know this until later in the show. In a regular hotel room, HANS has planned his most elaborate magic trick, the Great Disappearance. Strewn throughout the room are maps of Louisville marked with drawings of explosives, as well a plethora of dynamite. Also maybe a couple of mutilated toy penguins. Some partygoers think this is a cutting-edge art installation; others are disturbed and try alert the police. DEVIN, TANYA, and LUKE each bring small groups of audience members to this room; it's also possible for audience members to wander through the back hallway and find it themselves.

You also might see something intriguing or suspicious out of the corner of your eye, such as:

- BORIS PENGUROVICH seems to be following HANS SCHMIDT, the magician.

- The museum staff—ALICE, DIANE, and TANYA—seem to constantly be looking for ANDY POOLE, the hapless janitor, who seems to never be where he's supposed to be.

- Knockout TATIANA PENGUROVICH flirts with shy CLARENCE while he tries to play computer games.

- The renowned art critic TIMOTHY WYATT and a very stylish artist with a sketchpad, Q, seem to always be flirting in the corner. He looks smitten.

- DEVIN, arm-candy to CHELSEA COOLEY, tries to get ALICE's attention, trying to get her interested in his own unique brand of performance-art-installation-dance.

- ALICE instructs her Special Events Manager, VICTOR KUSIK, on how to replace the bourbon barrels in the back room.

- The rookie cop, CARL WEATHERS, frisks a scantily-clad party guest, JUSTICE, who seems to know COMMISSIONER FRANKLIN from "back in the day."

(See Appendix for a more complete list of conversations that happen between characters in the lobby and in the party, as well as suggestions for audience interaction ice-breakers.)

While all of the above is going on (and much, much more), the audience mingles, looks at the art, and is invited into three side galleries to view three cartoons that provide background to the key players in tonight's drama. Characters mingle too, with each other and with the audience—the atmosphere is festive, the best party in town.

This is THE place to be on a Friday night.

THE CARTOON GALLERIES.

At the entrance to each of the three side galleries, there is a bright red sign announcing a different time and place: "36 Years Ago," "6 Years Ago," and "600 Years Ago." In each of these rooms there is a cartoon running on a loop, providing the backstory and context for tonight's events. **(Please see Appendix for the scripts for these animations.)**

ACT 2: The Event Officially Begins.

A little after 11p.m. (the scheduled start time for the show), every character has made their entrance. You can feel the excitement rising in the room when…

ALICE WEATHERS *takes the podium.* ALICE *is impeccably dressed, and would fit in at any New York or London gallery opening—in other words, she is trying too hard and wearing too much asymmetrical black. She has the weariness of someone who wishes she were somewhere else—except, this is finally her moment to shine.*

ALICE. Hello. Good evening. I am Alice Weathers, Curator of Special Exhibitions here at 21c. It is my great honor to welcome you to the opening night soiree in honor of the newest piece by Archie Pellago, one of the finest and most exciting artists of his generation. I'd like to thank Chelsea Cooley for her generous support of this unique event.

(CHELSEA*, an over-exuberant debutante, rushes the podium. She is dressed up for her art party—a cross between a day at the races and Lady Gaga.*)

CHELSEA. (*On microphone.*) You're welcome! I love my painting! I'm just so happy to have you all here today to celebrate having this very very beautiful artwork here in Louisville! I'm so excited to have you all at my party!

ALICE. All right. Thank you Chelsea. This is the first Pellago exhibit in six years. Of course Archie is not able to join us tonight, being a notorious recluse and hermit. But he IS here in spirit. In his stead, he has sent his colleagues from Russia—

(*She gestures towards* THE RUSSIANS: BORIS *and* TATIANA PENGUROVICH *look like they just stepped out of a Cold War-era B-movie spy thriller. They never smile. She wears a hot red dress and an eye patch. He wears boots that could kill a man, and probably have.*

They wave to the crowd, awkwardly.)

ALICE. We are just thrilled to have such an international presence at this very important event. Thank you for being here. Now, I would like to introduce my good friend from Yale, Timothy Wyatt, esteemed art critic of *The Economist*, for some insights into Pellago's *oeuvre*. Timothy?

(TIMOTHY WYATT has flown in from New York, just for this event, and is impressed by nobody.)

TIMOTHY. Mr. Wyatt will be fine.

ALICE. All right then.

(Just as TIMOTHY begins to speak, ANDY POOLE—the goateed janitor of 21c—falls down near the podium. ALICE is embarrassed and appalled.)

Andy!

ANDY. I'm fine, it's okay.

(He runs away quickly, mop in hand.)

TIMOTHY. *(Rolls his eyes and looks at his notes.)* My first Pellago was the Venice Biennale some years ago, I'm sure you're all familiar with his room-sized installation "You Are Not Looking Where Your Eyes Are At." It is fair to say that Pellago has been pushing the form and pushing buttons since he first emerged as the idiot savant of the neo-minimalist movement of the early 21st century; I hope you know how lucky you are to have him here in your bourbon-soaked midst.

ALICE. Thank you, Tim—Mr. Wyatt—for that…rousing…

I know I shouldn't, but I suppose now, I should say a few words about the… controversy. You know, Archie and I go way back, and when Vista was released from jail he called me up, he said, "Alice, I don't know if I can go through with it." Because Archie firmly believes that his art is For the People, not For the Few. And I said, Archie, I said, listen to me. You can't be cobbled by a few con men in fancy suits. You can't keep your work in a dark studio. Brilliance needs light in order to shine. I said, Archie, I said, Art is more important than Fear.

Here to explain our extraordinary security precautions is Commissioner Jefferson Washington Franklin of the Louisville Metro Police Department. Commissioner, thank you for being here with us today.

COMMISSIONER. You're welcome.

(The COMMISSIONER takes the podium. He is a man who was born chomping a cigar: grizzled, official-looking, perennially confused, a strong believer in law and order and the rightness of justice, to comic effect.)

Okay enough with the chitchat, here's what's going on. We're the LMPD, and we're gonna keep you safe. We got friskers, we got that lady there, in the feminist power suit, she's from Scotland Yard, and that chick, Asian lady in khaki, she's from the FBI, and also we gots new hires coming out of our every orifice.

(*Suddenly,* VICTOR KUSIK, *the Head of Special Events at 21c, is trying to wheel a large barrel of bourbon from the far side of the room all the way to the back exit. He is making a big commotion and lots of people have to move out of his way.*)

COMMISSIONER. Oh, hey, look, the party has started!

VICTOR. (*As he crosses.*) Heavy load…excuse me, excuse me…sorry about this, coming through…

(*Meanwhile, the distraction has given the* COMMISSIONER *the chance to notice something alarming—his computer nerd son,* CLARENCE, *typing away on a laptop in a corner of the room.*)

COMMISSIONER. Clarence! Yo, Clarence!

CLARENCE. Me?

COMMISSIONER. Yeah, what do you think, I got another pussy son?

CLARENCE. What's your problem?

COMMISSIONER. Get off your internets and pay attention, this is important what I'm saying.

CLARENCE. Dad!

(*He slams his computer shut and stalks to the other side of the room.*)

COMMISSIONER. What, a father's not supposed to worry about his son? It's like on an airplane, if you don't listen to the lady about the yellow things with the oxygen in 'em, how're you gonna know how to breathe when the plane blows up?

(ALICE *grabs the microphone from the* COMMISSIONER.)

ALICE. Thank you, Commissioner. We are grateful for your help. But I would like to remind everyone that, above all, Art is more important than Fear. So, please, don't be frightened, and—

(*Suddenly,* ALICE *screams and points above the crowd to the top of the stairs. Everyone turns and looks to see—*PAUL VISTA *and* DUSTY PRESS *leaning over, surveying the scene below.*)

It's Paul Vista! And Dusty Press!

(PAUL *straightens his French cuffs.* DUSTY *pops a stick of gum in her mouth or blows a perfect pink bubble.*)

PAUL. Look at that, Dusty. It's good to be home.

DUSTY. Quite a sight. You ready for this?

PAUL. Ready as I'll ever be.

DUSTY. It's like Bricks used to say, right?

PAUL. Always gotta keep one eye open, and one eye closed.

DUSTY. Cheers to that.

PAUL. Shall we?

DUSTY. We shall.

(*They descend the stairs.*

HANS H.H.G. SCHMIDT, *the German magician who had been entertaining groups at the party, makes his way to the front of the room.*

Meanwhile, the COMMISSIONER *meets up with* PAUL *and* DUSTY *on the landing.*)

PAUL. Hey, old friend.

(*They embrace each other, like old friends, and pat each other down, like old enemies.*)

COMMISSIONER. Nice to have you back in Louisville.

PAUL. This is my friend, Dusty.

DUSTY. *Enchanté.*

COMMISSIONER. Yeah, hi, nice to meet you. Never heard of you.

PAUL. My partner in crime.

ALL. Ha ha ha

DUSTY. So what's a sister got to do to get a sandwich around here?

COMMISSIONER. (*Speaks into a tiny walkie-talkie on his wrist.*) Carl! Carl! Get this lady a sandwich.

CARL. (*Speaking into his wrist.*) Yes, sir.

(CARL *goes in search of a sandwich.*)

COMMISSIONER. So yeah, we're putting up a little exhibition thing.

PAUL. Archie Pellago.

COMMISSIONER. Yep. Archie Pellago.

DUSTY. Archie Pellago.

COMMISSIONER. You heard of him?

DUSTY. Can't say I have.

COMMISSIONER. So, you folks, here to see the old haunts?

PAUL. You know, I just got out of—

COMMISSIONER. We don't need to talk about that.

PAUL. How's Clarence?

COMMISSIONER. He's good. Good. Still a pussy. Aren't you, Clarence?

CLARENCE. What?

COMMISSIONER. Still a pussy! Isn't that right, Clarence?

CLARENCE. Da-ad! Jesus! Leave me alone!

PAUL. You've been saying that since he was two.

COMMISSIONER. Call it like I see it, don't I. All right, well enjoy the party and the arts and things. One more?

(They embrace warmly again, and frisk each other—the same routine as at the top of the scene.

When all of a sudden…)

ACT 3: The Panic.

A loud noise is heard from above: ANDY POOLE *has landed, face-down, on the glass ceiling of the atrium—he looks dead.*

Screams.

The lights go out.

More screams.

ANDY *stands up, shakes his head, and shrugs—sorry, my bad, I just fell.*

EVERYONE *sighs a sigh of relief—oh thank goodness, it's going to be okay.*

The lights come back on.

But then—

CHELSEA. OH MY GOD THE PAINTING! Somebody hit the alarm!

(CHELSEA points to where the Pellago should be—now, the red curtain has been torn away and all that is left is an empty frame.

Everyone screams again.

Alarms wail, somewhere in the building we hear gates clanging shut, and a computerized voice chirps "Lockdown. Lockdown. Lockdown." on repeat.

ALICE *makes horrible panicked noises.*

COMMISSIONER *barrel rolls, poorly, towards* VISTA, *in an attempt to catch him, but the* COPS *are there first and arrest both* PAUL *and* DUSTY.

Meanwhile, the RUSSIANS *kidnap* TIMOTHY WYATT *by karate-chopping him in the throat and carrying his body through the crowd, saying things like "Nothing to look at here" and "Excuse us please, this man fainted."*

KATE SHAPIRO, *a crack security expert from Scotland Yard dressed in a sharp power suit and heels to rival* DUSTY's, *takes control of the situation from the podium.*

Alarm sounds fade, lights are restored, but the energy in the room is still at high alert.)

KATE. *(On microphone.)* Are the suspects in custody? Paul Vista?

COP. *(From crowd.)* Check.

KATE. Dusty Press?

COP. Check.

KATE. Get them out of here.

(PENELOPE FRANCIS [PEN], a no-nonsense FBI agent, guides the COPS *in escorting* PAUL *and* DUSTY *up the stairs and out the door.*

As they go, PAUL *and* DUSTY *ad-lib with the cops and the audience.)*

PAUL. (*As he goes.*) Hey hey hey, no need to get rough, it's Armani. Watch the cuffs.

DUSTY. Don't forget to bring my sandwich...

KATE. (*On microphone.*) Hello, hello, may I have your attention please. Although we are on lockdown, there's no need to panic. I'm Kate Shapiro, here from Scotland Yard on behalf of Europol, representing Interpol. On behalf of the International Security Community, I am here to tell you that we've been monitoring Vista's movements for quite some time and were, alas, prepared for this eventuality. Some months ago we partnered with Dobson and Dorman Security Practitioners to ensure the safekeeping of Archie's near-priceless painting; and I am confident at this juncture that the painting, valued at roughly 200 million American dollars, is safe.

Now come along with me as I take you through the state of the art, foolproof and fail-safe security system.

(*She clicks on a screen above her head, which reads: The Top Secret Security System at 21c—Revealed!*

As KATE *narrates, we watch an animated tour through the state-of-the-art 21c security system, Perhaps she has a laser pointer to point out key details.*)

Approximately two minutes ago, when the lights went out, a computerized sensor was triggered, releasing the painting into a vault located two stories below where it was hung.

You see this floor, here, though it looks solid, actually has a trap door, leading directly to a bronze and concrete steel-reinforced shaft via which the painting dropped down into a sealed climate controlled vault. See, this is also where the barrels of rare bourbon are kept for special occasions.

Within this vault, there is a uniquely designed petroleum plastic pouch, which instantaneously forms a vacuum barrier around the painting.

At the instant of it clasping shut, so that no air or other elements may get in or out, a hatch is sprung, filling the room with water, which takes approximately four minutes.

As soon as the room is filled, the water level triggers a sensor, which releases the vacuum pack containing the painting, floating it across the Ohio River—landing the painting safely in Indiana where it is then sealed in another sealed climate-controlled vault, to be retrieved by myself or another proxy on behalf of Interpol.

Since it has now been approximately four minutes since the lights went out, and the painting disappeared, I would say that we can safely assume that the painting is now on its merry way to Indiana.

(*The animation ends. Pleased with her presentation,* KATE *snaps off the screen.*

CHELSEA, *completely distraught over the loss of her painting, grabs her mute personal assistant,* LOUISA.)

CHELSEA. (*To* LOUISA.) Be a proxy! Go! Be a proxy! Get the painting! To the river! To the river!

> (LOUISA *runs like the wind up the stairs, out the door, and towards the river, four blocks away.*
> PEN *takes the microphone.*)

PEN. Thank you for your attention. Thanks, Kate. I'm Penelope Francis, from the FBI.

We have been tracking the Vista Seven for years, and I am sorry to inform you that many of them were present tonight. You might recognize some of the following:

> (PEN's *slideshow of FBI mug shots consists of cartoon representations of all the major players on the heist team, some of whom we've already met at the party and some of whom we saw in the cartoons that played during the party.*)

Paul Vista, who you have heard so much about, and his partner, Dusty Press, both of whom were taken into custody just moments ago…

Additional suspected members of the Vista Seven include: Justice, their grease girl, known for fitting into small spaces; Q, a notorious French art forger; and Victor Kusik, who infiltrated the staff of 21c as Events Manager some months ago.

There are two additional members of the team who we have not yet been able to identify:

> (*For these, we see question marks or some other icon indicating "unknown persons."*)

—a computer wiz, known online as "Clarebear," real name unknown; and one more man we suspect was working on the inside.

We need your help identifying these crafty con men. We have set up a briefing room across the street with surveillance footage gathered over the past months and years, as Vista gathered his crew and plotted his crime.

I will need eight groups to go across the street. Kate, of course, will lead a group, and the staff—raise your hands so people can see you. Say your names for me please.

> (*She points out the 21c staff and they each introduce themselves: The kind-hearted docent…*)

TANYA. Tanya Steimer Feldman.

> (*Everybody's favorite curator…*)

ALICE. Alice Weathers.

> (*Her assistant, and rival…*)

DIANE. Diane Worthingbottom, Assistant Curator here at 21c.

PEN. Thank you. And I will need four additional volunteers. Who'd like to assist us in the investigation? Say your names for me please.

(*She points to certain party guests:*
The trendy young video blogger...)

CLARISSA. Clarissa Explains It All dot kick-ass dot org!

(*The friendly young man in gym shorts and a tie...*)

LUKE. Luke Michael Christianson!

(*Our distraught host...*)

CHELSEA. Chelsea Cooley...

(*Her hanger-on boyfriend, who is some sort of performance artist...*)

DEVIN. Devin.

PEN. Thank you.

(PEN *hands the microphone to the* COMMISSIONER.)

COMMISSIONER. Please, now, group leaders—collect your group, starting now.

(*The size of each group depends on the size of the audience—they should be divided evenly.*

The COMMISSIONER *and the rest of law enforcement helps the audience find a group, ad-libbing as needed.*

Once that's done:)

Everyone set? Great. I'm going to ask you to stick with your groups for the duration of the lockdown, for the safety of all involved. Should you get separated from your group, please ask the nearest law enforcement officer for assistance—police, can you please raise your hands?

(COPS *raise their hands.*)

Great, thank you. Finally, please be aware that there are no drinks allowed in HQ, so please finish your beverages before heading across the street.

You are dismissed.

(*Each group leader brings their group to the next location.*)

ACT 4: The Adventure.

After the COMMISSIONER *dismisses the crowd, each* GROUP LEADER *embarks on a journey through a number of scenes, some of which are happening in "real" time and some of which function as flashbacks to events past. These scenes take place in the galleries of 21c, as well as across the street in their annex "Museum Plaza Design and Sales Offices"; in our play, we called it "FBI Headquarters."*

The eight groups experience the scenes of Act 4 in different orders; the order of the experience is determined by the GROUP LEADER. *So, when* PEN *dismisses the groups at the end of Act 3, some groups go across the street right away, while others head into one of the side galleries.*

Each of the eight GROUP LEADERS *also have their own personal stories to tell; the stakes are different for each one, and therefore each group has an experience that is unique only to them.*

Every group gets to see the following scenes:

> A) **Planning The Heist**—a series of live museum exhibits, providing a peek into how PAUL VISTA assembled his crew.
>
> B) **The Russians Seek Their Penguin**—the subplot is revealed! Those shady Russians, BORIS and TATIANA PENGU-ROVICH, try to find the magical Red Penguin before it's too late.
>
> C) **The Commissioner's Training**—COMMISSIONER JEF-FERSON WASHINGTON FRANKLIN takes the audience through a series of absurd and ridiculous police training exercises.
>
> D) **Wild Card Group Leader Solo**—each GROUP LEADER has their own story to tell, which unfurls as they take their audience group from room to room. Each audience group only sees the Solo Scene of their GROUP LEADER—so, since you can only follow one group leader per night, *there are actually eight different ways to watch the show*: for example, ALICE WEATHERS' group has a different experience from CLARISSA's.

(See Appendix for Group Leader Texts, including the order of their tour through the different scenes and their Solos.)

As you watch scenes, learn about the theft of the Pellago and its possible connection to the missing Red Penguin, you are on a wild ride through the galleries and corridors of 21c and Louisville, as well as the unique world of your group leader. Part of the joy of HEIST! *is seeing other groups out of the corner of your eye, having an experience totally different from your own.*

ACT 4A: Planning The Heist.

Time to meet the VISTA SEVEN: *led by the fine and unflappable* PAUL VISTA *and his reliable partner-in-crime-and-all-you-can-eat-buffets,* DUSTY PRESS, *the crew also includes* JUSTICE, *a retired contortionist and sometimes-stripper;* Q, *an international art forger, who does it for love and a sense that her own talents were never appreciated in the cutthroat art world;* CLARENCE FRANKLIN, *who we have previously met as the* COMMISSIONER's *bumbling son;* VICTOR KUSIK, *the inside man who had been working in Special Events at 21c; and* ANDY POOLE, *who we met as 21c's klutzy janitor.*

To see these scenes, each group goes across the street to FBI HEADQUARTERS, *which is set up in 21c's Museum Plaza Design and Sales Offices, a showroom for luxury apartments high above Louisville. Each room is completely furnished in the highest style, with art on the walls, modern designer furniture, and fine crystal. The effect is of watching scenes from a movie happening live, more than of watching a play—the detail is that spot-on.*

Upon arriving at FBI Headquarters, each group is greeted by PENELOPE FRANCIS, *the no-nonsense FBI Officer. She has a megaphone.*

PEN. Hi. Hi. Welcome. Everyone here?

Hi. Nice to see you all here—sorry it's under such unfortunate circumstances. I promise this lockdown won't last too long.

Once again, I'm Penelope Francis from the Federal Bureau of Investigation. This briefing room is a joint project of the FBI, Scotland Yard, Interpol, and Europol.

We have been tracking Paul Vista for many years, but particularly ramped up our investigation when he was released from jail. Alas, while we wish that the Pellago unveiling had gone without a hitch, we were not surprised that he made an attempt to steal the painting.

These briefing rooms are an attempt to share with you some of our knowledge of how Vista's crew came together, in the hope of getting the painting back quickly from Indiana, and more importantly, making sure that a crisis of this magnitude Never. Happens. Again.

Vista, who we do have in custody, is a menace to our city, to our country, and to our ART.

As witnesses to an international crime, we need you to be vigilant and observant as you go through the briefing room. You will be seeing footage of Paul Vista, Dusty Press, Justice, Q, Victor Kusik, and two unknown persons. Should you recognize either of these unknowns, please don't hesitate to inform your group leader.

I'll be letting in two groups at a time. This group here, your group, I want you to go all the way to the back, and you guys—the second group, you stay in the front.

Here's how this works. There are two exhibits on either side. Watch the scene you're in front of, and then turn around and watch the scene on the other side. Then, I want you to rotate clockwise, so folks in the front move to the back and vice versa. Follow the arrows on the floor. Watch two more scenes—one on each side—and then, after you've seen all four scenes, please leave with your group leader.

Thanks for your cooperation. We hope you find these briefings as informative as we do.

(PEN *lets each group into the exhibit to watch Act 4A: Planning the Heist.*

Each of the four scenes are marked by a lightbox indicating both the time and location: i.e. RIO DE JANEIRO: 6 MONTHS AGO.)

In between loops, loud, sassy music plays, like would play during the opening credits of an <u>Ocean's Eleven</u> *movie, and our Vista Seven strut down the middle of the space as if walking on the tarmac. Wearing sunglasses. In unison. They are hot, sexy, and in control of the situation.*)

THE SCENES (on loop):

RIO DE JANEIRO: 6 Months ago.
Paul Vista and Dusty Press Reunite.

PAUL VISTA *sits on a white leather sofa in* DUSTY PRESS' *palatial Rio pad. Making himself quite at home.*

DUSTY *enters, with a jar full of snack mix. Sees* PAUL *and rushes him for a hug.*

DUSTY. VIIIIIIIIIIISTA!!

PAUL. Look at you.

DUSTY. Look at me? Look at you!

(*They hug warmly. He spins her around.*)

PAUL. You're a hard girl to find, you know that?

DUSTY. Always moving, always grooving, know what I mean?

PAUL. Well, you look great.

DUSTY. Know my secret?

PAUL. I know a lot of your secrets.

DUSTY. It's the Dust Off Those Abs Presser Machine 3000! You want a brochure? I sent one to the Bastille, but I never heard back from you.

PAUL. I wasn't at the Bastille.

DUSTY. J.K., Vista, J.K.! Brazil nut?

PAUL. Allergic.

DUSTY. So what now? You need a job? I got a whole back catalogue of Presser 3000's I need to unload...

PAUL. Actually, I think I got one.

DUSTY. Oh yeah? Doing what?

PAUL. How well do you know Louisville?

DUSTY. Um...where's that?

PAUL. Louisville? Kentucky?

DUSTY. Louisville...Louisville...sounds familiar, but I can't place it...

PAUL. Louisville Slugger? Galt House? I-65? The place I was born?

DUSTY. (*Still nothing.*)

PAUL. Churchill Downs?

DUSTY. I gave up on that shit when I started selling my workout systems.

PAUL. Dusty. I said I got a job.

DUSTY. I don't know, Paul, I love you like a brother, but I got me some thriving business centers here. Don't know if this is the right time to…enter into another…venture.

PAUL. Are you looking for a venture? Or an *adv*enture?

DUSTY. Paul Vista. Listen to me. Listen good. We all said we'd go straight. Remember? Scatter. Think of what happened to Bricks.

PAUL. I am thinking of Bricks. That's why I gotta do it. I gotta make it up to him. I loved him like a father and I let him down.

BARDSTOWN ROAD: 16 Months ago.
Andy Poole Recruits Clarence Franklin.

A local Louisville comic book store, in the back where they keep the games. CLARENCE FRANKLIN, *computer science major and son of Louisville's own* COMMISSIONER JEFFERSON WASHINGTON FRANKLIN, *is engrossed in an involved game of* Warhammer *with* ANDY POOLE, *the goateed janitor of 21c.*

ANDY. So, uh, you're in computers?

CLARENCE. Studying. Computer science. Four credits shy.

ANDY. Cool. I wish I could get into something employable.

CLARENCE. Where do you work?

ANDY. I'm at 21c, the art gallery downtown? It's cool. I'm the janitor—but it's cool.

CLARENCE. Oh yeah, I have some friends who work at Proof.

ANDY. Who's that? Maybe I know them.

CLARENCE. Oh—it was just—a girl I knew—but—

ANDY. Oh, yeah. Yeah.

(ANDY *makes a move in the game.*)

CLARENCE. So.

ANDY. Yeah. Actually, maybe you know about this, they're planning this new show? Some guy named—Archie Pellago?

CLARENCE. Archie Pellago?

ANDY. Apparently the painting is worth a ton of money. They're rigging up some special computer security system for it.

CLARENCE. I've heard of him—I know some people tried to steal one of his paintings, like six years ago or something, and he went into hiding.

(CLARENCE *makes a move.*)

ANDY. Actually—what I heard—I don't know if this is true, but—I heard that the security system is pretty easy to hack. I don't know a lot about that but—

CLARENCE. Who's the maker?

ANDY. The what?

CLARENCE. The company? The security system?

ANDY. Not sure—Dorman and Dobson? Something like that?

CLARENCE. No way, really? They went with Dobson and Dorman?

ANDY. What?

CLARENCE. Notoriously faulty, that's what.

ANDY. No shit.

CLARENCE. Oh, yeah. Infamous.

ANDY. Well, if you want to look at the security system, I can probably let you in—

CLARENCE. Okay, well—nah, I don't think—I don't want to—

ANDY. That's cool, it's a crazy idea.

> (ANDY *wins the game in a surprise move involving a stealth, unbeatable attack.* CLARENCE *is stunned.*)

But if you change your mind—I'm there Tuesday through Sunday. Third shift.

CLARENCE. Okay, cool. Cool. Thanks. Good game, man.

ANDY. Yeah, good game.

LISBON: 6 Months ago.
Paul and Dusty Recruit Q.

> Q's *apartment in Lisbon. Even more palatial than* DUSTY's *Rio place, if that's even possible. Paintings by the great masters adorn the walls. As is their habit,* PAUL *and* DUSTY *have let themselves in and are lounging in the kitchen.* DUSTY *is making herself some nachos.*
>
> Q *enters, her arms full of expensive shopping bags. Giant sunglasses cover most of her face.*
>
> (NOTE: *words that are* <u>underlined</u> *should be said in French.*)

PAUL. Excuse us.

DUSTY. We let ourselves in.

> (Q *nods and takes off her coat, unruffled.*)

PAUL. I heard she did a Rembrandt.

DUSTY. Those are easy. I heard she did a Pollack.

PAUL. No shit, a Pollack.

DUSTY. Nice collection you've racked up.

> (Q *pours shots of expensive vodka.*)

Q. <u>I only drink the hard stuff, I hope you don't mind.</u>

DUSTY. That's great.

PAUL. But the question is, which is the real and which is the copy?

Q. In my home, all originals. In museums across the world, my copies.

(*They toast and toss back their drinks.*)

PAUL. Paul Vista.

Q. I know who you are. And you must be Dusty Press.

DUSTY. We're huge fans of your work.

(*Q pours another round.*)

Q. And I, yours. If it wasn't for that old man on your team, you would have gotten away with the Paris Pellago. Small tragedy, that was.

DUSTY. Let's let bygones be bygones.

PAUL. Like Bricks always told us, always face the future with one eye open and one eye closed.

DUSTY. We've heard you've copied art all over the world.

Q. I prefer "replace." From the Louvre to LACMA, from Bilbao to Berlin.

DUSTY. Impressive.

Q. Thank you. I'm flattered by your interest, but I'm not looking for a partnership. Working alone, my work hangs everywhere—In fact, name me an important institution in the world that DOESN'T have one of my copies hanging on its walls...

PAUL. I got one.

Q. Oh, do you?

PAUL. 21c. Louisville, Kentucky.

Q. (*Suddenly enraged.*) That evil small woman, Alice Weathers.

DUSTY. You ready to get yourself into 21c?

Q. Tell me more.

DUSTY. How long did it take to do this one, here?

Q. A couple of months...there's an alchemy to it...

PAUL. And this one?

Q. Almost a year.

DUSTY. How'd you feel about...four minutes?

(*Beat. Q can't believe it, but can't resist the challenge.*)

PAUL. Deal?

Q. Deal.

ALL. Deal.

(*They do shots.*)

ISTANBUL: 6 Weeks ago.
Justice and Victor Get Sucked Back In.

VICTOR KUSIK *stands over a stainless steel pot in his beautifully tiled kitchen in Istanbul, savoring the aroma of his latest concoction. He is a master chef.*

Suddenly, he senses someone else in the room...grabs his knife, looking for the intruder. Knocks a rhythm on the counter. From somewhere below, a knock answers. Again, and then—

JUSTICE, *a former stripper whose expertise is fitting into small spaces, pops out of a cabinet.*

VICTOR. (*Warmly.*) Hey! Justice!

JUSTICE. Victor!

VICTOR. Scared the hell out of me.

(*She looks into the pot.*)

JUSTICE. I don't believe it! Victor From Everyone has gone and got himself an actual JOB!

VICTOR. Freelance.

JUSTICE. You sign a contract?

VICTOR. (*Shrugs.*)

JUSTICE. That's what I call going straight.

VICTOR. Health insurance, what can I say.

JUSTICE. You look good man, man.

VICTOR. So do you.

(*She twirls.*)

JUSTICE. Cabo, baby.

VICTOR. Taste this.

(*He holds up a spoonful of sauce to her lips. She tastes.*)

JUSTICE. That is the shit, man. You're good.

VICTOR. I'm happy, what can I say.

JUSTICE. If I keep eating like that, I won't be fitting myself into any small spaces anytime soon, you know what I mean?

(*Beat. An understanding passes between them.*)

VICTOR. You thinking of doing something that would require…

JUSTICE. You talk to Vista lately?

VICTOR. Did you?

JUSTICE. I asked you first.

VICTOR. You know he got out of jail, right.

JUSTICE. I heard some computer wiz kid got all that evidence erased. Clarence, Clarebear, something like that.

VICTOR. That was a bad time, in France. I don't like to think about it.

JUSTICE. I was stuck on the roof for three whole *days* before Dusty came to get me.

VICTOR. You and me, we got lucky. Six years in a French jail—Vista had it rough, man. But still—I always thought Bricks would have been disappointed if he knew we'd all gone straight.

JUSTICE. You know they want to put me in a bourbon barrel?

VICTOR. I heard that, yeah.

JUSTICE. I wouldn't trust anyone with that but you.

VICTOR. So you're going to do it?

JUSTICE. Are you?

VICTOR. Are you?

JUSTICE. I just said I can't do it alone.

VICTOR. So you are.

JUSTICE. You are.

VICTOR. You're in?

JUSTICE. You're in?

VICTOR. You are?

JUSTICE. You are?

VICTOR. One last job, yeah?

JUSTICE. And then we're out for good.

VICTOR. Deal.

JUSTICE. Deal.

BOTH. Deal.

(They shake on it.

End of Act 4A.

Once each group has seen all of the scenes, their GROUP LEADER *leads them back outside and across the street to the main 21c building. [See Appendix for these texts.]*)

ACT 4B: The Russians Seek Their Penguin.

We enter this scene from the main atrium gallery, where we've been spending some quality time with the COMMISSIONER *(more on that later).*

The COMMISSIONER *ushers two groups at a time into a side gallery, which is labeled "6 Minutes Ago."*

Inside the gallery are a bunch of the red plastic Penguins. It looks like someone has been hording them.

The COMMISSIONER *arranges the audience in two parallel clusters, creating an alleyway in which the action takes place.*

After the COMMISSIONER *leaves, the opposite door bursts open and the two mysterious Russian siblings,* BORIS *and* TATIANA PENGUROVICH, *enter carrying the art critic* TIMOTHY WYATT, *who has been knocked out cold.*

They are clearly agitated. They tie TIMOTHY *to a chair in the middle of the room while they try to figure out what to do.*

TATIANA. Four minutes…four minutes…is not long time.

BORIS. Four minutes for water, then whoosh to river…I do not really understand.

TATIANA. We have not much time to find correct Penguin. And also, to free the art critic man. And also, to save Louisville.

BORIS. I do not like these odds.

TATIANA. Wake up, art man! Wake up!

BORIS. What if he is not able to discern true Red Penguin identity?

TATIANA. Then we will not have our Penguin Powers back.

BORIS. The whole of Louisville hangs in our balance.

TATIANA. We promised Archie Pellago!

BORIS. We cannot fail.

(TATIANA *wakes up* TIMOTHY. *He takes one look at her attire and screams—*)

TIMOTHY. Tacky! Tacky!

BORIS. You are Timothy Wyatt, famous art critic.

TIMOTHY. What? What?

(*He starts to realize that there are more things to be scared of than* TATIANA's *cheap red dress.*)

TATIANA. Timothy Wyatt. Yes or no.

TIMOTHY. This is a statement, or a question? Question mark.

TATIANA. My brother and I do not have time for your, how do you say—snark.

BORIS. You are Timothy Wyatt, famous art critic, yes or no?

TIMOTHY. Who's asking?

BOTH. We are.

TIMOTHY. But who ARE you?

TATIANA. We are Boris and Tatiana Pengurovich.

BORIS. Tell us, which is the Red Penguin?

TIMOTHY. ALL of the penguins are RED!

TATIANA. One of these Penguins is not like the others.

TIMOTHY. WHO ARE YOU AND WHAT AM I DOING HERE????!!!!

BORIS. Tell me this. Which is the Penguin. Question mark.

TIMOTHY. Which is what penguin?

TATIANA. Yes. Exactly. Period.

TIMOTHY. That's a penguin and that's a penguin and that's a penguin.

TATIANA. Tell us, which one is different. Which one is real.

TIMOTHY. I will not.

BORIS. You will.

(TATIANA *rubs her hands together and places them on his shoulders. The heat of her hands seems to burn right through his jacket—he howls—*)

TIMOTHY. (*Howling.*) Who ARE you people?

TATIANA. We are Boris and Tatiana Pengurovich.

BORIS. The *Krasny Pengvin* has been in our family for thousands of years.

TIMOTHY. The Cranny what?

BORIS. *Krasny. Krasny Pengvin.*

TATIANA. It mean red.

BORIS. The Red Penguin is secret source of power throughout Russian History. It was there when Alexander freed the serfs—

TATIANA. —when the proletariat rose up against injustice—

BORIS. —when Tolstoy wrote his masterpiece—

TATIANA. —when Russia dominated the Winter Olympics, and the Summer. It is on our family crest.

BORIS. It is tattooed on my bottom.

TIMOTHY. But why me, why am I, a simple art critic, tied up in this dingy carpeted room with all this tacky "art" on the walls—

(BORIS *and* TATIANA *confer.*)

BORIS. You know this Archie Pellago?

TIMOTHY. Of COURSE I know Archie Pellago.

TATIANA. Very good artist.

TIMOTHY. Indeed.

TATIANA. And also, rumored leader of the Casa Nostra.

BORIS. And the Masons.

TATIANA. And the Rosicrucians of the Golden Dawn.

BORIS. And Skull and Bonies.

TATIANA. And Kiwanis Club.

BORIS. Archie Pellago brought us here from Russia to retrieve our rightful Red Penguin.

TATIANA. But there is small problem.

BORIS. We did not expect so many of Penguins.

TATIANA. This plastic replicating, we do not know of this.

BORIS. We need your discerning critical eye to tell us which is the real Red Penguin.

TIMOTHY. Just take a penguin, what's the big deal, they're all the same.

BORIS. If only that were true.

TATIANA. Only one has power to defuse bombs.

TIMOTHY. Bombs?? What BOMBS??

BORIS. If we do not find Penguin…all of Louisville will disappear.

TATIANA. Poof. Boom.

TIMOTHY. Louisville? Disappear? Good riddance!

TATIANA. You think this is joke?

BORIS. Tatiana. Time to show art man we are no joking.

(*TATIANA touches him with her hands.*)

TIMOTHY. Ow! Ow! Ow! What are you doing—???

TATIANA. Prepare to reveal which is the real Red Penguin—

TIMOTHY. But…but…

TATIANA. Or, prepare to die!

(*TATIANA touches him with her hands.*)

TIMOTHY. But ALL of the penguins are red!!!

TATIANA. This is very serious matter.

BORIS. If we cannot identify the real Penguin, we will not stop the bombs and Louisville and everyone in it will die. Including you, Timothy Wyatt.

TATIANA. Poof boom. Tonight.

TIMOTHY. I'm not ready to die! I never got a review in the *New York Times*!

(*Suddenly, the evil German magician, HANS H.H.G. SCHMIDT, bursts in. He wears a black and gold tuxedo and has a twirly mustache. He spent the party [Act 1] performing simple tricks for the audience using red foam balls and red cotton ropes—tools he now uses for evil.*)

HANS. Not so fast there, Russkies!

BORIS and TATIANA. Oh no! Hans Schmidt!

(*As HANS approaches, red foam balls pop out of BORIS' mouth and TATIANA's hands. They scream, terrified.*)

HANS. Abracadabra! There's something in your ear! *Scheisse!*

TIMOTHY. Oh, thank heavens! Untie me, please!

HANS. You! You want me to work my magic on you? Last I checked, you were not a fan of…magic.

TIMOTHY. I'll believe! I'll believe! Just get me the hell out of here—oh please help me Mr. Hans, please get me out of this chair. These crazy Russians kidnapped me and they want to steal a Red Penguin and take it back to Russia and they say there's bombs all over Louisville and I just want to go back to my home in New York and—

HANS. Ah, well, that part is true.

TIMOTHY. Which part?

HANS. There is dynamite planted all across Louisville.

TIMOTHY. (*Freaks out.*) What! What! What!

(HANS *gags* TIMOTHY.)

HANS. Abracadabra, now you are silent.

(*To the Russians.*) Hallo, I don't believe we've had the pleasure of my acquaintance.

TATIANA. We are Boris and Tatiana Pengurov—

HANS. And you have been following me around all night. You are friends, I hear, of Archie Pellago?

BORIS. We are.

HANS. I have come here to say stop following me and interfering willy nilly with my nefarious plans. Or I will kill you even before I kill the whole of Louisville.

TATIANA. No! We will stop you!

HANS. Oh will you ha ha? How will you do that?

TATIANA. With our powers of the Red Penguin!

HANS. Oh, you have secret Penguin Powers, do you? Then why am I still standing here?

BORIS. It is very delicate operation. Special powers require…special handling.

HANS. So sorry, little Russian dressing. As soon as the painting is returned, my plan will go into action. Ka-boom ha ha ha. Even your Penguin is no match for my greatest source of power…revenge!

(HANS *steps out to have an "aside" to the audience. But* BORIS *and* TATIANA *can still hear him.*)

You see, when I was nine years old, the war was just ending, and a U.S. Army magician came to our town. My mother volunteered to be sawed in half…but this man, he was not a very good magician…the blood spattered everywhere, soaking all of his ropes and sponge balls…she died that day…Mama…Mama…

BORIS. That is sad story.

TATIANA. And also gruesome.

HANS. That magician was from Louisville. And now Louisville must pay.

BORIS. You cannot destroy Louisville!

TATIANA. It is such nice place!

BORIS. Go Cardinals!

HANS. Too late for that, my fine feathered friends! I have already planted bombs throughout all of the major landmarks of this pit you call Kentuckiana…

the Louisville Slugger Museum…the bourbon museum…the creationist museum…as soon as the painting is returned, all the cameras of the nation and the world will be rolling, and I will detonate a daisy chain of dynamite, destroying you all! Prepare to say good-bye to Derby City…forever!

(CARL WEATHERS, *the enthusiastic rookie cop, bursts in to save the day. He makes a beeline for* BORIS.)

CARL. Not so fast there, Russkies! You are under arrest!

TATIANA. Good. That one. He is bad guy.

BORIS. Yes, yes, he is bad man.

HANS. I'm sorry, I can't hear you…

(HANS *pulls a coin out of* BORIS' *ear.*

TATIANA *rushes to help but is restrained by* CARL.)

CARL. They have two hostages! I'm calling in backup!

BORIS. No no, you do not understand!

CARL. Careful—or I'll arrest you too!

BORIS. Let go my sister!

TATIANA. No!

(*An expert gymnast,* TATIANA *cartwheels out of* CARL's *grip, kicking him down to the ground and knocking the wind out of him, and goes for* HANS.

HANS *flicks a giant playing card, which cuts her like a knife. She falls to the ground.* HANS *lunges at* BORIS *and breaks his neck [but he does not die]. All the while, he's shouting "Abracadabra! Abracadabra!" with glee.*)

TATIANA. (*On floor.*) I am wounded!

BORIS. (*On floor.*) I am wounded!

BOTH. We are wounded!

HANS. You come with me! Bwah ha ha ha!

(HANS *picks up* BORIS *and tosses him over his shoulder like a sack of potatoes. As he makes for the door,* BORIS *reaches his arms out towards his sister—*)

BORIS. Tatiana! Find the Penguin! Save me and save Louisville!

HANS. *Auf Wiedersehen*, Chickadee Kiev!

(HANS *runs out the door with* BORIS *on his back, into the main gallery atrium.* TIMOTHY *runs out after them, screaming, still tied to the chair. The door slams shut behind them.*)

CARL. I'm so sorry, Miss Pengurovich. Are you okay?

(TATIANA *picks herself up off the floor, and helps* CARL *to his feet.*)

TATIANA. It is all your fault.

CARL. Yes, I'm so sorry. What can I do?

TATIANA. I must save my brother!

CARL. All right. Let's go.

TATIANA. And also, get back the Penguin!

CARL. All right, gotta move fast then—

TATIANA. And also, stop Hans Schmidt! And also, return the Penguin to Russia! And also, restore honor to my family, to my country, and to brothers and sisters and gymnasts and ice skaters and trained assassins everywhere!

CARL. All right, all right, let's go, let's get out of here.

TATIANA. (*Feeling the grave responsibility.*) Louisville needs hero.

(*She leads him out the door.*

End of Act 4B. The COMMISSIONER *opens the door and the groups are either met by their* GROUP LEADER *[if s/he hasn't watched the scene] or led out by their* GROUP LEADER*, if s/he has been watching.*)

ACT 4C: The Commissioner's Training.

The COMMISSIONER *holds court in the main gallery space. As groups come through (two at a time, at first, until the end, when all the groups converge), he leads them through his very special version of police boot camp. His training course is always a little bit different for each group, since it is so dependent both on audience response and engagement and also on the group leaders.*

What follows is a blueprint for the actor's improvisation.

COMMISSIONER. All right everybody, all right peoples, line 'em up. If you and I haven't yet made your or my acquaintance, I'm Commissioner Jefferson Washington Franklin, and this here's my turf. We gots a dangerous situation going on, peoples, and I'm gonna need some help to keep the laws and the orders.

As you know, we are gathered here today under some…unfortunate… circumstance due to the arrival and shenanigans of one Paul Vista, International Art Thief Extraordinaire, con man, sexual ambiguity-maker, who just got out of prison and who already set his sights on this here Pellago painting—well, that there painting, well, where it was when it was here before it got stoled from us.

I've known Paul Vista since we was in diapers—in fact, we was born the very same day, and let me tell you, ever since that very first day he has been nothing but a slippery scofflaw, an electric eel, the kind of guy who steals your date for the Sadie Hawkins dance and doesn't even say sorry. He'll blind you with a smile while he's stealing your eyes out, know what I'm saying? He's all about the shortcuts, the cheats, the glad-handing and the black market.

That painting, it's worth a lot of money, and I'm not gonna rest easy till it's hanging back up on that wall. We gotta be vigilant when it returns. As long as Vista's in the same STATE as that painting, there ain't no rest for the rest of us fair-minded and rules-abiding folks.

So you know what it's gonna take? Physical and mental prowess, that's whats. And that's whats we pride ourselves in partaking in at the Louisville Metro Police Department, you knows what I'm saying?

This is the fight of my life, and you're gonna help me. I hereby enlist all of youse in Temporary Policeperson Training Camp, Starting Now.

Everybody, in a Diamond Shape. No, a Diamond! Into formation! Now! Four-sided, what are you deaf—?

> (*He arranges the audience into a large diamond-shaped floor pattern.*)

Now I'd like to introduce you to a very difficult maneuver. I call it the One-Sided Jumping Jack.

> (*This move is exactly what it sounds like. One side. Then the other. Then alternating sides. It's a little bit boot camp, a little bit Bob Fosse.*)

Great. Great. Now listen up. We got bigwigs, we got FBI down our throats and Interpol up our butts, been there for months. We gotta show 'em we can do this, we can get Vista, we can do it right.

Now we're gonna learn the Policeman's Creed. Repeat after me: Stab first!

> (*Audience repeats: "Stab first!"*)

Shoot first!

> (*"Shoot first!"*)

Look at what you're stabbing and shooting at later!

> (*"Look at what you're stabbing and shooting at later!"*)

Okay, good. Everyone passes. I hereby appoint you, by the power vested in me by the state of Kentucky and—some other things—you are temporary honorary honorarium police officers for the day. For the duration of this crisis. This is part of a program I designed to build policemen's out of nobodies.

> (*Suddenly,* HANS SCHMIDT *bursts out of a side gallery, carrying a mortally wounded* BORIS PENGUROVICH *on his back, and runs through the room laughing, exiting the other side.* TIMOTHY WYATT, *gagged and still tied to a chair, is close behind, wailing and crying.*)

COMMISSIONER. Whoa whoa whoa whoa—hold up there, soldier!

> (COMMISSIONER *chases them all, and catches* TIMOTHY *near the exit. He brings him around to be interrogated by the podium.*)

Okay, I wasn't really expecting this but this is a terrific opportunity to practice our Interrogation Skills. Very important for the Evidence Gathering and whatnot. All right sir. Now. Are you okay?

TIMOTHY. (*Blubbering.*)

COMMISSIONER. I'm sorry Sir, but I'm going to need you to give me a straight answer. For the benefit of these new recruits here. Now: what just happened to you?

TIMOTHY. (*Blubbering.*)

COMMISSIONER. All right, forget about it, get the hell out of here.

(TIMOTHY *runs away.*)

COMMISSIONER. (*To audience.*) Suspicious…very suspicious…I'm gonna have to ask for you alls help for a minute as we get to the bottom of this. Me, I gotta stay on the Paul Vista beat, catch the con man who took that Pellago painting, but you alls, if you can help me out, you will be richly rewarded with…well, we can see about that when the time comes. I need all of youse to look for clues to help us solve the case of the Half Man, Half Chair, that came out of that room there and then ran thataways. But where to look for clues…where…where…where…

(*A sign outside of a side gallery lights up: "6 Minutes Ago."*)

Oh! Lookie that here. It says 6 Minutes Ago! How very convenient. All right peoples, we're now going to experience what we in the business call "A Flashback." This is how we do our real and best detectiving.

(*He ushers the people inside, arranging the audience in two parallel groups— they're getting in place to watch Act 4B [The Russians Seek Their Penguin].*)

You be good, you hear? I'm going back on the trail of Vista. (Damn you, Paul Vista!)

(*Closes the door, and gets into place for the arrival of the next audience group. End of Act 4C.*)

ACT 4C—Alternative Ending.

As part of the final loop, each group winds up their tour and returns to the atrium. Since there is already a police training in progress, the COMMISSIONER asks each returning group to join in:

COMMISSIONER. Looky who's back! Line 'em up, in the back, move forward for these recruits, we got interrupted earlier…you're like half-temporary-police peoples. Come on in, line 'em up, line 'em up, we gots some work to do…

(*More groups return, and get in lines.*

In our production, this meant that by the end of Act 4, COMMISSIONER was leading over 200 people in a series of silly physical exercises—sort of like a giant Jazzercise class.)

I'm gonna keep training youse, and you're gonna keep liking it.

You guys are looking really terrific out there. Paul Vista better be scared, is what I'm saying. Strong bodies mean a strong mind, and that's how we're going to take down Vista. I've been training for this my whole life. You know how long I've known Vista? Since before I was born. And for all that time, he has been my mortal enemy.

Our police force is lucky to have you, and let me tell youse, Paul Vista and his crew should be scared, oh yes indeedy, he should be terrified to have all of you smart peoples out there looking for him. You make me proud. Let me tell you a story. I got me a son. Clarence. Any of youse out there gots childrens? You like your childrens? You proud of thems? I bet no matter what, there is no way on earth you are as disappointed in your childrens as I am in mine. Let me tell you. I don't think it's possible for a man to be more disappointed in a boy if the boy turned out to be a girl. He never wants to play cops and robbers, my Clarence. No sirree. Never wants to throw the ball around or shoot the guns at the little birdies or arrest the shoplifters at the Walmart. Nope nope nope. I even gave the boy a gun but he says he doesn't want it. Says he's a peacenik. Always on his computer games, always on his internets, he wouldn't know what to do with a girlfriend even if they was married already. All I wants is to put a little meat on his bones, toughen him out, shape him in my own image. Is that so much to ask?

ACT 5: The End.

The COMMISSIONER *gets word that* LOUISA *is on her way back with the painting. By now, all of the groups have returned to the main gallery, and he is leading the entire audience in a series of exercises.*

He interrupts his training course to announce—

COMMISSIONER. All right, alls rights everyones, settle yourselves down, we's gots some good news for you all. The PAINTING is BACK! Yep, that's rightie. That girl who ran away before swam all the way to Indiana, and in just a few moments, we can expect that she'll be here, all in one piece! And with the painting! Big cheers for—who was it?

CHELSEA. Louisa!

(Everyone cheers. PEN *takes the podium.)*

PEN. *(On microphone.)* Hello again, everyone. I am delighted to inform you that the painting has been recovered by…I'm sorry, what was her name?

CHELSEA. Louisa! She's my assistant! She SWAM to INDIANA! Through the whole entire Ohio River! It's amazing!

PEN. Indeed. At 11:45 p.m., the painting was picked up by…Louisa…in Indiana, who is now just moments away, with the painting.

CHELSEA. She swam as fast as she could! The painting is back! Look, see, there's Louisa! Yay! My painting!

(LOUISA appears at the top of the stairs, sopping wet and triumphantly displaying a plastic pouch, which supposedly contains the stolen painting.

Everyone cheers.

The COPS *bring in* PAUL *and* DUSTY *in handcuffs.*

ANDY POOLE *steps up to the microphone.*)

ANDY. Hello—can everyone hear me?

(*Murmurs from the Heist team—what's he doing up there? Why is he blowing their cover?*)

Many of you know me as Andy Poole, janitor here at 21c. But, in fact, my birth name is—

(*Rips off his goatee, revealing that he is really—*)

ALICE, DIANE, Q, TIMOTHY, PEN, KATE. Archie Pellago???!!??

ANDY/ARCHIE. That's right, everyone. I am—

ALL. Archie Pellago!

(*Everyone shares their reaction with their groups, or the audience immediately surrounding them.*

JUSTICE, VICTOR, *and* Q *gather in the back of the room and start to argue about whose fault this is, how did they get duped, etc.*)

ARCHIE. I beg your indulgence while I explain what you have seen tonight… you'll see that everything has been a piece of the artwork you came to see, my life-sized installation, "Art Is More Important Than Fear," in which I have endeavored to turn a crafty crime into artful art.

Inside that pouch—thank you, Louisa—is a forgery.

(*Throughout the following, all of the* GROUP LEADERS *react to each revelation, sharing their reactions with their groups—ad-libbing through the speech and slideshow.*)

The Vista crew, over there, nearly executed the perfect crime. Well done, I must commend you.

(*The* HEIST TEAM *try to slink away, Scooby-Doo style, but the* COPS *near the back of the room stop the team.*)

Let me take you back to the beginning.

(*He clicks on the screen, bringing up a slide that says: "How The Heist Went Down [right in front of your eyes, right here at 21c…]* © *Archie Pellago, 2010."*

As ARCHIE *narrates, we see a cartoon slideshow illustrating key moments of the Heist, some of which we saw happen in real time during Acts 1 and 2.* [*Images in* **bold** *are things that were staged.*])

Last November, I got myself hired, as Andy, as a janitor at 21c. Soon after, I called Alice Weathers, and asked if she would be interested in my new piece. Of course she said yes.

At this point, I contacted a young man about town, a local computer wiz, Clarence Franklin, and casually mentioned the painting over a game of Warhammer.

(*The "unknown person" slide from earlier becomes a cartoon of* CLARENCE.)

Of course I knew that he would be interested in embarrassing his father by connecting with his sworn enemy: Paul Vista.

(PAUL's *mug shot is shown.*)

CLARENCE. (*To* PAUL.) …I'm sorry, Paul…I had no idea!

PAUL. It's okay, kid, you got me out of jail, that's nothing to be sorry for.

COMMISSIONER. I guess you're not such a pussy, after all, Clarence.

ARCHIE. Knowing that a new Pellago would be bait for Vista, I sat and waited for the inevitable: for the Vista crew to walk through those doors. At which point, the plan went into action.

Earlier today, I planted a camera inside the climate-controlled vault where the bourbon barrels are stored, which Clarence has been monitoring on his computer all night long.

(*SLIDE:* ANDY *plants the camera by the vault.*)

Meanwhile, Victor, our undercover Private Events Manager, took up his station…you may have noticed him checking on patrons and the bartenders. Earlier this evening, he conveyed a large bourbon barrel into the climate-controlled vault…

(SLIDE: VICTOR, as events manager, brings in a bunch of bourbon barrels.)

VICTOR. You saw that? Who saw that? Nah…not possible. I am the Master of the Subtlety.

ARCHIE. Inside this barrel was Justice, our grease girl—

JUSTICE. Balls.

(*SLIDE:* JUSTICE *curled up inside one of these barrels.*)

ARCHIE. Victor deposited this barrel inside the climate-controlled room…where she was easily able to crawl out of the barrel, and let in Q, our forgery expert…

(*SLIDE:* VICTOR *deposits the barrels, including* JUSTICE*, inside the climate-controlled room, which happens to be the same climate-controlled room where the security vault resides, directly below the painting.*

SLIDE: JUSTICE *crawls out of the bourbon barrel, lets* Q *into the climate controlled room from the inside.*)

Q. (*In French.*) I don't know what you're talking about, I've never picked up a paintbrush in my life.

ARCHIE. Meanwhile, I knew that Paul and Dusty would hang back, as a diversion.

(SLIDE: PAUL and DUSTY at the bar.)

So that when I, as Andy, clumsily fell on the roof,

(SLIDE: ANDY falls on the glass roof of the atrium.)

Dusty Press knocked the painting, triggering the infrared lasers, but also sticking her chewing gum on the bottom of the frame.

*(SLIDE: DUSTY **knocks the painting,** sticks a wad of gum on the bottom of the painting before it drops down into the vault.)*

So that while you were all busy arresting Paul and Dusty, the painting was stuck in its track by the gum. While water rushed in, Q copied the painting—

Q. *Merde.*

(SLIDE: The painting drops into vault, gets jammed in the climate-controlled room.

SLIDE: Water starts to rush into the climate-controlled room.

SLIDE: JUSTICE hangs from the ceiling as a human easel as Q copies the painting [time stamp reads 3:59 minutes].

SLIDE: When Q is done, the water is almost to the top of the room— JUSTICE puts the painting back into the vault, allowing the Ziploc bag to seal, and the painting gets whisked away into the river.)

—in just under four minutes, at which point Justice switched out the copy for the real one, sending the fake off to Indiana, and putting the real painting inside the bourbon barrel…Leaving Louisa to collect the fake painting from beneath the Ohio River.

*(SLIDE: LOUISA, in her scuba suit, retrieves it under water, and **brings it back to the party where she is triumphantly congratulated.***

SLIDE: Meanwhile, JUSTICE puts the real painting into the empty bourbon barrel, and stacks it with the rest of the empties.)

And so, just moments ago, we all watched Victor take the real painting out the front door.

(SLIDE: VICTOR rolling a bourbon barrel out the front doors of 21c on a dolly.)

VICTOR. Son of a bitch…

(TIMOTHY starts a slow clap.)

TIMOTHY. Bravo. Bravo!

(Suddenly, HANS bursts into the room from a side gallery, still carrying BORIS on his back.)

HANS. Not so fast, Mr. Archie Pellago!

(TIMOTHY freaks out, yelling and pointing.)

TIMOTHY. Oh no! Oh no! Oh no! That's him! That's him! With the dynamite! Don't you remember? Didn't you see?

(HANS leaps up to the podium and takes the microphone. Drops BORIS on the floor.)

HANS. Oh, Archie Pellago, you think you're so clever…stand back!

(The GROUP LEADERS protect their groups.)

ARCHIE. Don't do it, Hans—

HANS. (*On microphone.*) Greetings, people of Louisville. You may not know this, but many years ago a young Louisvillian magician was responsible for my mother's untimely and horribly horrific death. Since that moment I have been plotting your demise. Never again will young boys suffer at the hands of Louisville…today is the day. With all the cameras of the world watching, I will tonight have my revenge on the man who killed my mother—Tonight I perform the Greatest Illusion Of All—the Great Disappearance—

> (HANS *holds up a Red Penguin, strapped with dynamite and a large cartoonish timer.*)

When I start this timer, you will have two minutes to telephone call your loved ones before all of Louisville goes up in smoke, along with the rest of your Kentucky…

> (*Crowd screams.*)

…and Indiana.

> (*Crowd screams louder.*)
>
> CARL *and* TATIANA *appear at the top of the stairs, guns drawn.*)

CARL. Stop that man!

TATIANA. Stop!

> (HANS *grabs the ailing* BORIS *and uses him as a shield.*)

HANS. Shoot me and you shoot your brother!

CARL. Go on, you've got a clear shot!

TATIANA. I can't…I will danger Boris!

CARL. What's it gonna take?

TATIANA. I must find Penguin…. But which is the Penguin? Does anyone know?

> (TATIANA *waves the gun at the crowd, everyone ducks except for* PAUL, *who reaches up to her.*)

PAUL. I have an idea—Bricks always used to say this, when he didn't know what to do. Look for what you're looking for with one eye open, and one eye closed.

> (HEIST TEAM *nods in agreement.*)

BORIS. Oh yes! Remember, like Papa told us. One eye open and one eye closed, the truth, it will be revealed.

HANS. Tick tock, tick tock, little Russkie…

> (TATIANA *reverses her eye patch.*)
>
> *A Red Penguin at the top of the stairs begins to glow.*)

TATIANA. Oh! It is that one!

> (*She puts her hands on it and it gives her secret strength. She aims her gun at* HANS.)

This is for my brother! And also, my country! And also, for Louisville!

(*She shoots him.*

Screams from the crowd.

HANS *drops* BORIS.)

HANS. You shot me! I'm dead!

(*He collapses.*)

TATIANA. Boris!

(*She runs across the room towards him. Just then,* HANS *rises from the dead.*)

HANS. Here Kid, catch!

(*Throws the Penguin-bomb to* CLARENCE. *Dies again.*)

CLARENCE. The timer! It's already going! We have sixty seconds before Louisville goes up in smoke!

(*The* COMMISSIONER *grabs the lethal Penguin from* CLARENCE.)

COMMISSIONER. Look out, this thing is gonna blow!

CLARENCE. Dad—

COMMISSIONER. I forgive you, Son! And you, Paul Vista, I pardon you—and all your peoples—to the river! To the river!

(*He gives* CLARENCE *his police cap, and races out with the Penguin.*)

ARCHIE. Let's go to the sidewalk-cam.

(*On the screen, we see a cartoon of the* COMMISSIONER *racing down the sidewalk towards the river, holding onto the dynamite-encased penguin—we see the skyline of Louisville as he leaps into the Ohio River, calling out—*)

COMMISSIONER. (*On screen.*) I always loved you, Clarence, even though you're a pussy! Vista—take care of my boy!

CLARENCE. (*Live.*) That's my dad!

(*Romantic music swells, reaching a fever pitch—until, BOOM!, the Penguin explodes into flames and the cartoon* COMMISSIONER *sinks into the river.*

Everyone gasps.)

ARCHIE. Clarence Franklin, your father is a true hero. He saved Louisville tonight. In his honor, let's all make his favorite shape: a diamond.

(ARCHIE *arranges the audience into a diamond shape. The* GROUP LEADERS *help.*

The cops release PAUL *and* DUSTY.)

For years I have known about Hans Schmidt and his plan to destroy Louisville. And so, for years, I have been seeking the perfect opportunity to take him down. And for that, I needed the Russian Penguroviches to find their Penguin and use it for good.

TATIANA. But I have the Penguin, and Boris is still hurt!

ARCHIE. It's what's inside that counts.

(*Music: Hallelujah!* TATIANA *goes to the Penguin, and lifts off the top half—discovers another Penguin, holds it aloft—and then, another, even smaller Golden Penguin—the "real" Red Penguin is a giant avian nesting doll.*

She gives the tiny Golden Penguin to BORIS, who now is able to stand up—)

BORIS. I am healed!

(ARCHIE, TATIANA, *and* BORIS *embrace.*

Meanwhile, stories wrap up in the crowd: TIMOTHY *and* Q *find each other;* DEVIN *proposes to* CHELSEA*;* ALICE *gets a text from the MoMA and offers the 21c curator job to* DIANE*;* DIANE *tells* CARL *she'll call him tomorrow;* KATE *thanks the Lord and Lady;* VICTOR *and* JUSTICE *high-five;* PEN *thanks the audience for their cooperation;* LUKE *tells his group that God worked through them tonight;* CLARISSA *videotapes it all—tells her group that it's the Best. Documentary. Ever.*

CHELSEA *takes the microphone.*)

CHELSEA. Well this is just amazing, everyone! Art *is* greater than Fear! What an amazing party! Let's dance! Clear the floor, I'm ready to bust a move! Hit it!

(*The* VISTA SEVEN *theme song plays, the one from Act 4.*

Everyone dances into the curtain call.

Credits roll.)

End of Play

APPENDIX:
Group Leader Texts and Journeys.

Below are texts for the eight different group experiences, sorted by Group Leader. In addition to visiting all of the scenes included in Act 4, each Group Leader character has a private scene (sometimes two) with just their small audience group. Once the audience has been divided, they stick with their group for the duration of the show.

For the performers, there's a lot of improvisation involved here—they have to keep the audience moving, literally, through the two buildings and multiple scenes; and also, they keep the audience interested in the story and the urgency of finding the painting, stopping the bombs, etc. **These texts are the bare bones of the Group Leaders' texts; it works best when the performers ad-lib and improv their way through their parts. This is true for all of Act 4 and also through the shenanigans of Act 5.**

There are four different possible orders of watching the scenes, so there are two groups on each track: Kate/Clarissa; Tanya/Diane; Chelsea/Devin; Alice/Luke. *However, their journeys are not the same, since the character of the Group Leader is different.*

Part of the fun is encountering other groups on their different journeys and seeing how yours overlap and diverge.

The private scenes are always unique for each group.

ALICE WEATHERS.

In many ways, ALICE WEATHERS *has the most to lose from the theft of the Pellago: her entire career has been building to this night, and even before the disappearance of the painting, she was starting to crack under the pressure. Over the course of her journey through Act 4,* ALICE *discovers that there are more important things in life than career success…in fact, maybe she has been approaching this whole "art" thing from the completely wrong perspective. In these scenes, she reveals a bit of her true self, and her true passion for a very special kind of music: a cappella.*

> ALICE*'s order of scenes:*
> *Solo Scene*
> *Act 4A (Planning The Heist)*
> *Act 4B (The Russians)*
> *Act 4C (The Commissioner Training)*

1. Gathering Group / Traveling to Solo Scene

ALICE *tries to hold it together and remain professional as she gathers her group.*

ALICE. Excellent, can everyone see me? Yes? Hello? Great. Hi. For those I haven't met, I'm Alice Weathers, curator of special collections here at 21c…I don't have a sign, so, um, I'll hold up my hand. Let's go upstairs, it will be quieter there, all right, follow me, don't be slow, we're going to be going up these stairs here…. Has anyone been through the upstairs galleries yet? No? There are some real gems of the collection we'll see, you really shouldn't miss it…

(Leading her group to an upstairs gallery, she gives a mini-lecture on a couple of key pieces of the collection.)

2. Solo Scene

Arriving at the upstairs gallery, ALICE *briskly ushers everyone in and shuts the door.*

Then, she turns on them with a vengeance.

ALICE. Down on the ground! Every last one of you! Get down. Now. This is a hostage situation.

Here's the deal. My job is on the line. My JOB and my FUTURE and I did not leave New Haven to come to Louisville fucking KENTUCKY to have my bright future TORPEDOED by some two-bit low-life criminals.

So you all just shut the fuck up and I'm going to—I'm calling information and then I'm going to get the number for the FBI and I'm going to call across the street so they can stop dicking around with some evidence room or whatever the shit, and get on with the business of getting the Pellago back from Indiana or whatever the fuck—

Down on the floor, I said. You! Down! I swear to God if you say a word, if you look at me strange—I will kick you in the shins, I totally will, I will pull your hair, I will put a flatiron on your face—

—this is going to be all over the news tomorrow and I—everything I've worked for flushed down the toilet by Paul Fucking Vista.

Oh he thinks he's all that, in his fancy suits and blah blah blah. He doesn't appreciate ART—to him it's all just a game, a commodity—not like us, not like ME, who has dedicated her whole life into the service of artists and—

Fuck.

> (*Beat. She slumps down, cross-legged on the floor, as if the wind has been knocked out of her. Complete change of tone.*)

You can sit up now. No, it's okay, I'm sorry, I—I don't even know what I would do with hostages. I don't know anything about it—I just curated an exhibit called Art Is More Important Than Fear, and what do I do the minute I get afraid, I get violent. Great.

I'm just as bad as Paul Vista.

I don't make art…I just buy it and sell it and talk about it.

I've always liked beautiful things. But I've never produced anything of beauty, like from my own self. I've been afraid to—that's it. I've been too afraid. My fear has been more important than my art—for a long time—

You know one of the most beautiful things I've ever heard? There's this bell tower at Yale, one of those old stone Gothic ones with the arch, you know—with the stained glass—and in the middle there's this pavilion, and at dusk people gather there to watch the sunset and listen to Whim-n-Rhythm, the all-female a cappella group…have you heard of them? They're great.

The first time I heard them, during orientation, I was so moved that I signed up to audition, I practiced in my room with my Walkman—you remember, those plastic ones with the yellow case? Oh—I'm having a total flashback. I'm sorry. Do you mind if I—well I'm just going to tell you. About the audition.

Because the day of the audition, you know, I went to the music building with my sheet music, and I sat in the chairs and I waited and I listened to my Walkman and I was ready—but when they called my name—I don't know, I don't know what happened, I just…I got all cold and…I pretended it wasn't me. I didn't go inside. I walked in the other direction, I walked out the door, I walked away, because it was easier to be scared than to take the risk.

I was filled up to here with fear.

And that's why—well I think it goes a long way to explaining how I got here, and why I yelled at you before—I'm sorry, I'm sorry for that, I was just so—scared? You know? I was just so scared. I'm really sorry.

Actually—you know what? Do you mind if…before we go across the street, maybe we could sing a little? I still remember my audition song, I still sing it in the shower sometimes, but by myself I can't do all the parts, so…You'll help me, though, right? Help me face my fear?

> (ALICE *divides the audience into four groups.*
>
> *The rest of this is ad-libbed—the text is a structure for improvisation.*)

I'll need four groups. You guys be the rhythm section, and you guys are gonna do vox. Voice. Vox? I don't know. But you know what I mean. Cool. And you guys, percussion. You're going to keep the basic beat, like this…

> (*She starts teaching the different parts, demonstrating and then getting the group to join in. She's a really good teacher, very patient and encouraging. As the parts start to come together, the audience will realize that they are learning the a cappella version of "Eye Of The Tiger," by Survivor. As the laughter [and groan] of recognition cascades through the group—*)

You guys know this one? Did you do a cappella in college? Don't lie, you're a natural!

> (*They sing, starting with the verse and leading up to a killer chorus. ALICE is on fire, she is delighted, everyone is so good and she is living her dream. She glows.*)

You guys this feels amazing! Thank you! I haven't felt this free in years!

> (*While the audience keeps singing…*)

I'm not going to be afraid any more. I'm not going to let Paul Vista or Chelsea Cooley or Archie Pellago or the Museum of Modern Art make me scared about anything! They can eat it, you know what I mean, because I am free and we are making music!

> (*A* COP *knocks on the door, says that Ms. Weathers is needed across the street at FBI HQ.*)

You guys, let's keep singing—this is the best thing we can do for Archie—he always said, Art is for the Many, not for the Few—let's bring our voices out into the streets—

> (*She leads them out of the gallery and onto the street, singing their hearts out for all of Louisville.*)

3. Watching Act 4A at FBI HQ

> *While watching these scenes,* ALICE *is crushed to discover that she's been betrayed by some people she really trusted—two of her employees,* VICTOR *and* ANDY, *are members of the Heist Team.*

4. Returning to 21c to watch Act 3C

> ALICE *shares her heartbroken-ness with her group, and continues to contemplate what it would mean to leave this crazy art business for good.*

ALICE. (*Ad-libs.*) I know those guys—I know them—one of them, Andy, I hired him. He was great. I treated him with such respect. And Victor, the caterer…I feel so betrayed…this is what I was saying about the cutthroat profession, it's not about art at all…

Did you see any of those others at the party? I think I saw that forger chick sketching in the main gallery…. Oh god oh god a forgery…. What if the painting they bring back from Indiana is a forgery? What am I going to tell Archie?

5. Back at 21c, Alice goes to check on Andy and Victor's files

Back in the main gallery, ALICE *leaves her groups to watch Act 3C (the Commissioner's Training) and Act 3B (the Russians) without her.*

After Act 3B, ALICE *picks them up at the gallery and brings them into the main gallery. They join the end of the final police training course, until* LOUISA *returns with the painting.*)

<u>LUKE MICHAEL CHRISTIANSON.</u>

LUKE MICHAEL CHRISTIANSON *is a local man about town, enthusiastic about sharing the good news about God with anyone who will listen. He is known for showing up at public events, just to make friends. During the party, he introduced himself to as many people as possible and volunteered his cheerful opinions on all of the art. During his journey through Act 4, he sees an opportunity to save some souls…an opportunity he's not going to let go to waste.*

LUKE's *order of scenes:*
Solo Scene
Act 4A (Planning The Heist)
Act 4B (The Russians)
Act 4C (The Commissioner Training)

1. Gathering Group / Traveling to Solo Scene

LUKE *gathers his group like a camp counselor:*

LUKE. If you can hear my clap, clap back!

(*They do.*)

Okay, you're my group. Get in a circle, okay—count off. Clap hands! Follow me! This way!

(*They duck into the closest side gallery.*)

2. Solo Scene

LUKE. Hi everyone. Okay. Circle up, you guys. Take a knee. Join hands. This is life and fate as a contact sport. Let's have a moment of silence together. Silent prayer, people. Close your eyes. Tune out the chaos. Tune out the mayhem. Find your inner happiness. There's too much noise going on—get in touch with your inner quiet.

I'm Luke Michael Christianson, of the United Church of Christ God. Everything is going to be okay. Because God has a plan and this is all part of it. I could be stressed out, by everything that's going on, but God is talking to us. Let's talk back. Let's let Him know that we do not believe in stealing things, in taking what is not ours. We have read our Ten Commandments. Even when it is a teeny tiny painting that Mr. Cooley in North Carolina paid 200 million dollars for. Even when those same 200 million dollars could be used to feed and clothe millions and millions of people all across the world, and animals. People and animals.

Even with art, there are still people starving.

But let's also let Him know that we do not condone the dark, dark impulses at the core of so much of the so-called art in these galleries. That even though so much beauty has been put before us, we see through the shiny exterior to the evil beneath, the dead animals, the exploitation of children—and we know that such depictions are merely a gateway to greater criminal activity. Paul Vista has succumbed to those dark impulses, to the craven greed and selfishness and superficiality that is as bad as a drug. We know that he is experiencing the darkest night of his soul, and it is our job to help bring him into the light. Even if he doesn't know it yet. Especially if he doesn't know it yet.

God is going to work through us tonight, to save Paul Vista, and to find those two unknown men. We're going to identify them and speak to them and see if we can bring them to our side. We are like the great aqueducts of Rome, bringing the sinners to God.

I feel for them. I really do. Did you notice how Dusty Press is always eating something? Because she's always hungry. Something is missing. She's trying to fill a void. I bet you know what that void is. I know I do. I get it, I really do. I used to be just like Dusty Press, I was always eating, I was so fat. I just ate ate ate all the time. But then I found someone who filled me up, not with carbs, but with love. I bet you know who that was.

Do you feel Jesus tugging at you to go and love on some art thieves? I feel it. I really do. We're going to go to FBI Headquarters, across the street, but the trip is not about us. It is not even about Paul Vista or Dusty Press or any of the rest of them. The trip is about Jesus' love. And if we can keep that knowledge in our hearts, then it's all going to be okay.

We know that this incident with the Pellago is a sign from God that the time to act is now.

Now repeat after me: Dear God.

(*Audience repeats: Dear God.*)

Thank you for your miracle today.
>(*Thank you for your miracle today.*)

Thank you for sending a sign.
>(*Thank you for sending a sign.*)

Art is a sin and theft is a sin
>(*Art is a sin and theft is a sin.*)

And we abhor both in equal measure
>(*And we abhor both in equal measure.*)

For sin begets sin.
>(*For sin begets sin.*)

Even without art, people are hungry.
>(*Even without art, people are hungry.*)

We hear and see your work, and we speak back
>(*We hear and see your work, and we speak back.*)

Through action and song.
>(*Through action and song.*)

That's right, through song! Everybody, up on your feet! Look alive, people, look alive!

>(LUKE *teaches the group the song,* "Our God Is An Awesome God.")

That's great, that's really wonderful, you guys are really fantastic.

The day is always darkest before the light, isn't it? When we get the sign, we're going to go to HQ, we're going to learn what they have to teach us— and we're going to use that knowledge to find the painting. Because no one deserves to have their things stolen. And then we will use it to find our way to Archie Pellago, because the most important thing we can do is to save Pellago and Vista from themselves. Art and criminality are two sides of the same coin.

Hate the sin, love the sinner.

Everybody, get a buddy, an animal buddy, we're going to go across the street like we're going into Noah's Ark—you'll be the Aardvarks, and you'll be the Bears...

>(*Etc. Each pair gets an animal name. If there is an odd number, the singleton is dubbed "The Unicorn."*)

All right everybody, let's go! Let's go across the street and find Paul Vista and help bring him to the light.

>(LUKE *has the group singing* "Our God Is An Awesome God" *as they go across the street to FBI HQ.*)

3. Watching Act 4A at FBI HQ

>*As he watches the scenes,* LUKE *calls attention to sinful things he observes— including* DUSTY's *abs presser machine (there's no substitute for self-discipline) and the Warhammer game (playing with the dark arts).*

4. Returning to 21c

LUKE *ad-libs around the following:*

LUKE. Couldn't you see how sin is a pervasive lifestyle? What's up with that—everything about them—the drinking and the strippers and the French people and the war games and the Presser 3000…there's no quick fix for fitness, we know that, right?

(Helps audience piece together the puzzle.)

Those two guys, they definitely work at 21c. What was she supposed to do in four minutes? Who were those two guys in the comic store? I've seen them around town—real nerds, a computer wizard, isn't he the Commissioner's son? *(Etc.)*

5. Watching Act 4C (The Commissioner Training)

LUKE *enthusiastically participates in the training course.*

6. Watching Act 4B (The Russians)

LUKE *does not watch this scene with his group. When it ends, he picks up his group and has them join in the end of the final police training exercises.*

They continue to train until LOUISA *returns with the painting.*

KATE SHAPIRO.

KATE SHAPIRO *is all-business as she gathers her group to go across the street to FBI Headquarters. However, as her journey unfolds, she slowly discovers how the tools of her trade have failed her—how the Vista crew exploited her beloved security system—causing her to reveal her deepest and most precious secrets to her group.*

KATE's *order of scenes:*
Act 4A (Planning The Heist)
Act 4C (Commissioner Training)
Act 4B (The Russians)
Solo Scene

1. Gathering Group / Walking Across to FBI HQ

As soon as the COMMISSIONER *dismisses everyone,* KATE *leads her group across the street to FBI HQ.*

KATE. All right, everybody, as you know I'm Kate Shapiro from Scotland Yard, on behalf of Interpol representing Europol. We're going to go across the street to be briefed by the FBI, who have been gathering information parallel to my offices. You all are going to be my witnesses and assistants, and I'm going to ask you to keep a sharp eye out to see if there is anyone in the FBI's files whom you recognize from this evening's fiasco.

(KATE *herds her group very official-like across the street to FBI HQ. Reminding them to be vigilant witnesses, this is a very important investigation, etc.*)

2. Watching Act 4A at FBI HQ

While watching the scenes of the VISTA CREW *planning the Heist,* KATE *realizes that the security system didn't work—during the scenes, she can even exclaim audibly at details like:* "Notoriously faulty?!"; "Four minutes—how did they know…?"

By the end of Act 4A, KATE *has realized that her beloved Dobson and Dorman security system did not work, and starts to unravel.*

As she leads her group back across the street to the main building of 21c, she asks them questions about the Heist, i.e. "Were any of those suspects at the party tonight?" *and* "They have a world-class art forger? I can't believe it…" *Also, this is a chance for the audience to ask* KATE *questions about what they saw at the party and in HQ, and connections they're starting to make between the scenes and the cartoons.*

3. Returning to 21c to watch Act 4C

When they return to 21c, KATE *leads her group to investigate the empty frame, where the Pellago had been.*

KATE. (*Ad-libs.*) All right—help me out here—so how did they do this? If Dusty reached for the painting here, it would have set off the lasers…

(*She feels around the bottom of the empty picture frame—notices a gummy residue.*)
Gum! Feel this!

(*Audience members can feel the gummy residue.*)
You know what this means. Dusty Press.

I'm sorry, I'll have to call Headquarters right away, you all stay right here with the Commissioner until I return…

(*She goes, leaving her group to be trained by the* COMMISSIONER.
KATE *goes to make a phone call.*)

4. Watching Act 4B (the Russians)

KATE *does not watch this scene with her group.*
At the end of the scene, she greets them at the door and leads them into a side gallery.

5. Solo Scene

KATE *is visibly rattled by what she found out on the phone (about how easy it is to jam the vault mechanism; also about Q's expertise as a forger).*
However, always a pro, she briskly and efficiently ushers her group into a small gallery room, and shuts the door behind them.

Asks them to form a circle.

KATE. Circle up everyone. I need to tell you something.

I need to tell you because I can't get through this on my own. I'm going to need your help. You know that whole plan I showed you, on the video, the state of the art video security system? It didn't work. You guys, it didn't work.

The painting was copied.

Nobody knows but you.

How could she copy it in four minutes? That's impossible! Impossible! And yet—and yet—

They're going to get it from Indiana and bring it back here and let everyone go and Vista and Dusty will just get a slap on the wrist but what they won't know is that they're going to have a copy. A copy! A forgery! It was forged!

Do you understand what I am saying?

Everyone was counting on me and I failed them. I counted on the rule of order and it failed me. Science failed me. Reason failed me. There's only one thing to do now. And I think you know what it is. We need to ask for help from a higher power.

(*She sits on the ground, and encourages everyone else to do the same.*)

We're just going to do a small little Wiccan ritual, just a small bit from the liturgy. We're going to return to our earth roots.

All right. Everyone—if you will, please, get up on your knees. Hands on your knees. Do as I do.

(*Everyone rises to their knees and follows her lead.*)

We're going to ask for assistance from the Lord and Lady. Start by rocking back and forth. I need you to really center yourself.

Let out a big sigh…. That's it, good. Open your eyes. Do as I do. Repeat after me.

(*She leads them in a vaguely Wiccan-style ritual: beating out a rhythm on the floor; singing out in high-pitched heavenly tones; etc.*)

Put your arms to the ceiling, raise your hands to the sky. The Sky! Call out, Huzzah! Repeat after me—huzzah! Huzzah!

Push out to the sky— Again— Huzzah! Huzzah! Huzzah!

Wonderful. Now, you can open your eyes. Breathe out. Breathe in. Breathe out. And in. Good.

Okay, now, I need another body, a pair of warm hands, can you help me? You? Good, thank you.

(*She selects a volunteer, brings him or her to the center of the circle, and clasps their hands together.*

She starts to sway, and gets the volunteer to follow in unison.)

I'm going to teach you a quick little prayer to the goddess. Keep your spirituality going, keep it focused to us, on us, on us…Here's the prayer:

Waxing, waxing
Waning, waning
Growing, growing
Diana's power
Is flowing, flowing

Repeat with me
Close your eyes

   (*They all repeat after her:*)

Waxing, waxing
Waning, waning
Growing, growing
Diana's power
Is flowing, flowing

   (*They all do it a few more times, speeding up and rising in forcefulness.*
   KATE *feels like the earth has moved a bit.*)

Do you all feel that? Great. Great. That was beautiful. Thank you. Thank you all so much for helping me. I really appreciate it, I feel less bad now, I do.

I think I can handle this now, now that I know you're all with me. We can do this. We can walk back out there and look them in the eye and tell them the truth, about Dusty Press and the French forgery, because we have the strength now.

You've all been such a help to me today. I know you weren't expecting this, but I would like to give you all your Wiccan names.

I'll start by introducing myself. I'm Golden Blossom.

   (*Bequeaths Wiccan names to everyone in the group, by going around and listening to their hair, their ear, their aura. Some names bequeathed in our production included: Dragonsong, Meadowlark, Prairiedawn, Grassniffer, Gimpingazalle, Beavertooth, Puppypetter, Parishiltonmiltonberle, Cheapdate, and Lindsaylohan. Please have fun with these.*)

Wow. All right. Thank you. This is really special. Doesn't that feel good? I feel so much better now. I'm ready to face the earthly world…with your support. Will you come with me?

6. Returning to the main gallery (atrium)

   With her newfound strength and sense of purpose, KATE *leads her group back to the main gallery space, where they encounter the* COMMISSIONER *in the middle of one of his trainings. They join the crowd in doing one-sided jumping jacks, and continue with the training (which becomes like a giant Jazzercise class as more and more audience members join in) until LOUISA returns with the painting.*

Which KATE's group knows is a forgery.

CLARISSA.

CLARISSA *is a local celebrity, famous for her video blogs of local hipster happenings, mostly art openings and concerts. She's always seen around town with her little camera, interviewing people on the street about anything and everything. She spends Act 1 interviewing various audience members about their impressions of Louisville and Archie Pellago, and so at least some of the audience has had some significant interactions with her. She is a hipster, but not sarcastic in any way—she's a big booster for Louisville, and wears her love for her hometown proudly on her sleeve. As her journey plays out in Act 4, she discovers that she is capable of more powerful forms of communication than just blogging.*

CLARISSA's *order of scenes:*
Act 4A (Planning The Heist)
Act 4C (Commissioner Training)
Act 4B (The Russians)
Solo Scene

1. Gathering Group / Walking Across to FBI HQ

CLARISSA *gathers up the closest people around her to be in her group.*

CLARISSA. Can you guys count off? I can only take, like, thirty of you. Sorry other peeps. Good luck!

(To her group:)

Cool cool. This is gonna be awesome. Can you say "Hey-yo"?

(The group says "Hey-yo!")

Great, good job, groupies. Awesome. Now for the camera! Hey-yo!

(She holds her camera on herself, and then at the group. The group says, "Hey-yo!" vamping like they're the audience on TRL, that seminal MTV countdown show that launched Carson Daly's career.)

So if you haven't met me, yo, I'm Clarissa, I got this blog, right, it's called Clarissa Explaining it All. Woo! Crazy shit going down, huh?

(She sees KATE SHAPIRO leading her group up the stairs.)

Hey, I got an idea—let's follow that chick from Interpol, I bet she knows what's up. We're gonna be FIRST on the SCENE! This is gonna be hot!

(She leads her group across the street to FBI HQ, following KATE's group. While crossing the street, she improvs—)

Stick with me, I know my way around, who's from here? Who's from Louisville? Who's not? Okay—we locals are gonna have to help out the out-of-towners, make sure they don't get lost.

Also, I'm gonna get this all on tape. This is gonna be rad. I've never been in the middle of an international incident before. I've never even been in a lockdown. This shit is gonna go viral!

Stick together, find your buddy, cool cool, wait for the light. Wow, we're on a lockdown but we're outside, how does that work? I love this part of town—

> (*Etc., until arriving at HQ.*)

2. Watching Act 4A at FBI HQ

> CLARISSA *watches the scenes of the Heist being planned, taking mental notes. Afterwards, she leads the group back across the street towards 21c, talking about what they just saw, did anyone see any of the Vista Crew at the party, "I could swear I know that Clarence guy from the University of Louisville…"*

3. Before getting to 21c, they see another building across the street.

CLARISSA. Ooh actually, let's go across the street on the way…there's something I want to show you.

> (*Brings her group across the street to another building, kitty-corner from the Museum Plaza Design and Sales Offices. This is the St. Charles Building, part of Brown-Forman Corporation; only CLARISSA's group visits this location.*)

This is the Brown-Forman building. They restored it ten years ago because this street was the original Whiskey Row, yeah there were a TON of bourbon distilleries here…this is just the office, I think, I don't really know…

> (*They look in the windows. But instead of historic bourbon memorabilia, they see boxes and boxes of Dyn-O-Mite…for anyone who also visited the Unterschlupf, it might look familiar.*)

Uh-oh.

Oh shit guys…is that what I think it is? Real live actual explosives?

Oh shit.

Maybe we're not supposed to see that…let's go back, um…let's just go…if we see any police or whatever, maybe we should say something?

> (*Hurries them along, back to the main building.*)

Okay okay okay um…

Was that really dynamite? Shit. Uh—let's go see if we can find a policeman or FBI lady or something.

> (*Etc.*)

4. Returning to 21c

> *As she reenters the atrium,* CLARISSA *sees the* COMMISSIONER *talking to* KATE.

CLARISSA. Oh—hey, hey, uh, Commissioner? I gotta tell you about something...

> *(But she doesn't get a chance to explain, as* COMMISSIONER *begins the training right away.*
>
> CLARISSA's *group watches Act 4C [the Commissioner's Training], while* CLARISSA *goes to find another cop who might be more helpful.*
>
> CLARISSA *returns for the end of the training, and goes with her group to watch Act 4B [The Russians].)*

5. CLARISSA watches Act 4B with her group.

> *Gets more and more agitated as she realizes that* HANS *planted the dynamite...*

6. Solo Scene

> *After the end of Act 4B,* CLARISSA *is freaking out. She hurries her group out into the hallway as quickly as possible, trying to find a safe corner of the building to figure out what to do.*

CLARISSA. Okay—shit—that's—whoa.

Everyone here?

Come with me. Come on, hurry—does everyone have your buddy? Uh—if you didn't have a buddy, and if you do, uh—well, you know—hurry, quick, this way—I'm not sure what to do.

Do you think the dynamite belongs to that German guy? Of course it does. Oh my god oh my god. WTF you guys—

> *(She ducks into the first empty room she sees, one of the side galleries, and pushes them inside.)*

Hurry—hurry—oh shit oh shit oh shit—come on, everyone in, let's go let's go.

Everyone in? Hurry, hurry, good, yeah, okay, nobody panic, we'll figure this out—I just gotta think—

So, this is the lowest down part of the building. Used to be a slaughterhouse, actually, did you know that? The front was a tobacco bank, and in the back they used to store bourbon barrels. Remember, I said, Whiskey Row. For real, yeah. They told me in school.

We should probably tell someone.

Dynamite! Fuck!

I've lived here my whole life and I've always felt totally safe and now some crazy magician is going to destroy everything I love...

Okay okay here's the deal. I don't really care about being a blogger. I mean, I really like to do all the things I do—it's a cool gig, I go to galleries, I go to shows. I am, like, the VOICE of the Louisville party scene, woo.

See, okay, I'm adopted, right? And I thought—okay this is silly but I thought that if I got really really good at blogging, then I would be one of those, like, *personalities,* like Perez Hilton or Ryan Seacrest, like on the red carpet, I'd be the girl who cracks the jokes with Robert Pattinson and whoever, and I'd get on Conan and my real mom and dad would see me and—and now Conan doesn't even have a SHOW anymore and we're all going to die, like, NOW, and what have I done with my life?

> *(At the time of this performance, 21c had a small exhibit by Lindsay Cameron, a local Louisville photographer who chronicled body piercings and tattoos in a small village in Ghana. This is the exhibit on the walls that* CLARISSA *refers to below.)*

I mean, look at these photos—I mean, wow. It says there she's from Louisville, the girl who took them? In Ghana—see it says Louisville has a sister city, in Ghana, and she went there, and—it's just really inspiring, you know what I mean? Damn.

Oh! Oh shit, people, I know what we're going to do! We're going to make a DOCUMENTARY! Fuck blogging. I'm going to make a record of all the things I want to remember about Louisville. Oh oh oh this is gonna be rad, people, and I need your help! This is gonna be awesome. We're gonna do something IMPORTANT. Yeah. Yeah. Get up. Help me out here. On your feet. Okay. Here's the deal.

I love Louisville. This is my *home,* man. So let's make a record of all the things that make it great—the things we're thinking about now, this moment, the last night of Louisville EVER in all of history, maybe. And after we're gone people will WATCH it and KNOW that we were here and we were awesome and Louisville is awesome and this documentary is gonna be awesome—

You get it? We're the story! We're here, right now, and we have all these memories and experiences and—

We don't have a lot of time. Here's what we're going to do—we're going to sing a song. Yeah.

> *(She starts to beatbox. Gets a groove going in the room.)*

Now what I want you to do is, we're going to go around the circle and shout out your favorite thing about Louisville. It doesn't matter if you've lived here your whole life or if you just got here yesterday—just call out something you love—it's okay to repeat what someone else says—

We're making a mosaic of experience! This is real art, people, this is great.

> *(Together, they sing an awesome song about Louisville, with* CLARISSA *holding down the beat and audience volunteers calling out their favorite things*

about Louisville. CLARISSA *videotapes the whole thing, gets really into it, does some breakdancing.*

As the party winds down…)

Great…wow, that's so inspiring…I am, like, so FILLED with the love right now, can you feel it? We are AWESOME you guys, that was awesome—

(*Suddenly, the door bursts open and* PENELOPE FRANCIS, *from the FBI, collapses in a sobbing heap in the doorway. She thinks she is in a private room or closet—doesn't see the others at first.*)

CLARISSA. Hey—hey, girl, are you okay?

(*Surprised,* PENELOPE *ducks into a defensive crouch and pulls her gun.*)

PEN. Who are you?

CLARISSA. I'm Clarissa…explaining it all…put the gun down, girl…shh…breathe…

(*After a brief standoff,* PEN *puts the gun away. She's still weeping.*)

Breathe…it's okay, it's gonna be okay…

PEN. NO IT IS NOT GOING TO BE OKAY! The Pellago is GONE! I was supposed to KEEP IT HERE but it is GONE and those assholes took it and I'm going to lose my JOB!

CLARISSA. That's rough, man.

PEN. Tell me about it.

CLARISSA. Behind every failure is an opportunity…we've been doing some thinking and some talking, my groupies and me, and we, we figured out some things. Didn't we, right, yeah, groupies?

(*The audience nods in agreement.*)

PEN. What did you figure out?

CLARISSA. I got it all on tape—

PEN. Got what on tape?

CLARISSA. Everything. The whole night. I tape everything. I'm a documentarian. Well, until recently I was a blogger. Clarissa Explains It All dot kick-ass dot org? Maybe you've seen it? No? Anyway—doesn't matter—because now, see, now I'm trying to move into the more serious realm of things, you know. Because life— you know, life could be over any minute now. And we were just, before you got here, we were taking stock of all the things we really love about, like, the world and specifically Louisville—see?

(*She plays some of the tape for* PEN, *who is very impressed.*)

PEN. Wow—you guys did all that? Tonight?

CLARISSA. Yeah we did. Me and my groupies.

PEN. That's so—that's so moving.

CLARISSA. We did all right.

PEN. And to think…while you guys were baring your souls, I was obsessing over a couple of two-bit criminals and a tiny piece of canvas…my life has gotten so small…

CLARISSA. It doesn't have to be! It's not too late—there's always time to refocus and open yourself to—to new experiences, and you know, things like that…

PEN. I've only been in Kentucky for two days but already I can relate to your love for it—it's so beautiful to see so much passion in one place.

CLARISSA. Thanks.

PEN. Hey, can I add something to your documentary?

CLARISSA. Okay, sure. But it has to be in song!

PEN. I don't know that song.

CLARISSA. That's okay. Sing anything. Do you know any songs about Kentucky?

PEN. I know one…

> (CLARISSA *presses "record" and begins to film as* PEN *sings a beautiful a cappella version of "Blue Moon Of Kentucky," or another song about Kentucky. Everyone cheers.*)

CLARISSA. Wow! Wow! That was amazing, that was so beautiful! You should like make a record or something! Wasn't that great you guys?

> (PEN *gets a text message.*)

PEN. Oh, I gotta get back to work—that was…that was fantastic…thank you so much, you guys. I really needed that. Thanks for this. This was really special.

CLARISSA. Any time, girl.

> (PEN *goes, rejuvenated and ready to face the world.*)

I didn't want to tell her about the dynamite…she seemed so upset already… she may as well be happy for a bit, you know what I mean?

> (*Depending on the mood,* CLARISSA *either tape-records audience members saying one thing they'd like to do before the bombs go off, or if it's a more reticent crowd, she brings them back to the main gallery to join the end of the* COMMISSIONER's *big all-group training, until* LOUISA *returns with the painting.*)

TANYA STEIMER FELDMAN.

New to her job, kindhearted junior docent TANYA STEIMER FELDMAN *was very excited to be working at 21c. During Act 1, she led small group tours of key works in the 21c collection and tried not to get in trouble with her bosses,* ALICE WEATHERS *and* DIANE WORTHINGBOTTOM. *However, she was late to work today and that set her nerves on edge even before the Pellago was stolen. As her journey unfolds, the theft of the Pellago is a catalyst for her to unload all of her insecurities about her new job, and about being so far from home.*

TANYA's *order of scenes:*
Act 4C (Commissioner Training)
Act 4B (The Russians)
Solo Scene
Act 4A (Planning The Heist)

1. Gathering her group

As Act 4 begins, TANYA *is near the back of the main gallery, and so gathers her group from the back of the crowd. She holds up her docent sign, which is a small paddle with the Red Penguin on one side and a photo of Chelsea Cooley on the other.*

TANYA. Everyone, over here, circle up! That's right, circle up, who's with me, great, let's step back a bit to separate from the others—make sure we're clear. Follow my sign. Everyone see the sign? Great.

All right, how many are we? Let's count off.

(They count off.)

Terrific. Great. Hi. I'm Tanya Steimer Feldman, I'm a docent here at 21c. You are in very good hands. Just follow the sign, okay? Penguin means go, and Chelsea Cooley's face means stop. Let's try it—Penguin, go! Chelsea face, stop! Penguin! Go! Chelsea face! Stop!

(They practice.)

Great job you guys. We're going to be great.

That's so crazy about the painting, huh? I can't believe it. I mean, of course I *believe* it, it's just—we were so prepared, you know? We hired the BEST security, did you *see* that thing? There's like a secret underground VAULT for the painting. Built special for the Pellago. Like at the Smithsonian, you know, where the Constitution goes at night? You ever been there? It's cool. You should go if you can.

Actually…I'm going to tell you a secret…Chelsea Cooley told me that apparently Dorman and Dobson security is notoriously faulty…so, do you think it's possible that the vault system didn't work? Oh! Maybe this cop knows—hey! Hey, hello there, um, Officer? Hello?

(CARL WEATHERS had been walking by, patrolling the hallway.)

CARL. Yes, Ma'am.

TANYA. Do you know—how long until the painting will be back?

CARL. I'm not at liberty to divulge that information, sorry.

TANYA. It's okay. I work here.

CARL. Sorry.

TANYA. *(Showing her nametag.)* No, I do, see?

CARL. I'll tell you this: it's a dangerous situation, but there's no need to panic.

TANYA. I work here. And I heard that the vault system for the painting might not have worked. Do you think that's possible?

CARL. Well, guess we just gotta wait to see if it comes back.

TANYA. If?

CARL. I mean, when.

TANYA. No, you said if…

CARL. (*Shrugs.*)

TANYA. Is there anything my group and I can do to help?

CARL. Help what?

TANYA. Get the painting back?

CARL. Oh. Right. No, nope, just gotta be vigilant. Never know what's lurking under the kitchen sink, know what I'm saying?

TANYA. This is an art gallery, not a kitchen.

CARL. So, you work here?

TANYA. It's my first week.

CARL. Do you know anything about those friends of Archie Pellago's?

TANYA. The Russians?

CARL. Oh, were they Russian? I didn't notice.

TANYA. Um, yeah, they were Russian. Kind of weird. Kept asking me about all the Red Penguins. They wanted to get to the roof—because there are so many Red Penguins up there.

CARL. To the roof? Did you tell them?

TANYA. Sure, it's easy, you just take the elevator to the 8th floor, and then at the end of the hallway there's a door—

CARL. Okay, great, thank you—gotta run—you all be careful, all right? You're in good hands with your leader…what was your name again?

TANYA. Tanya Steimer Feldman.

CARL. All right, Tanya, well, nice to meet you…gotta run…and the rest of you, don't forget: always keep your eyes open on both sides of your head.

TANYA. Okay—'bye, Officer, thank you!

(*Like a true hero,* CARL *barrel rolls down the hallway to the elevator.*)

Well he wasn't very helpful at all. Let's ask the Commissioner, he's right over there…

(TANYA *brings her group over to the* COMMISSIONER, *who welcomes them to his training course.*)

2. Watching Act 4C (Commissioner Training)

TANYA *leaves her group with the* COMMISSIONER, *and goes to make some tea in a break room.*

3. Watching Act 4B (The Russians)

> TANYA *does not watch this scene. She returns at the end to pick up her group and bring them to a side gallery, where she has prepared tea for everyone.*

4. Solo Scene

TANYA. I'm not really supposed to take people back here, but—everyone's breaking all kinds of rules, so, whatever…

> (TANYA *ushers her group into a small gallery, where there are small cups of tea laid out for everyone.*
>
> *On the walls is an exhibit by Lindsay Cameron, a local Louisville photographer who chronicled body piercings and tattoos in a small village in Ghana.*)

Does anyone need tea? I need a little tea. I'm pretty stressed out actually.

> (*Passes out little cups to the whole audience.*)

It's herbal. I don't have any sugar. Sorry.

Sorry there aren't any more seats…this is my safe place. Where I come when I just need to be quiet.

Except when my boss, Alice, tells me not to sit on the floor. But, I don't think anyone's paying attention. You should. Sit on the floor. I will in a moment.

This is my favorite exhibit in the whole gallery. This woman, Lindsay Cameron, she went to Ghana and took all these pictures of the people of Fooshegu. They all—see, on their faces? That's ritual scarring. It used to be a religious thing but now it's about beauty, the scars show pride. I have a scar too, here, see? I really like the idea that a scar is a kind of beauty—any time I'm feeling sad I come into this room, and I think about that.

Yeah—apparently Louisville has a sister city in Ghana. Isn't that cool? I think that's just great. I just moved here, from Idaho, I'd never been anywhere this far east before. It's kind of amazing to think how big the world is, you know?

> (*She takes her cell phone out of a pocket in her dress.*)

Do you mind if I listen to my messages?

> (*She puts the phone on speaker, and plays a message from* SEQUOIA, *her best friend from home who is so totally excited that she's at the Pellago exhibit.*)

She's my—I just moved here too, from Idaho? This is my first week on the job…

Has anyone ever been to Idaho? Oh great. Where? They're all really really excited for me that I have this job, with the Pellago…

> (*Plays the next message. It's from* DIANE, *her boss, ripping her a new one for being late today.*
>
> TANYA *shuts the phone and starts to cry.*)

I was late today. Do you think this happened because I was late? Was I supposed to be watching the Pellago or something? I don't really understand the whole security system…

Did anyone see? When I was late? It was really embarrassing. Diane—she's the other docent, the head one—she's not very understanding about…

Oh god. Oh no.

I can't get fired. I can't. I can't go back to Arby's—

I was transferred from the Twin Falls Arby's to Louisville because I was such a good worker. I am. I'm really diligent and hardworking—

But last week I was late—I just can't figure out the traffic in this town—I showed up late for my job, you know, it's the one on Third Street?—so I was late, and I had to rush everything, the patties and the toast and the apple pies, I was doing seventeen things at once, and you should never do more than three things at once in the kitchen, that's what it says in the manual—I KNOW what it says in the manual—but I was doing all these things, and you know the beef and cheddar chili, I turned up the heat too high and it all exploded, no I mean it really—burst out of the oven and was bubbling all over all of the counters and the floor and the ice cream machine and the fries and the coffee—and it was all over me, I was covered with beef and cheddar it was on my uniform and in my hair and IN MY MOUTH and I'M A VEGETARIAN…

And my boss came over and fired me right there, didn't even let me brush my teeth—so you see why I can't go back.

      (*Breathes…drinks her tea…tries to compose herself.*)

How's the tea? Okay, I have one more favor.

      (*Takes her phone out again, opens to a photo. Passes the picture around the room.*)

If you see this woman, Alice Weathers? She's my boss. If you see her tonight, can you all make a point to tell her that I did a really good job? My name is Tanya. Tanya Steimer Feldman. Tell her that you took my art tour—even if you didn't—and that it was really really good. Because I can't go back to Arby's. Tell her that Tanya Feldman is the best tour guide you've ever had, and that I'm an asset to her organization. You can use your own words…but that's the idea.

      (*A* COP *knocks on the door—tells her that it's time to bring her group to HQ.*)

5. Walking Across to FBI HQ

      As they cross the street, TANYA *is hopeful that these exhibits will reveal something about why the Pellago was stolen, and hopefully her job will be safe. She uses her docent sign to guide the group safely across the street ("Penguin means go, Chelsea Face means stop").*

6. Watching Act 4A at **FBI HQ**

Watching these scenes, TANYA *realizes that the people she worked with were part of the Heist Team—it's totally devastating.*

7. Returning to the main gallery (atrium)

Talking points for the walk back:

TANYA. Oh my god, I can't believe it—I worked with two of those guys—Victor, the really nice event manager, he always has cigarettes—and Andy, he's always the only one who's nice to me! Like, ever! It was his birthday on my first day of work, and on my lunch break I got him cupcakes because no one had gotten him anything…

What about those other people? Did you see any of them at the party?

What was this about the four minutes? I bet that's about the vault filling with water.

That's so scary about Victor and Andy…I feel so betrayed…

(Returns to the news that the painting has been found by LOUISA, *and is already on its way back.)*

DIANE WORTHINGBOTTOM.

DIANE WORTHINGBOTTOM, *the long-suffering Assistant Curator at 21c, has just about had it with her boss,* ALICE WEATHERS, *and her pretentious tastes.* DIANE *did her job during the party, shuttling audience members around the art, but is pretty disgusted by the big fuss being made over a two-bit poser like Archie Pellago. During Act 4, she will reveal her true passions, including her reverence for the late, great Ayn Rand and her devotion to applying the laws of the wild to everyday life.*

> DIANE's *order of scenes:*
> *Act 4C (Commissioner Training)*
> *Act 4B (The Russians)*
> *Solo Scene*
> *Act 4A (Planning The Heist)*

1. Gathering her group

DIANE briskly and efficiently points to the people she wants to follow her and takes them quickly into the nearest gallery. When she has reached maximum capacity, she brutally shuts out the rest, closes the door in their face.

DIANE. You, you, you, you, and you—this way. I need thirty, are you thirty? Yes. Good. I'm filled. Sorry, no more room. No following. Get your own group.

(On the walls of this gallery is an exhibit by Kara Walker.)

Everyone in. Shut the door. I said shut it!

Hi. I'm Diane Worthingbottom, Assistant Curator here at 21c. Let's start by introducing ourselves. First names only.

(*The audience introduces themselves. DIANE chooses her favorite and appoints him [or, her—but usually him] as her Number 2.*)

Great. Thanks. So, you may not have realized it, but you were chosen before you arrived. You are the smartest, the fastest, the most attractive. Yes. Everyone in this room is the cream of the crop, the top of the heap, the absolute best. And we're going to get through this evening; we are going to triumph over the criminals and the inept, mediocre, ill-equipped people in charge.

I'm not much of a Pellago fan, if you want to know the truth. The only reason we're having this exhibit anyway is because Alice wanted the publicity. If you want to know my opinion, Pellago is a hack. All smoke and mirrors, you know? There's no *there* there, no substance or content or—any of these kinds of things that make art worth having.

I know you know what I mean, because you're all so smart.

This room, this gallery, actually, this is my exhibit. I curated this room. Kara Walker.

This is, like, really important work about American identity—and Alice, what does she do, she just shoves it into a side gallery for what, so Archie Pellago can have more space. That's bullshit. She wanted the publicity, and boy oh boy is she gonna get it now.

I TOLD her that she needed better security. I TOLD her that Dobson and Dorman is notoriously faulty. I told her that having a Pellago exhibit at all was too risky—but no, no Diane, she said, she said, are you in charge? Art is more important than fear and blah blah blah blah. But what about art that portrays fear in its most basic, animal form?

(*She gestures at the fairly graphic art on the walls.*)

You know what I'm afraid of most of all? Mediocrity. That's why I like this art in here most of all, because it's not mediocre. Everything Alice likes, everything out there in the main gallery, that's mediocre, it's worse, it's shit. I mean, what are we learning right now except that Fear is actually greater than Art, right? I mean we're on lockdown, and not because it's *artistic*. Art can help us process our fear, sure, but if we are not vigilant, if we are not wary of the mediocre, then you know what? We're screwed.

We are all leaders, in this room. We are what rises above. The rest of the world is the floor, and we are the silver lining on the great mushroom cloud of civilization. And those mediocre people? We have to best them. And we do it for the good.

Repeat after me: I best you! Say it!

(*The audience shouts: I best you!*)

And I do it for the good!

(And I do it for the good!
She repeats this call-and-response a few times, as it grows in fervor.)

Okay great. Let's go out there, and if anyone tries to fuck with us, I'm going to put my hand up like this and I want you to say—I best you! And I do it for the good!

Let's find the Police Commissioner, I bet he knows what to do. Be mindful of what he recommends—he's a survivor.

2. Watching Act 4C (the Commissioner)

> DIANE *takes the group back out into the main gallery, where the* COMMISSIONER *welcomes them into his training course.*
>
> DIANE *loves it—soaks up every word.*

3. Watching Act 4B (the Russians)

> DIANE *watches this scene with her group.*
>
> *All riled up after learning about* HANS' *terrible plot,* DIANE *is all business at the end of the scene. She hurries her group out and to an upstairs gallery.*

DIANE. Hustle! Hustle! Look alive, no lagging, bring up the rear Number 2, all right, follow me—

> *(Etc.)*

4. Solo Scene

> *Militaristically,* DIANE *gets everyone into the room and slams the door behind them. Arranges them into a diamond-shaped formation.*

DIANE. Diamond shape! Diamond shape! Use what the Commissioner taught you, he knows how to survive on the mean streets, let's do this thing.

Okay. Everyone in?

Did you follow that? There is DYNAMITE planted throughout Louisville. As soon as we can get out of here, we are out of here.

I mean it. Remember what I was telling you earlier, about the silver lining on the mushroom cloud, well at the time I thought it was a metaphor but turns out that it's true. There WILL be a mushroom cloud, and we WILL survive. Why? Because survival is in our best interest. And according to my idol, Ayn Rand, it is not just *irrational* but also IMMORAL to act against one's self-interest. That makes sense, right?

Look. I have worked at 21c for 16 years. I started cleaning the bathrooms and now I am assistant curator. I was in line for Alice Weathers' job, until the board decided to swoop someone in from the East Coast and suddenly I'm in a holding pattern again. And you know what? That German magician, he might be crazy, but he's also on to something. We gotta hold people accountable for the damage they do. Alice came in here, with her fancy clothes and fancy lipstick and fancy friends, she got the Pellago and now all of Louisville is going to be embarrassed on a national level and maybe even way, way worse.

But you and me, we're going to survive the coming disaster because we are prepared. Because we are only looking out for ourselves. Sure, I'm the assistant here, but I have a whole other life aside from work in which I have been preparing for the inevitable.

Here—I'm going to read you something. I keep this quote in my pocket for inspiration at times like these. "Every man"—or, woman—"is an end to himself, not a means to the ends of others; he must live for his own sake, neither sacrificing himself to others nor sacrificing others to himself; he must work for his rational self-interest, with the achievement of his own happiness as the highest moral purpose of his life."

And by happiness, she means survival. She means getting up in the morning after the rest of the loser people are blown to bits or starved to death for lack of vitamins and resources. Because you know what, people are the only animals who would even do something like that, who would even be so stupid as to act against their own self-interest—if we were a pack of lions, we wouldn't even be having this conversation. Humans are the only animals who act as their own destroyer. You know I speak the truth.

So as we think about how to survive the impending apocalypse that we just heard all about downstairs, we need to think in practical terms of what's going to be best for me, and my own self-interest. And I fully expect you all to do the same for yourselves. Right, Number 2? I'm not going to have any dead weight near me when I'm sailing through the darkness, you hear me? You got that Number 2? You're not turning into dead weight on me, are you?

We're going to survive. What survival skills do you have?

> (Collects list of survival skills from group, including: Who knows how to find edible bugs? Collect rocks? Build a tent? Fish? Make a fire? Shoot a gun? Who has killed before? Who has a photographic memory? Who can drink poison? Who can turn tears into poison? Who can make clothes out of leaves? Etc....)

When shit does down, people of the world look to people like us to show them how to behave. But don't forget—those people are down there, and we are up here. We stand tall while they cower in fear. They sink down, while people like us, we rise up and become that silver lining. Some people will look to the sky from their hovels in the dirt and want to be like us. But NO! They CANNOT! There's no room for them on our ship!

If anyone tries to join us, or even to follow us down the street or ask us what we're doing—you know what we're gonna do? We're gonna have to beat them down. Why? Because that's the only way to survive.

That's our new mantra, people. Besting them is not enough. Repeat after me: I beat you!

(*I beat you!*)

And I do it for survival!

(*And I do it for survival!*

Call and response…rising to a fever pitch.)

Great, this is great. I think I'm really going to like having a civilization with all of you. You're making me so proud. Let's go over to HQ, and let's take notes with our photographic memories about how the Vista Crew got together, stayed together, and outsmarted the best security systems the world.

Let's do this thing.

5. Walking Across to FBI HQ

They cross the street, and if they see another group they shout: "I beat you! And I do it for survival!"

6. Watching Act 4A at FBI HQ

Watching the scenes, DIANE realizes that she worked with two inside men, ANDY and VICTOR. She develops a new respect for them. She points them out to her group and generally comes to revere the Vista Crew.

7. Returning to the main gallery (atrium)

Talking points for the walk back:

DIANE. Andy and Victor…I walked side by side with those guys for a long time, and you know I never gave them much credit, but you know, now they're in the book. I'll bring them into the ark, into our commune. Pretty damn impressive. All of those guys, if you think of that. That takes balls. And brains. A four-minute forgery! How do you even do that? Amazing!

(*Returns to the news that the painting has been found by LOUISA, and is already on its way back.*)

CHELSEA COOLEY and DEVIN THE GREAT.

CHELSEA COOLEY, the host and underwriter of this whole event, is basically in a puddle on the floor by the end of Act 3—her whole party in ruins. Her scheming boyfriend, DEVIN (known as "The Great" in his performance art pieces, which he seems to never actually do) tries to cheer her up but always says the wrong thing. They decide to combine their two audience groups together, but soon have a huge fight and break up, causing CHELSEA to take the women for a good cry in the ladies' room, while DEVIN is left with all the guys for some impromptu male bonding. All is well in the end, though, as the COMMISSIONER helps

DEVIN *find his way back into* CHELSEA's *heart, and her beloved personal assistant* LOUISA *saves the day by finding the painting (or so it seems).*

> CHELSEA/DEVIN's *order of scenes:*
> Act 4C (*Commissioner Training*)—*gets interrupted*
> Act 4B (*The Russians*)
> *Solo Scenes*
> Act 4A (*Planning The Heist*)
> Act 4C, *continued from where it got interrupted*

1. Gathering their groups.

> *After the* COMMISSIONER *says* "Dismissed," CHELSEA *calls over* DEVIN.

CHELSEA. Devy! Devy! I have an idea!

DEVIN. What babe?

CHELSEA. (*To her group.*) Have you all met Devin? This is Devin. He's an artist. Devy. Let's make a supergroup.

DEVIN. What?

CHELSEA. Let's mash our groups together and become like a big whole solar system group and we'll be like those birds that always fly together, you know, so they're safe and they don't get lost, you know, what's that called?

DEVIN. Flocks?

CHELSEA. Yes! Like flocks! Let's flock our groups!

DEVIN. I don't know if that's allowed…

CHELSEA. It's my party, we can do whatever we want.

DEVIN. Ummm…

CHELSEA. Circle up everybody. Come on. Come on. This is a very sensitive time for me, and I'm going to need y'alls help to get me through it. My daddy bought me the Pellago painting and now it's gone and I don't know what I'm going to do!

> (*Suddenly,* HANS SCHMIDT *bursts out of a side gallery, carrying a mortally wounded* BORIS PENGUROVICH *on his back, and runs through the room laughing, exiting the other side.* TIMOTHY WYATT, *gagged and still tied to a chair, is close behind, wailing and crying.*
>
> CHELSEA *and* DEVIN *move their groups out of the way and watch in shock.*
>
> COMMISSIONER *chases them all, and catches* TIMOTHY *near the exit. He brings him around to be interrogated in front of* CHELSEA *and* DEVIN's *groups.*)

COMMISSIONER. Whoa whoa whoa whoa—hold up there, soldier! Come with me!

> (*He brings* TIMOTHY *into the atrium [close to the stage?].* *Meanwhile:*)

CHELSEA. What was that! What was that! That was a crazy man with two heads and another weird thing that's half man half chair!

DEVIN. I'm sure there's a perfectly reasonable explanation!

CHELSEA. No Devin! There is NOT a perfectly reasonable explanation! My party is RUINED!!!

(COMMISSIONER *gets the attention of the group.*)

COMMISSIONER. Excuse me, excuse me. Sorry to disturb you peoples but we gots a bit of a situation here. Everyone if you can please gather back on that side of the room…very good…orderly, orderly, what do you think, this is a party? No, this is not a party, this is a crime scene. Back up, peoples. Excellent. Good work.

All righty. Did anybody here see where this man came from?

(*Audience says yes—he came from that door over there—*)

Excellent. Excellent. (*To* TIMOTHY.) Is this true, sir? Did you in fact come from that door over there?

TIMOTHY. (*Blubbering.*)

COMMISSIONER. I'm sorry sir, but I'm going to need you to give me a straight answer. For the benefit of these witnesses here. Now: what just happened to you?

TIMOTHY. (*Blubbering.*)

COMMISSIONER. I'm gonna ask you one more time: can you provide any useful information that can lead us to find the individuals who perpetrated this crime against you?

TIMOTHY. (*Blubbering.*)

COMMISSIONER. All right, forget about it, get the hell out of here.

(TIMOTHY *runs away—still gagged and tied to the chair.*)

COMMISSIONER. (*To audience.*) Suspicious…very suspicious…I'm gonna have to ask for you alls help for a minute as we get to the bottom of this. Me, I gotta stay on the Paul Vista beat, catch the con man who took that Pellago painting, but you alls, if you can help me out, you will be richly rewarded with…well, we can see about that when the time comes. I need all of youse to look for clues to help us solve the case of the Half Man, Half Chair, that came out of that room there and then ran thataways. But where to look for clues…where…where…where…

(*Sees the sign that says "6 Minutes Ago" outside of the gallery where Act 4B is performed.*)

Oh! Lookie that here. It says 6 Minutes Ago! How very convenient. All right peoples, we're now going to experience what we in the business call "A Flashback." This is how we do our real and best detectiving.

(*He opens the door and ushers the people inside—arranges the audience to watch the scene ["Shorties in front, tallies in the back…"]*)

CHELSEA *and* DEVIN *help their group move inside.*)

CHELSEA/DEVIN. (*Ad-lib.*) Go on, go on, help out the policeman, maybe we can save the party…go on, don't be scared, we'll wait for you out here! Buh-bye!

2. Watching Act 4B (the Russians)

While their group watches the scene, CHELSEA *and* DEVIN *stay outside and continue to bicker (ad-libbing).*

At the end of the scene, CHELSEA *and* DEVIN *open the doors and bring out the audience. They have obviously been fighting the whole time.*

3. The Break-Up

Bringing their group out of the Russian scene and into a back hallway, continuing to fight…

CHELSEA. I can't believe you didn't offer to help—the painting is GONE and that man was KIDNAPPED at my PARTY—

DEVIN. Yeah, like anyone here would ever listen to me.

CHELSEA. You're a man, Devin, you're supposed to be a man! Stick up for me! Stick your neck out for once instead of asking me to do all of the things all of the time—I do everything for you, you live in my house, I buy you clothes, I take you to parties and introduce you to people—

DEVIN. You do things for me? Yeah? Do you? Then why isn't tonight a night about unveiling one of MY art pieces, huh? Tell me that?

CHELSEA. You do installation art dance, Devin, you can't UNVEIL an installation art dance—

DEVIN. You never even tried to get Alice to look at my slides!

CHELSEA. That is NOT true!

DEVIN. She's never looked at my slides!

CHELSEA. Well maybe your slides aren't very good, did you ever think about that?

DEVIN. No, I didn't ever think about that, but clearly you did, you've been thinking that my art is bullshit since the beginning, right—

CHELSEA. I cannot have this conversation right now, I just lost a 200-million-dollar painting tonight, do you even have any idea how much money that is, 200 MILLION dollars, do YOU have 200 million dollars just lying around?

DEVIN. No, I don't, but thanks for rubbing my poverty in my face one more time—

CHELSEA. You make me feel like poverty when you give me gifts you found in the trash, tell me it's supposed to feel like a million bucks—

DEVIN. Vintage! It's vintage!

CHELSEA. It's trash! Trash scarf! You gave me a trash scarf! It's somebody else's DIRTY CLOTHES, DEVIN!

DEVIN. You know what—I don't need this shit. I prance around for you, I do the dog and pony show, I'm your arm candy, I give you CRED and that's not enough for you? I'm an ARTIST, I need to be able to come and go as I please…I need to be able to feel…things…without you breathing down my neck and making me commit to go to this party and that party—you know, not everyone likes PARTIES, Chelsea, that's not everyone's WHOLE LIFE…

CHELSEA. I can't take this—I can't take this from you right now—I need my girlfriends. Girls! Girls, I need some girl time, come with me please, please, I need you, come on.

DEVIN. Fine. Men, with me. This way.

(They each start to go in opposite directions down the hallways.)

CHELSEA. *(Going down the hallway with her group.)* Screw you and your installation art dance, Devin!

DEVIN. Screw you!

CHELSEA. Suck it!

DEVIN. No! You suck it!

4. Chelsea's Solo Scene

CHELSEA *brings all the women into the ladies' room. She sits on the floor, starts to pick at the hem of her dress.*

CHELSEA. I'm sorry y'all, this has been such a disaster. He's such a douchebag, I think that's romance, what is wrong with me? Do you have a boyfriend? You do? Do you still love him even when he acts like a douchebag?

(She girl-talks with the audience about boy troubles [improv].)

He thinks he's smarter than me, he's not smarter than me. Does that happen to you? Is he ever mean to you? What do you say when he's mean?

I was so excited about this party. I really love art. I read all about it, and I'm really proud that Louisville has 21c which is so cutting-edge, you know? I wanted to be a part of that…you know, art is so beautiful, why would anyone want to take it?

But I shouldn't have been so excited about the party. I've never had a good party. They always go wrong. I thought everything would be different after I graduated from school and lost all that weight—but it's still the same.

One time I had a party but it was a football game so nobody came and I had to eat the whole cake by myself. I got a dog that year and no one even saw my puppy. And this is just the same.

The painting is gone! And my best friend and personal assistant Louisa ran out into the river to get it but she's never been to Indiana before and she's mute so she can't even ask for directions!

(*Her phone rings. She looks at the caller ID.*)

It's my daddy.

(*Uh-oh.*)

I don't want to answer.

(*It keeps ringing. She answers the phone and gives it to an audience member.*)

Can you tell him that I'm not here?

(*She does. She has a conversation with the person on the other end of the line,* MR. COOLEY—*but the rest of the audience can only hear the volunteer's side of the conversation. Since this conversation happens live every night [we had a directing assistant play the role of* MR. COOLEY*], the scene with the audience volunteer is improvised. The basic gist is that* MR. COOLEY *insists on talking to* CHELSEA, *and he's so adamant that eventually even the most resistant audience volunteer gives the phone to* CHELSEA.

CHELSEA *puts the phone on speaker, so everyone can hear.*)

CHELSEA. Hi Daddy.

MR. COOLEY. How are you, Sweetie? How's your party?

CHELSEA. (*Starting to cry.*) It's fine, Daddy, it's perfect! It's such a good party!

MR. COOLEY. Why are you crying?

CHELSEA. It's just so fun, I wish you were here!

MR. COOLEY. Chelsea Marie, why are you lying to me?

CHELSEA. I'm not lying…

MR. COOLEY. Am I on speakerphone?

CHELSEA. No.

MR. COOLEY. You take me off speaker right now.

CHELSEA. But so many people here want to say hi. Say hi to my daddy—

(*Audience says "Hi."*)

MR. COOLEY. Hello.

CHELSEA. They want to thank you for a really great party. Say thank you—

(*They say "Thank you."*)

Mr. Cooley. His name is Mr. Cooley.

(*They say "Thank you Mr. Cooley."*)

MR. COOLEY. Why are you crying, Chelsea?

CHELSEA. I'm not crying.

MR. COOLEY. My ass you aren't crying.

CHELSEA. Daddy, it's gone!

MR. COOLEY. What's gone?

CHELSEA. It's in Indiana somewhere and someone took it and Louisa is missing!

MR. COOLEY. What's missing?

CHELSEA. The painting…

MR. COOLEY. WHAT??!! Do you know how much that painting cost me? Do you know? Do you?

CHELSEA. Yes…

MR. COOLEY. How much then? How much did it cost me?

CHELSEA. 200…

MR. COOLEY. 200 what?

CHELSEA. 200 million dollars…

MR. COOLEY. Do you think I have 200 million dollars just lying around…

CHELSEA. No, I know you don't have 200 million dollars just lying around…but Daddy it's not my fault —

> (*The conversation continues until a* COP *knocks on the door to move the group over to FBI HQ.*)

Okay Daddy, I gotta go, I gotta go…

> (*She hangs up on him.*
>
> *To the audience:*)

Devin's out there—what am I gonna—what am I gonna do—I can't, I can't…I can't see him…

> (*She crumples for a moment, but then stands up strong.*)

I have to. I'm gonna do it. I'm gonna stand proud. But I need your help. Here's how we do it at home. Follow me.

> (*They go out into the hallway, and* CHELSEA *teaches them how to walk a runway. She demonstrates:*)

It goes like this: right, left, right, step out, pivot, pivot, give a sassy look…and walk away.

Now do it with me. Put a hop into it.

> (*They practice.*)

Again! Right, left, right, step out, pivot, pivot, give a sassy look…and walk away.

Excellent! I love you girls! You're my new best girlfriends!

Because you know what? I lost my painting, and I lost my man, but my head is held up high! Let's go, girls!

> (*They sassy-walk out into the night.*)

5. Devin's Solo Scene

> *After* CHELSEA *peels away with all the women,* DEVIN *is left in the hallway with all the men. Shit. He just told his girlfriend (and sugarmomma) to suck it. This isn't how this was supposed to go.*

DEVIN. (*To group.*) All right, come on, we're getting the hell out of here—this is total bullshit, you know what I mean? Fuck that. She's gonna embarrass me? Well I'm gonna embarrass her—

> (*He starts to lead them down the hallway but* CARL WEATHERS, *the overeager rookie cop, stops them.*)

CARL. Excuse me, Sir, you can't go this way.

DEVIN. I just want to show these guys the fitness room.

CARL. Sorry, Sir, but it's a security issue.

DEVIN. We just need to let off some steam. It's getting a little close in here, you know what I'm saying?

CARL. Sorry about that. But the lockdown should be over soon.

DEVIN. We just need some air.

CARL. Sorry. Can't. Security. The painting should be on its way back from Indiana in the next ten minutes.

DEVIN. I don't give a shit about the painting.

CARL. Pardon me?

DEVIN. You heard me. I don't give a SHIT about that painting. Honestly, that painting can stay in the river, for all I care. It will serve her right for wasting all that money on a Pellago instead of investing in the local artistic community.

CARL. That's what my wife says.

DEVIN. Who's your wife?

CARL. Ex-wife. She's the assistant curator here. Diane.

DEVIN. The staff here is full of shit. I send them my slides every WEEK but do I even get a call back? From any of them? No. And I'm like, Chelsea, what the fuck? I can't even talk about her right now. I need to—I just need to get out of here—

CARL. All right—it's okay, man, hey follow me. We can't go down this hallway but let's duck in here—come on—

> (*They go into a side gallery.*)

DEVIN. Thanks, man. Appreciate it. You're all right.

CARL. Sure. All righty then, a cop will come to get you when it's time to go across to FBI Headquarters. I myself am on the trail of some suspicious-looking Russians.

DEVIN. Hey—Carl? Is it Carl?

CARL. Yup.

DEVIN. Devin. Let me ask you a question, Carl. You got a girlfriend?

CARL. Nope.

DEVIN. Good for you. (*To audience.*) See? This is what I'm saying. Unencumbered. No strings. No commitments. No entanglements.

CARL. I got a wife. Well—ex. Ex-wife.

DEVIN. This is what I'm talking about. Shed the baggage. Clear the drains. Dust-bust the dust. Get those ladies out of your business, out of your shit, then you can live as you're meant to live.

CARL. Yeah. Yeah. That's what I did.

DEVIN. 'Cause your wife, she was all up in your shit, right?

CARL. Yeah, she was.

DEVIN. (*To group.*) See, guys? This is what I'm talking about. You gotta be all "Chelsea, back off." I need some SPACE. Right?

CARL. Oh, yeah, man. It was always Carl do this, Carl do that. Carl take out the trash. Carl fix the roof. Carl pay your half of the rent. Carl get a job. Well you know what? I GOT a job!

DEVIN. You got a good job.

CARL. Damn right I do!

DEVIN. You got a nice uniform, responsibilities, a paycheck…

CARL. I get paid on the 15th. Today's my first day.

DEVIN. Well, congratulations, my friend. That's great. That's just great. Good for you. Did you tell your wife?

CARL. Yeah. She didn't care. I don't know.

DEVIN. Let it out, man. Shake it out.

CARL. What?

DEVIN. Let it go. Shake it out. Whenever Chelsea gets all up in my face, I shake it out and throw her name on the ground, like it's rolling off of me— like this—

(*He demonstrates shaking it out and yelling "Chelsea!" at the ground. It's more new-age touchy-feely than violent or macho. It's almost a dance move.*)

Your turn.

CARL. Nah—nah, I don't think so—

DEVIN. Try it. It will feel good.

(CARL *shakes it out—yells "Diane!"*)

DEVIN. How'd that feel?

CARL. It felt great actually.

DEVIN. Let's do it together!

(*They do. "Chelsea!" "Diane!"*)

DEVIN. (*To audience.*) Let's all do it. Let's shake it out—and think about someone who did you wrong. A girl, or a boss, or your dad—someone who doesn't see your whole potential, you know, someone who fills up your life like you don't have your own interests, like you don't have your own spirit, someone who thinks they can run your life like they're the boss of you—well you know what? They're not the boss of you! The only person who is the boss of you is YOU! So think of that person—hold their face in your head—and shake it out and throw their name on the floor! All together now!

> (*They all do it, shouting out names and shaking it out.*)

Again!

> (*They do it again.*)

One more time!

> (*Once more.*)

Awesome, everyone, I'm starting to feel better.

CARL. Me too.

DEVIN. Sometimes you just gotta say no—reclaim your self for your SELF, you know?

CARL. Absolutely. Oh, shit—I gotta go back on duty, or I'm gonna lose my job.

DEVIN. You go get 'em Carl.

CARL. I will.

DEVIN. Don't let anyone, female or otherwise, tell you that you can't do whatever it is you want to do.

CARL. I won't. Thanks, man. See you—

DEVIN. Good luck out there.

> (CARL *goes.*
> DEVIN *checks his cell phone.*)

Like—here's an example of what I'm talking about. She already left me like 15 messages TODAY and I can't, I haven't even had TIME to LISTEN to them. Like—okay, here. Check it.

> (*He plays the message on speaker.*)

CHELSEA. Hey Devy… It's Chelsea. I was just calling because today when I was looking at the Pellago, I was so moved. And it just made me think about you. And think about how much you changed my life, Honey. Like you have really, really changed it. I didn't know nothing about art until I met you. I mean everything I knew was just from books and stuff. And then you came and you changed my life. And you told me about how art is about the soul and the heart. And you CHANGED me Honey. That's why, when this is all over, I'm going to give the Pellago to you. And you can take it home, and you can look at it, and every time you see it it's a gift reminding you how you changed me. It's nothing but a big old circle of love, BABY! I LOVE YOU! I love you so much. Thank you for everything! You're the best, Devy. You're the best. I love you…I love you…I love you…

> (*Looks at the phone after the phone ends.*
> *Puts it in his pocket.*)

DEVIN. Oh. Okay, well—wow. Shit. Wow. That's kind of…

She's all right. That's kind of nice of her, right? She's all right, Chelsea. She is. She's—objectively speaking, she's an incredible lady, she always wants to make people feel good about themselves and—make me feel good about myself—even when I'm broke and living with my mom and—

Shit.

I kind of fucked this up, huh?

I gotta get her back. Shit. I don't even need the painting, I just want—I mean, I've never met anyone like her—

Let's go see if she's outside.

Okay. So here's what I want to do. And I'm going to need your help, because this is a hard thing for me to do, actually, it's not something I've ever done before…I'm gonna find her, and I'm gonna tell her I'm sorry. Yes. That's what we're going to do. You ready? Hey—and you, can you be sort of my buddy for this? Because we're such a big group, I'm going to need a scout. You bring up the rear as we're walking across the street, and if you see Chelsea, you can shout out—Chelsea! He's sorry! Can you do that? Great—thanks, man. I appreciate it. I do.

All right people, let's go get her back!

6. Walking Across to FBI HQ

DEVIN *brings his group outside and they head towards FBI HQ.*

CHELSEA *and her girlfriends are there, sassy-walking across the street and deliberately ignoring them.*

This is going to be harder than he thought…

7. Watching Act 4A at FBI HQ

Throughout these scenes, DEVIN *keeps trying to apologize but* CHELSEA *can't hear it.*

8. Returning to the main gallery

DEVIN *tries to talk to her but she is too upset, can't talk to him right now…*

CHELSEA *talks to her group about how now that they have information about the Heist, she's going to figure out how to get her painting back from the Vista Crew—she doesn't need no man to help her.*

DEVIN *says that now that they have info, he's going to try to get the painting back for Chelsea and thereby win her heart…Also, he encourages his group to tell* CHELSEA *that he's sorry…hoping that there is strength in numbers…*

9. Watching Act 4C—Alternate Version

Because these groups already have seen part of the COMMISSIONER's *training scene, this version is different from the others.*

Upon arriving in the atrium, CHELSEA *and* DEVIN's *groups are welcomed by the* COMMISSIONER, *who begins his training. Meanwhile,* CHELSEA *cries in the corner.*

As they arrive in the atrium:

COMMISSIONER. Welcome, welcome, come on in, no lagging. So you've been to HQ. Very interesting…very interesting…now, I'm going to teach you a little bit of how to apply this knowledge in the field of Law Enforcement.

(CHELSEA *cries in the corner.*

COMMISSIONER *starts to conduct his training as scripted [*"Diamond shape!" *etc.] but* CHELSEA's *sobbing is too loud. It's distracting everyone. Finally, he can't ignore it anymore.*)

COMMISSIONER. (*Calling over to* CHELSEA.) Lady, you're disturbing my Policepeople's Training Session here.

(*She cries more loudly.*)

Uh—hang on a sec, peoples, looks like we gots a domestic disturbance.

(*He goes to console her. Meanwhile,* DEVIN *steps up to the point of the diamond shape to address the group.*)

DEVIN. Hi guys. Sorry to interrupt—but, if I can have a moment of your time—

When I first met Chelsea, I was doing this modern dance installation outside of Starbucks, on Fourth Street, it was a stampede of jungle animals and she came up to me and was like, safari's cool and all, but what about the birds? What about the creatures of the sky? And I told her I'd make her an installation of seagulls—and I never did—

So I need you to be seagulls for her. Okay? Can you do this? Just—she's right over there, and I need you to put your arms up like this, like wings, and flap your wings, feel like you can touch the sky…

(*He ad-libs conducting the audience into a flock of seagulls—very childhood modern dance class.*)

Okay, do you see her, she's right over there, show her our flock, is she watching us yet, great, we're a flock of seagulls…keep going, flap those wings…flap them! Flap!

(CHELSEA *looks up from her crying.*)

CHELSEA. Oh—oh—do I see what I see? Do my eyes deceive me?

(DEVIN *leads the gulls so that they surround her in a circle of seagull love.*)

There are seagulls all over me! I'm living in the sky! I'm in the sky! What majestic birds! You're a majestic creature!

DEVIN. (*Flapping his arms like a seagull.*) I'm sorry for all the mean things I said. I love you Chelsea Cooley!

CHELSEA. I love you Devin! Even if I never get my painting back, I'm happy to have you babe!

(*They kiss. She jumps on his back and they become one two-headed seagull.*) We're a we-gull!!

(*Everyone applauds. The* COMMISSIONER *maybe even has a tear in his eye.* COMMISSIONER *gathers his recruits back in the center of the floor.*)

COMMISSIONER. All right, peoples, let's give the couple some privacy. I'm all for the happy times, but let's not forget that this girl here, she is the owner of that there painting, and that painting is still missing, and Paul Vista is still at large. And we're not gonna sleep till we catch him and make him pay and make him give this lady her painting thing back. Am I right, or am I right?

(*Continue here with "ACT 4C—Alternate Ending" as seen in the body of the script.*)

APPENDIX:
Act 1 Loops, Texts, and Suggestions For Improv During Party.

Act 1 is set up as an interactive party—when the audience arrives, they are immersed in a whole world, already in progress. These lists and scraps of text are part of the fabric of this world; they are a record of what we performed in Louisville. The goal is twofold: to create a party atmosphere with its own reality, and to set up character and style expectations to prepare the audience for the rest of the show.

Some characters have audience interaction as their primary party activity; others have scenes with each other that are meant to be caught out of the corner of your eye.

These lists are by no means complete—every single one of our 22 amazing actors filled in the world in their own way; each time I watched the show I delighted in seeing new little bits, gags, and details that I had never noticed before. Performers are encouraged to fully inhabit the skins of their characters and to be fully present in the "now," the present moment of the ridiculous things that are happening, to engage the audience in wild and particular ways, and to create new "bits" with other characters to flesh out the world of the play.

Suggestions for Audience Interaction
(by Character; in rough order of entrance).

CHELSEA COOLEY: The owner of the Pellago and our hostess for the evening, Chelsea begins the party as a greeter, and welcomes every audience member to her soiree. (Well, okay, it was her father who purchased the Pellago and donated it to the museum. But Chelsea acts like it's hers.) As various VIPs arrive, she calls out for Alice, her voice ringing across the space and causing Alice to scurry at her beck and call. As a notable member of the local community, she also has personal relationships with some of the guests and is given to exclaiming her love for everyone and everybody—most especially Devin, her performance artist boyfriend. The perfect hostess, there is nothing Chelsea enjoys more than circulating the party, making sure that everyone is having a wonderful time.

ALICE WEATHERS: Alice begins the party as a greeter, but is soon called away to make sure that everything is okay on the ground, what with the FBI scaring her party guests and the national art press descending to issue judgment—plus her own employees who show up late and seeking to undermine her at every turn, not to mention hapless janitor Andy Poole who never seems to be doing a good job. Alice deals with all of the above while also seeking out VIPs in the audience (or, just regular folk and treating them like VIPs) to show off parts of the 21c collection. Alice is an expert on the art, and nothing gives her more pleasure than talking about Pellago and the other artists with the audience. Unfortunately, she's always being called away to put out one fire or another, so these conversations often get cut short.

DIANE WORTHINGBOTTOM: As the proud Assistant Curator, Diane is an excellent docent, gathering groups of audience members for detailed and highly informative guided tours of the 21c collection. She is key for creating a sense that this is a nationally important museum, and that the Pellago is the most important piece the museum has acquired. She has trouble disguising her distaste for Alice, and her sense that she should have had the head curator's job; other thorns in her side are the janitor Andy Poole, who is always tripping; the new hire, Tanya Feldman, who showed up late; and her deadbeat ex-husband Carl Weathers, who is part of the security forces.

TANYA STEIMER FELDMAN: Poor Tanya. Her first week on the job, and she's already showed up late to the biggest event that 21c has ever hosted. She makes a dramatic entrance, racing past the security guards and bolting down the stairs, looking for Alice and Diane, both of whom bark at her. Tanya leads tours of the art collection, focusing particularly on the Pellago and how excited she is to be working near one. She gets lost on one of her tours, leading the group back to the mysterious room called the *Unterschlupf*, which just might be the lair of an evil German magician…but Tanya just thinks it's more kooky contemporary art and apologizes for not knowing more about the gems of the 21c collection.

ANDY POOLE: The hapless janitor, can't get anything right. Spends the party being ordered around by Alice and Diane, who always have three things they need done in the next two minutes. Andy is often seen politely navigating his way through the thickest part of the crowd, carrying a mop and bucket, trying to be unobtrusive but failing miserably. Of course, what nobody yet knows is that Andy is the most inside of the inside men, and is also helping Clarence Franklin hack into the 21c security system and helping Victor Kusik load Justice into the bourbon barrel.

COMMISSIONER JEFFERSON WASHINGTON FRANKLIN: The Commissioner tries to stay on top of all the security forces—Penelope Francis, Kate Shapiro, and Carl Weathers—but mostly succeeds in making a lot of noise. He loudly harasses his son, Clarence, embarrassing them both; reunites with his old flame, the sexy ex-stripper Justice; and performs "random security checks" which only succeed in making people feel uncomfortable, rather than safe.

CARL WEATHERS: Carl is present almost from the very beginning, briefing the audience on the high levels of security and the threat that looms over the party. While the audience waits on line to get their tickets, he gives them the rundown about Paul Vista, Archie Pellago, and the extreme security measures that have been taken to protect the art…so nobody should worry. He performs "random security checks," mostly of cute girls, stalks his ex-wife Diane Worthingbottom, and asks the audience to keep on the trail of the mysterious Russians.

LUKE MICHAEL CHRISTIANSON: Luke is here to spread the word of Jesus, but he's also the most joyful, fun-loving dude you've ever met. Luke interacts with characters and audience with equal enthusiasm, snapping photos with his phone (which he then texts to people, so they have a souvenir of the experience); compliments people's shoes and hairstyles; and leads small group aerobics in the hallway. He gathers a group for his own private Christian-themed tour of the art, and his tour accidentally discovers the *Unterschlupf*. Returning to the party, he tries to tell the docents, the curators, and law enforcement; but everyone is so obsessed with the Pellago that he is ignored.

DEVIN THE GREAT: Chelsea's art-world arm candy, Devin sees the party as his great opportunity to get in with the in-crowd, to get his face seen and his work known by the 21c staff and all the local art world luminaries. Unfortunately, nobody has any time for him, and all of his efforts to introduce himself are coldly rebuffed. Chelsea adores him, and introduces him to everybody and everyone; they even make out in the middle of the party. Like, multiple times. But this isn't enough for Devin, and over the course of the party, he gets increasingly frustrated with the scene and what he considers its inferior aesthetic values. He ends up recruiting his own "bootleg" tour of the art, showing a select group of audience members his own personal faves in the collection. When they find their way to the *Unterschlupf*, he thinks its weird German nihilism is the coolest thing he has ever seen, and bemoans Alice Weathers' lack of sophistication, sticking this work of genius in a back hallway where almost no one will ever see it rather than highlighting it as a seminal work of art.

TIMOTHY WYATT: Fresh off the plane from New York, the art critic everyone loves to hate has happily shaved and showered in his room at 21c Museum Hotel; Timothy enters the party with high hopes. However, these hopes are quickly dashed when he encounters the pedestrian and overbearing hosts, Chelsea and Alice. His heart sinks more when he regards the terrible fashion choices of so many Louisvillians. His heart sinks even more when Diane and Alice brazenly suck up to him. It's on the floor when the annoying German magician tries to pitch "magic" as "art." The one person who catches his eye is the drop-dead gorgeous Q, whom he spies sketching one of the photographs. He tries in vain to flirt, practically chasing her from one exhibit to the next.

CLARISSA: Video blogger extraordinaire, charming Clarissa is a fixture of the downtown scene, covering all the latest concerts, exhibits, and parties. Her shtick is that she does person-on-the-street interviews about their impressions and feelings about the event—of the "Everyone having a good time??" variety. Clarissa is a key to creating the party atmosphere, and to engaging with as many audience members as possible. Questions include "Where are you from?" "What do you think of Louisville so far?" and of course, "So is that Pellago rad or what?"

PENELOPE FRANCIS: Assigned to be the woman-on-the-ground by the FBI Special Task Force on Art Theft, Pen zealously guards the Pellago, pacing its perimeter and telling people to back off. Of course, her diligence is meant to communicate the extreme importance of the little tiny work of art behind the red curtain. She also keeps an eye out for members of the Vista Seven as they arrive, communicating with Kate Shapiro via Bluetooth and asking audience members if they have noticed anything suspicious (thus pointing out the thieves in the crowd).

KATE SHAPIRO: Direct from London, representing Europol, Kate Shapiro is a security maniac, asking to see people's ID's and interrogating them ("Did you pack your bags yourself?" "Did anyone ask you to carry anything for them into the party?" etc.). She spots each member of the Vista Seven as they arrive, growing increasingly dogged as they increase in number. She communicates with Pen via Bluetooth to make sure that they know the whereabouts of each member of the Heist team throughout the duration of the party.

HANS H.H.G. SCHMIDT: The tireless German performs simple magic tricks for anyone who will watch, usually gathering a small crowd around to watch him perform sleight of hand tricks with red foam balls, red ropes, and playing cards. He seems to be stuck in a time warp where the Nazis are still an active threat, and he thus takes great pride in his German heritage. He also is aware of being followed by Boris Pengurovich, and tries to drop him. As part of his act, he tells the audience to keep an eye on "that Russian boy." He desperately wants magic to be taken seriously as an art form and so tries to get Timothy Wyatt to pay attention…to no avail. This just feeds his rage, which he feeds into his art, making the stories he tells about the red foam balls and red strings even more violent and disturbing. Watching his magic show, you don't know whether to laugh…or call the cops.

BORIS and TATIANA PENGUROVICH: The seemingly evil Russian twins are caught in a time warp of their own, refugees from a 1960s spy thriller. As they prowl the party, looking for the Red Penguin, they make the unfortunate discovery that there are, in fact, dozens if not hundreds of Red Penguins all over 21c. They show photos of their Penguin ("Have you seen this Penguin?") to audience members, and are thus always pointed in a different direction. While Boris trails Hans Schmidt, Tatiana flirts with Clarence Franklin, trying to get access to the roof; by the end of the party, the siblings are certain that their only hope is the man with the discerning eye: Timothy Wyatt…and so they plot to kidnap him in order to save the world.

CLARENCE FRANKLIN: A quiet computer science student, Clarence spends most of the party working away on his laptop or trying to find a strong wireless signal somewhere in the building. While it looks like he's playing World of Warcraft, he is actually hacking into the 21c security system and making sure that everything is in place for Justice and Q to get into the vault. His biggest obstacles are his father, the Commissioner, who is hassling him to get offline and into the world; Tatiana, who comes on strong and invites him to the roof; and his own desire to meet cute girls. He asks women in the audience for their phone numbers and then will text them throughout the course of the show (we had a directing assistant send these texts). But every time he seems to be making progress, his dad interrupts and embarrasses him.

Q: The notorious art forger is always practicing her skills, visiting the gallery with an artist's eye and sketching what she likes. She strikes up an unusual flirtation with Timothy Wyatt, who quickly falls under her seductive spell, and speaks French with Tatiana about whether the Red Penguins are art. She checks in with Paul and Dusty at the bar; goes on Tanya's tour to learn more about the art, asking smart questions; and talks to the audience about the impressive 21c collection.

JUSTICE: Upon arriving, Justice instantly catches the eye of the law enforcement officers—Carl can't wait to frisk her, and Commissioner Franklin remembers her from a time in his distant past. She goes on Diane's tour; throws back drinks with the Commissioner; and checks in with Paul and Dusty at the bar. All this, of course, before she hides inside a bourbon barrel.

VICTOR: The consummate inside man, Victor takes his duties as Special Events Manager very seriously. Keeping the bourbon stocked, keeping the patrons happy, keeping Andy occupied…all in a day's work. He also strikes up a friendship with Alice and they take a smoke break together…until the moment comes for him to stash Justice in a bourbon barrel and sneak her into the secret vault.

PAUL VISTA and DUSTY PRESS: literally spend the entire duration of the party, before their entrance, at the Proof bar in the lobby of 21c, doing nothing but looking cool…which, in this world, is everything.

Selected Character Interaction Texts.

Here are some of the little snippets of text created by the ensemble for the scenarios mentioned above. Some of these were performed on loops; some were stand-alone scenes. No audience member ever saw all of these; probably each audience member saw just a few.

They are presented here in a very rough chronological order; well, as chronological as is possible when there are so many things happening at once.

Alice pre-scene with Chelsea

At the ticket pick-up table. Maybe even before anyone arrives.

ALICE. Are you excited?

CHELSEA. I'm excited, are you excited?

ALICE. I am.

CHELSEA. Are you ready?

ALICE. I am, are you?

CHELSEA. Let's give birth to our art baby!

(*Etc.—ad-libbing as audience arrives.*)

Alice and Chelsea Welcome Timothy

TIMOTHY *arrives with the first audience members, is greeted by* CHELSEA (*who doesn't know who he is*).

CHELSEA. Hi! Welcome to 21c, I'm Chelsea Cooley, and this is my party, it's for the Pellago my daddy bought me!

TIMOTHY. I'm looking for Alice Weathers?

CHELSEA. (*Screaming across the gallery floor.*) Alice! Alice! ALLLL-IIIIIIIICE!

(ALICE *comes running from wherever she is.*)

ALICE. (*Seeing* TIMOTHY WYATT, *is mortified.*) Yes, hi, I'm Alice Weathers?

TIMOTHY. Timothy Wyatt.

ALICE. Oh! Hello, so nice to meet you.

CHELSEA. You're Timothy Wyatt! She knows all about you. We've been eagerly awaiting your arrival.

ALICE. (*To* TIMOTHY.) We spoke on the phone.

TIMOTHY. I know.

CHELSEA. I'm Chelsea Cooley, and I paid for ALL of this! She made me read everything that you wrote, we are so honored to have you here, you are just fantastic!

ALICE. Okay, all right, thanks Chelsea.

CHELSEA. She is such a big fan of yours. I can't wait to read what you write about our party! This is so exciting!

ALICE. Okay, great, well um here's your press packet, there should be a badge in there…come with me, let me get you oriented to the space. The kick-off event will be at about 11:20… It's really very exciting, I must say, when

I was recruited for 21c I wasn't sure about the collection but it's really quite substantial... (*Etc.*)

(ALICE *and* TIMOTHY *go downstairs.*)

Alice Welcomes Clarissa

CLARISSA *enters, her camera already on.* CLARISSA *narrates everything she does.* (*"All right, everybody, now I am AT the Pellago opening, I'm walking through the lobby, I'm gonna pick up my rad press packet now, think they'll give me a sticker...?"*)

CLARISSA. (*To* CHELSEA.) Hey! What's up! It's Clarissa!

CHELSEA. Welcome! This is 21c...

CLARISSA. I know, yo! I'm Clarissa! I'm here to be Explaining It All for you! You got my press pack? (*Into her camera—*) Hey, I'm here now, I'm just arriving at 21c for the big Archie Pellago opening, and I'm about to get my press packet...this is so cool. Say hello to the nice welcome lady—

CHELSEA. (*Smiling into camera.*) Hello! Welcome!

CLARISSA. Say what's up Louisville!

CHELSEA. What's up Louisville! I'm Chelsea Cooley, welcome to my party!

CLARISSA. So, uh, can I get my press badge?

CHELSEA. Alice! Alice! Just one moment...

CLARISSA. So you think Paul Vista is gonna be here?

CHELSEA. We're trying to stay positive. Alice! ALLLLLL-IIIIIIIIICE!

(ALICE *returns—*)

ALICE. Chelsea?

CHELSEA. This is—

CLARISSA. Clarissa! You're Alice, awesome. We e-mailed!

ALICE. Oh. Right. Of course—here's your press packet, and down there is—

CLARISSA. The Pellago. Awesome.

ALICE. Do you need us to set anything up for you?

CLARISSA. Nope, I'm cool. Thanks. (*Into her camera—*) Now I am entering the party...the Pellago is behind a whole crazy security contraption, let's go check it out, yo...

(CLARISSA *goes downstairs, narrating as she goes.*)

Tanya Enters, Late

TANYA *flies through the doorway and races downstairs.*

TANYA. Hi Chelsea, hi, sorry, excuse me, sorry, I'm late.

(CARL *tries to check her in.*)

CARL. Ma'am? Ma'am! Sorry, I'm going to have to randomly security check you before you go in there.

TANYA. No thank you, sorry, maybe later—

> (*She runs to find* ALICE.)

Hi—hi—Alice, sorry I'm—

ALICE. Go find Diane, she'll get you set up.

Devin Arrives

> DEVIN *arrives, surveys the scene. He strides right up to the front of the line and swoops into* CHELSEA *for a surprise kiss.*

DEVIN. Hey babe.

CHELSEA. Devin! You're here! Isn't this amazing!

DEVIN. Big crowd, huh?

CHELSEA. I know! It's such a total success! (*Calls out over the atrium.*) Alice! ALICE!! Devin's here! Devin! (*Back with him.*) Hi baby I'm so so so happy to see you!

DEVIN. I'll have to bite your brain later about the guest list.

CHELSEA. Totally! I'm so excited!

DEVIN. I'm gonna take a look around…

CHELSEA. Make sure you see the cartoon rooms! They're so cool! I'm telling everybody!

DEVIN. You know I was up for that job.

CHELSEA. I know, Sweetie. But that doesn't mean that Adam and René didn't do a very good job.

DEVIN. I'll check it out, okay?

CHELSEA. You better! And I want a cucumber shake!

DEVIN. Catch you later.

CHELSEA. Love you honey muffin!

Penelope Arrives

> *All business,* PENELOPE *checks in with* CHELSEA, *mistaking her for someone important…or at least someone who knows what the hell is going on. In other words, not* CHELSEA.

PEN. Hi, I'm Penelope Francis, from the FBI, we spoke on the phone.

CHELSEA. Oh you must have spoken to Alice. Alice! ALICE! The FBI is here!

> (ALICE *comes up to help.*)

ALICE. Hello? Hi, I'm Alice Weathers, Curator of Special Exhibitions here at 21c.

PEN. Penelope Francis, Federal Bureau of Investigation.

ALICE. I didn't realize the FBI was going to—is the threat that serious?

PEN. I'm not at liberty to discuss.

ALICE. All right…well then come with me, I'll show you to the painting, and we have some local law enforcement…somewhere around here…

CHELSEA. Enjoy the party!

(ALICE and PEN go downstairs, where ALICE brings her to the Pellago.)

Chelsea Welcomes Luke

LUKE CHRISTIANSON *arrives, greets* CHELSEA.

LUKE. *(Calling out from across the room.)* Chelsea Cooley!

CHELSEA. Oh my God! How are you! So glad you decided to come!

LUKE. Thank you so much for your donation to the SPCA.

CHELSEA. I love puppies!

LUKE. We're all God's creatures.

CHELSEA. Especially you.

LUKE. Aw, you're the best, Chelsea Cooley.

CHELSEA. No, you are! Go, get yourself a drink, there's so much to see!

LUKE. You guys got any Sprite? Awesome!

(He bounds down the stairs and into the party.)

Kate Arrives

KATE SHAPIRO *arrives and checks in with* CHELSEA.

KATE. Hi there, hello, I'm Kate Shapiro, from Interpol, I'm looking for Commissioner Franklin.

CHELSEA. Oh! Interpol, that's in Europe, right?

KATE. I'm based in Scotland Yard, yes.

CHELSEA. Fascinating! Alice! ALICE! Interpol is here!!!

(ALICE scurries over and brings KATE into the party.)

Carl Frisks Justice

CARL *randomly security checks a particularly game visitor, who makes him blush.*

As JUSTICE *enters the party,* CARL *summons her over.*

CARL. Ma'am? Ma'am, excuse me, I'm gonna have to check you.

JUSTICE. You wanna check me out? Go right ahead, big boy…

CARL. It's a random selection.

JUSTICE. Yep, looks random to me.

CARL. Just doing my job. Spread your legs hip-width apart.

JUSTICE. Me too, I'm just doin' my job…

CARL. Arms against the wall.

JUSTICE. Whoa—whoa—watch yourself, mister.

CARL. All right, all set.

JUSTICE. Got twenty bucks? You can do it again.

CARL. All right then, enjoy the party.

JUSTICE. I'm already enjoying the party.

(JUSTICE *winks at him and goes.* CARL *is flustered, and tries to hide it from everyone else waiting on line.*)

Clarissa and Devin

Across the crowd, CLARISSA *spots her old friend* DEVIN *from art school.*

CLARISSA. No, shit, it's Devin The Great! Hell no, what are you doing here? How'd you get on the guest list?

DEVIN. It's my lady's party.

CLARISSA. I don't get it.

DEVIN. Chelsea and me. We're kind of a thing.

CLARISSA. You're shitting me.

DEVIN. (*Shrugs.*)

CLARISSA. Good for you, man, good for you.

DEVIN. Did you go to the Morrissey concert?

CLARISSA. Yeah I did, I freaking interviewed you, remember?

DEVIN. Oh, yeah, yeah…

CLARISSA. I gotta go get more footage. See you around?

DEVIN. Sure.

CLARISSA. Don't forget your friends the little people when you become a big art star…

DEVIN. I won't.

(*Disappointed, she turns and interviews someone else.*)

Diane Sucks Up To Timothy

TIMOTHY *is taking notes on a painting or photograph.*

DIANE. Timothy Wyatt?

TIMOTHY. Indeed, I am.

DIANE. Hi, I'm Diane Worthingbottom, I'm Assistant Curator here at 21c.

TIMOTHY. Quite a collection you have here.

DIANE. Is something not to your liking?

TIMOTHY. It's this frame, there's something…off.

DIANE. Off?

TIMOTHY. Crooked.

DIANE. I'll get someone to take care of it. Not everyone has such a sophisticated ...eye...as you.

TIMOTHY. I know.

DIANE. I'm a big follower of your column.

TIMOTHY. I have many followers.

DIANE. I'm sure you do, you're quite deserving.

TIMOTHY. Be a dear and get someone to fix the alignment on this frame, would you? I'm having a case of vertigo.

DIANE. Wouldn't want you to fall over—in the middle of the big Pellago opening—

TIMOTHY. You certainly would not.

(*He walks away. She swoons.*)

Tatiana and Boris—Good News

After each finding a Red Penguin, the RUSSIAN SIBLINGS *find each other to share their good news.*

BORIS. I have good news for you.

TATIANA. I have good news for you.

BORIS. You first.

TATIANA. No, no, you.

BORIS. No, you.

TATIANA. Together.

BOTH. I have found the Penguin. No, I found the Penguin. What?

BORIS. We have problem.

TATIANA. Very big problem.

BORIS. Who will know?

TATIANA. I have idea. The art man.

BORIS. (*Describes* DEVIN, *whatever* DEVIN *is wearing.*) With the ascot? And the hair?

TATIANA. No, the grumpy art man. With the eye.

BORIS. Oh. Yes. This is good.

(*They go out in search of* TIMOTHY WYATT.)

Devin Pitches Art To Alice

While ALICE *is in the middle of a hundred different things,* DEVIN *tries to ask her about the art he submitted to the museum. Now is obviously not the right time for this, but* DEVIN *doesn't have the best sense of propriety.*

DEVIN. Hey, Alice—

ALICE. Oh, hey Devin…

DEVIN. Did you get my slides?

ALICE. What? Oh—right, yeah, yep, got them on my desk.

DEVIN. Cool, cool, so, what do you think about…

ALICE. Can we talk about this tomorrow?

> (*She walks away.* DEVIN *is extremely frustrated and talks shit about* ALICE *to anyone who will listen.*)

Justice and Commissioner

Entering the party, JUSTICE *sees her old friend "Frankie" across the room. Weirdly, he's dressed up like a cop.*

JUSTICE. Jefferson Franklin? I don't believe it! Frankie!

COMMISSIONER. What what?

JUSTICE. No shit! It's me! Patty Jay! Justice? Remember?

COMMISSIONER. No way! Look at you!

JUSTICE. Look at me? Look at you! What are you doing dressed up like a cop?

COMMISSIONER. I *am* a cop.

JUSTICE. Yeah right, what is this, Dress Up Tuesday?

COMMISSIONER. No, no, I really am—

JUSTICE. Nice one, Frankie. You want a drink?

COMMISSIONER. Not right now—I'm in charge of this thing—

JUSTICE. Sure you are. Meet you by the bar in five?

COMMISSIONER. (*He can't resist her.*) …okay…

Diane and Clarissa

While DIANE *is giving a docent tour,* CLARISSA *recognizes her.*

CLARISSA. Hey! I know you! University of Louisville!

DIANE. No shit, Clarissa!

CLARISSA. How's it going, girl?

DIANE. Good, good, you know, staying alive.

CLARISSA. Totally.

DIANE. Are you filming here?

CLARISSA. Sure am. Catch you later.

Timothy and Q

Q and TIMOTHY *are at the same photograph, taking notes. (Note: these are three mini-scenes, which happen in different corners of the room.)*

TIMOTHY. Hard to concentrate with all this noise.

(*She looks at him like—Uh, now you're making noise too.*
He looks over her shoulder at her sketch.)

TIMOTHY. (*With disdain.*) Ohh…you're an artist.

(*She looks at his notepad.*)

Q. (*With even more disdain, in French.*) <u>Ohh…you are a critic</u>.

TIMOTHY. (*In bad French.*) *Vous etes Francaise?*

Q. (*In French.*) <u>Yes, I am. And you are American?</u>

TIMOTHY. Stupid question, huh?

Q. (*In English.*) Yes. Very stupid question.

(*She walks away from him. He keeps trying to talk to her and they flirt two more
times in front of two other paintings.*
Later, at a different part of the exhibit.)

TIMOTHY. So…you speak French?

Q. *Oui, bien sur.* Where I'm from, everyone speaks French.

TIMOTHY. Which would make you from…

Q. (*Bad American accent.*) France.

(*She walks away.*
Even later:)

TIMOTHY. Despite your tacky shoes, I think I may love you.

Q. Interesting. Because the shoes are Laboutin and they find you compellingly
tedious.

(*She gives him a sketch of a penguin and walks away. He melts.*)

Diane and Carl

CARL *calls out across the room while* DIANE *is in the middle of a tour.*

CARL. (*Yelling across the room.*) Stop that tour!

(*He barrel rolls over to the docent group.*)

DIANE. (*To tour.*) Jesus Christ. Sorry, people. Ignore him.

CARL. Diane.

DIANE. Not now.

CARL. It's a serious situation.

DIANE. I'm not supposed to talk about Vista.

CARL. Not that.

DIANE. What.

CARL. It's private.

DIANE. I'm at work, Carl.

CARL. So am I.

DIANE. Yeah, I know.

(*She yanks him close and they whisper in angry tones—we can't totally hear them but the gist is basically that* DIANE *stopped sending alimony checks now that* CARL *has a job, but he still wants her to send the checks. Awkward. Finally,* DIANE *pulls away—*)

No, Carl, you can't have it both ways, that was that point of you getting a JOB, remember— (*To tour.*) Sorry about that. Some people expect the world to give them handouts. Now, as I was saying…

(*She leads the group away, leaving* CARL *behind.*)

Tatiana and Clarence

CLARENCE *is working on his laptop in the back of the room.* TATIANA *leans over his shoulder to look. He tries to shield the screen but then notices that she is the most beautiful woman he has ever seen.*

TATIANA. What is this?

CLARENCE. Uh—uh—it's a game—

TATIANA. This is movie?

CLARENCE. Sort of…

TATIANA. This is 21c. This is roof. This is Penguins.

CLARENCE. Um—

TATIANA. Yes or no. Roof. Penguins. You know it?

CLARENCE. Well, uh, sure, there are penguins everywhere—

TATIANA. Roof. I need roof. Zoom in.

(*She starts poking at the keyboard.*)

CLARENCE. Hey—hey—hold up. Okay. Here.

TATIANA. Yes. Good. You tell me how to go there.

CLARENCE. You just go in the elevator, and then there's a door, it's probably locked, there's a computer system—

TATIANA. You know how to unlock? With computer?

CLARENCE. Sort of, yeah—

TATIANA. Good. You show me.

CLARENCE. I can't right now…

TATIANA. We go now. To roof.

CLARENCE. Maybe later? Can I—do you have a phone number? I can call you—

TATIANA. Now. Big things happen on the roof.

(*He follows her.*)

Hans Schmidt's Magic Show

HANS *gathers an audience for his magic act. This is just an outline for a sense of timing and tone—there is a lot of ad-lib here, depending on the tricks chosen.*

HANS. *Guten tag,* I am Hans Schmidt, and this is magic.

(*He sets up the foam ball trick.*)

Please hold this ball in your hand if you will, thank you...My mother, she loved this trick. Mama, Mama.... Now connect with me, look in my beautiful German eyes.... Good, good. *Schweinsteiger!*

(*Now there are two balls where there was one.*)

Oh! Two! This is the part where you clap. You figured that out *ja?*

(*The audience claps.*

He continues with the trick of having multiple sponge balls appear in an audience member's hand.

Next: the rope trick.)

Three ropes, *ja?* You see them? This was my mother's favorite trick, may her soul rest in peace.... The short rope, this will be yours, Sir. You take the long, you take medium...good, good. Make sure they are not magical ropes, they don't stretch, no tricks up my sleeve ha ha...

(*He makes the ropes the same length, and then reveals them again to be the different lengths. Magic! Applause, etc.*)

Before you go, I have a question for you. Have you seen that Russian boy following me? Over there. You know the Russian with the stupid haircut? No? Very suspicious. Very very suspicious. Just keep an eye out for him. And if you do that, I will do one more trick for you...in about eight minutes, I'm going to make all of Louisville disappear. Yes indeed. See you then. Or perhaps, not.

(*Applause. He goes and finds a new audience for his tricks.*)

Alice and Victor Take a Smoke Break

As things get going, ALICE *might relax enough to take a smoke break with the only employee she can stand,* VICTOR.

ALICE *finds* VICTOR *by the bar.*

ALICE. Do you have any cigarettes?

VICTOR. Sure—

ALICE. You want to—?

VICTOR. (*To bartender.*) I'm gonna take my break now.

(*They go for a walk-and-talk.*)

ALICE. Thanks—I didn't bring any today.

VICTOR. No problem.

ALICE. How are we on supplies?

VICTOR. Good, good.

ALICE. Is the bourbon all stocked?

VICTOR. We're good, we have Woodford Reserve out and there's about twenty more barrels in the storage unit.

ALICE. Good, good…maybe we should bring out a backup, people seem to be hitting it hard, which is good I guess it's a party as long as no one gets rowdy ha ha…

VICTOR. Sure, sure.

ALICE. Just don't be obvious about it, you know, I hate when the mechanics of the party are made visible.

VICTOR. Of course.

ALICE. Bring it in the back, okay?

VICTOR. Got it.

THE CARTOONS.

After arriving, looking at the art, and getting their drinks, the audience is encouraged to watch three cartoons, which can be viewed in any order. The scripts for these animations are as follows.

Animation #1: 36 Years Ago.
PAUL + THE COMMISSIONER – THE EARLY YEARS.

TITLE CARD: Louisville, KY—Yesterday.

VOICEOVER. As far as tales of rivals go,
I thought I'd heard them all:
Of enemies and frenemies,
Games won and lost;
Heartbreak caused by lovers, by siblings,
By plain old down and dirty foes
History's full of stories worth repeating—but this one,
I believe,
This one more than most.

INT. COMMISSIONER's OFFICE—DUSK.

COMMISSIONER FRANKLIN *at his big wood desk in his big noir-ish office. He has a big mustache and chomps his ever-present cigar. He reads a TOP-SECRET FILE.*

Caption: THE ACTUAL REAL-LIFE LOUISVILLE METRO POLICE DEPT.

VO. This is the tale of
Jefferson Washington Franklin,
Louisville's own Policeman in Chief.
A quixotic original devoted to law,
Especially the arrest
Of one crooked thief.

COMMISSIONER. Vista!

PAUL. Hey…

CLOSE on the newspaper headline: "PAUL VISTA, CELEBRITY THIEF, RELEASED."

The content we can see of the newspaper article: "Paris, France, Yesterday. Beloved celebrity thief Paul Vista was released from jail here yesterday due to lack of evidence and gross negligence on the part of Interpol, Europol, Scotland Yard, and the Louisville Metro Police Department of Louisville, KY..."

VO. Paul Vista's his name,
And he's known around town
As Franklin's adversary,
The cause of all strife
A lover, a fighter,
A charming young man—
Paul famously gave Franklin
The worst day of his life:

The first one.

In a town known for horses,
For bourbon, for baseball bats;
For drama and hot browns
And big derby hats;
On a bright spring day,
Two babies were born
Not two minutes apart,
Two little boys
Who give our story its heart.

You see, on the day of their birth,
One boy got lucky...

Nurses, doctors, and photographers swarm around a smiling baby boy: BABY PAUL. He smiles a gleaming smile. Sparkles shoot out from teeth.

VOICES. (*Overlapping—a crowd.*)Oh he's so beautiful! Congratulations! Oh look at that smile. What a beautiful baby boy! Here, can I have your autograph? Can I hold him? Oh smile for the camera itty bitty baby waby! Do you want to take my car?

To the side, on the ground, on a dirty blanket: BABY COMMISSIONER sits in a diaper, totally ignored. He already has his mustache and is reaching out for a stray discarded congratulatory cigar that has been dropped by the celebratory crowds.

VOICE. Well you certainly have the very most beautiful baby boy that has EVER been born in this hospital in the HISTORY of the world of ALL TIME, EVER!

VO. And one boy, well, not.

BABY COMMISSIONER chomps on the cigar.

BABY COMMISSIONER. Vista!

BABY PAUL. Hey...

VO. This day set the pattern
That continued for years.
Paul's daily routine
Got nothing but cheers.

COMMISSIONER *as crossing guard; in the background a car approaches spraying mud in its wake.*

VO. So what's a little corner cut
When you've got hands to hold?

PAUL *knocks* COMMISSIONER *out of the way to escort a* GIRL *across the street; in this image the car is closer, spewing mud.*

VO. Paul's bending and breaking the rules
Left Franklin ice cold.

COMMISSIONER *splashed with mud, the car now past—*PAUL *and the* GIRL *safely and cleanly on the other side of the street, holding hands. Hearts.*

VO. And so, while Vista won hearts and minds,
Franklin sang a different song.

COMMISSIONER *sweating a really hard math problem while* PAUL *flirts with the girl at the next desk over, switching their papers...*

VO. In reading, writing, and arithmetic,
He saw nothing but wrongs
To be righted and rules to be fixed.
As time passed, he cried foul
In the face of Paul's tricks.

COMMISSIONER *stands proudly by a lemonade stand. The neatly printed sign reads: "Lemonade, 40¢"*

PAUL *with a flashy lemonade stand. Sign reads "Lemmin-aid $4.75." Lines of kids around the block.* PAUL *is there handing a* PRETTY GIRL *lemonade in a martini glass.*

COMMISSIONER. Vista!

PAUL. Hey...

COMMISSIONER, *deflated and scowling, his sign now reads:*
"Lemonade ~~40¢,~~
~~30¢~~
~~25¢~~
~~15¢~~
~~free~~
~~please~~
I'll pay you."

VO. Yes, whatever he did,
Wherever he went
He was determined to straighten
Every rule bent
By that Vista, that fool,
That charlatan of charm,
Who got by with some improvisation...
And a hot girl on his arm.

PAUL *hitting on a group of* GIRLS.

PAUL. Hey...

GIRLS. (*Giggling.*)

COMMISSIONER *as hall monitor gallantly opening a door for a cute girl. Moments later,* PAUL VISTA *and the* GIRL *under a banner reading*

"Homecoming King and Queen," mobbed by other kids like paparazzi—
autograph-seekers, photographers, etc.

VO. And so, the years passed,
And as adulthood approached
Young Franklin set his sight
On being Policeman in Chief

COMMISSIONER *sweating through a grueling physical exam at
Louisville Police Academy.*

VO. While Paul...well, Paul found
That living was easiest
Living the life of a thief.

PAUL *as a cat burglar in the Harvard Admissions Office, stealing
the SAT scores of "Barry Obama" and "Steve Jobs" and "Bill Gates."*

COMMISSIONER *as security guard while* PAUL *gives the Harvard
valedictory speech.*

Montage of headlines, all including glamour pics of PAUL
VISTA *through the years:*
   "CAT BURGLAR SUSPECTED IN ROME"
   "CARD SHARK ALSO SUSPECTED LADIES' MAN"
   "CELEBRITY THIEF DOES IT AGAIN"
   "VISTA TOPS PEOPLE's *50 MOST BEAUTIFUL PEOPLE LIST—AGAIN!"*
   "FORBES TOP 100 MOST SUCCESSFUL INTERNATIONAL ART THIEVES"

VO. But everything that's easy
Eventually comes with a price.
At least that's what Franklin believes...

CLOSE on COMMISSIONER's *eyes.*

VO. Now Commissioner For Life.

PAN OUT from COMMISSIONER's *EYE and we see that it's the
grown-up* COMMISSIONER, *in his office as at the beginning,
looking out the window at 21c. His gaze turns to his desk
and a placard on the desk: "COMMISSIONER FOR LIFE."*

END.

Animation #2: 6 Years Ago.
THE HEIST THAT FAILED.

TITLE CARD: Paris, France—6 years ago.

*A nostalgic, fictional skyline of Paris emerges, crowding
many of Paris's key landmarks into one strip: the Eiffel
Tower, Arc de Triomphe, Champs Elysees, etc.*

*As we track along the skyline, the sun in the sky rises and
sets in an arc, going from morning to night.*

and then...the LOUVRE.

SUPERIMPOSED: Musee de Louvre...

At the entrance to the Louvre is a WHITE VAN, from which
VICTOR *unloads a wine barrel.*

INT. DOMED GALLERY—NIGHT

*Archie's Prism, the famed and priceless piece of art, sits
on a pedestal in the middle of the domed gallery. The room*

is surrounded by arched doorways, all outfitted with lasers blocking entry.

The CAMERA pushes in on the art...

THEN, FROM THE CORNER OF THE FRAME, DUSTY's FACE SLIDES IN, OUTFITTED WITH A TELEMARKETING HEADSET.

DUSTY. How close are we ladies and gents? We only have about a minute left.

DUSTY blows a big bubblegum bubble real fast that fills the whole frame and POPS, causing the CAMERA to pull out of the domed room through an arched doorway and down a long hall through a series of lasers, an impossible stretch of space to cover.

FROM THE RIGHT CORNER OF THE FRAME, PAUL's FACE SLIDES IN, THE RED GLOW OF LASERS THROUGH HEAVY SMOKE THE ONLY THING ILLUMINATING HIS FACE. SLIGHT COUGHING CAN BE HEARD OFF-FRAME.

PAUL. (*Unsure.*) Ummmmmm, pretty close I would say.

FROM THE OTHER SIDE OF THE FRAME, BRICKS' FACE SLIDES INTO THE PICTURE.

BRICKS is an ancient-looking guy straight out of On The Waterfront. He's got a cigarette in his mouth and another tucked behind his ear and a third lit and ready to go in his hand; he brings it up to his mouth and takes a puff, filling his frame and PAUL's with smoke.

BRICKS. What's the guard situation Dusty? (*Cough cough.*)

PAUL. You okay, Bricks?

BRICKS. No problem. (*Cough cough.*)

WHIP PAN to an overhead shot of the halls of the Louvre, security guards walking their route. A "Family Circus"-style dotted line footprints their path on the hall floors.

DUSTY's FACE SLIDES INTO THE SIDE OF THE FRAME, STILL CHEWING GUM.

DUSTY. What's the guard sitch?

FROM THE OTHER SIDE OF THE FRAME, ANDY's FACE SLIDES IN, WEARING A GUARD'S HAT AND AN EARPIECE, BUT HIS FACE IS SHADOWED FROM THE HAT.

ANDY. 3...2...1...

In a wide shot, the guards pass a hallway that leads to the hallway with the lasers. The lasered hallway can be seen behind them as they pass it.

ANOTHER GUARD hears the INSIDE GUY and says "Quoi?" The CAMERA in the INSIDE GUY's FRAME goes to that GUARD quickly and then back to INSIDE GUY.

DUSTY reacts by pausing on a bubble she is blowing.

INSIDE GUY. Oh, *rien...*

DUSTY's BUBBLE POPS AGAIN, CHANGING THE LOCATION.

BRICKS is hunched over a device with glowing green numbers and he connects two wires, while blowing smoke over the whole affair. The lasers in the hallway turn off. BRICKS and PAUL run down the hallway, BRICKS lagging behind somewhat and wheezing slightly.

They get to the DOMED GALLERY and PAUL looks up toward the ceiling.

PAUL. Where's Justice?

WHIP PAN to the inside of the barrel that VICTOR brought in...
CORNER OF THE FRAME, VICTOR's FACE SLIDES IN.

VICTOR. I made sure the barrel would open easily...
The side of the barrel becomes transparent and we see JUSTICE inside banging on the top of it to get it out.

JUSTICE. Fricken Victor.

Finally the top pops off and we see a quick montage of close-ups, the camera just barely missing JUSTICE jumping through lasers, cat walking up air shafts and the like.

THEN, the CAMERA slowly pushes in to the dome of the gallery, a saw cutting a circle through from the top. The circular hole then drops the length of the gallery, but with a rope ladder attached, just falling short of the work of art in the center.

A big grin stretches across PAUL's face.

BRICKS is kneeling by the arched doors, disarming the last of the things that need disarming.

A TIMER starts in the corner of the frame, 15 SECONDS.

PAUL grabs the art.

PAUL. Let's go.

BRICKS does not respond. He clutches his chest, coughing.

PAUL. Shhh, shush. Bricks!

PAUL turns to BRICKS, and he is doubled over, grabbing at his chest.

PAUL. Bricks?

PAUL looks up toward the hole in the ceiling, JUSTICE looking down on him. PAUL looks toward BRICKS.

PAUL. Come on man.

PAUL looks toward the ladder. THE CLOCK IS TICKING.

PAUL leans down toward BRICKS and holds him in his arms. BRICKS dies, a victim of old age, bad health and this high-stress lifestyle.

FROM A CORNER OF THE FRAME, JUSTICE SLIDES IN, staring down the hole.

FROM ANOTHER CORNER, VICTOR slides in, listening intently through his earpiece.

FROM ANOTHER CORNER, INSIDE GUY slides in, still walking and holding his earpiece.

FROM ANOTHER CORNER, DUSTY slides in, slowly chewing gum.

THE CLOCK ticks down its final seconds, and DUSTY stops chewing her gum, all the frames of people dissolving out.

PAUL is holding BRICKS in his arms, the rope is dangling and suddenly, when the clock hits zero, the security systems kick in and steel doors begin slamming down in the arched doorways. Red light alarms begin flashing and sirens begin squealing. A bank of security monitors turn on, all pointed on PAUL and BRICKS on the floor. More doors slam shut, then...

JAIL BARS SLAM SHUT over PAUL's shrinking frame.

END.

Animation #3: 600 Years Ago.
THE RUSSIAN BACKSTORY.

Note: with the exception of the character-based images, all of the historical images in this film should be pulled from historic archival images—i.e., the photo of Lenin should be an instantly recognizable picture, digitally altered to include the Red Penguin.

Rousing military/historical epic music.

White letters on a black screen:
TRADITION.
HONOR.
HISTORY.
FAMILY.
RUSSIA.

PROFESSORIAL VOICEOVER. The fraught and storied history of the great nation of Russia might be best understood as an epic, centuries-old fight between the powerful and the powerless. And throughout this ongoing struggle, there has always been one individual present, for all the tumultuous tides of history, who remained standing proud and tall in even the strongest storm, who distinguished himself as a hero to both the haves and the have-nots.

This individual was known as *Krasny Pengvin*, translated roughly as: The Red Penguin.

Sometimes, the Red Penguin was in the foreground of history, politics, and culture...

SLIDE: THE PENGUIN LEADING A MOB DURING THE RUSSIAN REVOLUTION.

...and sometimes, he was a footnote.

SLIDE: POSTER OF DR. ZHIVAGO, with penguin in the bg.

But one fact bears repeating, known by all Russian schoolchildren, from Siberia to Brighton Beach: the Red Penguin was present at Ground Zero of every major development of Mother Russia.

SLIDE: RED PENGUIN WITH STALIN

SLIDE: PENGUIN-SHAPED BIRTHMARK ON GORBACHEV'S HEAD

But who is this Penguin, and what has happened to him since the dawn of Perestroika and the fall of the House of Yeltsin?

The secret might lie with one little-known family. You see, behind every great Penguin, there is a Pengurovich.

SLIDE: 1970S-ERA FAMILY PORTRAIT: TWO PARENTS, TWO GAP-TOOTHED BLONDE KIDS, AND THEIR PET RED PENGUIN, THE SIZE OF A SMALL CHILD

The Pengurovich clan—Pengurovich roughly translates as "Penguin Keeper"

SLIDE: FAMILY CREST, WITH PENGUIN

though less visible, were the keepers of the Penguin's red flame, their family mascot a penguin-shaped passkey to the corridors of power.

The Penguroviches wrangled the Penguin through Russian history's darkest and brightest hours. Dating back to the times of Ivan the Terrible,

SLIDE: IVAN THE TERRIBLE, WITH RED PENGUIN

the Red Penguin tended to every tyrant's terrible desire,
   SLIDE: PETER THE GREAT, WITH RED PENGUIN
and every do-gooder's act of doing good. From freeing the serfs
   SLIDE: ALEXANDER II FREEING THE SERFS, AND THE PENGUINS
to sharing Catherine the Great's great big bed...
   SLIDE: CATHERINE THE GREAT DOING THE DEED WITH A RED PENGUIN
...and tending to the whims of the whimsical Rasputin,
   SLIDE: RASPUTIN CONSULTING A RED PENGUIN
the Red Penguin always found himself on the right side of history.
Alas, it was not Anastasia who was the Last of the Romanovs, but
their fickle friend the Red Penguin
   SLIDE: THE ROMANOVS, WITH THEIR PET RED PENGUIN
who was already on the other side of the Revolution, marching
for the proletariat
   SLIDE: LENIN WITH THE RED PENGUIN BY HIS SIDE
and somehow avoiding exile in Siberia.
   SLIDE: STALIN AND THE RED PENGUIN
In fact, did you know that the Communists adopted the red color
as their sign of solidarity in honor of the Red Penguin, that
persevering bird? True fact.
But alas, all was not rosy in the House of Pengurovich.
As Stalin's Reign of Terror rained terror across the entire
Soviet Union
   SLIDE: A MAP OF THE U.S.S.R.
even the Red Penguin, for the first time in Russian History,
was not safe.
   SLIDE: RED PENGUIN LANGUISHING IN A SIBERIAN JAIL
And as the Red Penguin began to fade from glory, so too did the
fortunes of the Pengurovich clan.
   *SLIDE: FAMILY HUDDLING UNDER BLANKETS IN A SNOW HUT; THE
   PENGUIN IS THERE, ALSO FREEZING*
Until one day, the Red Penguin was gone
   *SLIDE: SAME PICTURE, BUT WITH A BLACK PENGUIN-SHAPED HOLE
   WHERE THE PENGUIN SHOULD BE*
Many thought that the Red Penguin had escaped to the West, like
that joker Baryshnikov...
   SLIDE: SCREEN SHOT FROM WHITE NIGHTS
...but the Penguroviches knew the truth. The Red Penguin had
been...stolen!
   SLIDE: GORBACHEV HEAD WITH PENGUIN-SHAPED BIRTHMARK
   SLIDE: GORBACHEV HEAD WITHOUT PENGUIN-SHAPED BIRTHMARK
   *SLIDE: THE FAMILY SNAPSHOT IN HAPPIER DAYS, THE PENGUIN RIPPED
   OUT OF IT*
Born as the last in the long line of Penguin keepers, the twin
children Boris
   CLOSE ON BORIS

and Tatiana Pengurovich

CLOSE ON TATIANA

were raised to be their family's last great hope, with one purpose in life: to retrieve the Penguin and restore Honor to the Pengurovich family...and thereby, to Mother Russia.

SLIDE: DECADENT CONTEMPORARY GANGSTER-FILLED MOSCOW

When Father trained Boris to hunt, shoot, and smoke cigars, this gangster-in-training was a gangster with a mission.

SLIDE: BORIS *TAKING AIM WITH A RIFLE AND A CIGARETTE IN HIS MOUTH*

When Tatiana competed in the Olympics, she was disqualified

SLIDE: TATIANA *AS TONYA HARDING*

bringing great shame on her country and her team, but great pride to her parents

SLIDE: PARENTS *BEAMING WITH PRIDE*

who knew she was just training for the ultimate battle against the unknown but lethal international Penguin thief.

So when Boris found a familiar-looking face in the gutter

SLIDE: BORIS *LEANING DOWN TO PICK UP SOME TRASH IN THE STREET*

SLIDE: CLOSE ON AN INVITE TO ARCHIE'S OPENING AT 21c, WITH THE RED PENGUIN LOGO PROMINENTLY DISPLAYED

They knew their fate was once again decided by the Red Penguin.

So the brother and the sister set sail for America

SLIDE: A BOAT IN THE NEW YORK HARBOR, THE STATUE OF LIBERTY ON THE HORIZON

Stopping at Sea World to feel less alone

SLIDE: SEA WORLD

And checked into 21c

SLIDE: BORIS *AND* TATIANA, *LOOKING LIKE THE POSTER FOR* DR. ZHIVAGO, *CHECKING IN AT THE 21C FRONT DESK*

Planning to restore the Red Penguin to Mother Russia

And to restore honor to the Pengurovich clan.

SLIDE: FINAL, HEROIC SHOT OF THE RED PENGUIN

END.

End of Appendices

FISSURES (LOST AND FOUND)
by Steve Epp, Cory Hinkle,
Dominic Orlando, Dominique Serrand,
Deborah Stein, and Victoria Stewart

ABOUT *FISSURES (LOST AND FOUND)*

This article first ran in the January/February 2010 issue of Inside Actors, *and is based on conversations with the authors before rehearsals for the Humana Festival production began.*

Have you ever noticed that every time you recall a memory, you've both forgotten and reinvented more of it? Why is it that looking at an old photograph, or walking into a house where you once lived, can bring the past rushing back so vividly—or leave you bewildered when the picture in your imagination doesn't match? With whimsical humor and a searching fascination for these mysteries, the six co-authors of *Fissures (lost and found)* have teamed up to roam through the corridors between loss and rediscovery, creating a theatrical world that playfully embodies the ever-shifting landscape of memory.

To discover a theatrical vocabulary that could capture the experience of remembering, the authors embarked on an innovative collaboration. The experiment began in Minneapolis, where Dominique Serrand and Steve Epp, former co-Artistic Directors of the visionary Theatre de la Jeune Lune, joined forces with playwrights Cory Hinkle, Dominic Orlando, Deborah Stein and Victoria Stewart—all members of Workhaus Collective, a writer-run company devoted to producing adventurous new plays. When the playwrights' diverse storytelling talents met the Jeune Lune artists' physically expressive improvisational methods, all found themselves in new creative territory, making a play whose form is inspired by the way that memory fades, morphs and accumulates. "One of the challenges was to push the poetic rather than the intellectual approach," explains Serrand, "to find a way that the concept would always be translated into a playful gesture that retained its energy and complexity. To encounter journeys which are very moving, but never lose a sense of humor."

After months of research and conversation, the authors began to generate material by bringing "seeds" to the group—pieces of text, raw ideas—which became springboards for everyone (including the playwrights) to improvise on their feet. "We were learning a new language," says Orlando, describing how seeds were explored through improvisation, then written and reworked by multiple writers. "There were pieces that kept emerging that were common touchstones for the group," Epp adds. "It was like panning for gold, sifting through the material until we'd see something we could crack open to create an amazing moment or revelation." Over time, the threads that remained developed into a web of encounters that felt central to the play. "It's actually very similar to the way memory works," observes Stewart, "in that we're sifting through all these ideas and keeping the important ones, while others have fallen away. The ideas that stayed tended not to be about historical situations, or politics, but instead were grounded in the archetypal and universal, like memories of home or childhood—memories we all have."

The authors gravitated toward an immediate present to convey the delicate feeling of memory. "We discovered that the piece wanted to exist in the room where we were, in real time—so that actors and audience would be here in this moment, and the moment would be constantly peeling away," says Stein. Because memory is unstable, the people who inhabit this world are always struggling to reconstruct it: they're missing a complete context. "The idea of the lost character onstage goes back to the clown, who embodies the vulnerability of being in a world where you don't know where you fit," Serrand points out. With the playwrights' instincts for dramatic context in productive tension with the Jeune Lune artists' desire to keep uncertainty afloat, the group located a style of character that's wholly suited to the play. "Remembering is about not knowing what's next or what came before—you try to remember because you've forgotten, something isn't there," explains Hinkle. The absurdity of this human predicament is both funny and poignant: like all of us, the characters in this landscape are constantly unraveling and reimagining their memories.

What is the geography of such a world? "Our task was to *create* memory onstage, rather than *talk* about memory," recalls Orlando, and so the authors have mapped the places and objects where memory resides: in a once-familiar neighborhood, a house, an old keepsake, along the path to finding lost keys. "A place, an object or a room contains layers of memory," says Epp. "You walk into certain rooms, and you say, 'Think of all the things that happened here.' It's palpable, and makes them alive in a way." The play itself builds this sense of accumulation in a room: "We wanted to find a way to track the memory of the audience," says Serrand, "so that this open page of the theatre space becomes occupied by *their* memories."

As the six authors remember creating *Fissures (lost and found)*, all describe a process that's been truly collective and rigorous, one that's led to a singular theatrical world that none would have imagined without the perspectives of the others. "Because there were six minds negotiating what memory is, the piece has a mysterious, haunting quality," reflects Hinkle. "The play will be a lot of fun throughout, but remembering also involves moments we're never going to get back, a return to places that aren't what we thought they were. The unique feeling of the piece comes from working together to understand a bunch of unanswered questions."

—Amy Wegener

BIOGRAPHIES

Cory Hinkle's plays include *Little Eyes, SadGrrl13, Phosphorescence* and *Cipher,* and have been produced or developed at American Repertory Theater, the Guthrie Theater, Williamstown Theatre Festival, Summer Play Festival (SPF), Bay Area Playwrights Festival, Illusion Theater, Rattlestick Playwrights Theater, Salvage Vanguard, Workhaus Collective, Page 73 Productions, Hangar Theatre, and Red Eye Theater, among others. Cory is a co-creator of *Fissures (lost and found),* which was co-commissioned by Actors Theatre of Louisville and The Playwrights' Center and premiered at the 2010 Humana Festival of New American Plays. He has twice been commissioned by the Guthrie Theater, has received multiple MacDowell Colony fellowships, is a former resident at the Hermitage Artist Retreat, and is a recipient of a Jerome Travel and Study Grant. He received two Jerome Fellowships through The Playwrights' Center, where he is a Core Writer and a member playwright of the Workhaus Collective. He earned his M.F.A. in Playwriting from Brown University.

Dominic Orlando is a co-creator of *Fissures (lost and found)* (2010 Humana Festival); other plays include *Danny Casolaro Died for You* (Wellfleet Harbor Actors Theatre, 2010), *Juan Gelion Dances for The Sun* (Crowded Fire Theater, 2006) and *Life During Wartime* (HERE, 2002). Commissions include Actors Theatre of Louisville, the Guthrie Theater, Berkeley Repertory Theatre, The Playwrights' Center, History Theatre, Nautilus Music-Theater, BVT Children's Theater and Teatro del Pueblo. His work has been presented/developed at New York Theatre Workshop, HERE (multi-year), The Samuel Beckett on Theatre Row (Off-Broadway), Aurora Theatre Company, Kitchen Dog Theater (multi-year), Bay Area Playwrights Festival (multi-year), The New York International Fringe Festival (multi-year), The Prague Fringe, The Pasinger/ Fabrik Theater in Munich and The Tokyo International Arts Festival. He's been a writer-in-residence at the MacDowell Colony (multi-year), Yaddo, The Edward Albee Foundation (multi-year), and the Atlantic Center for The Arts (with Paula Vogel). He was awarded two Jerome Fellowships and a McKnight Fellowship through The Playwrights' Center, where he is currently a Core Writer and co-founding producer of The Workhaus Collective, the Center's company-in-residence.

Paris native **Dominique Serrand** was Artistic Director and one of the co-founders of Theatre de la Jeune Lune from 1978 to 2008. He studied at the National Circus School and the École Jacques Lecoq in Paris. Mr. Serrand has acted, conceived, directed and designed for most Jeune Lune productions for over 25 years, concentrating primarily on directing. His directing credits include *The Kitchen, Lulu, The Bourgeois Gentleman, Romeo and Juliet, Red Noses, 1789, Children of Paradise: Shooting a Dream, 3 Musketeers, The Pursuit of Happiness,*

Queen Elizabeth, Tartuffe, Gulliver, The Seagull, The Miser, The Little Prince, and *Amerika, or The Disappearance.* He has staged several operas, including *The Magic Flute, Cosi Fan Tutte, Don Juan Giovanni, Figaro, Carmen, Maria de Buenos Aires* and *Mefistofele.* Mr. Serrand's directing stages include Berkeley Repertory Theatre, La Jolla Playhouse, Yale Repertory Theatre, American Repertory Theater, Actors Theatre of Louisville, the Guthrie Theater, and the Children's Theatre Company, among others. He is a USA/Ford Foundation and Bush Foundation fellow. Mr. Serrand has been knighted by the French Government in the order of Arts and Letters.

Deborah Stein's plays include *God Save Gertrude, Wallflower, Bone Portraits,* and *Natasha And The Coat.* Her work has been produced and developed nationally at Actors Theatre of Louisville, The Theatre @ Boston Court, the Guthrie Theater, Seattle Repertory Theatre, Stages Repertory Theatre, Women's Project and Productions, The Wilma Theater, Live Girls! Theater, Bay Area Playwrights Festival, and Theater Artaud; in New York at the Public Theater, Dance Theatre Workshop, and Ars Nova; and internationally in Poland, Ireland, Edinburgh (the Traverse) and Prague. She has created original ensemble works with a number of collaborators, including Joseph Chaikin, Dominique Serrand, Lear deBessonet, and most frequently the Pig Iron Theatre Company, with whom she has collaborated since 2000. Her writing is published in *TheatreForum, Play: A Journal of Plays,* and *The Best American Poetry of 1996.* She has been a resident artist at Hedgebrook, Swarthmore College, Princeton University, and the Tofte Lake Center, and has taught writing at New York University, Northeastern University, St. Olaf College, Parsons School of Design, and Brown University, where she received her M.F.A. Deborah is the recipient of the 2010-2011 McKnight Advancement Grant at The Playwrights' Center in Minneapolis, where she was also a two-time Jerome Fellow and co-producing director of the Workhaus Collective. Currently, she is a resident artist at HERE, the recipient of a 2009-2011 Bush Artist Fellowship, and a resident playwright at New Dramatists.

Before graduating from the Playwrights Workshop at the University of Iowa, **Victoria Stewart** was a professional stage manager, working with David Rabe, Anne Bogart and Peter Sellars, among others. For her writing, Victoria has received a McKnight Advancement Grant, Francesca Primus Award, the Helen Merrill Award for Emerging Playwrights, the Martha R. Ingram Artist-in-Residence: New Work for the Theatre Fellowship, a Jerome Fellowship, and was a finalist for the Susan Smith Blackburn Award. She's been in residence at Ucross/Sundance, Donmar Warehouse, the Hermitage and Hedgebrook. Her plays include *Rich Girl, Hardball* (Summer Play Festival, Live Girls! Theater), *800 Words: The Transmigration of Philip K. Dick* (Workhaus Collective, Hourglass Group, Live Girls! Theater, named one of the top ten productions of 2009 by *City Pages*), *LIVE GIRLS* (Urban Stages, Wellfleet Harbor Actors Theater, Stage Left), *Leitmotif* (South Coast Repertory, Page 73 Productions), *Nightwatches* (Overlap Productions), *The Last Scene* and an adaptation of Henry James' *The Bostonians*. She is a producing member of the Workhaus Collective. She is now working on a screenplay for HBO about the recording industry's battle with Napster, and a play based on the Mercy Watson series for the Children's Theatre Company in Minneapolis.

ACKNOWLEDGMENTS

Fissures (lost and found) premiered at the Humana Festival of New American Plays in February 2010. It was directed by Dominique Serrand with the following cast:

Casey Greig
Megan Hill
Emily Gunyou Halaas
Nathan Keepers
Dominique Serrand

and the following production staff:

Scenic Designer	Michael B. Raiford
Costume Designer	Sonya Berlovitz
Lighting Designer	Jeff Nellis
Sound Designer	Benjamin Marcum
Properties Designer	Joe Cunningham
Video Technician	Philip Allgeier
Stage Manager	Melissa Rae Miller
Dramaturg	Amy Wegener
Directing Assistant	Jay Briggs
Scenic Design Assistant	Ryan Wineinger
Costume Design Assistant	Jordan Bivens
Lighting Design Assistant	Paola Rodriguez
Stage Management Intern	Jessica Potter
Assistant Dramaturg	Emily Feldman

Fissures (lost and found) was commissioned and developed by Actors Theatre of Louisville and The Playwrights' Center.

NOTES

Fissures (lost and found) was conceived and created by Steve Epp, Cory Hinkle, Dominic Orlando, Dominique Serrand, Deborah Stein and Victoria Stewart, with text by Hinkle, Orlando, Stein and Stewart.

Special thanks to the actors who participated in workshops of *Fissures (lost and found)*: Jennifer Baldwin Peden, Lisa Clair, Jon Ferguson, Nathan Keepers and Amanda Whisner.

Fissures (lost and found) was developed by the creators and the participating actors during a series of workshops under the auspices of The Playwrights' Center and Actors Theatre of Louisville.

The piece had its premiere at the 2010 Humana Festival of New American Plays. The cast included Casey Greig, Megan Hill, Emily Gunyou Halaas, Nathan Keepers and Dominique Serrand.

They are the characters as well as the performers.

The show was rehearsed and presented in the round at Actors Theatre of Louisville's Bingham Theatre—the scenes were tailored to the specificity of the space. The piece should be somewhat reconceived for every space in which it is performed.

The show was performed on a blank white floor, which was written upon, in black marker. There was a staircase in the middle of the space going down under the stage, and four doors, one at each corner of the stage. There was also a bank of bare light bulbs hung above the stage.

The play begins before you realize it's beginning.

There are no scene changes or blackouts until the end.

Megan Hill and Dominique Serrand
in *Fissures (lost and found)*

34th Annual Humana Festival of New American Plays
Actors Theatre of Louisville, 2010
Photo by Harlan Taylor

FISSURES (LOST AND FOUND)

1. Casey's Keys

CASEY *enters before the lights go down, while the Audience is still settling in.*

CASEY. Did someone lose their keys?
It looks like there's a car key here,
And a bike lock key
A house key, or no, maybe it's an apartment key?
Oh, wait. These are mine.

Do you remember where your keys are?
Can you find them now?
Is it the left pocket, or the right?

Do you have an apartment key, or a house key?
And when you return home, do you enter through the front door, or the back door?
Does the door open in or out?
When you reach for the light, is it on your wall to the left, or the right?
Or maybe there's not a switch, there's a lamp?
Or maybe you have a pull chain like I do.
With the little bumps on it, almost like beads,
rosemary beads—*rosary* beads…
Beads that help you remember… "Hail Mary, full of…"
If you're Catholic, maybe you know…
I'm not—Catholic. Maybe you are…

Did you leave the stove on?
Is it gas or is it electric?

Now walk to your bedroom.
How do you get there?
Down a hallway?
Or do you go up the stairs?
Or do you go up the stairs and then down a hallway?
Do you have stairs?
Maybe you live on a single floor?

Is your bed in the center of the room?
Or under a window?
What color are the sheets?
Is it a single?
Is it a double, a queen? a king?

Do you sleep alone?
Is there room for someone beside you?
Is anyone there?
Is the bed lifted up off the floor?
Is there space down below?
Can you crouch down
and look—look under the bed?

Is there dust? Socks? A book you forgot to finish?

Or maybe there's a box?
Can you reach it?
Can you pull the box out and put in on the bed?

Is it a large box, or small?
A shoebox or an old gift box
or a box left over from
the last time you moved?

Maybe you marked it "kitchen,"
or "library"?
No, you probably don't have a library, do you?

When was the last time you opened it?
Do you even remember what you put in there?
Could you open it now?
Could you open it,
and look inside?

       (He sits on the sidelines, watching.)

2. Nathan's Keys

      NATHAN *rushes breathlessly into the space.*

NATHAN. Sorry, sorry.
Just give me a second to catch my breath…
I'm sorry, really. I lost my keys.
They weren't on the desk—I have a desk—

      (He shows us the spot where his desk is, against the wall. He acts out his story
      as he speaks it.)

That's where I usually put them—I walk through the door and throw my coat
on the chair and my keys on the desk—it's more of a table, really, oak, but I
call it a desk—but my keys weren't there so I went to see if they were still in
the door, but when I step outside, the door shuts behind me and now, I'm
locked out.

So I have to climb up the water thing and through this broken window screen—gotta get that fixed—and I go to the kitchen where I have a glass of milk and a brownie. Then I remember, I have to be somewhere. So I check my calendar. The page for today is missing. Sometimes I tear it off and keep it in my wallet, so I check my wallet. There's a receipt in my wallet for a lot of money, but I can't remember what I bought...

That reminds me I have to pay my credit card bill. So I look for a pen—there's usually one on the desk—well, the table.

(It's on the floor.)

Oh, there it is, it fell. And I pay my credit card bill and I put it in an envelope. And then I remember what I bought, my new coat. So I put on the coat to go downstairs to mail the credit card bill—oh, there are my keys, they're in my coat, great—but then, I forget where I parked my car...

So I take a walk, south past the Mexican taco place and the laundromat—and I see this woman, walks past me. That's my wife. But, that's not possible. She's gone now.

So I follow her. And she turns a corner and then another corner and then she's going into a house that's right across the street from my house—she walks right in—

(He goes into the house.)

The door is open.

The house is empty. No furniture, nothing. Except—some books, scattered on the floor, like they fell out of a box and nobody bothered to pick them up, or forgot to—there are people wandering about, but it's really really quiet, there's like no sound at all—sssh...

(He looks around.)

Oh.

(Takes off his shoes.)

Because nobody is wearing any shoes. The floors are really, really nice. There's a pile, here—

(He sets his shoes next to CASEY's feet.)

I have no idea where she went. So I go into the other room and on the mantle there's a picture frame, and inside the frame—is a picture of me, with my wife, the frame is one of those really nice silver-y things you get at a crafts shop in a vacation town, you know.

It's not a picture I remember. The flash in the picture was so bright that there's a weird burst of silver all around our faces and our eyes are red and it's not very flattering, but we look happy. What the hell is this picture doing here?

It's a shame, our eyes are red, because otherwise you would see, she had really beautiful eyes—

"Somewhere, beyond the sea…" She loved this one song, her favorite song. "Somewhere, beyond the sea…" No that's not it. "Somewhere, waiting for me…" Well now I can't get it out of my head, but that's not the one, it's like that but not it…I know this song but it's the other song, the other song was her— "Somewhere, beyond the sea…"

I have no idea.

So…a man is standing in his socks in an empty house, with an unflattering picture he doesn't recognize, with no idea of how he got there, or how the picture got there, and he's trying really hard to (*He hums the song.*) remember his wife's favorite song…

And then, just as he's about to give up, he remembers where he parked his car.
　　　(*He exits with his keys as* EMILY *marches confidently onstage.*)

3. Half-Life of Memory

EMILY. I read this somewhere—or somebody told me—I don't remember—that every time you remember something, you only remember half of what you remembered the last time you remembered it. So every time you remember something, you're also forgetting it. It gets farther away. Faces become shapes become splotches, paragraphs become sentences become words become sounds. Hills become dots and then I don't know.

Can I borrow your program?
　　　(*She takes a program from an audience member.*)
So, you have the thing, and the memory is half of that thing,
　　　(*Tears the program in half.*)
and then your next memory is half of that, and the next time half of that,
　　　(*She tears and tears as she speaks.*)
then half of that and half of that and half of that, and so on and so on, until you're only holding the barest essential.
　　　(*Hands the audience member the tiny piece that remains.*)
So think about what you did yesterday. Got it? Great. Hold it there…because the next time you think of it, you'll only have half. But another thing! If you remember something wrong, that still becomes part of the way you'll remember it next time. So you're remembering something that never really happened, but it becomes part of your memory anyway. Something that never really *was* becomes as real as something that actually *happened.*

So if a man is walking down the street and thinks he sees his dead wife, and he follows her, then there's always a part of him that will remember his wife walking down that street, even if she never actually did.

(*She backs slowly off as* CASEY *rises, exiting with her.*)

CASEY. Do you know where your wife is?

Do you even have a wife?

Are *you* a wife?

Maybe you're single

(nothing wrong with that).

Maybe you're an only child?

A sister?

A brother?

What *are* you?

(*He is gone.*)

4. The Visit

MEGAN *and* NATHAN *enter the space.*

MEGAN. Wow.

NATHAN. Wow.

MEGAN. It's bigger than I remember.

NATHAN. It's huge.

(*They walk over to a short wall.*)

MEGAN. This is totally different.

NATHAN. Didn't there used to be a wall here?

Yeah, I could swear it was—like—it was this tall.

(NATHAN *backs up toward a taller wall while looking at the smaller one.*)

Like up to here.

(*He puts his hand out at the exact height of the wall behind him.*)

Huh.

(*He leans against the taller wall.*

He sits on it.)

You know, our feet would dangle…

(*He looks down at his feet. Then, at the wall he's sitting on.*)

Oh, here it is.

MEGAN. They switched it.

NATHAN. That's a big job.

(MEGAN *walks to the side of the stage opposite the staircase.*)

MEGAN. There were stairs here.

NATHAN. Oh, yeah.

MEGAN. They were really steep—Mom always said be careful—

NATHAN. Yeah, she used to go down to the cellar—

> (*Without realizing it, he's walking down the actual stairs.*)

—Oh. Here they are.

MEGAN. They moved them.

NATHAN. That's a big job.

Didn't there used to be a mural here.

> (*They look out into the audience..*)

People in rows and chairs, watching something.

MEGAN. Right.

NATHAN. Remember…

> (*They go into an improvisation, describing a very specific person in the front row of the audience behind them.*
> *They're puzzled at the change, then slowly turn around, seeing the person they described.*)

NATHAN. Oh—there she is!

> (*They go through the description again to be sure.*)

MEGAN. They moved it.

NATHAN. That's a big job.

MEGAN. Remember the best part is that when you move, the eyes follow you.

> (*They walk and watch the audience follow their movements.*
> MEGAN *almost bangs into the bench—*)

There used to be a door here.

NATHAN. Yeah, but it was at an angle. Oh—there it is. Oh yeah, and there's the other one—the one we came in through. Actually, I remember now there were two. But for some reason, I pictured them on the other side.

> (*Turning around.*)

Oh I see…there's four?!

MEGAN. Yes, because this is the pantry. Oh.

> (*She opens the door—nothing there.*)

NATHAN. They made it a hallway.

> (*Nathan walks into the hallway—he's off.*)

MEGAN. Yeah: if you go right, you're in the piano room.

NATHAN. What's left?

MEGAN. If you go left, and then take another left you end up in the ballroom.

> (*She exits through the door as Nathan enters through the opposite door.*)

NATHAN. WOW, look at this.

> (*Calling.*)

Hey, hey—you gotta see—hey—

(She doesn't answer. He looks around.)

Was it? The ballroom?

(Dances a bit.)

No, no…

(Dances more fluidly.)

Yeah—yeah, it was definitely the ballroom.

(His dance takes him to the edge of the stage: something's missing.)

Didn't there used to be a table here?

(MEGAN comes up the stairs.)

MEGAN. How'd you get up here?

NATHAN. What?!?

MEGAN. How'd you get up here? GO!

(She pretends to run but stops short—this is an old game. He has run halfway across the stage before he remembers the game and stops, mad at himself for being fooled again. She, meanwhile, hides under the table that's gone now.)

NATHAN. There's no table there anymore. I can see you.

(He pounds her back with his fist.)

MEGAN. The old man, he used to hit the table when he was angry!

NATHAN. Yeah, he used to pound the table—

(Hits her again.)

and run out of the room—

MEGAN. But he kept the door open so we could hear him shouting.

(NATHAN goes to the door to confirm—the door swings, it won't stay open. Hmm.)

NATHAN. He must have had a—a whatchamacallit, a—

MEGAN. A book—

NATHAN. No, a, uh—

MEGAN. A shim—

NATHAN. No, a, a—

MEGAN. A cane.

NATHAN. What!? No, no, it was a wedge, but where did he keep it? Did he have it in his pocket? Was it—where was the wedge?

(Trying to find the movement.)

Oh, yeah—

(NATHAN goes through the body memory: he pounds on "the table" angrily as he speaks, heading for the door and without thinking finds the wedge, which sits

on the lintel above the door. He looks at it, says "there it is," slams it into place and marches out the door, still screaming:)

You do so many good things for your kids, you clothe 'em, you give 'em shoes, you send 'em off to school, you put food on the table—meat and vegetables—ice cream even, you let 'em watch TV, go camping upstate, you buy 'em textbooks, comic books, SAT prep books, you varnish the furniture, you bail 'em out of jail and what do they do? The turn around and kick you in the ass!

5. The Brother and Sister (attempt to) Explain Systems

The old man's angry sentence is so long, NATHAN *has returned through the other door. He finishes the screed—stops, confused.*

NATHAN. Is that right? Did that happen?

MEGAN. When we went back to the old house, we remembered everything differently from what we found. Which made no sense, because we had so many ways of remembering: photographs, old letters, books handed down—

We make these objects to help us remember—but sometimes the objects disappear and you're left with only the memories. On the other hand, sometimes the memories disappear and you're left with only the objects—

NATHAN. Like when you make a to-do list, like the one I have here.

(*He reaches into his pocket. There's nothing there.*)

MEGAN. Right—because you make a to-do list to help you remember what to do.

But really the first thing you need to do
is remember the list.

6. The Missing Friend

CASEY. If I'm going to tell it, I should start simply…
So, I was sitting in my chair—

Wait.

(*He looks around for a chair. There isn't one.*
He pulls out a pack of Post-it notes.
He writes "chair" on a Post-it and sticks it on the bench.)

Okay, this is my chair.

So one night, I was sitting in my chair, at my writing desk—well, really it's more of table—wait.

(*He writes "table" on a Post-it and sticks it to his leg.*)

So one night, I was sitting in my chair, at my writing desk—with my back to the window—

(*He turns to look behind him—no window.*)

I have a window here, see—

(*Indicates where the window should be.*

Looks around for a substitute—finds it nearby in the door.)

Okay all right, so *this* window is my window.

(*He writes "window" on a Post-it and sticks it on the actual window in the door.*)

Oh, but my chair is right below my window—

So this

(*The actual window.*)

is actually here

(*Behind him.*)

And I—am actually there

(*Under the actual window.*)

So, okay—one night, I'm sitting at my writing desk—

And I'm writing, writing, working intensely on an e-mail (I don't remember who I was writing, but it was important) and I'm really into it, it's really going well and in the back of my mind I know my friend is going to arrive, but I'm so into the writing that I lose track of time and then I look at the clock and see it's 8:20 and I think, "Where the heck is he?" he was supposed to be here twenty minutes ago—

So I stand and I look out the window—

Wait. I forgot something.

It's not daylight. It was actually night.

(*Writes "night" on a Post-it, puts it on window.*)

So, one *night*, I'm sitting in my chair, at my desk and I'm writing on my laptop and I realize my friend's late, so I stand to look out the window but—Wait.

I forgot. It was also snowy.

(*Writes "snowy" on a Post-it, puts it on window next to "night."*)

So, one snowy night, I'm sitting in my chair, I'm writing on my laptop—hold on.

(*He writes "laptop" on a Post-it.*)

Laptop.

So one snowy night, I'm sitting in my chair, at my desk and I'm—wait—my lamp. I never write without my lamp.

(*Writes "lamp" on a Post-it, sets it on the floor nearby.*)

Okay, so one night—oh, the lamp was "on."

> (*He writes "on" on a Post-it and puts "on" over "lamp."*)

So one—hang on—

> (*He moves the "lamp" slightly closer to get better light.*)

So one snowy night, I'm sitting in my chair, at my desk and I'm writing on my laptop, working on this e-mail, very focused and I realize my friend's late, so I stand to look out the window into the snowy night and then I reach into my pocket to call him on my cell phone—

> (*Writes "cell phone" on Post-it, uses it as a phone.*)

So, I dial his number as I'm standing there, but just as it starts ringing I see him, out there, or I think I see him, through the snowy night. So, the phone rings once and I hang up and I sit back down and start working again. I think, good, he's here he should come up any time, let me get back to this, but then I lose track of time again and it's been fifteen more minutes and I think where the heck is he? and then I stand up and look out again, down to the street…

> (*He stops.*)

Wait. This isn't working. None of you can see the street. Um. Hold on.

> (*He looks at the whole floor.*)

Okay…

> (*He draws on the floor of the stage with the marker—simple line drawings—boxes, circles, etc.*)

This is my street—it goes on, but there's a lake over there, so…here's my apartment building. I live here in the bigger part, here—I don't know who lives here, so that's not important—

> (*He crosses out half of his building, the "not important" part. He stands up and looks at his street and his house.*)

Across the street is my neighbor's house.

> (*Another box.*)

I've never talked to her, but I see her all the time, here—

> (*—drawing—*)

at the community garden and here's a Baptist Church—but I'm Lutheran so that's not important.

> (*Crosses out the Baptist Church.*)

This is Phillip Jackson Avenue. And this is—well, this would be Up North, so here's Canada. And South of Canada would be Mexico.

> (*He labels two doors, one on the North end of the theater "Canada," the other on the South end, "Mexico."*)

Okay.

> (*He grabs all his Post-its, putting them in his "apartment."*)

Here's my desk, chair, lamp, laptop. So! One snowy night, I'm sitting in my chair, and I'm writing on my laptop, very focused and I realize my friend's late so I stand to look out the window, I dial my cell phone, but just as it starts ringing I see him, Joe—

(He writes "Joe" on a Post-it note. He places it on the street where he last saw Joe.)

—out there, or I think I see him, through the snowy night, he's not looking up at me, but anyway, okay good, he's here and so I go back to work, but again I lose track of time and when I look back again he's gone, if that was him, but I know it was.

I saw him right here. And then he disappeared. At least, from where I'm standing, here, at my window he did.

(He stands in his "apartment" at his "window" and looks down at the street.)

But from his perspective, if he was looking up at me—

(He switches and stands in Joe's spot and looks up at the apartment.)

I disappeared when I sat back down.

(He switches again, back to his apartment.)

But all I know is when I stood again and looked out the window he was gone.

(He stands frozen at his window, looking out onto the street.

MEGAN *has been watching for most of the scene.*

She steps forward.)

MEGAN. I watch him standing
At his window
Almost every single day.

He looks as if
He sees nothing
Except the snow
And the cold
The darkness
Like he's completely frozen
Watching the world move from his window.
I watch him for hours
I see him
From the front window of my apartment.

Which is right across the street.

(She stands in her "apartment" across the street.)

I don't often look out the front window
usually I'm at my kitchen table in the back
reading, or talking on the phone.

On nice days, I read in the community garden
Under a big cottonwood tree—
Well, that's not important.

I'm so curious about him.

I decide one day to move my kitchen table
Out of my kitchen
And into my front room

Now I can sit near the front window
And occasionally while reading
I glance up
And watch him standing.
What is he looking at?

What is he thinking?
I can't know.
I can't read his mind
Or imagine what's inside it.

I think,
He'll move, someday soon he'll move
But he just
Continues to stand and watch and wait
As winter storms start up
And then stop
And it snows again
And then again
The world thaws
All of the winter snow melts
Spring arrives
And still he stands there
Watching
And waiting

I imagine his apartment
What it looks like on the inside
All the things inside of it.
I imagine living there

I imagine we're madly in love and fighting,
Growing old together.
And then one of us dies…

      (CASEY *walks out into the street.*)

One day,
I'm not sure exactly when, I see him walk outside
To the end of our street—
He turns a corner
And disappears from view.

So: a woman watches her neighbor day after day after day.
Years go by.
Without her realizing it, he becomes a part of her life.
So much so, that when he moves away
she mourns for him.

> (MEGAN *backs slowly off.*)

7. The Messenger Arrives

> CASEY *shouts from underneath the stage.*

CASEY. Excuse me!

> (NATHAN *enters.*)

Excuse me! Is this you?

> (NATHAN *looks down the stairs.*)

NATHAN. What?

> (CASEY *throws up a box*—NATHAN *catches it.*)

CASEY. The name on the box—is it you?

NATHAN. Oh. Right.

> (*Looks at the box.*)

No. Sorry.

> (*He throws the box back at* CASEY *and exits.*
> CASEY *comes up the stairs, knocks on a door—no answer.*
> *He knocks on another—no answer.*
> *He is about to knock on a third door when* EMILY *opens the door across the way.*)

EMILY. Hello?

CASEY. Hello.

CASEY. Is this you?

EMILY. Me?

CASEY. Is this your name? On the box?

EMILY. Yes.

CASEY. Well, then.

> (EMILY *looks at it, looks up at the audience.*)

EMILY. So, there was a knock at my door.

Wait, was there a knock? Maybe I just opened the door and—no—yes. There was a knock at the door. And I opened the door and—there was a man standing there. So he said:

CASEY. Is this you?

EMILY. Me?

CASEY. Is this your name? On the box.

EMILY. Yes.

CASEY. Well, then.

EMILY. He had a package with my name on it. But there was no return address. Thank you.

> (*She opens the box.*)

What is this stuff?

You don't know who this is from?

> (*Nope.*
> *She pulls a photo out of the box.*)

Oh. Oh my God.

That's me, here, in the photo. See? Next to some guy. Oh, wow—my hair— that was—that must be the summer I went to Europe—I was still in school. I cut my hair really short to look like Jean Seberg, you know, from that movie, what's it called? I got it cut just before I left for Paris, in Barcelona, because I wanted to look already French when I got to France…but that's not Barcelona… I don't think—and the guy…

> (*She looks at the back of the photo.*)

"O what a day we had." B.

"O what a day we had."

B.

Who's B?

Did B *take* the photo? Or is that B *in* the photo?

> (*Turns the photo over.*)

Where are we?

CASEY. Trains.

EMILY. What?

CASEY. It's a train station.

EMILY. How can you tell?

> (*He sighs, walks over, looks.*)

CASEY. Everything's in France. And there's a bit of the track.

EMILY. *Gare Montparnasse?*

CASEY. Maybe.

(*She looks at the photo again.*)

EMILY. I don't remember this day at all. It was clearly important—to him. If he's B. Did I sleep with him? No…I would remember that. Wouldn't I?

(*Back to the box: she finds a tin of candies.*)

Oh, I love these!

—I bought them at every town we stopped in—

You want one?

CASEY. Sure. Thanks!

(*He takes a candy. They suck on the candies.*)

EMILY. Whenever I taste orange…

I smell trains.

(*She gets lost a moment, trying to remember.*)

CASEY. I love trains. I love movies about trains, and books about trains—reading train schedules—oh, and maps! I take one with me everywhere I go—see, like this one, big ones with the accordion folds—

(*He takes a map out of his pocket and demonstrates as he talks.*)

I can spend hours and hours looking at maps. Spread it out on a nice big table—

(*He looks for a table but there isn't one. Lays it out on the floor or on a bench. It is a map of the United States.*)

I've been here, in Dubuque, and also here, Des Moines, and here in Duluth. But I've never been anywhere outside the United States. Well, I've been to Canada. But that doesn't count. If I folded this map down so it was only the places I've been, it would be very, very tiny. But if I fell through the middle of the map—

(*He turns the map over and it is a map of the world.*)

—then I would be here, looking at the pyramids in Giza. I want to go there, I want to eat a persimmon in Beijing—and to sink my feet into the Sahara—

EMILY. Did he give me one of these on the train from Barcelona to Paris? Did we sit next to each other?

This can't be the same tin—from back then—

wouldn't they be stale?

CASEY. It's a little stale.

EMILY. Yeah. Sorry.

CASEY. It's okay. It's still good.

EMILY. I can't remember…

It was just a summer, just two months, but…he's not there at all. Not even a shadow.

If I was still this girl—the girl in this photo—would I remember him now? And if I did, what else would be different?

So, there was a knock at my door
And the man standing there
had a package with my name on it
I open it
And none of it makes any sense
Not even the picture of me.

But it's mine now.

I have so many boxes put away:
some of them were given to me
some of them I took
some I packed away myself.
I re-use the boxes—the labels get confused—
but every one of them must be important.

9. Fedunk

> MEGAN *hands boxes up the staircase for* NATHAN *to stack onstage.*
> *She will continue handing up boxes throughout.*
> *As* NATHAN *enters with his first box, he draws* CASEY *in:*

NATHAN. So our old man, he ran into the hall screaming "You do so many good things for your kids, you clothe 'em, you give 'em shoes, you bail 'em out of jail, and what do they do? They turn around and kick you in the ass!" And he comes running back in here and he just—keels over.

> (*Setting the box down.*)

Fedunk.

CASEY. Huh?

NATHAN. What? Our old man, he was running through the hallway screaming and he came back in here and he just—keeled over. Right on this spot.

> (*Setting down a box.*)

Fedunk.

CASEY. What was that?

NATHAN. What're you thinking about? He keeled over on this spot. Fedunk.

CASEY. There—you did it again.

NATHAN. Did what?

CASEY. When you put the box down and you said something like dunk.

NATHAN. No I didn't. I took the box and I put it down like this.

> (*Places the box very carefully.*)

See?

(Moves it back into position.)

Fedunk.

CASEY. There! you did it again!

(Takes a box from MEGAN.*)*

You put the box down and went "Fedunk"—I swear—

NATHAN. No I didn't.

CASEY. *(Setting down the box.)* Fedunk. Oh god I do it too.

NATHAN. That's weird…

MEGAN. Fedunk? What does that mean?

NATHAN. Don't ask me, he's the one who said it.

(Puts his box down.)

Fedunk. Oh, God, I did it! What is that?

EMILY. *(Still holding her box from the previous scene.)* Maybe it's one of those whatchamacallits—

MEGAN. Cipher?

EMILY. No—

CASEY. Enigma?

EMILY. No—what's the word?

NATHAN. Haiku?

(Setting down a box.)

Fedunk. Goddammit.

EMILY. No like…Fred Eats Donuts Until Crying Kips.

NATHAN. That's "feduck."

CASEY. *(Setting down a box.)* Fedunk. What the—

EMILY. No, no, it's—oh yeah. "Crying Kips"…

(Rejected, she starts off.)

MEGAN. How do you spell—

EMILY. *(Sets her box beside the staircase as she goes down.)* Fedunk.

NATHAN. F-E-D-U-N-K.

(CASEY circles the stage thinking about it.)

CASEY. There's not a PH?

NATHAN. Puh-fcdunk?

CASEY. No it's more of a pfffedunk.

NATHAN. Maybe.

(They put their last boxes down together—)

BOTH. Fedunk.

(—and turn around to exit down the stairs.)

NATHAN. Yeah, it's definitely more of a PH when you say it.

CASEY. And you're more of a traditional hard Ef.

NATHAN. Yeah.

> (*They stop a moment on the stairs, puzzled—then continue down.*
> *Leaving* MEGAN *alone onstage.*)

10. Sister and the Books

MEGAN. Photographs

Maps

Keys

Me.

Me? Did I write me? Who's "me" is this?

> (*Opens the box. Picks out pile of books.*)

Is this stuff mine?

> (*Kneels down, sets the books in front of her. Picks up first book—*
> *There's a bookmark.*)

What's this?

> (*She pulls it out. Reads:*)

"I underlined this sentence, so you'd never forget. It sums you up."

> (*She looks at the book—of course the page isn't marked anymore:*)

Fuh…

> (*She flips through the pages.*
> *She flips through them again.*
> *She reads a sentence.*)

"There was nothing there. Just a void. Absolutely nothing." That can't be it.

> (*Flips some more pages, finds another.*)

"And slowly you killed him with your suffocating personality that killed him just like a pillow over his face."

Definitely not mine.

> (*She puts the book down—she's curious now and wants to get through the whole pile.*
> *Another book.*)

Oh yeah. It rained—all day.

> (*Puts it down.*)

And this one we kept under the table leg to keep it from wobbling

> (*Puts it down.*
> *Another book—picks it up—it smells.*)

Falafel and fries—yow. The bodega.

(She sets it down—she's surrounding herself with books.
She picks up another. Notices the dog-eared page.)

Ooo... "He whispered now and then, telling her to raise her legs as she had never done, until her knees touched her chin. He whispered to her to turn and he spread her cockatoo's cage needed cleaning and the maid was nowhere to be found."

(Wha'? She goes back.)

"He whispered to her to turn and he spread her cockatoo's cage needed cleaning and the maid was nowhere to be found."

"He spread her..."

(She looks at the next page—)

"...cockatoo's cage needed cleaning—"

(Goes back again, reads, silently.)

96, 97, 100. Definitely mine...but what did I do with the page?

(She sets it down. Picks up another—reads a quote:)

"The question is one not merely of what kind of distance is preferable, but of what kind of distance is possible, meaning how much distance people must put between themselves and their past in order to remain psychically viable, which very often, as Freud showed, is no distance at all." That's circled and then, next to it in the margin, I wrote "bullshit."

Look at my L's, they're so severe—
"BuLLLLshit."

(Puts the book down.
Last book in the pile: she finds a handkerchief under the front cover.)

Our grandmother always used to give us a handkerchief with a knot tied in it, to help us remember things.

(Ties it. Tries to remember.
Nothing.
Throws it in the box.)

Some things are just lost...they disappear.

(Meaning the books:)

But other things return to you...

Or maybe you only thought they were lost, but really they were just somewhere else—without you, but not lost.

For example, if I were to walk out this door, I would disappear—well, for you I would.

11. The Missing Friend Returns

CASEY *enters through the door marked "Canada."*
He sees the way the boxes and the books are arranged—they become a map of the city.

CASEY. I never should've gone to Canada.
But now I'm here.
And this is the highway through downtown.
This is the exit
This is the street
There's the school.
There's the Best Western.
That insurance company with the weird awning.
And over there—oh, I remember, the zoo—
And here's—a bodega.
Is this the right street?
But yes, it is. There's the church! And the community garden, which is kitty corner to where my friend lives. There's a bodega where his house used to be. So he moved. How could he move without telling me?

We were really good friends. The last time I saw him was right here. It was a snowy night and I was driving in—wait a minute. This isn't working.

You know, he always used to say that, my friend. He'd start telling a story and then he'd say, wait a minute, this isn't working and then he'd start from scratch.

I have to come at this a different way.

The last time I saw him was through his window. Here was his desk, his chair, and he had this crappy lamp from a trip to Taiwan—
 (Sees the Post-its left there and throws each one away as he says:)
But the desk isn't here, the lamp isn't here, neither is the chair and he's not here.
 (Sees the Post-it in the street.)
And here's Joe. That's me.
But I'm not there, I'm here.
 (Throws it away.)
Okay…follow me.
 (Goes to the end of the street.
 Picks up the book he called "the school.")
So this is my car and I was on the highway driving—no wait. That doesn't work.
This is still the school.
 (Sets it back in place. A moment—he takes off his shoe.)

This is my car.

It's a Toyota Corolla Hatchback.

328,000 miles on it.

I've had it since college.

> (*Puts his shoe on the floor,*
> *Starts to push it along.*
> *Doesn't like that.*
> *Puts his shoe back on his foot and moves his car along.*)

I get off at the exit.

Past the school, the Best Western, the insurance company with the weird awning…I park right here in front of my friend's house.

I get out of the car, I see his light, that lamp from Taiwan—in my peripheral vision I see a light from across the street, but that doesn't matter.

My cell phone starts ringing, I get back in the car, I answer it and there's no one there.

No wait. Didn't I go up then? I did.

I get out of my car, I walk up the walkway, ring his bell, and I walk up the stairs and into his house…

It's a sweet little two-bedroom. We have a great time, we drink whiskey, we watch football.

I'm sitting on his sofa, he puts some nuts out on his coffee table, but then I remind him that I'm allergic to nuts. And so he puts out some Tostitos and thank God because I'm starving. He has some cognac, oh it wasn't whiskey, it was cognac. He has a big glass and I have a small glass, no actually, the glasses are the same size he just fills his up full and I have just a little bit of cognac. I don't know why, maybe I was on one of my kicks. So I take all night to drink this really small glass of cognac.

His big screen TV is on, actually, it's not a big screen TV, it's a regular size TV…there's a football game, or hockey I can't remember who's playing, but it's on mute, so we're not really paying attention. He's telling me a story (I don't remember what it was about, but he was very upset), he does all the talking, I'm mostly listening. And finally, I say, I have to get back on the road, I should go.

And there's that moment at the door, you know, it's always awkward, are you gonna hug or shake hands? I just pat him on the back and say, good night, buddy. No, I didn't say buddy. I said, "Good night, pal." That seems weird too. I just said, "Good night." I got back into my car.

(*He puts the shoe back on.*)

And then I drove away.

Back down the street, past the insurance company, the Best Western, the school, the zoo, to the exit, well now the entrance ramp, and onto the highway.

And now we haven't spoken in twelve years.

Is that right?

If that was the last time I saw him and we had such a great time (the cognac, nut allergy, football or hockey game on mute, and the small TV) why haven't we spoken since then?

(*He sees the Post-its on the window, takes them off.*)

It was a snowy night, or no wait, it wasn't snowing at all. And it wasn't night, it was daytime,

and this isn't a window, it's my hand—

(*He throws them all away.*)

Was that this night with this friend, or a different night with a different friend in a different city?

Did I go to Canada?

Am I from here?

(*He looks toward "Mexico."*)

Tal vez necesito volver a México
para ver de donde soy
y para comprender a donde voy…

(*He goes through the door marked "Mexico."*)

12(A). The Wife Returns

EMILY. I'm walking—well, I'm not actually walking, because that's not possible, I'm gone now. But I'm walking in my husband's memory because he thinks he sees me in the street.

I turn a corner and then another corner and then I'm going into a house.

The door is open and it's really quiet and I notice there's a pile of shoes in the corner. I look around. What am I doing here?

(*Singing.*)

"Somewhere, beyond the sea…"

What's that? Why am I in this strange house and why am I singing that song? Why does he remember me here? Oh.

He's remembering me doing something I never did. This happens sometimes.

See, now that I'm dead, I'm a fixed point in time. I don't have any new experiences.

Let me explain.

I'm like an old globe or an old map of Berlin, separated down the middle, East and West. Even though things have changed since, this map never changes: I'm always young, I'm always beautiful.

As long as my husband remembers me that way.

I know—
> (*Goes to the same audience member she approached earlier.*)

Hi, do you have that piece of paper? That really really small one?
> (*She shows it to the audience.*)

One day, this is all my husband will remember of me.
> (*She puts the piece of paper in the palm of her right hand.*)

This is me. Where we lived when I was alive.
> (*She opens her left hand and puts it beside her right: both her palms are open.*)

But his life keeps unfolding, like a map…
> (*She "unfolds" her left hand away from her right, imitating a map unfolding.*)

1 year, 2 years, 3 years, 4 years, 5 years—

His life keeps getting larger. But I'm still there—and he's here.

I want to fold the map back—but of course that's impossible.
> (*She starts to fold the map back—stops herself.*
> *Instead of "refolding" her map, she raises her hands up and brings her palms together, making the two ends of her map side by side.*)

But when I fold the map like this—we are here, now, together again.
> (*Singing.*)

"Somewhere beyond the sea…"
> (NATHAN *enters.*)

12(B). Chorale

NATHAN. "Somewhere beyond the sea
> Somewhere"

No that's not it—that's not the one—it's like that one, but not it.
> (*The other performers enter, one by one, creating new conversations from the same dialogue.*)

CASEY. If I'm going to tell it, I should start simply:
I've never been outside the United States.
I've been to Canada—but that doesn't count.

NATHAN. I'm trying to tell you the story:

EMILY. He had a package with my name on it, I open it—

CASEY. It's a train station.

EMILY. None of it makes any sense.

CASEY. Everything's in France.

EMILY. Oh.

NATHAN. Just give me a second to catch my breath.

MEGAN. I imagine his apartment.
What it looks like on the inside
all the things inside it—

CASEY. This window is my window. This is my chair and this is my writing desk.

NATHAN. Well, really it's more of a table, oak, but I call it a desk.

MEGAN. I imagine living there, we are madly in love and fighting.

CASEY. I've never talked to her, but I see her all the time.

MEGAN. Wow.

NATHAN. On the mantle there's a picture frame, one of those nice silvery things.

EMILY. It's a shame our eyes are red, because you would see I had really beautiful eyes.

CASEY. I forgot. It was also snowy.

MEGAN. It rained all day.

EMILY. It was really quiet.

NATHAN. Because no one is wearing any shoes.

    (CASEY *and* MEGAN *with the books:*)

CASEY. This is a school—the Best Western—

MEGAN. I underlined this sentence, it sums you up.

CASEY. —the insurance company with the weird—

MEGAN. He whispered to her the cockatoo's cage needed cleaning and the maid was nowhere to be found—

EMILY. "B," who's "B"?

NATHAN. That can't be, she's gone now.

MEGAN. That's the door that leads to the pantry.

NATHAN. Wasn't it a hallway?

EMILY. Wait, was there a knock?

MEGAN. How'd you get up here?

CASEY. Do you go up the stairs?
Or do you go up the stairs and then down a hallway?

NATHAN. They moved it.
That's a big job.

CASEY. That's me, but I'm not there, I'm here.

EMILY. I'm still here—he's there—but when I fold the map back,
we're here, together again—

MEGAN. Our grandmother used to give us a handkerchief
with a knot tied in it
to help us remember things.

12(C). The Last Return

DOMINIQUE *enters.*

DOMINIQUE. That's why people don't remember anything nowadays,
they use Kleenex.

I remember everything.
I remember when I was born.
They always say you can't, but I do.

Sorry, sorry. I should start simply:

I wasn't born here.
There.
Let's start with that.

> (*The other actors begin writing on the floor of the stage, on the benches, on the doors—they write their lines from the play, perhaps the lines of others. A single light bulb begins to drop from the ceiling, very slowly, almost imperceptibly.*)

My mother and I came over on a boat
with only a few things
some books,
a table.

The table my father built.
The wood split from its tree
ripped from its home and transformed by his hands.

He came from the school that if you build something,
you need to leave a bit unfinished
or you will bring a curse upon your family.

So he would never tell me or my mother but
somewhere in our house was an undone piece.
I looked for it everywhere, and after we came here
I found it—on the table.

I would finger the grain.
I got several splinters,
some are still in my finger
they never worked their way out of the skin.

We came over when I was a boy,
to a new world with no memories.
I can't even tell you my name
because I never learned it.

And I never learned my father's way with wood.
Because he never joined us here.
Years later we received a letter with no return address
only a postmark, telling us he was gone.

But the splinter is still here.

My mother finds work as a housekeeper—
I grow up in someone else's home.

> (*During the following,*
>
> DOMINIQUE *refers to each actor as he talks about them.*)

There's a little girl, we play together.
When we become older, I marry her.

I have a friend, no, he's her friend.
Maybe I have it wrong, maybe he married her.

When she dies, I have very little to remind me of her.
Except for him.

I look at pictures of them
And I almost see myself.

I have another friend—he disappears or maybe it's me who disappears
But when it snows, I think of him and taste whiskey, no, cognac—

In Beijing I eat a persimmon.
I find a knotted handkerchief buried in the sands of the Sahara.
East Berlin, I see a woman who reminds me of my wife. So I follow her onto
a train, not knowing where it is going. We have a day filled with the taste of
oranges. Later, I send her a box of mementos—

> (*He accidentally kicks* EMILY's *box.*)

Fedunk.

She reminds me of my neighbor across the street
who watched me from her window—
Who reminds me of my wife.

I think I was in love with her.
I think.
I want to retrace,

to retrieve, extract,
make sense of all these things—

So I take a walk.

With each block, I travel into my past—
But the lines on the map shift under my feet.

And then I find it—the way back.
As I approach the door
I realize the keys are in my pocket, have always been
but the door is open.

An open house.
So I take off my shoes and walk in.
Or do I walk out?
Am I inside, or still outside in the street
Do the doors lead in or do they lead out?

The library is full of streets,
The books have become buildings (the Best Western, the insurance company
with the weird awning)—
the walls have moved and the sea of faces is never the same—

      (*With joyful sorrow*—)
But the table is still here.

I used to hide beneath it as a child.
It sheltered me, a tree from a rainstorm.
The table contained me, became my world.

Why do I still see my table when there's no table there—
Or is this my table?

If only I could open it up, a thing like this
which has memory stretching all the way back,
all the way to forests I've never seen,
an object that can't make mistakes but only witness—

I want to sit down at this table and write.
I want to write everything down. Everything.

But then I notice
there are bumps, ridges, cuts in the wood
from pens, from pencils
a knife, a crack—

I lay a sheet of paper on the table
and rub my pencil over the scars—

the scars become words,
the words become faces
become stories

What are they saying to me?
I reach for the light to bring them closer
so that I can read, hear, see—
understand—

But as I do—

> (*Music.*
>
> *Lights begin to fade.*
>
> *One naked bulb, hanging just above* DOMINIQUE, *remains bright as the rest of the stage darkens.*
>
> *The others stop writing, stand, and watch* DOMINIQUE.
>
> *He tries to connect with them, but they recede into the shadows.*
>
> *It grows darker. He turns and reaches for the light—*
>
> *And it drops, disappearing through the floor.*)

End of Play